CONTENTS.

CONTENTS.

BALANCE SHEETS AND LEGER ACCOUNTS.

DAY-BOOK IN JOURNAL FORM—CASH ENTERED SOLELY IN THE CASH-BOOK, AND TRANSFERRED MONTHLY TO THE DAY-BOOK.

STEAMBOAT BOOKS.

PRACTICAL FORMS TO SAVE LABOR IN KEEPING BOOKS.

COMMERCIAL CALCULATIONS, OR MERCANTILE ARITHMETIC.

PREFACE.

In the fall of 1845, a treatise on Book-Keeping was published, entitled, "An Inductive and Practical System of Double Entry Book-Keeping," in two editions, one for the Counting-House, and the other (being an abridgment of the Counting-House edition) for High-Schools and Academies. In the preparation of that work for the press, the author of the present treatise was associated with his brother, A. F. Crittenden. In 1849, having purchased all his brother's interest in the former work, he prepared for publication as sole author a new treatise, (also in two editions,) similar in many respects to the former, but much more extended, embracing Single as well as Double Entry Book-Keeping, and made to conform more fully to the actual practice of our best accountants. Both these publications ran through several editions, and the latter especially has met with the most favorable reception in all parts of the United States, each succeeding year having shown a greatly enlarged demand for it.

The favor thus shown the work did not cause the author to lessen his endeavors to improve it, but rather stimulated him to increased effort to merit the favor bestowed upon it, and led to the publication of the present edition, which, as compared with the former, is improved in every way which the additional experience of several years in teaching in a large city, daily intercourse with practical accountants, and almost constant exercise in adjusting intricate accounts for others could suggest to him. In his efforts to improve the work he has been kindly and liberally aided by his publishers, who have spared no expense which would tend to make it more useful and acceptable.

It must be apparent to every careful observer that the science of Book-Keeping has of late received much more attention in our country than in former years, not only among merchants and business men generally, but in schools, both public and private; and the author confidently believes that the time is not far distant when it will be considered as essential a branch of an English education as Arithmetic or Grammar now is. Entertaining this opinion, he prepared for the press "An Elementary Treatise on Book-Keeping by Single and Double Entry, designed for Common Schools," which was published in April of this year, and which he trusts may prove a valuable auxiliary to teachers.

The three publications on Book-Keeping above named are now so arranged as to harmonize with each other, and to supply a series of text-books adapted, it is believed, for the use of learners at different stages of advancement, from the school-boy and mere tyro in commercial knowledge, to the man of mature years and cultivated business habits; while the more advanced work of the series will, the author hopes, be found to be not unworthy a place on the desk of the experienced accountant, as a book of reference.

The following is a concise summary of the leading features of the Counting-House edition, as now presented to the public:

1. Each set of books is so short that the pupil will be enabled to comprehend and trace out the connection between corresponding entries in the several account books of the set, and will not become fatigued with the extent of his business before ascertaining its result.
2. A sufficient number of sets is given to illustrate the *opening* and *closing* of books, both individual and partnership, under the various positions of gains and losses, capital and insolvency.
3. Plain and philosophical principles, to guide the reasoning faculties, are presented, instead of mere arbitrary directions and unnecessary classifications; and in the part by Double Entry, all elucidations of debits and credits are based on one *general rule deduced from the definition of debtor and creditor.*

4. Many of the entries are so classified as to bring those of a similar nature or of a directly opposite nature together, and thus to impress them upon the mind by strong *similarities* and *contrasts*.
5. Each successive exercise is intended to be a step of progress in the science, but yet so short and easy a step that what has already been explained shall be inductive thereto, and aid in its achievement.
6. The Day-Book, or the original history of transactions, is all that is furnished for several sets, *to prevent the possibility of merely copying*, and to compel the pupil to depend upon his own mental resources for his entries. Trial Balances, and other proofs, are however given to test the correctness of his work.
7. Each set is followed with questions for review, which will afford teachers an opportunity of ascertaining the amount of knowledge which their pupils have acquired, and will aid the pupil in fixing that knowledge permanently in his mind.
8. The nature and object of the different Leger accounts are discussed *after* the student has been made acquainted with the premises for reasonable conclusions.
9. The method of transferring accounts from one Leger to another is illustrated. Also, a business is shown, in which two partners are interested at starting, but afterward a third is taken into the concern.
10. A *foreign shipping* business is introduced. In preparing this important portion of the work, the author consulted with many practical accountants, and he feels assured he has presented the matter in a form well adapted to the wants of learners, and which will claim the approval of experienced book-keepers.
11. The space occupied with the *Italian method* of Book-Keeping (a form now obsolete in practice, although the foundation of all other forms) is barely sufficient to give those general ideas of journalizing, posting, &c., which must first be learned, and which can be better acquired under this form than any other; while the main portion of the work is devoted to *improved methods*, such as are now in use in counting-houses in the various branches of business.
12. An extended variety of *practical labor-saving Forms for keeping books* follows that portion of the work intended for imparting a general knowledge of the science; the object of each Form and the kind of business to which it is best suited being particularly described. These Forms, it is believed, far exceed in number and real utility those embraced in any other publication. They have been revised with rigid criticism, and some which were formerly inserted have been thrown aside as too theoretical, while others have been modified to make them the better suited to the specific business intended; and the author's endeavor has been to furnish *all*—the teacher, the mechanic, and the professional man, as well as the most extensive wholesale dealer, manufacturer, and commission merchant, with such information as each severally needs.
13. A series of *Commercial Calculations* are given, worked by the shortest and most approved methods; also, a *Table of the Coins and Moneys of Account* of the principal commercial nations of the world, showing their intrinsic values estimated according to the United States Mint valuation.
14. A *Key* to the work has been published for the use of teachers and private students, which contains the different Journals, Legers, Balance Sheets, &c., that are omitted in the treatise itself. Some books which are omitted in the High-school edition, and therefore given in the Key, will be found inserted in this edition, for the convenience of those who use it as a book of reference, and who do not wish to procure the Key.
15. *Blank books*, for writing up the sets, with printed explanations, have also been published.

The distinctive characteristics of the High-School edition are noticed in the *Brief Plan* of the work, which follows this Preface.

The author returns his sincere thanks to the many gentlemen, comprising in the number merchants, book-keepers, captains of vessels, and others, in various cities, (particularly in New York and Philadelphia,) who kindly aided him in his labors, both by their advice and by furnishing such business details as could be acquired only by a long pursuit of their several callings.

S. W. C.

PHILADELPHIA, Sept. 1st, 1853.

BRIEF PLAN OF THE WORK.

THIS work embraces illustrations of accounts kept by both Single and Double Entry. In the Single Entry, contained in the first 57 pages, four sets of books are shown, with entries for four different kinds of business, each set being preceded by explanatory remarks, descriptions of the books used, &c., and followed by exhibits of gains or losses, and of net capital or insolvency, resulting from the business, and by questions for review.

The author has endeavored to reduce the keeping of books by Single Entry (which is at best only a series of memoranda) as nearly to scientific principles as possible; but in his opinion the system of *Double Entry* alone deserves the appellation of *Book-keeping;* and any one who becomes thoroughly master of it, will not relinquish it, but will keep his accounts in accordance with its principles, whether engaged in business on a limited or an extensive scale. The greater part of this treatise has therefore been devoted to Double Entry Book-keeping.

In this Counting-House edition, the elementary portion of Double Entry, designed to impart a general knowledge of the science, embraces *three different methods* of keeping books. The first is the Italian method, so called from its supposed origin, and by this method three sets of books are given. The second is a method of dispensing with the Journal, and using a Day-Book in Journal form, from which postings are made direct to the Leger:—two sets of books are thus shown. The third method is similar to the second, with this variation, that the Cash-Book is the only book of original entry for moneys received or paid out, these entries being transferred from the Cash-Book to the Day-Book at the end of each month. This method is embraced in Set VI, which illustrates a *foreign shipping and commission business*, continued for three years—two partners for the first two years, and three partners for the third year. In the third year a new Day-Book and Leger is introduced, and the method of transferring accounts from one Leger to another is exhibited. In connection with Set VI, the various auxiliary books requisite in business are also given and explained.

Following the above-named six sets, is a set of *Steamboat* books, which will be found particularly serviceable to clerks on our Western rivers and lakes.

Lastly, in order to show how a knowledge of Book-keeping may be most advantageously applied to any specific branch of business, *six Practical Forms* are given, embracing *labor-saving* methods of keeping books, suited to mechanical, professional, retail, wholesale, jobbing, importing, manufacturing, and commission business. These Forms show how the general principles laid down in the elementary portion of the work may be applied to any particular method of keeping books which shall suit the taste of the book-keeper, or be best adapted to the specific kind of business. They exhibit plans for posting from one or more books of original entry, *without journalizing*, making the postings to the various property accounts in monthly totals, while personal accounts are posted daily—*for journalizing monthly*—for keeping commission books, *without opening Sales accounts in the Leger*, &c. &c.

Full explanations of the nature and use of the different books belonging to each set; the manner of opening and closing the Leger for individual or partnership business, commencing with capital or without capital, and winding up with gains or losses—capital or insolvency; directions for writing up the books, and also for the detection and correction of errors; questions for review; Balance Sheets, with instructions how to make them out; a discussion of the nature and object of the different Leger accounts, their modes of treatment, and the manner in which each is closed; and a Vocabulary of commercial terms, together with explanations of the abbreviations and characters made use of in commercial transactions, will all be found in their appropriate places, and may be readily referred to by means of the Table of Contents, pages 3 and 4.

At the close of the book, Commercial Calculations, Tables of Foreign Coins and Moneys of Account, and Time Tables are given.

The SERIES OF PRACTICAL TREATISES ON BOOK-KEEPING BY SINGLE AND DOUBLE ENTRY, of which this volume forms a part, comprises the following works:—

1. ELEMENTARY TREATISE ON BOOK-KEEPING FOR COMMON SCHOOLS.
   KEY to the same.
   BLANK BOOKS, for writing up the exercises contained therein.
2. INDUCTIVE AND PRACTICAL TREATISE ON BOOK-KEEPING: HIGH-SCHOOL EDITION.
   KEY to the same.
   BLANK BOOKS, for writing up the exercises contained therein.
3. INDUCTIVE AND PRACTICAL TREATISE ON BOOK-KEEPING: COUNTING-HOUSE EDITION.
   KEY to the same.
   BLANK BOOKS, for writing up the exercises contained therein.

No. 1, of the Series, was prepared with reference to the capacity of pupils of "Common" or "Grammar" schools, of from twelve to sixteen years of age, and elucidates the principles of the science, and the application of those principles to the more simple modes of keeping accounts, so that they may, it is believed, be fully understood by the class of pupils referred to. It contains four sets of books by Single Entry, illustrating four different kinds of business; and six sets by Double Entry, the first three of which are kept by the Italian method, the fourth and fifth have a Day-Book in Journal form, so as to dispense with the Journal, and the sixth is upon the plan of journalizing monthly.

No. 2, of the Series, is suited to pupils of a more advanced age, and a higher state of progress, and is designed for use in the higher schools, academies and other institutions of learning, in the United States, both male and female, public and private. All of the Single Entry and the first three sets of Double Entry (by the Italian method) are nearly the same as in the treatise for Common Schools, but the subsequent sets are varied and more extensive. It contains seven sets by Double Entry. The fourth, fifth and sixth sets are without a Journal, the Day-Book being in Journal form. The fifth illustrates domestic shipping, and the sixth foreign shipping business. The seventh is a plan for journalizing monthly, and illustrates a jobbing and importing business.

No. 3, of the Series, is intended as a book of reference for practical book-keepers, as a text-book for commercial schools, or institutions designed to prepare young men for immediate entrance upon the active duties of accountants, and as an aid to private students who wish a full and complete treatise. It is precisely like the High-School edition to the end of the sixth set by Double Entry. Following this, is a set of *Steamboat* books, and *six different Practical Forms, or shortened methods for keeping books*, suited to mechanical, professional, retail, wholesale, jobbing, manufacturing and commission business. The third of these Practical Forms is the same as Set VII of the High-School edition. This edition also embraces numerous Commercial Calculations, a knowledge of which is essential to the practical accountant, and Tables of Foreign Coins and Moneys of Account.

One word as to the *style* used by the author in this work. Knowing, from experience, the great advantages to be derived from adopting the *direct address* in teaching, he has, at the risk of incurring the charge of *egotism*, made use of pronouns of the first and second person, (I and You,) instead of the third person; and is confident that those who peruse with a desire to obtain information will be pleased that all formality has thus been laid aside, and the *conversational style* adopted in its stead. To those whose sole object is *criticism*, it need only be said, the book was not written for their pleasure.

VOCABULARY

OF

ABBREVIATIONS, CHARACTERS, AND MERCANTILE TERMS,

USED IN THIS WORK.

ABBREVIATIONS.

Adv.	Adventure.
Ac't	Account.
Amer.	American.
Am't	Amount.
Ans.	Answer.
Apr.	April.
Ass'd or *As'd*	Assorted.
Aug.	August.
Bal.	Balance.
B.-B.	Bill-Book, Bank-Book.
Bbl.	Barrel.
Bills Pay.	Bills Payable.
Bills Rec.	Bills Receivable.
B'k	Bank.
Blk.	Black.
Bo't	Bought.
Bro't	Brought.
Cap.	Capital.
C.-B.	Cash-Book.
Co.	Company.
Col'd	Colored.
Com.	Commission, Commerce.
Cons't	Consignment.
Cr.	Creditor.
D.-B.	Day-Book.
Dec.	December.
Dep.	Deposited.
D'ft	Draft.
Dis.	Discount.
Do.	[Ditto.] The same.
Doz.	Dozen.
Dr.	Debtor.
Dray.	Drayage.
d's	Days.
ea.	Each.
E. E.	Errors excepted.
E. & O. E.	Errors & omissions excepted.
Emb'd	Embroidered.
Eng.	English.
Ent.	Entry.
Ex.	Example.
Exch.	Exchange.
Exp's	Expenses.
fav.	Favor.
Feb.	February.
Fig'd	Figured.
fol.	Folio.
Forw'd	Forward.
Fr.	French.
fr.	From.
Fr't	Freight.
Gal.	Gallon.
Guar.	Guarantee.
Hhd.	Hogshead.
I.-B.	Invoice-Book.
i. e.	[Id est.] That is.
Ins.	Insurance.
Insol.	Insolvency.
inst.	[Instant.] The present month.
Int.	Interest.
Inv't	Inventory.
Jan.	January.
Jour.	Journal.
J. F.	Journal folio.
Lab.	Labor.
lbs.	Pounds.
Leg.	Leger.
L. F.	Leger folio.
Mar.	March.
Mdse.	Merchandise.
m. or *mo.*	Month.
Mols.	Molasses.
Mut.	Mutal.
N. B.	[Nota Bene.] Take notice.
No.	Number.
Nov.	November.
Oct.	October.
O.-I.-B.	Outward-Invoice-Book.
p.	Page.
Pay't	Payment.
P.-C.-B.	Petty-Cash-Book.
P'ch's	Purchases.
P'd	Paid.
P'k'g's	Packages.
P. & L.	Profit & Loss.
Per.	Personal.
Pr.	Pair.
pr.	[Per.] By.
pr. ct.	[Per centum.] By the hundred.
Prem.	Premium.
Prof.	Profit.
prox.	[Proximo.] The next month.
Ps.	Pieces.
Rec'd	Received.
R.-R.	Rail-road.
S.-B.	Sales-Book.
Sept.	September.
Sh.	Share.
Ship't	Shipment.
St'b't	Steamboat.
Stor.	Storage.
Sund's	Sundries.
Super. or *S. F.*	Superfine.
ult.	[Ultimo.] The last month.
viz.	[Videlicet.] To wit—namely.
vs.	[Versus.] Against.
Weigh.	Weighing.
Yds.	Yards.
yr.	Year.

CHARACTERS.

@	At.
℅	Account.
¢	Cents.
%	[Per centum.] By the hundred.
#	Number.
$+$	Sign of addition.
$-$	" " subtraction.
$\times$	" " multiplication.
$\div$	" " division.
$=$	" " equality.
"	[Ditto.] The same.
1^1	One & one-quarter.
1^2	One & one-half.
1^3	One & three-quarters.

MERCANTILE TERMS.

Abatement, a deduction or discount for damages on goods, or for payment of demands before due, etc.

Acceptance, 1st. The receiving of a bill of exchange or order, in such a way as to bind the acceptor to payment. It consists in the acceptor's writing across the face of the bill "Accepted," and signing his name. If drawn payable at a certain number of days' sight, the date of acceptance should also be given. 2d. A bill of exchange accepted.

Accommodation, a loan of money. When applied to bills of exchange it is where the *drawee* lends his *name* for the use of the drawer.

Account-Current, an exhibit in detail of a running account between two or more parties.

Account-Sales, an exhibit of the sales of goods disposed of on commission, with the charges incurred thereon.

Ad valorem, according to value. An *ad valorem duty* is a certain percentage on the first cost, or invoice price.

VOCABULARY.

Advance, additional price; profit; premium. Money paid on property or goods expected, or on goods held in possession for security.
Adventure, goods sent to a distance to be sold on commission. Any speculation in Co.
Advice, mercantile intelligence.
Annuity, a sum of money payable periodically, usually yearly.
Ante-date, to date before the present time; to date beforehand.
Arbitration, the hearing and determination of a cause between parties in controversy, by a person or persons chosen for the purpose. A hearing before arbitrators though they make no award.
Assets, available means for payment of debts; goods, estate, and indebtedness of others.
Assignee, one to whom an assignment is made. One appointed or deputed for some specific purpose.
Assignment, conditional transfer of property to another. The property so transferred.
Assignor, one who makes an assignment.
Attachment, a claim on property legally executed.
Aune, a French cloth measure, one yard and a quarter.
Average, sums allowed for losses at sea. A medium time found by equation.

Balance, to close an account in the Leger. Difference between the debits and credits. An account in the Leger, into which all balances are closed.
Bankrupt, insolvent. One unable to pay his debts.
Bill, or *Bill of Parcels,* a statement in detail of goods bought or sold.
Bills, a term applied to drafts, notes, etc.
Bill of Entry, a list of goods entered at the Custom-house.
Bill of Exchange, an order for the payment of money; usually applied to drafts on persons in another state or country from the drawer.
Bill of Lading, a written account of goods shipped, having the signature of the master of the vessel on which shipped.
Bill of Sale, a contract, under seal, for the sale of goods.
Bill of Store, a Custom-house license for carrying to sea ship-stores and provisions free of duty.
Blank Credit, permission granted by one house to another to draw on it at pleasure to a specified amount.
Bona fide, in good faith.
Bond, a note. An obligation or deed by which a person binds himself, his heirs, executors, and administrators, to pay a certain sum on or before a certain day.
Bonded goods, those for the duties on which bonds are given at the Custom-house.
Bottomry Bond, a mortgage or lien upon a vessel.
Brace, a measure of $\frac{5}{8}$ of a yard.
Broker, a money or stock trader. Factor; agent.
Brokerage, a percentage for the purchase and sale of money and stocks.

Capital, stock in trade.
Cargo, the lading or freight of a vessel.
Catty, a Chinese weight of $1\frac{1}{3}$ lbs. avoirdupois.
Carrying trade, the transportation of goods by vessels from country to country.
Charter-party, a written agreement between the owner of a vessel and the person to whom she is chartered.
Circular letter, a printed notice issued by a house, relative to its business.
Clearing a vessel, entering at the Custom-house all particulars relating to her when she is ready to sail, and paying clearance charges.
Clearance, a certificate from a Custom-house that a vessel has been cleared.
Closing an account, making an entry to balance it, and drawing lines underneath to indicate that it is closed.
Cocket, a Custom-house warrant to show that goods have been entered.
Commission, a percentage allowed for the sale of goods.
Compound, to settle with a creditor by agreement, and discharge a debt by paying a part of its amount.
Compromise, an adjustment of differences by mutual concessions.
Consignee, one to whom goods or wares are consigned.
Consignment, goods sent to an agent to be sold for the consignor.
Consignor, the person making a consignment.
Contraband goods, articles prohibited by law to be imported or exported.
Contra, on the other side; opposite.
Convoy, ships of war sailing with other vessels as a protection.
Co-partnership, the union of two or more persons for purposes of trade.
Counter order, a revocation of a former order.
Credit, that side of an account which shows the amount due to the person or thing represented. The amount of confidence reposed in another.
Custom-house, the house where vessels are entered and cleared, and where the duties on goods are paid.

Days of grace, the days allowed for the payment of a bill after it becomes due. In the United States, and in Great Britain and her dependencies, the number of days of grace is *three;* but it varies very much in other commercial states, reaching 30 days in Genoa, there being none allowed at Leghorn. Bills drawn at sight are usually paid when presented, without grace.
Debenture, drawback of duties on goods imported, when afterward exported according to law.
Debit, that side of an account which shows the indebtedness of the person or thing represented.
Defalcation, deduction; diminution. That which is deducted or cut off.
Demurrage, forfeit money for detaining a vessel beyond the time specified in her Charter-party.
Depot, a place where goods are deposited; a depository; a magazine.
Deviation, the voluntary departure of a vessel, without necessity, from the regular and usual course of the specific voyage insured, which frees the underwriters from obligation.
Discount, any deduction from the stipulated price of goods, or from a sum due or to be due at a future time.
Dividend, gains on stock, shares in trade, etc.
Dock, a place to build, repair, or lodge vessels.
Draft, an order from one person on another for the payment of money; a bill of exchange.
Drawer, the one who draws a bill or draft on another. The maker of a note.
Drawee, the person on whom a bill is drawn.

Drawback, amount paid back. Any loss of advantage, or deduction from profit.
Duplicate, a copy.
Duty, a government tax on exported or imported goods.

Effects, money, property on hand, and debts due.
Ell Flemish (E. Fl.), a measure of $\frac{3}{4}$ yd.
Embargo, a restraint on ships by Government; or prohibition of sailing either out of port, or into port, or both.
Emporium, a mart. A town or city of trade; particularly a commercial city.
Endorse, to write one's name on the back of a bill; to become obligated for its payment.
Entry, a record made in an account book. The depositing of a ship's papers at the Custom-house, to procure license to land goods.
Engross, to monopolize; to purchase the whole or large quantities of commodities, in market, so as to enhance the price.
Equity of redemption, the advantage allowed to a mortgager, of a reasonable time to redeem lands mortgaged.
Exchange, the giving of one commodity for another. The place where merchants, bankers, and brokers meet, at certain hours, to transact business. Discount and premium arising from the purchase and sale of bills and money.

Face, the amount for which a bill is drawn.
Fac-Simile, an exact copy.
Factor, an agent employed by merchants to buy and sell, or transact business, on their account.
Failure, a breaking or becoming insolvent.
Favor, a bill is said to be drawn in *favor* of the person to whom it is payable.
Finance, or *Finances,* revenue; funds in the public treasury. The resources or income of individuals.
Financier, one skilled in money matters. A revenue officer.
Firm, the name or title under which a company transact business; a partnership, or house.
Flat, low, [as to the prices of goods;] or dull, [as to sales.]
Foreclose, to *foreclose* a mortgage is to cut a mortgager off from his equity of redemption.
Folio, page of an account book; both the right and left hand pages expressed by the same figure.
Freight, lading; that which is carried by water. Sum charged by a vessel for the transportation of goods.

Guarantee, or *Guaranty,* indemnity or security against loss; a pledge for the fulfilment of stipulations; one who binds himself to see the stipulations of another performed.
Grace, see *Days of grace.*

Honor, as applied to drafts, means to accept and pay when due.
Hypothecate, to pledge; to give as security.
Hypothecated, pledged, as security for money borrowed.

Importation, the bringing of goods from another country to one's own country. The commodities imported.
Insurance, security against loss. The premium paid for insuring property or life.
Insolvent, not having money, goods, or estate sufficient to pay all debts. A debtor unable to pay his debts.
Instalment, a part of a sum of money paid, or to be paid, at a particular period.
Interest, a percentage paid for the use of money.
International, relating to the mutual intercourse between different nations.
Inventory, an account in detail of property.
Invoice, see *Inventory.* *Inventory* is generally applied to a catalogue of goods on hand; *Invoice,* to goods purchased, received from abroad, or about to be shipped.

Land Waiter, a Custom-house officer whose duty it is to *wait* or attend on the landing of goods.
Lease, a contract granting possession of property for a stipulated time.
Letter of Attorney, a writing by which one person authorizes another to act in his stead.
Letter of Credit, a letter authorizing one person to receive funds on the credit of another.
Letter of License, a written permission to a person under embarrassment to conduct his business for a time without molestation.
Letter of Marque, a written commission or authority given by government to private vessels, to make reprisals on the vessels of another nation.
Liabilities, debts of an individual, or claims against him.
License, a legal permit to sell certain articles of merchandise.
Lien, legal claim, as a lien upon land, houses, &c.
Lighter, a craft used to lighten vessels in shoal water.
Lighterage, a charge for carrying goods to and from a vessel in a lighter.
Liquidation, the act of adjusting and paying debts.

Manifest, an exhibit of a vessel's cargo.
Mart, a place of public sale and traffic.
Maturity, the time when a bill falls due.
Maximum, the highest price of an article.
Merchandise, the usual articles of trade.
Metre, a measure of $1\frac{1}{12}$ yds.
Minimum, the lowest price of an article.
Mint, a place where money is coined.
Mortgage, the grant of an estate in fee, as security for the payment of money.
Mortgager, the person who grants or pledges property, for security of debt.
Mortgagee, the person to whom an estate is mortgaged.

Net proceeds, the remainder after deducting all charges from the amount of gross sales.
Net weight, the weight of a commodity after deducting tare, and all other allowances.
Non claim, a failure to claim within the time limited by law. Omission of claim.

Notary, or *Notary Public,* a person legally authorized to attest contracts, or writings of any kind; also to take note of the non-payment of bills, promissory notes, &c., which is called protesting.
Note, a written obligation to pay money. A memorandum.

Obligation, indebtedness. A bond, with a consideration annexed, and a penalty for non-fulfilment.
Obligee, the person to whom another is bound.
Obligor, the person who binds himself, or gives his bond to another.
Order, a request to deliver or pay to a person certain moneys or goods. Any request made of another in writing.

Par of Exchange, the intrinsic value of money, when compared with that of other countries, both in weight and fineness.
Partnership, see *Co-Partnership.*
Payee, the person to whom money is to be paid.
Per annum, by the year.
Picul, a Chinese weight of 133⅓ lbs. avoirdupois.
Policy, or *Policy of Insurance,* the writing, or instrument, by which a contract of indemnity to the insured is effected between him and the insurer.
Portage, the incidental sums paid by a Captain in running his vessel.
Postdate, to date after the real time.
Posting, transferring the Journal entries to the Leger.
Power of Attorney, authority given to a person to act for another.
Price Current, a list of various articles of Mdse., with their market values.
Principal, the chief of a commercial house or firm. Capital sum due, lent, or owed, in contradistinction to interest.
Primage, a percentage allowed to the master of a vessel on the amount of freight transported.
Procuration, the act of procuring. The instrument by which a person is empowered to transact business for another.
Pro forma, according to form. Thus a *pro forma* Account-Sales is an imaginary Account-Sales, made out in form of a real one, to send to parties abroad, to give information of prices, charges, commission, &c.
Promissory Note, a writing which contains a promise of the payment of money, or the delivery of property at or before a specified time.
Protest, a Notary's document, declaring that a bill was not accepted when presented, or was not paid when it fell due.

Quarantine, restraint of intercourse to which a ship is subjected, for a limited term, on the presumption that she may be infected with a malignant, contagious disease.

Rate of Exchange, the per centum above or below the par value of a bill of exchange.
Rebate, or *Rebatement,* abatement of price; deduction for prompt payment.
Receipt, a writing acknowledging the receipt of money or goods.
Remittance, bills or money sent from one house to another. The act of sending the same.
Renewal of a Bill, prolonging the time of payment.
Resources, funds, money, or that which may be converted into supplies. See *Assets.*

Salvage, a reward allowed for saving property from loss at sea.
Schedule, a piece of paper or parchment containing an inventory of goods.
Sea-worthy, fitted in every respect for a voyage.
Seize, to take possession by virtue of a warrant, or legal authority.
Set of Exchange, a number of *Bills of Exchange,* (usually three,) drawn of the same tenor and date. Each bill is forwarded by a different conveyance, to prevent failures, and one of them being paid, the remainder are of no value.
Shipment, the act of putting goods on board a vessel. The goods shipped.
Sight, or *at sight,* the time when a bill is presented to the drawee.
Signature, the name of a person written or subscribed by himself.
Sine die, without fixing the day.
Sine qua non, without which a thing cannot be; hence an indispensable condition.
Smuggling, passing goods into a country clandestinely, without paying duties.
Solidity, the estimate a mercantile house bears as to property.
Solvent, able to pay all debts.
Staple Goods, the principal produce of a country. Goods not liable to perish.
Stock, capital invested in trade. Goods on hand. The name of a person in business.
Surety, security against loss or damage. One bound for the payment of another's debts; bondsman; bail.

Tare, an allowance for the weight of boxes, barrels, &c., in which Mdse. is put up.
Tariff, a list or table of duties or customs on Mdse. imported or exported.
Teller, an officer of a bank, employed to receive deposits or pay money on checks.
Tide-waiters, officers who watch the lading and unlading of vessels, to secure duties, as a check on contraband trade, &c.
Tonnage, the weight or measurement of goods carried in a vessel, or the capacity of a vessel.
Transfer, to carry from one account to another. To make over; to convey from one to another.
Trustee, a person to whom any thing, or business, is committed.

Underwriters, persons who insure property against loss.
Usury, formerly interest—in present usage, *illegal* interest.

Voucher, a book, paper, or document, which serves to vouch the truth of accounts.

Wharfage, money paid for the use of a wharf.
Wreckers, persons employed in saving property from shipwreck.

Book-Keeping

BY

SINGLE ENTRY.

INTRODUCTION

TO

SINGLE ENTRY BOOK-KEEPING.

BOOK-KEEPING *is the science of accounts*, and teaches how to preserve a correct record of all business transactions. There are two distinct methods of keeping accounts, termed Book-Keeping by *Single Entry* and Book-Keeping by *Double Entry*.

In *Single Entry* Book-Keeping, each entry is a *single entry*, that is, consists of *but one debit*, or *one credit;* while in *Double Entry* Book-Keeping, every entry contains *both a debit and a credit.*

The principles of Single Entry are so easy of comprehension as scarcely to need explanation. Accounts are usually kept only with the *persons* with whom you have dealings, and although a Cash account, Merchandise account, and other *property* accounts may be kept, yet just so far as you introduce any other accounts except those with *persons* who owe you, or whom you owe, so far do you encroach upon the peculiar province of Double Entry, as is more fully explained on page 60.

The principal books of entry are a *Day-Book* and *Leger.* Besides these there are several smaller books which are convenient, and some of which are absolutely essential to be kept. These are usually termed *auxiliary* books, and vary in number and form according to the business. They will all be described and shown in the subsequent pages of this book. Of these the CASH-BOOK is the most important, and should never be dispensed with where there are any considerable dealings in cash. In it all receipts and payments of cash are entered, and it is a constant check upon your cash transactions to test their accuracy.

THE DAY-BOOK.—All transactions are entered in this book which require a debit or credit to any person with whom you have dealings. The form of entry is very simple, thus: "John Brown Dr. To 6 lbs. Nails @ 7¢, 42¢," or "Samuel Henry Cr. By Cash on a/c $5.00;" in every case specifying the details which constitute the debit or credit. This is the only book from which posts are made to the Leger.

THE LEGER.—Into this book all sums entered in the Day-Book are transferred, an account being opened with each different person, into which every debit and credit made to that person is collected. This process is called posting, and the advantages derived from it are, that, by looking at any person's account in the Leger, you can see at a glance your whole dealings with that person, and also the balance which is due him or you, which you could not find without much trouble and great liability to error, if the amounts of debit and credit were all left standing scattered through the Day-Book.

SET I, SINGLE ENTRY.

EXPLANATORY REMARKS, SET I.

CASH-BOOK, SET I.

The Cash-Book [see page 19] is a simple memorandum-book for keeping the Cash account correctly. There are various ways of keeping the Cash-Book, but the form here shown is perhaps as simple as any, as easily kept, and as little liable to mistakes, for persons whose cash transactions are not very numerous, and who are not scientific accountants. It contains two columns for dollars and cents.*

Whenever money is received from any source whatever, it must be entered in this book as "Rec'd," (describing for what,) and the amount must be extended into the *left* hand dollar and cent column, which is called the *debit* column; and whenever money is paid out for any purpose whatever, it must also be entered in this book as "Paid," (telling for what,) and the amount extended into the *right* hand dollar and cent column, called the *credit* column. Thus, if the account is kept correctly, the difference between these two columns will show at all times the *balance* of cash on hand, and will agree with the actual amount of money in possession, counting that which is deposited in bank, as well as what is in the store or shop; and if it does not so agree, there has been some error, which must be searched for and corrected. The credit column can never be the larger, since it is impossible to pay out more money than you receive.

The Cash-Book should be balanced at the end of each week—or daily, when much business is done—by entering in the credit column the balance of cash on hand, (usually done in *red* ink,) ruling and footing both columns, and underneath the closure entering the balance on hand (in black ink) in the debit column.

The Cash account may be tested at any time, without balancing the Cash-Book, by finding the difference between the debit and credit columns, on a scrap of paper, and comparing that difference with the cash on hand. This should be done daily, when the Cash-Book is balanced only once a week.

DAY-BOOK, SET I.

Whenever you do a job of work for any person, or sell him any thing, or pay him money, or he in any other manner becomes indebted to you, he must be charged (or debited) with the same in this book, to show that *he owes you*. And whenever any person sells you any thing, pays you money, or does work for you, or you in any other manner become indebted to him, he must be credited with the same in this book, to show that *you owe him*. [See form of entry, page 20.]

This is the only book from which you post, and therefore every entry which you wish to bring into any account in the Leger must be entered here. *Erasures* are *not allowable* in the Day-Book, as they look suspicious, and frequently render invalid the evidence of entries therein. [See remarks on detection and correction of errors, page 111.]

In entering *purchases*, it is allowable to say, "Am't as pr. Bill," or "Am't as pr. Invoice," and omit the detail of items, since you have the Invoice filed away, or pasted in a book, so that you can refer to it at any time; but in entering *Sales*, the *items* should *always* be mentioned in your Day-Book, as this is your legal evidence of the transaction; and in order to be taken as evidence, each article must be distinctly named.

LEGER, SET I.

This Leger contains the accounts of persons only, and is used for collecting in one place all the items of debit and credit belonging to any one man, which are found scattered in separate entries over many pages in the Day-Book; and thus presenting the account before us complete, for ascertaining the gross amount of debit and credit, and the balance due either party; and also affording an easy reference to the various items, by the date and page of the Day-Book.

* The pupil will observe that throughout the book, in speaking of the money columns, I designate the space for dollars and the space for cents, united, as but one column.

DEFINITIONS.

As some may be at a loss to know the true meaning of the words *debtor* and *creditor*, *debit* and *credit*, I will here define them as used in Single Entry.

DEBTOR, the person who owes you.

CREDITOR, the person whom you owe.

DEBIT—*as a verb*—to make the proper entry of a person's indebtedness to you:—*as an adjective*—that side of a person's account which shows his indebtedness to you.

CREDIT—*as a verb*—to make the proper entry of your indebtedness to another person:—*as an adjective*—that side of a person's account which shows your indebtedness to him.

For a more perfect definition of these words, and a fuller explanation of their true philosophy, see the Introduction to Double Entry, pages 61 and 62. Also, for the definition of any terms, words, or abbreviations which you do not understand, refer to the Vocabulary, pages 9–12.

INSTRUCTIONS FOR WRITING UP CASH-BOOK AND DAY-BOOK, SET I.

The intention is, that Sets I and II shall be written on loose sheets of paper for practice, and then Set III may be written in the blank books which accompany this work. This previous practice on loose sheets will enable the pupil to fill his blank books neatly and correctly. Ruling the sheets will be also very useful to the pupil, as he will be able to rule his Legers and other books much more book-keeper-like after this practice. The rulings in books, except the ordinary faint lines for writing on, look better to be in red ink.

Prepare some paper, ruled after the patterns given for the different books. Then in the Cash-Book enter the amount of cash at commencing business, on the 1st day of September, and the amounts paid out for paints, &c., on the same day; and in the Day-Book enter the debit to B. T. Stokes. Next, enter in the Cash-Book the payments out for gold leaf, step ladders, and muslin on the 2d inst.; and in the Day-Book the debits to Mayland, Morris & Co., and to T. Templeton. Follow this with the receipt of cash in the Cash-Book, on the 3d inst. —— and this, again, with the entries in both Cash-Book and Day-Book, on the 4th inst.

Having completed the first week, balance your Cash-Book, and bring the balance down to the beginning of the subsequent week. Continue the entries of this week in the Cash-Book and Day-Book, *in order of date*, the same as the preceding, and so on, successively, balancing your Cash-Book at the close of each week, until you come to the end of the month.

It makes no difference in which book the entries of any given day are *first* made, as in a real business the entry would be put down at the time of the transaction, and would be sometimes placed in the Cash-Book and sometimes in the Day-Book, according to its nature. Some transactions, however, require an entry in each book at the same time; as, for instance, on the 4th inst., Geo. L. Searles is credited with his wages, and charged with cash on account in the Day-Book, and then the cash is recorded also in the Cash-Book. A little observation and thought, however, will enable you to discover which transactions require entering in both books, and which only in one.

You will perceive some of the hands employed have accounts opened with them in the Leger, and some have not. Those paid in full at the end of each week, have not.

INSTRUCTIONS FOR WRITING UP LEGER, SET I.

After having finished writing up the Cash-Book and Day-Book, as just described, the next step is to post the entries from the Day-Book to the Leger. This is done as follows:—The first entry in the Day-Book is a debit to Stokes, for whom you open an account on the Leger, thus: "*Dr.*———*Bailey T. Stokes*———*Cr.*;" [see page 22;] then on the debit side, underneath this heading, place the date, description, Day-Book folio, and amount, as found in the Day-Book, which completes the post of the 1st inst. Next *post-mark* the entry, *i. e.* place the folio of the Leger to which it is taken, in the left-hand marginal column of the Day-Book.

Underneath the account of Stokes in the Leger, open, in the same manner, an account for *Mayland, Morris & Co.*, leaving a sufficient space for all the entries that will probably be posted to Stokes. On the debit side of this account post the entry of the 2d inst., post-marking it in the Day-Book, to show that it is posted. Follow this with the account of *Thomas Templeton,* and so on, successively, opening an account in the Leger for each different name. But when entries to any person occur subsequently to having opened an account with that person in the Leger, post all such subsequent entries into the account already opened. *Credits* must be posted to the *credit* side of the account; and where there is both a debit and a credit in the same entry, as in the entry to Searles on the 4th inst., it requires two posts, one on each side of the account. Any accounts which are paid in full, as that of Stokes on the 7th inst., *may be closed* at the time, and entries occurring subsequently must then be posted underneath the closure.

When the whole month has been posted, you may re-examine each item, checking the entries with a pencil in the Day-Book and Leger, to be sure that no mistakes have been made. This is the only test of correctness that exists in Single Entry Book-Keeping, and is quite essential if you would avoid errors, which are very apt to occur in posting. After satisfying yourself of the accuracy of your work, you may proceed to close up your Leger, as you would at the expiration of a year in actual business. Those accounts which have been paid in full, if not closed at the settlement, may now be closed by ruling them according to the sample given, and adding up the accounts, if they need adding up. Those accounts which have debit or credit balances still unsettled, may also be closed by making a *red ink* entry, (indicated by *Italics,*) on the smaller side of the account, saying, "*To Bal. to new a/c,*" or "*By Bal. to new a/c,*" ruling and footing up the account, and placing the balance underneath the closure, on the opposite side of the account.

In the printed Leger given, you will observe that the *perpendicular lines* are interrupted by spaces left for inserting each name, which cannot well be avoided in printing, although, in blank books ruled for the counting-house, the lines generally extend connectedly the whole length of the page. In most blank books ruled for Legers, the only *horizontal lines* across the page (except the faint lines for writing upon) are the double lines at the top of the page. The other single lines above and double lines underneath each account are ruled by hand, and I think it is quite as well to dispense with them altogether, and open accounts after the following sample.

Dr.——————*Mayland, Morris & Co.*——————*Cr.*

This form is neat, easily done, and, I think, looks better than so much ruling. All rulings on the Leger should be in *red ink.*

The number of accounts to be opened on a page in actual business must be determined by the judgment of the book-keeper. An account that is likely to fill up soon, should have a whole page left for it: smaller accounts may be placed two on a page, and in some cases, though seldom, three or four.

In writing up these sets for practice, you can place as many accounts as you have room for on each page; but be careful not to crowd one account on another, as this looks excessively awkward.

The accounts may be arranged in the Leger in any order that suits the taste of the accountant, as will be seen more fully hereafter.

The *Alphabet* or *Index,* a small book that always accompanies the Leger, will be explained in Set II. The pupil need not make it out in this set.

Sets of books, in actual business, are usually closed yearly, and the continuance of Sets I and II for one month each is to be understood as for one year.

NOTE.—In the closure of all the Sets in this volume, I have supposed that no bad debts exist on the Leger. But if any debts are known to be bad, or are even thought doubtful, an ample allowance should be made for them, in estimating your profits.

CASH-BOOK, SET I.

		Cash.	*Dr.*		*Cr.*	
1852.						
Sept.	1	Am't of Cash on hand at commencing business	500	00		
“	“	Paid for Paints, Oils, Glass, Brushes, &c., pr. Adam's Bill			105	32
“	2	“ “ 2 Books Gold Leaf				75
“	“	“ “ Making Step Ladders			5	00
“	“	“ “ Muslin				37
“	3	Rec'd of S. Lambert for Glazing 27 Lights 10 by 12 @ 25 ¢	6	75		
“	4	Paid Geo. L. Searles on a/c of Wages pr. D.-B.			3	00
“	“	“ Wm. Boyd, Jr., 3 days' Work @ $1.50			4	50
“	“	“ Hiram Smith 2 “ “ @ .75			1	50
“	“	**Balance in Bank*, $345.00, *in Safe*, $41.31			386	31
			506	75	506	75
Sept.	6	Balance Cash on hand	386	31		
“	“	Rec'd of John Payson for painting Sign as pr. agreement	30	00		
“	7	“ “ Bailey T. Stokes in full of a/c	6	75		
“	8	Paid Jonathan Long & Co. on a/c			25	00
“	11	“ “ “ “ “ “			10	00
“	“	“ George L. Searles on a/c of Wages pr. D.-B.			9	00
“	“	“ Hiram L. Smith 5^2 days' Work @ 75 ¢			4	13
“	“	*Balance in Bank*, $364.93, *in Safe*, $10.00			374	93
			423	06	423	06
Sept.	13	Balance Cash on hand	374	93		
“	17	Rec'd for 37 lbs. Blue Paint @ 25 ¢	9	25		
“	18	Paid George L. Searles in full pr. D.-B.			7	50
“	“	Rec'd for 2 Lights 10 by 20 Stained Glass @ $4.50	9	00		
“	“	Paid Hiram Smith 6 days' Work @ $1.00			6	00
“	“	*Balance in Bank*, $374.43, *in Safe*, $5.25			379	68
			393	18	393	18
Sept.	20	Balance Cash on hand	379	68		
“	“	Rec'd of Timothy Stone for 120 lbs. White Paint @ 11 ¢	13	20		
“	“	Paid for Repairs of Shop			2	12
“	“	“ “ making Transparency Frame			4	38
“	24	Rec'd of J. F. Goodwin, for Stained Glass, as pr. agreement	25	00		
“	“	“ “ Harry Biddle for painting Church, “ “	210	00		
“	25	Paid Foster B. Jones 6 days' Work @ $1.50			9	00
“	“	“ Walter Hughes 5^2 “ “ @ $1.50			8	25
“	“	“ Hiram Smith 5 “ “ @ $1.00			5	00
“	“	“ Peter Lundy 4^2 “ “ @ $ .75			3	38
“	“	*Balance in Bank*, $541.75, *in Safe*, $54.00			595	75
			627	88	627	88
Sept.	27	Balance Cash on hand	595	75		
“	“	Paid Peter Lee, Carpenter, for Sundry Jobs, as pr. Bill			22	50
“	28	“ for 10 galls. Linseed Oil @ $1.62²			16	25
“	29	Rec'd for Tin Sign	10	00		
“	“	Paid for Tin and Japanning			4	25
“	30	“ Hiram Smith 6 days' Work @ $1.00			6	00
“	“	“ Rent of Shop one month			16	67
“	“	*Balance in Bank*, $521.43, *in Safe*, $18.65			540	08
1852.			605	75	605	75
Oct.	1	Balance from Sept. 30th /52	540	08		

* *Italics* denote *red ink.*

DAY-BOOK, SET I.

Philadelphia, September 1*st,* 1852.

L. F.				
*1	Bailey T. Stokes	Dr.		
	To Lettering Tin Sign		1.75	
	" 1 Light Stained Glass		5.00	6.75
	2d			
1	Mayland, Morris & Co.	Dr.		
	To Bronzing Candelabra			2.00
	3d			
1	Thomas Templeton	Dr.		
	To Bronzing Valve		50	
	" 6 lbs. Blue Paint @ 25 ¢		1.50	
	" 18 lbs. White " @ 12½ ¢		2.25	4.25
	4th			
1	Camden & Amboy Rail-Road Co.	Dr.		
	To Lettering Sign 60 feet, @ 20 ¢ pr. foot		12.00	
	" Gilding Border of Sign		2.00	
	" Putting up Sign		2.50	16.50
	"			
1	George L. Searles	Cr.		
	By 4 days' Labor @ $1.50			6.00
	Dr.			
1	To Cash on a/c			3.00
	6th			
1	Camden & Amboy Rail-Road Co.	Dr.		
	To Lettering Sign 15 feet, @ 20 ¢		3.00	
	" Making Board and putting up		4.25	7.25
	"			
2	Henry Talbott	Cr.		
	By Making Sign for Camden & Amboy R.-R. Co.			3.00
	7th			
1	Bailey T. Stokes	Cr.		
	By Cash in full of a/c			6.75
	8th			
2	Jonathan Long & Co.	Cr.		
	By Paints, Oils &c., as pr. Bill			52.64
	Dr.			
2	To Cash in Part			25.00
	"			
2	Wm. G. Bradbury	Cr.		
	By Bill of Glass and Putty		17.50	
	" " " Paints and Oils		122.50	140.00

* Omit the figures in the left-hand marginal column, until you post. These figures are the postmarks.

DAY-BOOK, SET I. 2

Philadelphia, September 9th, 1852.

L. F.				
1	Thomas Templeton Dr.			
	To Glazing 1 Light 11 by 18			37
	— 11th —			
2	Jonathan Long & Co. Dr.			
	To Cash on %	10.00		
	" Glazing 10 Lights 10 by 18 @ 25¢	2.50	12	50
	— " —			
1	George L. Searles Cr.			
	By 5½ days' Labor @ $1.50		8	25
	Dr.			
1	To Cash on %		9	00
	— 13th —			
2	Philadelphia Exchange Dr.			
	To Glazing 4 Lights 10 by 16 @ 25¢	1.00		
	" Painting 3 Rooms, 2 Coats, as pr. Agreement	15.00	16	00
	— 15th —			
1	Camden & Amboy Rail-Road Co. Cr.			
	By my Order on them, favor of J. Long & Co.		15	14
	— " —			
2	Jonathan Long & Co. Dr.			
	To my Order, their favor, on Camden & Amboy R.-R. Co.		15	14
	— 18th —			
1	George L. Searles Cr.			
	By 3½ days Labor @ $1.50		5	25
	Dr.			
1	To Cash in full (discharged)		7	50
	— 22d —			
2	Sargeant & Willis Dr.			
	To Stained Glass for Transparency, Frame, and putting up as agreed		40	00
	— 25th —			
1	Bailey T. Stokes Dr.			
	To Glazing New Sash at Manufactory, as pr. Agreement, to wit,			
	56 Lights 11 by 15 @ 9¢	5.04		
	139 " 10 by 12 @ 7¢	9.73		
	1920 " 8 by 10 @ 3¢	57.60		
	" 20 " Old Glazing 11 by 17 @ 35¢	7.00		
	" Painting 110 Window Frames @ 45¢	49.50		
	" " Reception Room	5.25	134	12
	— 27th —			
1	Thomas Templeton Cr.			
	By 1 Blk. Cloth Dress Coat	15.00		
	" 1 Pr. Blk. Cass. Pants	6.00	21	00
	— 30th —			
2	Sargeant & Willis Dr.			
	To Painting office as pr. Agreement		30	00

1

LEGER, SET I.

Dr. *Bailey T. Stokes.* *Cr.*

Date.		Description.	D.-B. Folio.	Amount.		Date.		Description.	D.-B. Folio.	Amount	
1852. Sept.	1	To Sundries	1	6	75	1852. Sept.	7	By Cash	1	6	75
1852. Sept.	25	To Glazing, &c.	2	134	12						

Dr. *Mayland, Morris & Co.* *Cr.*

Date.		Description.	D.-B. Folio.	Amount.		Date.		Description.	D.-B. Folio.	Amount	
1852. Sept.	2	To bronzing candelabra	1	2	00						

Dr. *Thomas Templeton.* *Cr.*

Date.		Description.	D.-B. Folio.	Amount.		Date.		Description.	D.-B. Folio.	Amount	
1852. Sept.	3	To Sundries	1	4	25	1852. Sept.	27	By Sundries	2	21	00
"	9	" Glazing	2		37						
"	30	" *Bal. to New %*		16	38						
				21	00					21	00
						1852. Oct.	1	By Bal. fr. Old %		16	38

Dr. *Camden & Amboy Rail Road Co.* *Cr.*

Date.		Description.	D.-B. Folio.	Amount.		Date.		Description.	D.-B. Folio.	Amount	
1852. Sept.	4	To Sundries	1	16	50	1852. Sept.	15	By Order on them	2	15	14
"	6	" "	1	7	25		30	" *Bal. to New %*		8	61
				23	75					23	75
1852. Oct.	1	To Bal. fr. Old %		8	61						

Dr. *George L. Searles.* *Cr.*

Date.		Description.	D.-B. Folio.	Amount.		Date.		Description.	D.-B. Folio.	Amount	
1852. Sept.	4	To Cash	1	3	00	1852. Sept.	4	By Labor	1	6	00
"	11	" "	2	9	00	"	11	" "	2	8	25
"	18	" "	2	7	50	"	18	" "	2	5	25
				19	50					19	50

Dr. *Henry Talbot.* *Cr.*

Date.		Description.	D.-B. Folio.	Amount.		Date.		Description.	D.-B. Folio.	Amount.	
						1852. Sept.	6	By Making Sign	1	3	00

Dr. *Jonathan Long & Co.* *Cr.*

Date.		Description.	D.-B. Folio.	Amount.		Date.		Description.	D.-B. Folio.	Amount.	
1852. Sept.	8	To Cash	1	25	00	1852. Sept.	8	By Paints, Oils &c.	1	52	64
"	11	" Sundries	2	12	50						
"	15	" My Order	2	15	14						
				52	64					52	64

Dr. *Wm. G. Bradbury.* *Cr.*

Date.		Description.	D.-B. Folio.	Amount.		Date.		Description.	D.-B. Folio.	Amount.	
						1852. Sept.	8	By Bill of Glass &c.	1	140	00

Dr. *Philadelphia Exchange.* *Cr.*

Date.		Description.	D.-B. Folio.	Amount.		Date.		Description.	D.-B. Folio.	Amount.	
1852. Sept.	13	To Sundries	2	16	00						

Dr. *Sargeant & Willis.* *Cr.*

Date.		Description.	D.-B. Folio.	Amount.		Date.		Description.	D.-B. Folio.	Amount.	
1852. Sept.	22	To Stain'd Glass &c.	2	40	00	1852. *Sept.*	30	*By Bal. to New %*		70	00
"	30	" Painting Office	2	30	00						
				70	00					70	00
1852. Oct.	1	To Bal. fr. Old %		70	00						

DEDUCTIONS FROM SET I.

As this business has now been brought to a close, it remains to be seen whether it has been profitable or unprofitable.

Take off a list of the debit and credit balances standing on the Leger, and you will find the following results.

Balances due me.			*Balances I owe.*		
Bailey T. Stokes	134	12	Thomas Templeton	16	38
Mayland, Morris & Co.	2	00	Henry Talbot	3	00
Camden & Amboy R. R. Co.	8	61	Wm. G. Bradbury	140	00
Philadelphia Exchange	16	00		159	38
Sargeant & Willis	70	00			
	$230	73			

Now suppose that the Cash on hand constituted the only capital at commencing business, except a stock of tools, amounting (say) to $75, as shown by the Inventory-Book, which are worth as much now as when you commenced, the new ones purchased being an offset against damage by use. Suppose, also, that the stock of paints, oils, glass, &c., remaining on hand, amounts to $65.50, as shown by the Inventory-Book.

You will then have the following details.

Cash on hand, as pr. Cash-Book, at starting - - -		500.00
Stock of tools, as pr. Inventory-Book* - - -		75.00
Capital at starting		$575.00
Cash on hand, as pr. Cash-Book, at closing - - - -	540.08	
Stock of tools, as pr. Inventory-Book " - - - - -	75.00	
Stock of paints, &c. " " " - - - - -	65.50	
Personal accounts due me as pr. Leger " - - - - -	230.73	
Resources or *assets*	$911.31	
Deduct liabilities, viz., personal accounts I owe as pr. Leger,	159.38	
Net capital or present worth	$751.93	

It appears from the above that my net capital at closing business is	$751.93
While my capital at commencing business was only	575.00
Showing that my *gains in business* have been	$176.93

From these statements, you will perceive that:—

The amount invested by you at starting business is termed *capital.*†

Your available means at closing are termed *resources* or *assets.*

Your indebtedness at closing is termed *liabilities.*

The difference between your assets and liabilities is termed *net capital* or *present worth.*

Also,

By taking your capital at starting from your present worth, you may ascertain your gains in business.

In a losing business,

By taking your present worth from your capital at starting, you may ascertain your losses in business.

* The Inventory-Book will be explained hereafter.

† The various items which make up this capital are called *Effects;* and if you owed debts also at starting, the difference between the amount of your effects and debts would be called *net* capital, or, if the debts were the greater, *net insolvency.*

QUESTIONS FOR REVIEW.

These Questions review the whole of Single Entry thus far, and the pupil should be required to commit the answers thoroughly to memory and answer them, before proceeding farther. This questioning is one of the very best exercises for fixing in the mind what is intended to be learned by the previous practice; and I think the teacher will find that the series of questions prepared through the work are sufficiently extended to embrace nearly or quite the whole subject expounded, and not, as is too often the case, so meagre as to impose on him half the work of framing questions.

What is Book-keeping?
What two distinct methods are there of keeping accounts?
In Single Entry Book-keeping, of what does each entry consist?
In Double Entry, what does every entry contain?
What accounts are usually kept in Single Entry?
So far as you introduce Cash, Mdse., and other *property* accounts, upon what do you encroach?
What are the principal books of entry?
What are the smaller books kept besides these, in business, termed?
Which is the most important of these? What do you enter in the Cash-Book?
What transactions are entered in the Day-Book? Describe the form of entry.
What sums are transferred to the Leger?
What is the process of transferring from the Day-Book to the Leger called?
What are the advantages derived from it?
What is the Cash-Book?
How many columns for dollars and cents has Cash-Book, Set I?
How must money received be entered? How must money paid out be entered?
What must the difference between the two columns show?
If this difference does not agree with the actual amount of money in possession, what is shown?
Why cannot the credit column be larger than the debit?
How often should the Cash-Book be balanced? How is it done?
How can you test the Cash account without balancing the Cash-Book?
When do you debit a person in the Day-Book? When do you credit a person?
Why must every entry which you wish to bring into any account in the Leger be entered in the Day-Book?
Why are erasures not allowable in the Day-Book?
Is it allowable, in entering purchases, to say "Am't as pr. Bill," and to omit the items? Why is it?
Is it proper thus to do in entering sales? Why not?
For what is the Leger used?
Define *debtor*. Define *creditor*.
Define *debit*—as a verb:—as an adjective.
Define *credit*—as a verb:—as an adjective.
What colored ink looks best for rulings in the books?
In what *order* should the entries in the Cash-Book and Day-Book be entered?
Mention a transaction which requires an entry in both Day-Book and Cash-Book.
What is the next step, after writing up the Cash-Book and Day-Book?
Describe the process of posting. How do you post-mark the entry?
What may be done with accounts paid in full, as that of Stokes on the 7th inst.?
What do you do, after completing the posting, to assure yourself that no mistakes have been made?
What do you do with the Leger, after satisfying yourself of its accuracy?
How do you close accounts paid in full?
How do you close accounts which have debit or credit balances, still unsettled?
How does the ruling of the printed Legers given differ from that of blank-books ruled for the counting-house?
How many accounts should be opened on one page of the Leger?
In what order should accounts be arranged in the Leger?
What is the Alphabet or Index? How often are books usually closed?
What does the continuance of this Set for one month represent?
Mention the accounts on your Leger* which have balances due you. What is the gross amount of them?

* The pupil may have his own Leger and other books before him, in answering this and the following questions. Also the statements which he has drawn up to show his net capital, net gains, &c.

Mention the accounts on your Leger which have balances you owe. What is the gross amount of them?
What was the amount of cash on hand at starting? Where found?
What was the value of tools at starting? Where found?
What was the total capital at starting? How ascertained?
What is the amount of cash on hand at closing? Where found?
What is the value of tools at closing? Where found?
What is the value of paints, oils, &c., at closing? Where found?
What amount of personal accounts is due you? Where found?
What are the total assets at closing? How ascertained?
What amount of personal accounts do you owe? Where found?
What is the net capital or present worth? How ascertained?
What have been your gains in business? How ascertained?
What is the amount invested by you at starting termed?
What are the various items which make up this capital called?
What would the difference between your effects and debts at starting be called?
What are your available means at closing termed?
What is your indebtedness at closing termed?
What is the difference between your assets and liabilities termed?
How do you ascertain your gains in business. How your losses?
What is to be done, if bad debts exist at closing? [See Note on page 18.]

SET II, SINGLE ENTRY.

EXPLANATORY REMARKS, SET II.

When you have carefully pondered over the contents of Set I, so as to impress upon your mind all the principles that are therein contained, you may then proceed with the second Set in a similar manner, first writing up the Cash-Book and Day-Book connectedly in order of date, and then posting from the Day-Book to the Leger. You will find frequent reference, in this Set, to the *Inventory-Book*, *Bill-Book*, and *Time-Book*, none of which are here given, but you can find examples of them all in the work, by referring to the Table of Contents, pages 3 and 4.

CASH-BOOK, SET II.

In this Cash-Book, *one page* or *folio* of the Cash account occupies *two* pages of the book, Cash *debits* being placed on the *left* hand page, and Cash *credits* on the *right* hand page.

This form of Cash-Book is more used than that given in Set I, and is better, except in quite a limited business. The balances are brought down weekly, as in Set I; but when the entries are numerous it would be better to balance the Cash account daily.

Several new entries occur in this Cash-Book—as the receipt of Cash for a Note held by the firm—taking up a note of the firm outstanding—payment of a Gas Bill, &c.; but they will be readily comprehended by a little thought. The wages of hands employed, you will perceive, is paid weekly, in cash, the time which they work being kept in a Time-Book. Sometimes hands are employed by the piece or job, and then a memorandum book, similar to the Time-Book, is required, to keep account of the work done.

You will notice that money paid or received *on account* requires an entry in this Book, and also in the Day-Book, at the same time.

DAY-BOOK, SET II.

This book is the same in form and general treatment as the Day-Book to Set I.

The statement of the forming of a partnership, and the terms thereof, at the commencement of the Day-book, is not usually inserted in actual business, but is contained in the articles of agreement between the parties, which should always be drawn up and signed by each partner.

LEGER, SET II.

THIS Leger is precisely similar to Leger, Set I.

When the space left for an account in the Leger is filled, it should be transferred to a new folio, as shown in the case of James Margrave. But if entries have been made only upon one side of the account, the method of transferring differs somewhat from this, as may be seen in the case of Philip Mendenhall. An account should always be transferred before it crowds upon the one below it.

THE ALPHABET OR INDEX.

This is a small book which is used in connection with the Leger, to afford a ready reference to any account therein contained. It usually has a leaf allowed for every two letters of the English alphabet, and sometimes, in large Legers, one or more leaves for each letter. Each leaf is marked, upon its outer edge, with the letter or letters for which it is intended to be used, and then the different Leger titles are entered thereon, as indicated by their initials. The initial to the *surname* of a person is generally used, this part of the name being written first in the Alphabet.

The account should be entered in the Alphabet at the time it is placed in the Leger.

The Alphabets shown in this Set, and in subsequent Sets of this book, have been condensed on one page, to save room.

After having prepared paper for the different books as directed for Set I, page 17, commence to transcribe the Cash-Book and Day-Book, connectedly, in order of date, balancing the Cash-Book weekly, and thus progress until you have finished them.

Next, post from the Day-Book to the Leger, as before described, pages 17 and 18, being careful, however, to remember, whenever you open a new account on the Leger, to insert its title also in the Alphabet, with the page of the Leger on which it may be found. This gives ease in future reference, and prevents the opening of duplicate accounts to the same parties.

Open the two partners' accounts first upon the Leger, and after posting the entries of 1st inst., you may close B. L. Archer's account, and bring the balance, which is his net capital, down to new account, so that, in making statements from the Leger, each partner's investment may be readily seen.

When the posting is completed, and you have re-examined, to be certain of accuracy, rule and close up such accounts as balance themselves, or have the debit and credit sides equal. Then draw up statements on a separate sheet of paper, after the manner shown on page 39, to ascertain the present worth and the net gains of the firm, and of each partner. Pay particular attention to this, and try to make the method of arriving at these results perfectly familiar, as it is a very important branch of the accountant's duties, and frequently not well understood.

After completing these statements, *enter each partner's share of net gain to the credit of his account in the Leger*. Make this an original entry in the Leger, which is the simplest and best way; and not enter it in the Day-Book, and post to the Leger, although some good accountants pursue this latter plan. The difference between the two sides of each partner's account will now show his net capital, and you may close his account and bring down this net capital to new account, as it is called,—that is, write it down in the same account underneath the closure. You may likewise close all the other accounts remaining open on the Leger.

Dr. *Cash.*

1852.				
Nov.	1	To B. L. Archer, invested by him		50 00
"	"	" C. T. Marion, " " "		648 08
"	3	" James Margrave, on a/c		60 00
				758 08
Nov.	8	To Balance on hand from 6th inst.		674 98
"	"	" 1 Bureau, Mahogany Veneered		22 00
"	9	" Bills Receivable, B. Pinkley's Note, Archer's favor		125 00
"	11	" James Mortley, Arm Chair for Office		5 00
				826 98
Nov.	15	To Balance on hand from 13th inst.		648 60
"	"	" 1 Pint of Varnish		50
"	17	" Staining Cupboard		75
"	18	" 1 Reclining Chair for Invalids		25 00
"	19	" 2 Ottomans		7 00
"	20	" 1 French Bedstead, Birds'-Eye Maple		4 50
				686 35
Nov.	22	To Balance on hand from 20th inst.		598 23
"	"	" Steamboat Ohio Belle, part Bill of date		150 00
				748 23
Nov.	29	To Balance on hand from 27th inst.		474 83
"	"	" 2 Mahogany Rocking Chairs, Plush covered, @ $12.50		25 00
"	"	" 2 Birds'-Eye Maple French Bedsteads, @ 4.50		9 00
"	"	" 1 Doz. Cane-Seat Walnut Chairs	24.00	
"	"	" 1 Child's High Chair	1.25	
"	"	" 1 " Rocking "	1.25	26 50
"	30	" James Margrave, in full		62 75
"	"	" Repairing Tables		2 38
"	"	" " Chairs		1 62
				602 08
1852.				
Dec.	1	To Balance from Nov. 30th/52		471 98

CASH-BOOK, SET II.

Cash. *Cr.*

				$	cts
1852. Nov.	2	By Richard Baker, Bill of Lumber		75	60
"	6	" Wages paid hands, pr. Time-Book		7	50
"	"	" *Balance in Bank*, $650, *in Safe*, $24.98		674	98
				758	08
Nov.	8	By S. Brinkley, Carpenter, Repairs of Shop		51	50
"	"	" Jonas Smith, Painting Shop		22	00
"	"	" John Johnson & Son, in full of %		67	00
"	"	" Glazing 1 Light of Glass			38
"	13	" Wages paid hands, pr. Time-Book		37	50
"	"	" *Balance in Bank*, $620, *in Safe*, $28.60		648	60
				826	98
Nov.	16	By John Johnson & Son, part Bill of Paints, &c.		50	00
"	20	" Wages paid hands, pr. Time-Book		38	12
"	"	" *Balance in Bank*, $525.50, *in Safe*, $72.73		598	23
				686	35
Nov.	22	By Bills Payable, Archer's Note, P. Wall's favor	200.00		
		Less Discount from date, to Jan. 6th /53	1.50	198	50
"	23	" B. L. Archer, on %		10	00
"	24	" Bill of Varnish		13	50
"	"	" Gas Bill		14	25
"	"	" Drayage of Furniture			50
"	27	" Wages paid hands, as pr. Time-Book		36	65
"	"	" *Balance in Bank*, $470, *in Safe*, $4.83		474	83
				748	23
Nov.	29	By Bill of Veneering		25	60
"	"	" Charles T. Marion, on %		25	00
"	"	" Repairs of Lock			25
"	30	" Rent of Shop, one month		40	00
"	"	" Wages paid hands, as pr. Time-Book		39	25
"	"	" *Balance in Bank*, $460.50, *in Safe*, $11.48		471	98
				602	08

DAY-BOOK, SET II.

Pittsburg, *November* 1*st*, 1852.

L. F.				
	Barney L. Archer, Cabinet-Maker, associates with himself Charles T. Marion;—Archer transferring to the firm such portion of his resources and liabilities as is mutually agreed upon, and Marion investing their equivalent in Cash. The parties are to share alike in gains and losses.			
1	Barney L. Archer, Cr.			
	By Cash invested	50.00		
	" Sundry Notes he holds against others, pr. B.-B.	350.00		
	" Bal. of James Margrave's ⁰⁄c	55.75		
	" " of Peyton Gardner's "	37.40		
	" Materials & Unfinished Work, as pr. Inventory	356.50		
	" Stock of Furniture, " " "	210.43		
	" " Tools " " "	151.20	1,211	28
	Dr.			
1	To Sundry Notes he owes, pr. B.-B.	421.00		
	" Bal. due John Johnson & Son, on ⁰⁄c	67.00		
	" " " Peters, Fithian & Co. " "	75.20	563	20
1	Charles T. Marion Cr.			
	By Cash invested		648	08
	1st			
1	James Margrave Dr.			
	To Bal. of his ⁰⁄c due B. L. Archer		55	75
	"			
1	Peyton Gardner Dr.			
	To Bal. of his ⁰⁄c due B. L. Archer		37	40
	"			
1	John Johnson & Son Cr.			
	By Bal. of B. L. Archer's ⁰⁄c assumed by us		67	00
	"			
2	Peters, Fithian & Co. Cr.			
	By Bal. of B. L. Archer's ⁰⁄c assumed by us		75	20
	3d			
1	James Margrave Dr.			
	To 1 Hair Cloth, Mahogany Sofa		20	00
	Cr.			
1	By Cash on ⁰⁄c		60	00
	4th			
2	Mrs. Matilda Warterby Dr.			
	To 9 Mahogany Chairs, Cane-Seats, @ $1.25	11.25		
	" 6 " " Hair-Cloth Seats, " 3.00	18.00		
	" 2 Cherry Dining Tables " 6.00	12.00		
	" 1 Maple French Bedstead	4.25		
	" 1 " Low-Post Bedstead	2.75	48	25

Pittsburg, November 5th, 1852.

L.F.					
2	Jeremiah McCabe, pr. wife,	Dr.			
	To 1 Doz. Windsor Chairs		12.00		
	" ½ " " " @ $15.00		7.50		
	" ½ " " " " 10.00		5.00		
	" 1 Spring-Seat Black Walnut Sofa		21.00	45	50
	8th				
1	John Johnson & Son	Dr.			
	To Cash in full			67	00
	9th				
2	Peters, Fithian & Co.	Cr.			
	By Bill of Lumber			135	00
	Dr.				
2	To our Note @ 30 days, in full of their ⁰⁄₀			210	20
	"				
1	James Margrave, pr. daughter	Dr.			
	To 1 Black Walnut Footstool			1	50
	"				
2	Lewis Laflin, Jr.	Dr.			
	To 3 Patent Pivot Chairs for Office, @ $5.00			15	00
	11th				
1	James Margrave, pr. wife	Dr.			
	To 1 Black Walnut Extension Dining-Table			40	00
	13th				
2	Philip Mendenhall	Dr.			
	To 2 Children's High Dining-Chairs, Mahogany, @ 2.00			4	00
	"				
3	Miss Betsy Crim	Dr.			
	To 3 Doz. Windsor Chairs, @ $11.00		33.00		
	" 1 Rocking Chair, Second-Hand		9.00	42	00
	15th				
1	James Margrave	Dr.			
	To ⁰⁄₀ of J. McCabe, assumed by him			45	50
	"				
2	Jeremiah McCabe	Cr.			
	By transfer of ⁰⁄₀ to J. Margrave			45	50
	16th				
1	John Johnson & Son	Cr.			
	By Bill of Paints, Varnish, Brushes, &c.			175	26
	Dr.				
1	To Cash in part			50	00
	18th				
2	Philip Mendenhall	Dr.			
	To 1 Black Walnut Book-Case			15	00

Pittsburg, November 19*th*, 1852.

L. F.			
3	James Margrave, pr. son Dr. To 1 Hat-Stand, Mahogany Veneered		10.00
	20th		
2	Philip Mendenhall Dr. To Varnishing 1 Table		.50
	22d		
3	Steamboat Ohio Belle Dr. To 3 Mahogany Sofas, @ $15.00 " 2 " Tete-a-Tetes, " 16.00 " 1 " Rocking Chair, " 4 " Arm Chairs, " 8.00 " 2 Doz. " Chairs, " 30.00 " 14 Cherry Wash-Stands, " 2.00 " 14 Looking-Glasses, " 2.00	45.00 32.00 12.00 32.00 60.00 28.00 28.00	237.00
3	Cr. By Cash in part payment		150.00
	23d		
1	B. L. Archer Dr. To Cash on a/c		10.00
	"		
3	Oscar P. Lewis & Co. Cr. By Bill of Lumber		96.40
	26th		
3	James Margrave, per wife Dr. To 1 Mahogany Bureau, with Glass		25.00
	29th		
1	Charles T. Marion Dr. To Cash on a/c		25.00
	"		
3	Miss Betsy Crim Dr. To 1 Mahogany Bureau		19.00
	30th		
3	Philip Mendenhall Dr. To 1 Black Walnut Centre Table		15.00
	"		
3	Miss Betsy Crim Cr. By 1 Mahogany Bureau, returned because it was too large for the room		19.00
	"		
3	James Margrave Cr. By his Note @ 60 days " Cash to Bal. a/c	75.00 62.75	137.75

ALPHABET OR INDEX,

LEGER, SET II.

1

LEGER, SET II.

Dr. *Barney L. Archer.* *Cr.*

1852. Nov.	1	To Sundries	1	563	20	1852. Nov.	1	By Sundries	1	1,211	28
"	"	" *Net. Cap. at starting*		648	08						
				1,211	28					1,211	28
1852. Nov.	23	To Cash on a/c	3	10	00	1852. Nov.	1	By Net Capital brought down		648	08
"	30	" *Net Cap. to New a/c*		778	38	"	30	" ½ Net Gains*		140	30
				788	38					788	38
						1852. Dec.	1	By Net Cap. fr. old a/c		778	38

Dr. *Charles T. Marion.* *Cr.*

1852. Nov.	29	To Cash on a/c	3	25	00	1852. Nov.	1	By Cash invested	1	648	08
"	30	" *Net Cap. to New a/c*		763	38	"	30	" ½ Net Gains*		140	30
				788	38					788	38
						1852. Dec.	1	By Net Cap. fr. old a/c		763	38

Dr. *James Margrave.* *Cr.*

1852. Nov.	1	To B. L. Archer	1	55	75	1852. Nov.	3	By Cash	1	60	00
"	3	" Sofa	1	20	00						
"	9	" Footstool	2	1	50						
"	11	" Dining Table	2	40	00						
"	15	" J. McCabe	2	45	50						
		Am't to folio	3	162	75			*Am't to folio*	3	60	00

Dr. *Peyton Gardner.* *Cr.*

1852. Nov.	1	To B. L. Archer	1	37	40						

Dr. *John Johnson & Son.* *Cr.*

1852. Nov.	8	To Cash	2	67	00	1852. Nov.	1	By B. L. Archer	1	67	00
1852. Nov.	16	To Cash	2	50	00	1852. Nov.	16	By Bill of date	2	175	26
"	30	" *Bal. to New a/c*		125	26						
						1852. Dec.	1	By Bal. fr. Old a/c		125	26

* See Statements, page 39.

Dr. *Peters, Fithian & Co.* **Cr.**

1852. Nov.	9	To Bills Payable	2	210	20	1852. Nov.	1	By B. L. Archer	1	75	20
						"	9	" Bill of date	2	135	00
				210	20					210	20

Dr. *Mrs. Matilda Waterby.* **Cr.**

1852. Nov.	4	To Sundries	1	48	25						

Dr. *Jeremiah McCabe.* **Cr.**

1852. Nov.	5	To Sundries	2	45	50	1852. Nov.	15	By J. Margrave	2	45	50

Dr. *Lewis Laflin, Jr.* **Cr.**

1852. Nov.	9	To Pivot Chairs	2	15	00						

Dr. *Philip Mendenhall.* **Cr.**

1852. Nov.	13	To Children's chairs	2	4	00	1852. Nov.	20	*By Bal. to folio*	3	19	50
"	18	" Book Case	2	15	00						
"	20	" Varnishing	3		50						
				19	50					19	50

Dr. *Miss Betsy Crim.* **Cr.**

1852. Nov.	13	To Sundries	2	42	00	1852. Nov.	30	By Bureau	3	19	00
"	29	" Bureau	3	19	00	"	31	" *Bal. to New %*		42	00
				61	00					61	00
1852. Dec.	1	To Bal. fr. Old %		42	00						

Dr. *James Margrave.* **Cr.**

1852. Nov.	15	To Am't fr. folio	1	162	75	1852. Nov.	15	By Am't fr. folio	1	60	00
"	19	" Hat Stand	3	10	00	"	30	" Sundries	3	137	75
"	26	" Bureau	3	25	00						
				197	75					197	75

Dr. *Steamboat Ohio Belle.* **Cr.**

1852. Nov.	22	To Sundries	3	237	00	1852. Nov.	22	By Cash	3	150	00
						"	30	" *Bal. to New %*		87	00
				237	00					237	00
1852. Dec.	1	To Bal. fr. Old %		87	00						

Dr. *Oscar P. Lewis & Co.* **Cr.**

						1852. Nov.	23	By Bill of date	3	96	40

Dr. *Philip Mendenhall.* **Cr.**

1852. Nov.	20	To Bal. from folio	2	19	50	1852. *Nov.*	30	*By Bal. to New %*		34	50
"	30	" Centre Table	3	15	00						
				34	50					34	50
1852. Dec.	1	To Bal. fr Old %		34	50						

DEDUCTIONS FROM SET II.

UNSETTLED BALANCES ON THE LEGER.

Debts due the Firm.	$	cts.	*Debts the Firm owe.*	$	cts.
Peyton Gardner	37	40	John Johnson & Son	125	26
Mrs. Matilda Waterby	48	25	Oscar P. Lewis & Co.	96	40
Lewis Laflin, Jr.	15	00		$221	66
Miss Betsy Crim	42	00			
Steamboat Ohio Belle	87	00			
Philip Mendenhall	34	50			
	$264	15			

You now need some facts contained in auxiliary books, which are omitted.

Suppose, then,

The Stock of furniture on hand amounts, pr. Inventory-Book, to	$776.75
" " " materials and unfinished work, " " "	239.79
" " " tools, depreciated by use, " " "	141.95
The amount of Bills Receivable in possession of the firm, pr. Bill-Book	300.00
" " " Bills Payable outstanding, " " "	431.20

You have now the materials for the following statements.

Assets.	$	cts.	*Liabilities.*	$	cts.
Cash on hand, pr. C.-B.	471	98	Debts the firm owe, pr. Leger	221	66
Debts due the firm, pr. Leger	264	15	Bills Payable, pr. B.-B.	431	20
Bills Receivable, pr. B.-B.	300	00	Total liabilities	$652	86
Furniture, pr. Invt.-Book	776	75			
Materials, &c. " "	239	79			
Tools, " "	141	95			
Total assets	$2,194	62			
Deduct liabilities	652	86			
Firm's *net capital* or *pres't worth*	$1,541	76			

Assets, including Partners' debits.	$	cts.	*Liabilities, including Partners' investments.*	$	cts.
Total assets, pr. above statem't	2,194	62	Total liabilities pr. above statement	652	86
Cash paid B. L. Archer	10	00	B. L. Archer's investment	648	08
" " C. T. Marion	25	00	C. T. Marion's "	648	08
	$2,229	62		$1,949	02
Deduct	1,949	02			
Firm's *net gains*	$280	60			
Each partner's ½ $140.30					

Again,

Net gains of B. L. Archer	$140.30	
Add credit Bal. of his % pr. Leger	638.08	
B. L. Archer's net capital		778.38
Net gain of C. T. Marion	$140.30	
Add credit Bal. of his % pr. Leger	623.08	
C. T. Marion's net capital		763.38
Firm's net capital, as above		$1,541.76

Therefore,

The difference between the total assets and total liabilities of a firm shows the *net capital* or *net insolvency* of the firm.

The difference between the assets, including partners' debits, and liabilities, including partners' investments, shows the *net gains* or *net losses* of firm.

Each partner's share of net gains, added to his account, shows his *net capital.**

The net capital of the several partners, being added together, shows the firm's net capital.

* In a losing business, the losses of each partner, deducted from the credit balance of his account, shows his net capital; or if the net losses are greater than the credit balance of his account, the difference shows his net insolvency.

QUESTIONS FOR REVIEW, SET II.

How are the Cash-Book and Day-Book of this Set to be written up?
From what book do you post to the Leger?
How can you find examples of the *Inventory-Book, Bill-Book, Time-Book,* and other auxiliaries not given in this Set?
What is the form of the Cash-Book, in Set II? How does it differ from that in Set I?
How often is the wages of hands employed paid? How is the time they work kept?
How is money paid or received *on account* to be entered?
In what is the statement of the forming of a partnership, and the terms thereof usually contained?
When the space left for an account in the Leger is full, what is to be done with it?
What two accounts are transferred in this Leger?
Is the method of transferring them the same in both cases? How different?
What is the Alphabet or Index? Describe its usual form?
Which part of the name of a person is generally written first in the Index?
When should the title of an account be placed in the Index? Why is it important to insert it in the Index as soon as the account is opened in the Leger?
What two accounts are first opened in the Leger?
What is done to B. L. Archer's account, after posting the entries of 1st inst.?
After completing the posting, what do you do? What, after re-examining the Leger, and closing such accounts as balance themselves?
What is the object in drawing up statements, as shown on page 39?
Where do you enter each partner's share of the net gain? How?
What will the difference between the two sides of each partner's account now show?
What do you do with this net capital?
How do you treat other accounts remaining open in the Leger?
Mention the several accounts in the Leger having balances due the firm?
What is the gross amount of them?
Mention those having balances the firm owe. What is the gross amount?
What is the value of the stock of furniture remaining on hand?
What is the value of materials and unfinished work?
What is the value of tools?
What amount of Bills Receivable have the firm in possession?
What amount of Bills Payable are outstanding against the firm?
What are the total assets of the firm? What the total liabilities?
What is the firm's present worth?
What are the total assets, including partners' debits?
What are the total liabilities, inculding partners' investments?
What are the net gains of the firm?
What is each partner's half of the net gains?
What is shown by the difference between the total assets and total liabilities of the firm?
What is shown by the difference between the assets, including partners' debits, and the liabilities, including partners' investments?
What is shown by adding each partner's share of net gains to his account?
In a losing business, what is shown by deducting the losses of each partner from the credit balance of his account?
If the net losses are greater than the credit balance of his account, what does the difference show?
What is shown by adding together the net capital of the several partners?

SET III, SINGLE ENTRY.

EXPLANATORY REMARKS,

AND

INSTRUCTIONS FOR WRITING UP SET III.

There are blank books for this Set intended to accompany the work, and in these I wish you to write up the materials found on pages 44 to 49 inclusive. These materials will afford you a complete and connected history of the business of farming for a year, (except that some of the petty details, which are of constant occurrence, are omitted, to avoid an unnecessary and tiresome repetition.) In most cases the gross amounts of debit or credit are omitted, but the number of acres, bushels, &c., bought or sold, and at what price, are in all cases mentioned; and you can calculate the amounts for yourself. This will give just the kind of practice which is needful to prepare for the actual keeping of books—for no one is qualified to keep a set of books, however well he may understand the theory of accounts, unless he is quick and accurate in making extensions, additions, and such calculations as usually occur in business.

You will find at first, underneath each transaction recorded, an elucidation of the manner in which you are to enter it in your Cash-Book, or Day-Book, or both. But when there are several records of similar transactions, elucidations are given to one or more of the first, and omitted in the subsequent ones, in order that you may exercise your power of thought, and be benefited thereby, instead of being a mere copyist, leaning entirely and constantly upon a support, and ready to fall as soon as that support shall be removed.

The *Cash-Book*, *Day-Book*, and *Leger* used in this Set are the same in form and mode of entry as those in Set II. The blanks prepared have printed explanations on their covers, which will enable you to use them correctly, and the practice which you have now had on loose sheets of paper should give you accuracy and neatness in all your work. It is no small accomplishment to be able to keep books free from mistakes, erasures, and blots; and yet all books of account (especially books of original entry) should be thus kept, for they are frequently the only means of proving important dealings between man and man, and if doubts be cast upon their accuracy and truthfulness, by a careless (not to say dishonest) manner of keeping them, innocent parties will thereby oftentimes be sufferers.

First examine critically the history of every separate transaction, before looking at the elucidation, and determine, if possible, how you would make the entry, and then compare your own ideas with the elucidation given, and ascertain whether you are right—and make the entry or entries accordingly. Proceed thus, entering in both Day-Book and Cash-Book, in order of date, until you have completed the whole year. Then post the Day-Book—re-examine, to see if rightly posted—close it—and draw off statements as before directed. The statements and deductions on page 53 will enable you to see whether you have performed all your work with accuracy.

Teachers will find the Cash-Book, Day-Book, Alphabet and Leger, complete, in the Key to this work, which, with the directions here given, will enable even those unacquainted with the science of accounts to guide their pupils aright in the prosecution of this study. But all the aid an intelligent pupil needs, except such suggestions as his teacher will of course give him, is intended to be furnished in the treatise itself, and it is far better that he should not consult the Key.

FARM ACCOUNT, SET III.

This account, given on pages 50 and 51, exhibits in detail, on the debit side, the whole of your expenditures for the farm, including the expenses of your family; and on the credit side, the whole of the proceeds accruing and arising therefrom; and is an exemplification of a regular *Double Entry property account,* except that in Double Entry, instead of being embraced under one head, it would more commonly be divided into several separate accounts, as "Dairy Account," "Wheat Field," "Family Expenses," "Interest," and the like, and thus enable you to know precisely, truly, and minutely, the whole state of your affairs, and what branches of your business are more or less profitable. This account, as here shown, however, enables you to ascertain how much you have gained by your whole farming operations, and operates as a proof upon the correctness of your books, by producing the same result.

INVENTORY-BOOK, OR ACCOUNT-STOCK-BOOK, SET III.

On page 52, I have given an Inventory-Book. This is a small book, used for taking an account of the value of property owned by you, at any given date, in order that you may use it in estimating your net capital, net gains, &c. Merchants take an inventory of their goods, or, as they usually call it, "*take an account of stock,*" once a year at least, and every business man should inventory his property as often as this. It must of necessity be done whenever you would ascertain the true state of your business affairs. In taking an inventory, there must be a careful estimate of the value of the property, of whatever kind, and it is perhaps as safe a rule as any to affix such a price as the article would bring in market.

To ascertain on what pages the *Check-Book* and other *auxiliaries* needed in actual business are exhibited, refer to the Table of Contents, pages 3 and 4.

1 HISTORY AND ELUCIDATIONS, SET III.

Lancaster, Penn'a, January 1st, 1852.

My Capital at the present time consists of Cash on hand, $6,275, and Notes which I hold against other persons to the Am't of $2,629.50.

You must enter in your Cash-Book, on the debit side, the money here mentioned as on hand, thus, "To Am't on hand at commencing business," giving the date and amount.

The notes would, in actual business, be recorded in a Bill-Book; but you may omit any record of them, as no Bill-Book is given in connection with this Set. Or, if you prefer so to do, you can rule, on a sheet of paper, a Bill-Book like that in Set VI. Double Entry, and make therein the proper entries of these notes, and others which occur in this Set. You can find the name of drawer and the time when due, in these notes, by the history of the payment.

1st

Bo't of Jonas A. Leech a Farm, containing 125 Acres improved Land, and 25 Acres wood Land, with Stone House, Barn & Out-buildings complete = 150 Acres @ $100 pr. Acre. $15,000.00

Paid him in Cash, $5,000, and gave him my two Bonds for the Bal., secured by Mortgage on the Farm, one for $5,000, payable in five years, and one for $5,000, payable in ten years, each on Int. @ 6 % pr. annum, payable semi-yearly.

As Jonas A. Leech has been paid in full for the farm purchased of him, no entry need be made necessarily to his account; but in so large transactions as this, it is well to show them in the person's account in your Leger, even though paid in full: therefore you may credit Jonas A. Leech (in your Day-Book) with the farm, and debit him with the cash and bonds given in payment, making the entry full and explicit as to its details. When this entry in your Day-Book is posted, you may rule and add up the account in the Leger, before posting any more into it.

In the Cash-Book, on the credit side, enter the money paid, thus, "By Jonas A. Leech, paid in part for Farm," giving the date and amount.

"

Bo't of Jonas A. Leech 20 Acres of Wheat, in the ground, @ $12 pr. Acre, to be paid for 4 mos. after it is harvested.

This requires a credit to Leech in the Day-Book. Make the correct extension of the amount, which is here omitted.

"

Bo't of Jonas A. Leech, his Horses, Cattle, Dairy Stock, Farming Implements, &c., as below enumerated:—

1 Span Horses, one 7, the other 8 years old, $200; 1 Yoke Oxen, 5 years old, $70; 5 Steers, yearlings last Spring, @ $10; 1 Durham Bull, 4 years old, $100; 1 Alderney Bull, yearling last Spring, $50; 3 Alderney Heifers, 2 years old last Spring, @ $28; 17 Cows, at an average price of $23; 10 Hogs, @ $6; 12 Pigs, @ $3; 1 Large Two-horse Wagon, with Cover, $110; 1 Ox-Cart, $30; 2 Ploughs, @ $10; 1 Harrow, $8; 1 Horse Rake, $5; Dairying Utensils, Fanning Mill, Corn Cultivator, Pitch Forks, Spades, Shovels, Rakes, Hoes, Flails, and all other Farming Implements now on the place, for the gross sum agreed between us of $65; Stock of Hay, supposed to be 40 Tons, @ $10; a quantity of Corn Fodder and Straw, $30; 110 Bush. Wheat @ $1, 250 Bush. Corn @ 50¢; 100 Bush. Oats @ 35¢; 1,000 Bush. Turnips @ 12^2¢; 10 Bush. Ruta Bagas @ 25¢; 20 Bush. Carrots, @ 35¢. $2,113.50

Paid him in Cash, $625, and a Note against Geo. Wheaton, my favor, @ 6 mos., due Feb. 10th, proximo, for $355; agreed to pay him in Cash, on the 1st of next Mar., $500, and the Bal. 8 mos. from date.

In the Day-Book, credit Jonas A. Leech for all the above purchases, giving full particulars in systematic order. Take a separate line for each separate item enumerated, placing the amount of it at the left of the dollar and cent column. Add up these several amounts, and extend the total into the dollar and cent column. Debit him with the Cash, and with the note of Wheaton which you pay him.

In the Cash-Book, enter the money paid him, on the credit side.

"

Agreed with John Jones to work for me on the Farm, at any and all kinds of Farm work, for one year, @ $12 pr. mo.; Bernard Samson do., @ $10 pr. mo.; Patrick McFarland @ $8 pr. mo.; and Lewis W. Gregory, boy, @ $3 pr. mo.; also hired

Lancaster, Penn'a, January 1st, 1852.

Margaret Wilson as Dairy-woman, @ $5 pr. mo.; Peggy Morrison, Milk-maid, @ $4 pr. mo.; Charlotte C. Bryant, Cook, @ $5 pr. mo.; all to be paid monthly. Total, $47 pr. mo.

This requires no entry in either Day-Book or Cash-Book. It is merely inserted here to preserve the connected history of the whole business.

The paying monthly is introduced in order to lessen the number of similar entries through the Set; although usually females employed, and sometimes men, are paid weekly.

2d

Bo't for Cash, 75 Bush. Potatoes, @ 35¢, and 1 Bbl. Sweet Potatoes, @ $2.25.

Enter the above upon the credit side of your Cash-Book.

3d

Bo't for Cash, 10 lbs. Beef, @ 10¢, and 5 lbs. Nails, @ 5¢.

Enter this precisely similar to the last. In the next transaction of the same kind, I shall give you no suggestions as to entering it.

Such entries would be of almost daily occurrence in actual life, but I shall give only a few, as specimens. If I should write out *all the details* of a farmer's life for a year, it would extend this Set to an unreasonable length, without any real advantage.

"

Sent 30 Bush. Wheat and 25 Bush. Corn to Wm. Jacob's Grist Mill, to be ground.

The miller takes toll out of the grain sent, to pay for grinding. No entry required.

10th

Bo't of Orrin Woolworth, 1 Rockaway Wagon, with two seats, which can be used with one or two horses, for $150, to be paid for in grain.

Sold him on a/c, 20 Bush. Wheat, @ $1.05 pr. Bush.

Credit Mr. Woolworth in your Day-Book, with the wagon purchased, and debit him with the wheat furnished. Specify also that he is to be paid in grain. As a general rule, it is well to mention any important fact in reference to the bargain in making entries in your Day-Book.

"

Bo't for Cash of Sundry Persons, as pr. Bills, ½ Bbl. Pickled Mackerel, $6; 3 Bbls. Pork, @ $12; 200 lbs. Sugar, @ 5¢; 200 lbs. Sugar, @ 7¢; 20 lbs. Loaf Sugar, @ 11¢; 5 Gals. Molasses, @ 30¢; 1 Gal. Sugar-house Syrup, 50¢; 10 lbs. Tea, @ 50¢; 2 Sacks, 320 lbs. Coffee, @ 10¢; 2 lbs. Saleratus, @ 12^2¢; 4 lbs. Raisins, @ 12^2¢.

24th

Sold to Ebenezer Failing, 5 Tons of Hay @ $15 pr. Ton.

He paid me in part by 20 Bush. Buckwheat, delivered at Jacobs' Grist Mill, @ 55¢.

Mr. Failing must be debited with the hay, and credited with the buckwheat.

31st

Paid in full all the Hands employed by me, according to agreement, of 1st inst., $47.

When the record is "Paid" simply, as in this case, without mentioning how, you are to consider it a cash payment, and enter it accordingly.

February 4th

Bo't for Cash, 1 quarter of Veal, 15 lbs., @ 7¢; and 4 lbs. Beef Steak, @ 10¢.

17th

Exchanged my horse Bill (8 years old) for a better match to my other horse, of the same age, (7 years,) and paid in Cash the difference in value, $10.

Here you need only to enter in the Cash-Book the difference in value of the horses, paid in money.

21st

Gave to my wife as Shopping Money $25.

Enter, same as any other expense, on the credit side of the Cash-Book.

Lancaster, Penn'a, February 28th, 1852.

Isaac McGuigan has paid me his Note, my favor, due this day, $500.

Enter on debit side of Cash-Book.

"

Paid Hands in full, pr. agreement, $47.

1852 is leap-year, and February has 29 days, but the 29th is Sabbath, and all payments falling due on that day must be made the day previous.

March 1st

Paid Jonas A. Leech, on ℅ of Stock, Farming Implements, &c., Bo't Jan. 1st, $500.

Place this on the credit side of your Cash-Book; and also debit Mr. Leech with it in the Day-Book, as he was credited with the whole stock and implements when they were purchased of him on 1st January.

16th

Bo't for Cash, to use as manure, 2 Tons Peruvian Guano @ $45 pr. Ton; 2 Tons Patagonian Guano @ $25; 1,000 Bush. Lime @ 10 ¢; and 100 Bush. Bone Dust @ 50 ¢.

Enter in Cash-Book only.

31st

Paid Hands in full, pr. agreement, $47.

Discharged Patrick McFarland, because I find him untrustworthy.

April 5th

Sent 60 Bush. Wheat to Wm. Jacobs' Grist Mill to be ground.

No entry required.

13th

Sold my Durham Bull to Caleb L. Rodgers, for $125.

Received of him Cash $50, and his Note @ 4 mos. for Bal.

As Mr. Rodgers has paid in full, you need not open any account with him; and the only entry here is to debit the cash received, in the Cash-Book. In actual business, the note would also be recorded in the Bill-Book.

"

Killed one of my Steers. Sold for Cash the 2 Fore-quarters of Beef, 200 lbs., @ 7 ¢; 1 Hind-quarter, 95 lbs., @ 8 ¢; 10 lbs. Tallow @ 8 ¢; and reserved the Bal. for use. Gave the hide to the Butcher for Killing and Selling.

Enter receipts of money in the Cash-Book.

30th

Paid Hands their Wages in full, $39.

May 1st

Sent my Horses to Ebenezer Failing, Blacksmith, and had 4 New Shoes put on @ 31^1 ¢ ea.; 4 reset @ 12^2 ¢ ea.

Credit Mr. Failing in the proper book.

19th

Ebenezer Failing has put New Coulter in my Plough and 2 New Teeth in the Harrow @ $2.50.

25th

Sold Ebenezer Failing, on ℅, 8 Bush. Seed Potatoes, @ 50 ¢.

Debit Mr. Failing in the proper book.

31st

Paid Hands in full, $39. Also Paid 6 d's.' Work of Day Laborers @ 75 ¢; Hired Two New Hands for 3 months from date, at $14 pr. mo.—names, George Munson, and Wm. Patterson, Jr.

Enter in the Cash-Book only what is paid. It would be well for every farmer, and every other business-man, to have a memorandum-book, in which he can state such facts as the hiring of these two new hands, and other matters which he cannot enter in his regular book of accounts, and which ought nevertheless not to be left entirely to the memory, because this often causes disputes and broils, when a few lines in writing, done at the time, would satisfy all parties.

Lancaster, Penn'a, June 1st, 1852.

Rec'd Cash of Timothy Tumbleston for his Note, my favor, due this day, $520.

All receipts to be placed on the debit side of Cash-Book.

1st

Bo't 6 First-rate Milch Cows, with Calves, Alderney Stock, @ $50 ea., of Geo. T. Lipman.
Paid Cash, $150; Bal. due 1st Sept.

Credit Lipman with the cows, and charge him with the money paid, in the Day-Book. Also enter in Cash-Book correctly the money paid out.

30th

Paid Wages in full, $67.
Also paid to Jonas A. Leech the Interest on my 2 Bonds, given in pay't of Farm, ea. for $5,000 = $10,000 @ 6 %, for 6 mos., $300.

All payments to be entered on the credit side of Cash-Book.

July 9th

Rec'd of James McClain, Cash in full for his Note, my favor, due this day, $625.

10th

Bo't of Peter A. Phillips a Market Wagon and Horse for $175.
Paid in part by a Note I hold against Mulford & McKee, due Aug. 15th, for $110, and agreed to pay the Bal. on the 1st of Jan. /53.

Credit Phillips with the wagon purchased and debit him with the Note.

15th

Paid 4 days' Work of Men to help at Harvesting @ $1.25.

31st

Paid Wages in full, $67.

August 17th

Paid Cash for Marketing, $3.50.

25th

Sold Caleb Cope 2 of my Steers @ $25 ea.

When no mention is made of payment, take it for granted nothing is paid, and debit the person accordingly.

28th

Sold for Cash, to a Drover, my 2 remaining Steers @ $15 ea., and 12 Calves (all except my Alderneys) @ $5 ea.

31st

Paid Wages of Hands to date, $67.
George Munson and Wm. Patterson, Jr. left to-day.

September 3d

Rec'd of G. M. Wharton, Esq., Cash in full for Notes, placed in his hands Mar. 11th for collection, to wit:—
One drawn by John Thomas, due Mar. 3d, for $250.00
Int. on same to date, $7.50.
One drawn by James B. Babcock, due Apr. 3d, $269.50
Int. on same to date, $6.74.
Paid him fee for Professional Services, $50.

Enter in the Cash-Book, on the debit side, the money received for notes and interest, and on the credit side the money paid for professional services.

4th

Paid Jonas A. Leech in full for Bal. due on Stock, Farming Implements, &c. Bo't of him on 1st Jan. last, $633.50.

The elucidation of Mar. 1st will apply to this entry.

Lancaster, Penn'a, September 16th, 1852.

E. B. Holden & Co. have this day sent me a Bill of Sundry Articles of Children's Clothing and other Mdse. obtained at their Store since April 1st, Am't $62.25.

E. B. Holden & Co. must of course be credited with this bill of Mdse.

30th

Paid Wages of Hands in full to date, $39.
" 12 days' Work @ 75¢

October 2d

Bo't of E. B. Holden & Co., on %, Mdse. as pr. Bill, $10.75.

Purchases on account to be credited the person of whom you buy.

"

Sold E. B. Holden & Co. on % 600 lbs. Butter, in Firkins, @ 16¢; and 225 lbs. Cheese, @ 8¢.

Sales on account to be debited the person to whom you sell.

12th

Sold Mrs. Sarah C. Dermott 50 Bush. Potatoes, @ 35¢.
(Will pay in three mos.)

15th

Stedman & Williston have this day finished threshing my Wheat, furnishing a Threshing Machine, 1 Man and 2 Horses. They threshed 600 Bush. and charged 6¢ pr. Bush.

Credit the firm who did the work.

23d

Peggy Morrison, the Milk-maid, left me this day sick. Think I shall be able to get along without hiring another at present, by letting Patrick and Lewis milk.

Paid Peggy 3 weeks' wages, $3, and made her a present of $3, as she had been a good girl, and is now sick.

Enter same as any of the other payments of wages.

26th

Sold for Cash to Wm. R. Patterson, 375 Bush. Wheat, @ $1.

30th

Paid Wages of Hands in full, $35.

The 31st is Sabbath.

November 3d

Sold Orrin Woolworth, on %, 50 Bush. Potatoes, @ 35¢; 50 Bush. Wheat @ $1; and 50 Bush. Oats @ 35¢.

"

Paid Cash for a Suit of Clothes for self, $30; Dresses for Wife, $25; Children's Clothing, $20.15; Crockery, $15.40; and Groceries, $18.25.

17th

Paid Jonas A. Leech for Field of Wheat Bo't on Jan. 1st, as pr. agreement, $240.

See entry of the purchase, Jan. 1st, and elucidation of Mar. 1st.

27th

Richard P. Simpkins finished chopping wood on my Farm to-day. He has cut 50 cords, @ 50¢ pr. cord.

Paid him in part by an order on E. B. Holden & Co., for Dry-Goods out of their store, to the Am't of $10; and Cash $10.

The Bal. remains unpaid.

Credit Richard P. Simpkins with whole amount of the chopping, and debit him with order and cash. Then credit E. B. Holden & Co. with your order, favor of Simpkins.
Enter the Cash also in Cash-Book.

30th

Paid Hands their Wages in full, $35.

Lancaster, Penn'a, December 3d, 1852.

Sold E. B. Holden & Co. on %, 20 Cords Wood, delivered at their Store, @ $3.

7th

Rec'd of Caleb S. Rodgers Cash in full for his Note of Apr. 13th, @ 4 mos., due Aug. 16th, $75, and for Int. from Aug. 16th to date, $1.39.

Enter in Cash-Book the whole amount received for note and interest. As no account was opened with Mr. Rodgers on the 13th April, (which see,) he is not to receive any credit here.

"

Paid Geo. T. Lipman Bal. of his %, in full, due Sept. 1st, $150; and Int. on same from Sept. 1st to date, $2.40.

Credit Mr. Lipman with interest on his account, and debit him with the payment in full.

14th

Rec'd of Caleb Cope Cash in full of his %, $50.

"

Sold Stedman & Williston on %, 100 Bush. Corn @ 50¢.

20th

Sold Richard P. Simpkins on %, 5 Bush. Wheat @ $1.

25th

Sold Caleb Cope 2 Alderney Calves @ $15; 1 Alderney Cow @ $60; 1 Yoke Oxen @ $75.

See Aug. 25th.

28th

Sold for Cash to Wm. Jacobs, 750 Bush. Oats @ 35¢; 800 Bush. Corn @ 55¢; 50 Bush. Buckwheat @ 60¢.

"

Paid the following contributions to charitable objects:

Bible Society, $20; Tract Society, $20; Foreign Missions, $20; Home Missions, $20; Sabbath School Union, $20; For building Churches, $100; To our Pastor, $50.

Also paid Schooling of William and Mary for one year @ $75 ea.

Cash-Book entries.

30th

Sold in the City of Philada., for Cash, 1,725 lbs. Cheese, @ 9¢; and 900 lbs. Firkin Butter, @ 18¢.

Paid Freight and other Expenses on same, $11.55.

31st

Ebenezer Failing has this day rendered me a Bill for repairing Wagons and Farming Implements, Shoeing Horses, and other Blacksmithing to date, $53.75.

"

Paid Anson Holcomb, Cooper, for Bill of Butter Firkins, Cheese Boxes, and Coopering, during the past year, $26.25.

"

Paid Wages in full, $35.

"

Paid Int. on Bonds & Mortgages, favor of Jonas A. Leech, $300.

"

Rec'd of Simpson Treat, Milk-man, Cash for 9,500 quarts Milk furnished him during the year, as pr. agreement, taken by him from the Farm each morning, @ 3¢ pr. quart.

FARM ACCOUNT.

Dr. *Farm.*

1852.				
Jan. 1	To Cost, 150 Acres @ $100		15,000	00
" "	" 20 Acres Wheat in the ground @ $12		240	00
" "	" Horses, Cattle, Dairy Stock, Farming Implements, &c.		2,113	50
" 2	" 75 Bush. Potatoes	@ 35¢	26	25
" "	" 1 Bbl. Sweet Potatoes		2	25
" 3	" Beef & Nails		1	25
" 10	" 1 Rockaway Wagon		150	00
" "	" Mackerel, Pork & Groceries		107	95
" 24	" 20 Bush. Wheat	@ 55¢	11	00
" 31	" Wages of Hands		47	00
Feb. 4	" Veal & Beef		1	45
" 17	" Difference in Exchange of Horses		10	00
" 21	" Shopping Money		25	00
" 28	" Wages of Hands		47	00
Mar. 16	" Guano, Lime & Bone Dust		290	00
" 31	" Wages of Hands		47	00
April 30	" " " "		39	00
May 1	" Blacksmithing		1	75
" 19	" "		2	50
" 31	" Wages of Hands		43	50
June 1	" 6 Alderney Cows with Calves	@ $50	300	00
" 30	" Wages of Hands		67	00
" "	" Int. on Bonds to Leech		300	00
July 10	" Market Wagon & Horse		175	00
" 15	" Wages of Hands		5	00
" 31	" " " "		67	00
Aug. 17	" Marketing		3	50
" 31	" Wages of Hands		67	00
Sept. 3	" Professional Services of Geo. M. Wharton		50	00
" 16	" Clothing & other Mdse.		62	25
" 30	" Wages of Hands		48	00
Oct. 2	" Mdse., of E. B. Holden & Co.		10	75
" 15	" Threshing 600 Bush. Wheat	@ 6¢	36	00
" 23	" Wages of Hands		6	00
" 30	" " " "		35	00
Nov. 3	" Clothing, Crockery & Groceries		108	80
" 27	" Chopping 50 Cords Wood	@ 50¢	25	00
" 30	" Wages of Hands		35	00
Dec. 7	" Int. paid Geo. T. Lipman		2	40
" 28	" Contributions $250.00, Schooling $150		400	00
" 30	" Freight & Expenses to Market		11	55
" 31	" Blacksmithing $53.75, Coopering $26.25		80	00
" "	" Wages of Hands		35	00
" "	" Int. on Bonds to Leech		300	00
			20,436	65
	Net Gains, as shown on page 53		315	67
			$20,752	32

FARM ACCOUNT.

Farm. *Cr.*

				$	¢
1852.					
Jan.	10	By 20 Bush. Wheat	@ $1.05	21	00
"	24	" 5 Tons Hay	@ $15.	75	00
April	13	" Durham Bull		125	00
"	"	" 2 Fore-quarters, 200 lbs. Beef	@ 7¢	14	00
"	"	" 1 Hind-quarter, 95 lbs. Beef	@ 8¢	7	60
"	"	" 10 lbs. Tallow	@ 8¢		80
May	25	" 8 Bush. Seed Potatoes	@ 50¢	4	00
Aug.	25	" 2 Steers	@ $25.	50	00
"	28	" 2 " sold Drover	@ $15.	30	00
"	"	" 12 Calves " "	@ $5.	60	00
Sept.	3	" Interest on Notes collected		14	24
Oct.	2	" Butter & Cheese		114	00
"	12	" 50 Bush. Potatoes	@ 35¢	17	50
"	26	" 375 " Wheat	@ $1.	375	00
Nov.	3	" 50 " Potatoes	@ 35¢	17	50
"	"	" 50 " Wheat	@ $1.	50	00
"	"	" 50 " Oats	@ 35¢	17	50
Dec.	3	" 20 Cords Wood	@ $3.	60	00
"	7	" Interest on C. L. Rodgers' Note		1	39
"	14	" 100 Bush. Corn	@ 50¢	50	00
"	20	" 5 " Wheat	@ $1.	5	00
"	25	" 2 Alderney Calves	@ $15.	30	00
"	"	" 1 " Cow		60	00
"	"	" 1 Yoke Oxen		75	00
"	28	" 750 Bush. Oats	@ 35¢	262	50
"	"	" 800 " Corn	@ 55¢	440	00
"	"	" 50 " Buckwheat	@ 60¢	30	00
"	30	" 1725 lbs. Cheese	@ 9¢	155	25
"	"	" 900 " Butter	@ 18¢	162	00
"	31	" 9,500 qts. Milk	@ 3¢	285	00
				2,609	28
		Value of Farm, Stock, &c., pr. Inventory		18,143	04
				$20,752	32

Inventory of my Property, Dec. 31st, 1852:			
1 Farm of 150 Acres, worth $10 an Acre more than when I bought it, owing to good cultivation; but which I will value at the original cost, $100. pr. Acre			15,000 00
1 Span Horses		$250.00	
1 Horse		100.00	
1 Alderney Bull, 2 years old,		120.00	
2 " Cows,	@ $60.	120.00	
6 " Do.	" $45.	270.00	
16 Common Do. (1 died)	" $20.	320.00	
7 Alderney Calves,	" $15.	105.00	
8 Hogs,	" $6.	48.00	
20 Pigs,	" $3.	60.00	1,393 00
1 Rockaway Wagon		142.00	
1 Large Double Wagon, with Cover		100.00	
Market Wagon $70., Ox-Cart $25.		95.00	
2 Ploughs,	@ $7.50	15.00	
Harrow $7., Horse-Rake $4.50		11.50	
Fanning Mill & Corn Cultivator		23.00	
Dairying Utensils, Forks, Spades, Shovels, Rakes, Hoes, Flails, and other Implements, valued at		40.00	426 50
170 Bush. Wheat,	@ $1.	170.00	
250 " Corn,	" 50¢	125.00	
150 " Oats,	" 35¢	52.50	
40 " Buckwheat,	" 55¢	22.00	
115 " Potatoes,	" 35¢	40.25	
48 Tons Hay,	" $10.	480.00	
3 Stacks Straw,	" $9.	27.00	
Quantity of Corn Fodder		42.00	
210 lbs. Butter,	@ 18¢	37.80	
154 " Cheese,	" 9¢	13.86	
1,125 Bush. Turnips,	" 12½¢	140.63	
130 " Ruta Bagas,	" 25¢	32.50	
25 Cords Hickory Wood,	" $3.	75.00	
Quantity of Stable Manure		65.00	1,323 54
	Total		$18,143 04

DEDUCTIONS FROM SET III.

UNSETTLED BALANCES ON THE LEGER.

Debts due me.		*Debts I owe.*	
Ebenezer Failing	10.00	Orrin Woolworth	44.00
Caleb Cope	165.00	Peter A. Phillips	65.00
E. B. Holden & Co.	91.00		$109.00
Mrs. S. C. Dermott	17.50		
Stedman & Williston	14.00		
	$297.50		

Capital at Starting.

Cash on hand, pr. Cash-Book, at starting - - - - - - -		6,275.00
Notes held against others, " " - - - - - - -		2,629.50
	Capital	$8,904.50

Present Worth.

Cash on hand, pr. Cash-Book, at closing - - - - - - -		888.63
Property owned by me, pr. Inventory-Book, - - - - - -		18,143.04
Personal accounts due me, pr. Leger, - - - - - - - - -		297.50
	Assets	$19,329.17
Deduct liabilities, viz.:—		
Personal accounts I owe, pr. Leger, - - - - - -	109.00	
Bonds & Mortgages Payable, [See entry of the purchase of Farm, on the 1st of Jan., 1852.] - - - - -	10,000.00	$10,109.00
Present worth, or net capital at closing		$9,220.17

Net Gains in Business.

Net capital at closing business - - - - - - -		$9,220.17
Deduct net capital at commencing - - - - - - - -		8,904.50
	Net gains	$315.67

From the above statements, you will perceive that:—

The amount invested by you at starting business is termed *capital.**

Your available means at closing are termed *assets.*

Your indebtedness at closing is termed *liabilities.*

The difference between your assets and liabilities is termed *net capital* or *present worth.* (Or, if the liabilities be the greater, *net insolvency.*)

Also,

By taking your capital at starting from your present worth, you may ascertain your gains in business.

In a losing business,

By taking your present worth from your capital at starting, you may ascertain your losses in business.

* The various items which make up this capital are called *effects;* and if you owed debts also at starting, the difference between the amount of your effects and debts would be called *net capital,* or, if the debts were the greater, *net insolvency.*

QUESTIONS FOR REVIEW, SET III.

Of what business do the materials on pages 44 to 49, inclusive, afford a history?
How are you to ascertain the gross amounts of debit or credit in any transaction?
To qualify a person to keep a set of books, what is necessary besides understanding the theory of accounts?
Where will you find an elucidation of the manner of entering any transaction recorded in the history to Set III?
Of what form are the *Cash-Book, Day-Book, and Leger* used in this Set?
Where are the explanations requisite for the blank books which accompany this treatise to be found?
Why should all books of account be kept free from mistakes, erasures, and blots?
What are you to do before looking at the elucidation of any transaction, and how are you to make the entry?
What is to be done after the Cash-Book and Day-Book are completed?
What after finishing the posting?
What after re-examining the posting?
What after closing the Leger?
What test of accuracy have you?
What is the Inventory-Book?
Of what use is this estimation of the value of property owned by you?
How often do merchants "take an account of stock?" Should every business man do the same? How often must it necessarily be done?
What is the best rule as to the value to be affixed to your property?
What is exhibited on the debit side of the Farm account?
What on the credit side?
Of what is this account an exemplification?
What does the account as here shown enable you to ascertain?
Of what is it a proof?
Mention the persons who owe you on closing business.
What is the gross amount?
Mention those whom you owe.
What is the gross amount?
What amount of cash was on hand at starting?
What amount of notes did you hold against others?
What was the total capital at starting? How ascertained?
What amount of cash is on hand at closing? What amount of property is owned by you? What amount is due on personal accounts?
What are the total assets at closing? How ascertained?
What amount of personal accounts do you owe? How much on bonds and mortgages?
What are the total liabilities? How ascertained?
What is the present worth or net capital at closing? How ascertained?
What have been your gains in business? How ascertained?
What is the amount invested by you at starting termed?
What are the various items which make up this capital called?
What would the difference between your effects and debts at starting be called?
What are your available means at closing termed?
What is your indebtedness at closing termed?
What is the difference between your assets and liabilities termed?
How do you ascertain your gains in business. How your losses?
What is to be done, if bad debts exist at closing? [See Note, page 18.]

SET IV, SINGLE ENTRY.

I HAVE given a *Crew's Leger* in connection with the Western river Steamboat Set of books, pages 200–203, for keeping accounts with the hands on board the boat, and the form of accounts there shown is so simple, that I concluded, in revising for this edition, to give here an illustration of the same method, for the use of persons whose business is very limited, and who may prefer to adopt it. It is to use a Leger only, ruled like the Cash-Book to Set I, [page 19,] and to enter directly in it all the debits or credits to the different parties with whom you have dealings, without the intervention of the Day-Book. The Cash account may be kept in a portion of the Leger, instead of having a separate Cash-Book, and any property accounts may be also kept, if desired, as well as in the preceding Sets given.

I have omitted the Cash account, because its form and treatment would be precisely like Cash-Book, Set I, above referred to; and also, to save room, have omitted all statements, deductions, &c. Indeed, I have not endeavored to make the Set complete, as I do not intend it to be written up. You will be able at once to comprehend it, by a mere examination, after having progressed thus far.

The Index (here omitted) would of course be needed, for convenient reference to the Leger.

James B. Loughead. Dr. Cr.

			Dr. $	¢	Cr. $	¢
1852. Dec.	3	To Re-setting 4 Tires to Wagon	3	00		
"	"	" Mending King Bolt		25		
"	"	" 2 Nuts to Bolts		13		
"	23	" Shoeing Oxen, $1.50, Clevis 37 ¢	1	87		
"	"	" 6 Iron Wedges, different sizes,	3	38		
"	"	" Mending Eye to Trace Chain		10		
"	27	By 4 Bush. Potatoes @ 35 ¢			1	40
"	31	" 16 lbs. Butter @ 20 ¢			3	20
"	"	" *Bal. to New ᵃ/c*			4	13
			8	73	8	73
1853. Jan.	1	To Bal. from Old ᵃ/c	4	13		

Herman Logan. Dr. Cr.

			Dr. $	¢	Cr. $	¢
1852. Dec.	4	By 4 days' Work @ $1.			4	00
"	11	" 5^2 " " " $1.			5	50
"	"	To Cash on ᵃ/c	6	00		
"	18	By 4^3 days' Work @ $1.			4	75
"	25	" 5 " " " $1.			5	00
"	31	" 3^1 " " " $1.			3	25
"	"	To Cash in full	16	50		
			22	50	22	50

Orlando Chase. Dr. Cr.

			Dr. $	¢	Cr. $	¢
1852. Dec.	10	By 4 lbs. Tea @ 45 ¢			1	80
"	"	" 1 " Allspice				13
"	"	" 2 " Raisins @ 12^2 ¢				25
"	16	To 5 " Wrought Nails for Doors @ 25 ¢	1	25		
"	21	" Iron Bar for Store Windows		88		
"	24	By 20 lbs. Brown Sugar @ 7^2 ¢			1	50
"	30	" 10 " Coffee " 9 ¢				90
"	"	" 1 Gal. Molasses				40
"	31	" 14 Yds. Merrimac Prints @ 12^2 ¢			1	75
"	"	" 30^2 " Lowell Sheeting " 10 ¢			3	05
"	"	" *Bal. to New ᵃ/c*	7	65		
			9	78	9	78
1853. Jan.	1	By Bal. from Old ᵃ/c			7	65

Mrs. Mary Pennington. Dr. Cr.

			Dr. $	¢	Cr. $	¢
1852. Dec.	28	To Ironing Sleigh, as agreed	15	00		

Wendall A. Lyons. Dr. Cr.

			Dr. $	Dr. ¢	Cr. $	Cr. ¢
1852. Dec.	6	To 4 New Linch-Pins		38		
"	7	" 1 Pr. Iron Hinges for Barn		75		
"	"	" 1 " " " " "		62		
"	9	" Ironing Cart, as pr. agreement	10	50		
"	"	" Mending Plough	1	25		
"	17	" Repairs to Carriage	3	13		
"	"	By 10 Bush. Wheat @ $1.			10	00
"	20	" 4 " Corn " 50¢			2	00
"	22	" 20 lbs. Cheese " 7¢			1	40
"	"	To Mending Log Chain		25		
"	25	" Shoeing Horses, 5 New Shoes	1	56		
"	27	" Ironing York Wagon in the best manner, as agreed,	25	00		
"	"	" Making 3 Screws and Nuts		45		
"	"	" Mending Stirrup to Saddle		10		
"	28	" 4 New Teeth in Harrow		75		
"	29	" Irons on Whipple-trees	1	00		
"	"	By Cash on a/c			20	00
"	"	" 15 Bush. Potatoes @ 35¢			5	25
"	"	" 3 " Oats " 40¢			1	20
"	30	To Log Chain	2	50		
"	"	" 1 Small Bolt		16		
"	"	" Mending Iron Kettle		44		
"	"	" Repairing Sleigh, as agreed	4	25		
"	"	By Cash on a/c			5	00
"	31	To Putting Bands on Beetle		50		
"	"	" 3 Strong Latches to Barn Doors	1	13		
"	"	" 1 Bolt for Pump		19		
"	"	" Mending Shovel		31		
"	"	" " Manure Forks		62		
"	"	" Staple & Ring for Hitching-Post		38		
"	"	" Repairing Wheel-Barrow		94		
"	"	*By Bal. to New a/c*			12	31
			57	16	57	16
1853. Jan.	1	To Bal. from Old a/c	12	31		

Wilson P. Jones, Jr. Dr. Cr.

				Dr. $	Dr. ¢	Cr. $	Cr. ¢
1852. Dec.	1	To Shoeing Horses,					
		4 New Shoes @ 31[1]¢	1.25				
		4 Shoes, reset, " 12[2]¢	.50	1	75		
"	10	" Repairing Wagon		2	25		
"	15	By Cash in full				4	00
				4	00	4	00

Book-Keeping

BY

DOUBLE ENTRY.

INTRODUCTION

TO

DOUBLE ENTRY BOOK-KEEPING.

BOOK-KEEPING by *Double Entry* is the keeping of accounts in such a manner that each entry contains *both a debit and a credit*, and hence the name.

BOOK-KEEPING by *Single Entry*, as already explained, embraces only the accounts of persons; but, in DOUBLE ENTRY Book-keeping, *persons* and *things* are alike debited and credited, and accounts are kept, not only with individuals, but also with the different species of property in your possession, and with the different branches of your gains and losses in business. All accounts are *representative*, of whatever name or description; thus, accounts kept with persons represent your business relations with those persons, accounts kept with the different species of property in your possession represent your business relations with those different kinds of property, and accounts with the various branches of your gains and losses represent *you* as gaining or losing in business.

The *distinguishing feature* of Double Entry Book-keeping consists in carrying out a mathematical principle of equilibrium, under the titles of debtor and creditor, or of debits and credits. It is this: IN AMOUNT, EVERY DEBIT MUST HAVE A CREDIT, AND VICE VERSA, EVERY CREDIT A DEBIT.* The particular *method* or *form* in which books are kept is not essential, so that they conform to the principles of Double Entry, and preserve strictly the equilibrium of debit and credit.

The Origin of the science of keeping books by Double Entry has been a matter of much speculation by different writers on the subject, but nothing definite can be ascertained respecting it. McCulloch, in his Commercial Dictionary, says "it was first practised in Venice, Genoa, and other towns of Italy, where trade was conducted on an extensive scale at a much earlier date than in England, France, or other parts of Europe." Kelly, in his treatise on Book-keeping, published in London in 1833, (first edition in 1801,) says, "it is generally supposed to have been first practised at Venice in the fifteenth century, when that city was the grand emporium of Europe:" although he adds, "it is remarkable that the first European who translated Algebra from the writings of the Arabians is also supposed to have written the first treatise on Book-keeping. It was published in the Italian language at Venice, about the year 1495, by Lucas de Burgo, a friar, who likewise wrote several useful works on mathematical subjects." Colt, in a lecture delivered at Boston, says that the Italians "most likely picked up, among other things, all they ever knew of Double Entry Book-keeping, at Constantinople, Alexandria, or some other eastern city, whose traders more anciently may have practised it in their commerce with northern Africa, Hindostan, and the countries bordering upon the Red Sea:"—and thinks it more likely that the Hanseatic merchants are the inventors of Double Entry than the Italians.

To whomsoever the credit *properly* belongs, the *Italians* have pretty generally received it, and that system of Double Entry which is shown in the first part of this

* Recollect that this equilibrium is an equilibrium of *amount*, and not in the number of debits and credits. One debit may be balanced by several credits, or one credit by several debits, if the gross amounts in each case are equal.

treatise—embracing the Day-Book in history form, (originally called Waste-Book or Blotter,) the Journal, and Leger, as the main books of entry—is usually denominated the *Italian method.*

Since the publication of the first work at Venice, there had been, previous to 1810, according to *Isler*, of Brussels, "150 authors on Book-keeping in different parts of Europe, among whom he enumerates 70 in Germany, 25 in France, 7 in Holland, 3 in Italy, and 30 in England. Subsequent to that time, it is not improbable there have been as many writers on the subject; and this country has recently had its full share. The author of this work has examined upwards of 20 different treatises on Book-keeping published in the United States since 1815, exclusive of a large number of small works on Single Entry.

There have been constant improvements in the method of keeping accounts, and very many changes made in the *form* and *use* of the different books, so as the better to adapt them to any specific class of business required; but these improvements have been made, for the most part, by practical accountants, and writers on the subject have by no means kept pace with the progress that has been made.

The old Italian method has been adopted in the first three Sets here shown, because it is the basis of all other forms, and therefore the best form from which to learn the first principles of the science. The main books of entry, as already stated, are the Day-Book, Journal, and Leger. More or less auxiliary books are used in connection with these, according to the nature of the business transacted; but as a knowledge of these auxiliaries is easily obtained, it is not thought best to encumber the mind of the student with them at first, and they are accordingly omitted until a subsequent part of the work. In the fourth and fifth Sets, I have shown another method of keeping accounts, which somewhat shortens the work, and lessens the labor of the accountant; and in the sixth Set nearly the same method is continued. Set VI, however, had been prepared with particular reference to its practical character, as suited to a foreign shipping and commission business; and the various auxiliary books are here introduced for the first time. Set VII, of the High-School edition, illustrates one of the best forms for actual use, and one perhaps more used in the different kinds of business than any one form:—while in the Counting-House edition, a large number of *practical forms of accounts* are given, some now used by and obtained from accountants in the various departments of trade and commerce in the United States, and others original with the author, which will materially lessen the amount of writing and labor requisite in keeping books. Thus the design has been, from the simplest commencement, to attain to the most thorough and practical results by a plain, easy, and gradually progressive process.

DEBTOR AND CREDITOR DEFINED.

Debtor signifies the *person* or *thing* which is held bound, which owes, or which is under obligation.

Creditor signifies the *person* or *thing* which holds bound, which is owed, or which has conferred an obligation.

Therefore, whenever any personal account, property account, or account of gains and losses is debited on your books, it signifies that the person or thing represented thereby owes you; and whenever any account is credited on your books, it signifies that you owe the person or thing so represented.

GENERAL RULE

FOR JOURNALIZING TRANSACTIONS, OR

FOR DETERMINING WHAT TO DEBIT AND WHAT TO CREDIT.

Transactions or trades have their foundation in exchanges of value. In every trade in which you are interested, value (real or supposed) goes from your possession, and value is also received by you. The value with which you part is either given for the use and benefit of some person, without his immediately remunerating you for it, thus making him your debtor; or else it is given for some species of property or some branch of your gains and losses, which thus becomes your debtor, for this cost or outgo. The value which you receive is either furnished by some person, without your immediately remunerating him for it, thus rendering him your creditor; or else is paid for through the medium of some species of property or some branch of your gains and losses, which thus becomes your creditor, for this value produced.

As *value exchanged* is the basis of all trade, it should also be the basis of any rule or rules for entering transactions which occur in the course of trade; and the great value of *good rules* consists not in their arbitrarily producing results, but in their containing within themselves the *reason* for such results, so that the learner cannot *apply* the rules without *understanding* the subject-matter.

The following GENERAL RULE for *journalizing transactions*, (or *for determining what to debit and what to credit*,) is believed to be of such a character, and to be applicable to every transaction that will occur in the ordinary course of trade, whether on a limited or on an extended scale.

RULE.

IN STOCK BOOKS.

Any person or thing is DEBTOR when you give value or become obligated for it.
Any person or thing is CREDITOR when it produces value or renders service for you.

IN PARTNERSHIP BOOKS.

Any person or thing is DEBTOR when the firm give value or become obligated for it.
Any person or thing is CREDITOR when it produces value or renders service for the firm.

Or Briefly.

IN STOCK BOOKS.

DEBIT *what* COSTS *you value.*
CREDIT *what* PRODUCES *you value.*

IN PARTNERSHIP BOOKS.

DEBIT *what* COSTS *the firm value.*
CREDIT *what* PRODUCES *the firm value.*

NOTE.—The above Rule will not apply for determining the opening Journal entry of individual or stock books, since the Rule is only applicable to transactions between two or more parties in business; but it will apply to the opening entry of partnership books, as there must necessarily be an agreement or bargain between the parties at the commencement of business.

SET I, DOUBLE ENTRY.

It should be borne in mind that each set is intended to represent a business by itself, independent of the others; and particular attention should be paid to the opening and closing of each, to discover clearly the various exhibits made of capital invested, gains or losses in business, and net capital or insolvency resulting therefrom. The continuance of each set for one *month* is intended to represent a *year*, this being as often as books are closed in a majority of houses, although some close every six months.

EXPLANATORY REMARKS, SET I.

THE DAY-BOOK.

The Day-Book, in the Italian method, is a plain history of your business transactions, written in the order and date of their occurrence. It is necessary to open the Day-Book by giving therein a statement of your effects at the commencement of business, and also of what debts you owe. Afterward record in detail every transaction that occurs in the course of business, making the entry, in *history form*, in as few words as possible, and have it complete. [See Day-Book, page 66.]

THE JOURNAL.

The Journal is used for arranging under Leger titles the entries that have been previously made in the Day-Book, and for affixing to each Leger title the correct amount of debit or credit, which is called journalizing. This is done that the accounts may with ease be collected under their proper heads in the Leger.

There are various styles of Journal. The one given with this Set has two dollar and cent columns, one for the debits and one for the credits. The debtors are written first, commencing at the left-hand marginal line, and having their amounts extended into the debit column. The creditors are designated by commencing at a short distance from the left-hand marginal line, by being prefixed with the word "To," and by having their amounts extended into the credit column. [See Journal, page 68.]

THE LEGER.

The Leger may be appropriately styled the *grand reservoir* of accounts, into which all records in the other books flow as naturally as streams to the ocean. It may also be styled *the business-man's directory*, from which he can refer to the details contained in the books of original entry, with the same ease as he would trace out the residence of a friend by searching the street and number in the City Directory. Its principal use is to collect under one head all sums belonging to the same account. Copying from the Journal to the Leger is called Posting. By examining the Leger, and tracing out a few postings, you will see that there are spaces ruled for particular purposes—viz. for the date, the name of balancing entry to each debit or credit, the folio of Journal, and the amount—and that the form and mode of entry in a Double Entry Leger is very nearly similar to Single Entry.

NOTE.—"By," whenever used in any of the books, is the *prefix of* the *debtor*, although generally placed on the creditor side of an account; and "To" is the *prefix* of the *creditor*, although generally placed on the debtor side of an account.

BILLS RECEIVABLE.

Bills Receivable may be defined as follows:

1st. A note in our possession, drawn by another person, payable to us or order.

2d. A note drawn by another person, purchased by us, although not originally made payable to us.

3d. A draft or bill of exchange drawn by one party on a second, and coming into our possession as a third party, whether accepted or not.

4th. Our draft on another, accepted by him and retained in our possession.

BILLS PAYABLE.

1st. Our note payable to another person.

2d. A draft or bill of exchange on us, and accepted by us.

3d. Any bond or obligation in contract, with our signature, and requiring payment of us.

NOTE 1.—Notes are said to be *negotiable* when they are drawn in such form as to be *transferable* from one party to another, and may be collected by the last party to whom transferred.

NOTE 2.—The above definitions of Bills Receivable and Bills Payable have been here given, to enable the student more readily to comprehend them in future entries; and when he has any difficulty in determining what should be called Bills Pay. or Bills Rec., he will do well to read them over.

INSTRUCTIONS FOR WRITING UP SET I.

Write Set I on loose sheets for practice, (prior to writing Sets II and III in the blank books which accompany this treatise.) Rule sufficient paper for the purpose after the forms shown, and then copy off all the entries in the printed Day-Book.

JOURNALIZING.—From this Day-Book, so copied, make out your Journal, relying as far as possible upon your own reasoning powers, in the application of the *general rule* for journalizing and of the explanations contained on the preceding pages. When you cannot determine the correct entry yourself, you may refer to the printed Journal, and pattern after it, but in every such case, as well as where you make your own entry, you should carefully read over the elucidation found underneath the entry, in the printed Journal; and make the *reason* of each debit and credit perfectly understood before you proceed to the subsequent entry. I cannot too firmly impress this upon your mind, for the clear comprehension of the whole science of Double Entry hinges, as it were, upon a thorough acquaintance with the principles of journalizing; and although the Journal is now often laid aside in actual business, yet you must thoroughly understand how to use it, in order to be able to do without it.

OPENING THE JOURNAL.—The name usually given to an individual in business by himself is *Stock*, and his books are called *Stock books*, in contradistinction to *Partnership books:* you may therefore consider *Stock* as your *alias*, and debit and credit yourself under that title. On opening the Journal at the commencement of business, debit each person that owes you for the amount of his indebtedness, and each species of property in your possession for its value, thus expressing their obligation to you; and credit Stock (yourself) for the whole amount of your effects invested, consisting of this indebtedness of persons and value of property. Again, debit Stock (yourself) for all your indebtedness; and credit each person the amount you owe him, and each property account the amount of your obligation, as shown under that head. Your own name can be used instead of Stock, if preferred.

When two or more persons are associated in business, their books are called Partnership books; for the method of opening which, see Set IV.

☞ For instructions on posting, see page 73.

NOTE 1.—The total footing of the Day-Book must agree with that of the Journal. Also, the footings of the debit and credit columns of the Journal must be equal.

In practice, these additions of the money columns in Day-Book and Journal are frequently omitted; but great care must then be taken to see that each Journal entry has an equal amount of debit and credit, for if this equilibrium does not in all cases exist, the Leger will be out of balance.

NOTE 2.—The Index to Leger, Set I, is omitted, but the pupil can make one for his Leger, as he posts. For form, see page 35.

DAY-BOOK, SET I.

Philadelphia, January 1*st*, 1852.

✓ *	Inventory of my effects on commencing business				
	400 Yds. Blk. Eng. Cloths @ $3.	1,200.00			
	460 " Ass'd " Do. @ $2.50	1,150.00			
	720 " Blk. " Cassimeres @ $1.50	1,080.00			
	385 " Ass'd " Do. @ $1.	385.00	3,815.00		
	Cash on hand		2,000.00	5,815	00
	2d				
✓	Sold, for Cash, to Isaac Bates				
	100 Yds. Ass'd Eng. Cloths @ $3.		300.00		
	160 " Blk. " Cassimeres @ $2.		320.00	620	00
	3d				
✓	Sold to James Melrose, for his Note @ 30 days,				
	190 Yds. Ass'd Eng. Cassimeres @ $1.16			220	40
	5th				
✓	Sold to Philip Somers on a/c				
	175 Yds. Blk. Eng. Cloths @ $3.75			656	25
	"				
✓	Bought of Nathan S. Faxon, for Cash,				
	225 Yds. Blue Eng. Cloths @ $3.25			731	25
	6th				
✓	Bought of James Walton, on my Note @ 60 days,				
	350 Yds. Blk. Fr. Cloths @ $4.		1,400.00		
	195 " " " Cassimeres @ $2.		390.00		
	200 " " Eng. Do. @ $1.		200.00	1,990	00
	8th				
✓	Bought of Elihu Barnes on a/c, @ 90 days,				
	238 Yds. Ass'd Fr. Cassimeres @ $1.25			297	50
	9th				
✓	Sold to Wm. Alexander 250 Yds. Blk. Fr. Cloths @ $5.			1,250	00
	Received in Payment, Cash,	450.00			
	His Note, @ 30 days, for the Balance	800.00	1,250.00		
	12th				
✓	Sold to Thomas Carpenter & Co. 195 Yds. Blk. Fr. Cassimeres @ $2.25			438	75
	Received Cash in part payment		300.00		
	The remainder sold on a/c		138.75		
	13th				
✓	Paid Cash to L. W. Camden, for repairs of Store			50	00
				12,069	15

* These check-marks indicate that the entries have been journalized, and should be placed opposite each entry as soon as it is transferred to the Journal. Some use the Journal folio instead.

DAY-BOOK, SET I.

Philadelphia, January 19*th*, 1852.

	Am't Bro't forward			12,069	15
✓	Sold to Martin Pemberton, on ℀, 125 Yds. Blue Eng. Cloths @ $4.			500	00
	20th				
✓	Sold to Philip Somers 230 Yds. Ass'd Eng. Cloths @ $3.			690	00
	Received payment in part by Elihu Barnes' Note, in favor of P. Somers, due March 4th, Am't		350.00		
	The Balance sold on ℀		340.00		
	22d				
✓	Bought of Elihu Barnes 400 Yds. Ass'd Eng. Cassimeres @ $1.50			600	00
	Paid in part by his Note, favor of P. Somers, due Mar. 4th		350.00		
	The Balance purchased @ 30 days' credit		250.00		
	23d				
✓	Bought of Ezra Peterson 240 Yds. Ass'd Fr. Cloths @ $3.			720	00
	Paid Cash in part	400.00			
	Balance on ℀	320.00	720.00		
	24th				
✓	Received Cash of Philip Somers on ℀			656	25
	26th				
✓	Sold to Thomas Carpenter & Co. 220 Yds. Ass'd Fr. Cloths @ $3.40			748	00
	Received an Order of Samuel W. Fairburn on me		400.00		
	Cash		200.00		
	Balance on ℀		148.00		
	27th				
✓	Appropriated Cash for Personal Expenses			60	00
	29th				
✓	Sold to Thomas Carpenter & Co.				
	225 Yds. Blk. Eng. Cloths @ $3.75		843.75		
	130 " Ass'd " Do. @ $3.00		390.00		
	200 " Blk. " Cassimeres @ $1.25		250.00		
	195 " Ass'd " Do. @ $1.16		226.20	1,709	95
	Received in payment, Cash	569.98			
	Their Note @ 60 days	569.98			
	Balance on ℀ @ 30 days	569.99	1,709.95		
	31st				
✓	Paid Ezra Peterson Cash in full of his ℀			320	00
	"				
✓	Paid Cash for Rent of Store one month		75.00		
	" Clerk hire " "		75.00		
	" Gas Bill " "		5.00	155	00
				18,228	35

JOURNAL, SET I.

Philadelphia, January 1st, 1852.

L.F.		Dr.	Cr.
*1	Sundries Dr. To Stock		5,815.00
1	Merchandise	3,815.00	
1	Cash	2,000.00	
	You must imagine this to be your own business, and bear in mind that "Stock," *as here used,* does not mean goods on hand, but represents *you,* instead of your own name. This entry means simply *Sundries Dr.,* and *Stock* (yourself) *Cr.* Under the heading "Sundries," the several items which make up the sundries are always enumerated:—in this case, as you see, the items are *Mdse.* and *Cash,* each of which is considered as obligated, or indebted to you for its value. *You* are credited, under the title of *Stock,* for the Effects invested by you in business. See remarks on the opening of the Journal, page 65.		
	2d		
1/1	Cash Dr. To Merchandise	620.00	620.00
	The Cash which you get in this trade has cost you Mdse. to the value of $620, and is considered as owing you for its cost. The Mdse. which you have sold has been the means of your receiving $620 in Cash, and you are considered indebted to it for the value produced; therefore, *Cash* is *Dr.* because it has *cost* value.—*Mdse.* is *Cr.* because it has *produced* value. ☞ Be careful to notice the *form* of each entry, and the manner of extending the amounts into the columns. In this case you perceive both a debit and credit extension on the same line. Notice, also, that several items of the *same kind* of property do not constitute sundries in the Journal, but the term *Sundries* is the caption when there are several *Leger titles.*		
	3d		
1/1	Bills Receivable Dr. To Merchandise	220.40	220.40
	By this transaction a *Note* is received for Mdse., instead of Cash, as in the preceding entry. *Bills Rec.* Costs† value, and is *Dr.*—*Mdse.* produces value, and is *Cr.*		
	5th		
2/1	Philip Somers Dr. To Merchandise	656.25	656.25
	You do not here receive immediate payment for the Mdse. sold, as in the two preceding entries; value *has not,* therefore, been given for Cash or Bills Rec., or any other species of property, and *no property account is Dr.*—But value has gone from your possession in Mdse. to the amount of $656.25, for the use and benefit of *Philip Somers,* without his remunerating you for it: therefore he has been the occasion of an outgo, or expense, to you; in other words, has *cost you value,* and is *Dr.* *Mdse.* has produced value in his indebtedness, and is *Cr.*		
	"		
1/1	Merchandise Dr. To Cash	731.25	731.25
	This and the two following entries are the exact counterparts of the three preceding ones. Here Mdse. costs value in Cash:—Cash produces value by paying for the Mdse.		
	6th		
1/2	Merchandise Dr. To Bills Payable	1,990.00	1,990.00
	Mdse. costs value in your Note:—Bills Pay. produces value by paying for the Mdse.		
	8th		
1/2	Merchandise Dr. To Elihu Barnes	297.50	297.50
	Mdse. costs value in your indebtedness to Barnes:—E. Barnes produces value by furnishing you with the goods without pay.		
	9th		
1	Sundries Dr. To Merchandise		1,250.00
1	Cash	450.00	
1	Bills Receivable	800.00	
	Sundries—to wit, Cash and Bills Rec.—have cost you value in Mdse, and each is Dr. for its cost. Mdse. has produced value in the Cash and Note, and is Cr.		
	12th		
1	Sundries Dr. To Merchandise		438.75
1	Cash	300.00	
2	Thomas Carpenter & Co.	138.75	
	Cash and T. Carpenter & Co. have each caused you to part with Mdse., and have thus been a cost to you. Mdse. has produced you value in Cash and the indebtedness of Carpenter & Co.	12,019.15	12,019.15

* Omit the Leger folio until you post.

† Whenever, as in this case, I am speaking of the Leger account of "Bills Rec." or "Bills Pay.," I use the singular verb, because the noun is really singular, although the word "Bills," of itself, is plural.

Philadelphia, January 13*th*, 1852.

L.F.		Dr.		Cr.	
	Am'ts Bro't forward	12,019	15	12,019	15
2/1	Store Expenses Dr. To Cash	50	00	50	00
	Store Expenses have cost you value, and are Dr.—Cash has produced you value, by paying for repairs, and is Cr.				
	19th				
2/1	Martin Pemberton Dr. To Merchandise	500	00	500	00
	The elucidation of the entry of the 5th inst. will fully explain this transaction.				
	20th				
1	Sundries Dr. To Merchandise			690	00
1	Bills Receivable	350	00		
2	Philip Somers	340	00		
	You have given Mdse. to the value of $690 for Barnes' Note and for Somers' obligation; therefore, Bills Rec. and P. Somers are Dr. for what they cost you, and Mdse. is Cr. for the value it produces you.				
	22d				
1	Merchandise Dr. To Sundries	600	00		
1	To Bills Receivable			350	00
2	" Elihu Barnes			250	00
	Mdse. costs $600, and is Dr.—Bills Rec. and E. Barnes produce value; Bills Rec. by paying for part of the goods, Barnes by furnishing part without pay.				
	23d				
1	Merchandise Dr. To Sundries	720	00		
1	To Cash			400	00
3	" Ezra Peterson			320	00
	Mdse. costs value.—Cash and E. Peterson produce value.				
	24th				
1/2	Cash Dr. To Philip Somers	656	25	656	25
	Cash has cost you the former indebtedness of Somers.—Somers has produced value by paying his account.				
	26th				
1	Sundries Dr. To Merchandise			748	00
3	Samuel W. Fairburn	400	00		
1	Cash	200	00		
2	Thomas Carpenter & Co.	148	00		
	An Order is a request in writing that you will pay a certain sum for another person. Here you have parted with Mdse. to the value of $400, at the request of S. W. Fairburn; thus he has cost you that much, and owes you for it, or is Dr. For remainder of entry, see elucidation of 12th inst.				
	27th				
3/1	Personal Expenses Dr. To Cash	60	00	60	00
	Personal Expenses cost value; Cash produces value by paying these expenses.				
	29th				
1	Sundries Dr. To Merchandise			1,709	95
1	Cash	569	98		
1	Bills Receivable	569	98		
2	Thomas Carpenter & Co.	569	99		
	Sundries cost value in Mdse.				
	31st				
3/1	Ezra Peterson Dr. To Cash	320	00	320	00
	Peterson costs you $320 in Cash.—Cash produces value by paying the debt.				
	"				
2/1	Store Expenses Dr. To Cash	155	00	155	00
	Store Expenses cost value in Cash.				
		18,228	35	18,228	35

LEGER, SET I.

Dr. ***Stock.*** ***Cr.***

Date.		Balancing Entry.	J. F.	Amount.		Date.		Balancing Entry.	J. F.	Amount.	
1852.						1852.					
Jan.	31	*To Bal. (Net Cap.)*	3	6,752	10	Jan.	1	By Sundries	1	5,815	00
						"	31	" Profit & Loss	3	937	10
				6,752	10					6,752	10

Dr. ***Merchandise.*** ***Cr.***

Date.		Balancing Entry.	J. F.	Amount.		Date.		Balancing Entry.	J. F.	Amount.	
1852.						1852.					
Jan.	1	To Stock	1	3,815	00	Jan.	2	By Cash	1	620	00
"	5	" Cash	1	731	25	"	3	" Bills Rec.	1	220	40
"	6	" Bills Pay.	1	1,990	00	"	5	" P. Somers	1	656	25
"	8	" E. Barnes	1	297	50	"	9	" Sundries	1	1,250	00
"	22	" Sundries	2	600	00	"	12	" "	1	438	75
"	23	" "	2	720	00	"	19	" M. Pemberton	2	500	00
		8,153.75				"	20	" Sundries	2	690	00
"	31	" *Prof.&Loss (gain)*	3	1,202	10	"	26	" "	2	748	00
						"	29	" "	2	1,709	95
								6,833.35			
						"	31	" *Bal. (Inv't.)*	3	2,522	50
				9,355	85					9,355	85

Dr. ***Cash.*** ***Cr.***

Date.		Balancing Entry.	J. F.	Amount.		Date.		Balancing Entry.	J. F.	Amount.	
1852.						1852.					
Jan.	1	To Stock	1	2,000	00	Jan.	5	By Mdse.	1	731	25
"	2	" Mdse.	1	620	00	"	13	" Store Expenses	2	50	00
"	9	" "	1	450	00	"	23	" Mdse.	2	400	00
"	12	" "	1	300	00	"	27	" Per. Expenses	2	60	00
"	24	" P. Somers	2	656	25	"	31	" E. Peterson	2	320	00
"	26	" Mdse.	2	200	00	"	"	" Store Expenses	2	155	00
"	29	" "	2	569	98			1,716.25			
		4,796.23				"	31	" *Bal. (on hand)*	3	3,079	98
				4,796	23					4,796	23

Dr. ***Bills Receivable.*** ***Cr.***

Date.		Balancing Entry.	J. F.	Amount.		Date.		Balancing Entry.	J. F.	Amount.	
1852.						1852.					
Jan.	3	To Mdse.	1	220	40	Jan.	22	By Mdse.	2	350	00
"	9	" "	1	800	00	"	31	" *Bal. (unpaid)*	3	1,590	38
"	20	" "	2	350	00						
"	29	" "	2	569	98						
		1,940.38									
				1,940	38					1,940	38

Dr. *Philip Somers.* *Cr.*

1852.			J. F.			1852.			J. F.		
Jan.	5	To Mdse.	1	656	25	Jan.	24	By Cash	2	656	25
"	20	" "	2	340	00	"	31	" *Bal. (due me)*	3	340	00
		996.25		996	25					996	25

Dr. *Bills Payable.* *Cr.*

1852.						1852.					
Jan.	31	*To Bal. (unpaid)*	3	1,990	00	Jan.	6	By Mdse.	1	1,990	00

Dr. *Elihu Barnes.* *Cr.*

1852.						1852.					
Jan.	31	*To Bal. (due him)*	3	547	50	Jan.	8	By Mdse.	1	297	50
						"	22	" "	2	250	00
				547	50			547.50		547	50

Dr. *Thomas Carpenter & Co.* *Cr.*

1852.						1852.					
Jan.	12	To Mdse.	1	138	75	*Jan.*	31	*By Bal. (due me)*	3	856	74
"	26	" "	2	148	00						
"	29	" "	2	569	99						
		856.74		856	74					856	74

Dr. *Store Expenses.* *Cr.*

1852.						1852.					
Jan.	13	To Cash	2	50	00	*Jan.*	31	*By Prof. & Loss (loss)*	3	205	00
"	31	" "	2	155	00						
		205.00		205	00					205	00

Dr. *Martin Pemberton.* *Cr.*

1852.						1852.					
Jan.	19	To Mdse.	2	500	00	*Jan.*	31	*By Bal. (due me)*	3	500	00

Ezra Peterson.

Dr.			J. F.			Cr.			J. F.		
1852. Jan.	31	To Cash	2	320	00	1852. Jan.	23	By Mdse.	2	320	00

Samuel W. Fairburn.

Dr.						Cr.					
1852. Jan.	26	To Mdse.	2	400	00	1852. *Jan.*	31	*By Bal.* (*due me*)	3	400	00

Personal Expenses.

Dr.						Cr.					
1852. Jan.	27	To Cash	2	60	00	1852. *Jan.*	31	*By Prof. & Loss* (*loss*)	3	60	00

Profit & Loss.

Dr.						Cr.					
1852. Jan.	31	To Store Expenses	2	205	00	1852. Jan.	31	By Mdse.	1	1,202	10
"	"	" Per. "	3	60	00						
		265.00									
"	"	" *Stock* (*net gain*)	1	937	10						
				1,202	10					1,202	10

Balance.

Dr.						Cr.					
1852. Jan.	31	To Mdse.	1	2,522	50	1852. Jan.	31	By Bills Pay.	2	1,990	00
"	"	" Cash	1	3,079	98	"	"	" E. Barnes	2	547	50
								2,537.50			
"	"	" Bills Rec.	1	1,590	38	"	"	" *Stock* (*net cap.*)	1	6,752	10
"	"	" P. Somers	2	340	00						
"	"	" T. Carpenter & Co.	2	856	74						
"	"	" M. Pemberton	2	500	00						
"	"	" S. W. Fairburn	3	400	00						
		9,289.60									
				9,289	60					9,289	60

ON POSTING.

Having journalized all the transactions recorded in the Day-Book, the next step is to *post* them, *i. e.* transfer them from the Journal to the Leger. This process I will endeavor to explain to you.

Look at the first entry in your Journal, "Sundries Dr. To Stock," and you will perceive that Stock is Cr. $5,815.00, which is now to be transferred to the account of Stock on the Leger. After *opening* this account thus, "Dr.——Stock——Cr.," as shown in the Leger here given, place underneath this heading, on the credit side, the date of Journal entry, what Stock is Cr. by, the Journal folio from which the post is made, and the amount. Having done this, you post-mark the entry; *i. e.* place, in the left hand margin of the Journal, the folio of the Leger to which it is posted. This completes the first post. Next comes the Drs. of this entry, of which Merchandise is the first. Open an account for it thus, "Dr.——Merchandise——Cr.," below Stock on the same folio, leaving enough lines intervening between the two to receive all the posts which are to be made to the Stock account. Underneath this second heading, on the debit side, place the date, description, Journal folio, and amount, as directed for Stock, and lastly post-mark it in the Journal. Next take the debit to Cash: open an account for Cash in the Leger, and post as directed for Merchandise. The whole of the first entry in the Journal is now posted.

The second entry requires two posts, one to the debit of Cash, and one to the credit of Merchandise, which two accounts you have already opened on the Leger. This entry will also require two post-marks, the upper one for the debit, and the lower one for the credit.

Proceed in this manner regularly, opening new accounts as you come to them, until the whole Journal is posted, when you will be ready to take a Trial Balance; for an explanation of which see the following.

TRIAL BALANCE, LEGER, SET I.

L. F.	Leger Titles.	Dr. Amount Columns.		Cr.		Dr. Difference Columns.		Cr.	
1	Stock - - - - -			5,815	00			5,815	00
1	Merchandise - -	8,153	75	6,833	35	1,320	40		
1	Cash - - - - -	4,796	23	1,716	25	3,079	98		
1	Bills Receivable - -	1,940	38	350	00	1,590	38		
2	Philip Somers - - -	996	25	656	25	340	00		
2	Bills Payable - -			1,990	00			1,990	00
2	Elihu Barnes - - -			547	50			547	50
2	Thomas Carpenter & Co.	856	74			856	74		
2	Store Expenses - -	205	00			205	00		
2	Martin Pemberton -	500	00			500	00		
3	Samuel W. Fairburn -	400	00			400	00		
3	Personal Expenses -	60	00			60	00		
		17,908	35	17,908	35	8,352	50	8,352	50

The *Trial Balance* of the Leger is made when the Journal is all posted to it, to ascertain whether equal amounts of debits and credits have been posted, or if the whole Leger balances.

It is made in the following manner:—First, add up the debit and credit side of each account in the Leger, and place their amounts to the left of the dollar column, with a pencil, as shown by the small figures in the Leger given. Then, having headed the Trial Balance, write down in it the titles of the several Leger accounts, commencing with Stock; and place opposite each title, in the amount columns, the debit and credit footings, as set down with a pencil in the Leger: also, place in the difference columns the differences between these debit and credit footings. Accounts that balance in the Leger need not be brought in. The left hand marginal column is for the Leger folio.

Add up the several columns of the Trial Balance. Now, since for every debit made upon the Leger there has been an equal amount of credit, and for every credit an equal amount of debit; and since the amount columns of the Trial Balance embrace every debit and credit upon the Leger, (except those accounts whose debits and credits are equal;) therefore, the debit and credit totals of these amount columns must be equal. And, if the totals of the amount columns are equal, then the totals of the difference columns must also be equal. If this equilibrium does not exist, there is an error, which must be sought.*

A Trial Balance may be taken with the amount columns only, or with the difference columns only. The latter is the usual mode in business; and, in subsequent Trial Balances in this work, the differences of the Leger accounts will only be used. In a real business, the Trial Balance *may* be taken monthly, and *should* be taken as often as once in three months, even though the books are closed but once a year.

You will next find use for the Inventory.

INVENTORY-BOOK, OR ACCOUNT-STOCK-BOOK, SET I.

Inventory of Merchandise remaining unsold Jan. 31, 1852:				
100 yds. Blk. Fr. Cloths,	@ $4.		400	00
20 " Ass'd " do.	@ $3.		60	00
100 " Eng. Blue do.	@ $3.25		325	00
560 " Blk. Eng. Cassimeres,	@ $1.50		840	00
400 " Ass'd " do.	@ $1.50		600	00
238 " " Fr. do.	@ $1.25		297	50
			2,522	50

This is a small book used to take down the Inventory of goods remaining unsold at any time, generally called by merchants "taking an account of stock,"—*stock, as here used,* meaning goods on hand, and *not* your own name in business, as it does in the Journal and Leger. This Inventory, or account of stock, is taken by actual observation and estimate of the goods or other property remaining on hand, either at cost price or at the estimated value; and is usually made out once a year, as most houses close their books yearly; but houses that close their books semi-yearly, must take an account of stock once in six months, as the property on hand is always made use of in closing the Leger.

In *this set,* if you will go over the Day-Book, carefully selecting the goods of each kind bought, adding them to those of the same kind on hand at commencing business, and deducting therefrom those of the same kind sold, you will find whether the Inventory here given is correct. This test of correctness would not generally be practicable in business, owing to the diversity and number of items bought and sold.

Having thus described how the Inventory is taken, I will now explain what use is made of it in closing the Leger.

ON CLOSING THE LEGER.

Preparatory Steps. After making a Trial Balance, open a Profit and Loss account, (unless previously opened,) and a Balance account. Next *bring in the property on hand, i. e.* place to the *credit* of each speculating† property account, in the Leger, the amount of property belonging to that account, as shown by the Inventory-Book. Enter this in *red ink,* giving the date on which you close, and saying "*By Balance* (*Inv't.*),"

* For manner of detecting and correcting errors, see page 111.

† Each account representing any species of property which you buy and sell to speculate upon—as Mdse. or Real Estate.

to show that it is to be transferred to the Balance account; and make the *opposite* entry immediately on the *debit* side of Balance account, in *black ink*, saying "To Mdse.," or "To" whatever property account you have just made the red ink entry. In the column usually occupied by Journal folios, place the Leger folio of the account indicated by the entry.

This entry of the property unsold is sometimes made through the Day-Book and Journal, but considering this useless labor, I have adopted the shorter and simpler method of placing it directly upon the Leger.

All speculating property accounts must have the balances of property unsold credited to them in this manner, before they are closed. In this set there is only one such account—Merchandise; and the whole of the goods unsold must be credited to it.

The Leger is now ready for closing. Leave Stock open for the present. Commence at the first account after Stock, and close each account which shows a gain or loss into Profit and Loss, and each account which shows a balance that will add either to your assets or liabilities into Balance. It will suffice my present purpose to state, in short, that Merchandise, Bank Stock, and all other speculating property accounts—Premium, Interest, and Discount—Personal Expenses—Store Expenses, and all similar accounts, show gains and losses, and are closed into Profit and Loss: while Cash—Bills Receivable—Bills Payable—Bank—accounts with individuals, and the like, show assets and liabilities, and are closed into Balance.

To close an account, find the difference between the debit and credit side of it by subtraction, and enter this difference on the *smaller* side of said account in *red ink*, saying "To" or "By" that account into which you wish to close it; and then enter the same amount in *black ink* on the opposite side of the account into which you close it, saying "To" or "By" the account you are closing. Then rule the account with red ink, and add it up with black ink, after the pattern given you, and the closure is complete.

Make all closing and transfer entries and all rulings in the Leger in red ink. *Italics* in the Legers given in this work indicate red ink. Continue thus to close the accounts successively, until only Stock, Profit and Loss, and Balance remain open.

In order to prove that your work thus far has been done correctly, you may now take another test, which I shall call a Second Trial Balance.

SECOND TRIAL BALANCE, LEGER, SET I.

L. F.	Leger Titles.	Dr. Amount Columns.		Cr.		Dr. Difference Columns.		Cr.	
1	Stock - - - -			5,815	00			5,815	00
3	Profit & Loss - -	265	00	1,202	10			937	10
3	Balance - - - -	9,289	60	2,537	50	6,752	10		
		9,554	60	9,554	60	6,752	10	6,752	10

This Second Trial Balance, as you see, consists of the three accounts now open, and its debit and credit totals must be equal, since, throughout the closure of the Leger, every debit has had its credit, and every credit its debit.

In real business, neither the Balance account is used, nor the Second Trial Balance, as here shown. But of this you will be informed in Set IV.

Finally.—After proving your work thus far, close Profit and Loss into Stock, thus transferring your net gains or losses in business to the account which is your own representative. The difference between the two sides of the Stock account will now show your net capital or your net insolvency, which you must close into Balance, making the last entry in Balance account also in *red ink*, as it becomes the closing entry to that account. This completes the closing of the Leger.

STATEMENTS, SET I.

If you have carefully considered what is embraced in the foregoing pages, you will have acquired, I think, a pretty clear idea of the business represented in Set I; but, to make it still plainer, and also to give you more general ideas of what is embodied in the Leger, I will now show you some abstracts from it, in the form of statements, (worded as if drawn off by yourself from your own Leger,) by which your capital at commencing business, your gains during business, and your net capital at closing, will be clearly represented.

Statement 1st, showing Net Gains.

I have *gained*, as shown on the *credit* side of *Profit & Loss* account,		
By trading in Merchandise - - - - - - - - - - -		$1,202.10
I have *lost*, as shown on the *debit* side of *Profit & Loss* account,		
By payment of Store Expenses - - - - - -	$205.00	
" " " Personal do. - - - - - - -	60.00	
Deduct *total losses* - - - - - - -		265.00
My *net gains* in the business are - - - - -		$937.10

Which is the excess of credit in Profit & Loss account.

Statement 2d, showing Net Capital at closing.

My *available means*, called "Resources," or "Assets," are shown upon the *debit* side of *Balance* account, and consist of		
Merchandise remaining unsold to the am't of - - - - - -		$2,522.50
Cash on hand - - - - - - - - - - - - -		3,079.98
Bills Receivable, or other persons' Notes held by me - - - -		1,590.38
The indebtedness of P. Somers - - - - - - - - -		340.00
" " " T. Carpenter & Co. - - - - - - -		856.74
" " " M. Pemberton - - - - - - - -		500.00
" " " S. W. Fairburn - - - - - - - -		400.00
Total resources or assets - - - - - - -		$9,289.60
My *indebtedness*, called "Liabilities," is shown upon the *credit* side of *Balance* account, and consists of		
Bills Payable, outstanding against me - - - - -	$1,990.00	
Amount due E. Barnes - - - - - - - - -	547.50	
Deduct *total liabilities* - - - - - - - -		2,537.50
My *net capital*, or *present worth*, is - - - - - - - -		$6,752.10

Which is the excess of debit in the Balance account.

Statement 3d, proving Statements 1st and 2d.

The *amount of Effects invested* by me at the commencement of business as shown by the *credit* side of *Stock* account, is - - - - - - -	$5,815.00
The *net gains*, shown on *credit* side of *Stock*, and by Statement 1st, are	937.10
Thus, the *net capital* or *present worth* (as by Statement 2d) is - -	$6,752.10

Which is seen also in Stock account.

NOTE.—If any additional investment had been made by you during the business, it would find its place also upon the *credit* side of Stock account.

The *debit* side of Stock account contains the amount of your *indebtedness* at commencing, any sums withdrawn by you during the business, and your *net losses* in business: but, in Set I, nothing has occurred requiring a debit to it.

STATEMENTS (*continued*).

Therefore:—

In a gaining business, commencing with net capital,

To find your present worth, or net capital at closing:

1st. Add the net gains in business to the net capital at starting.
2d. Deduct the total liabilities from the total assets.

To find your net gains in business:

1st. Deduct the total losses from the total gains.
2d. Deduct the net capital at starting from the present worth.

QUESTIONS FOR REVIEW, SET I.

The following questions are intended as a review of all that has been written thus far on Double Entry. Answers to all questions asked can be found on some of the foregoing pages, and teachers will do well to require their pupils to search them out and learn them.

What is Book-Keeping by Double Entry? How does Double Entry Book-Keeping differ from Single Entry?
What do accounts with persons represent?
What do accounts with the different species of property represent?
What do accounts with the various branches of your gains and losses represent?
What is the *distinguishing feature* of Double Entry?
Is an equilibrium in the number of debits and credits required? What then?
Why is the *old Italian method* of Book-Keeping adopted in the first three Sets of Double Entry?
What are the main books of entry in the Italian method?
Define *debtor*. Define *creditor*.
In what have transactions or trades their foundations?
Repeat the *general rule* for journalizing transactions. Repeat it briefly.
Does this rule apply for determining the opening Journal entry of individual books?
Does it apply to the opening entry of partnership books?
What is each Set intended to represent?
Why should particular attention be paid to the opening and closing of each?
What is the continuance of each Set for *one month* intended to represent?
How often are books closed in a majority of houses?
Describe the Day-Book in the Italian method of Book-Keeping.
For what is the Journal used? Why is this done?
Describe the Journal given with this Set. In making entries therein, how do you distinguish between debtors and creditors?
What may the Leger be styled? What is its principal use?
Of what is "By" the prefix? On which side of an account is it generally placed?
Of what is "To" the prefix? On which side of an account is it generally placed?
Define Bills Receivable. Define Bills Payable. When are notes said to be negotiable?
What name is given to an individual in business by himself? What are his books called?
Explain the opening of the Journal for Stock books.
What would you debit, and what credit in journalizing each of the following transactions, and for what reasons?

1st, Sale of Mdse. for cash.—2d, Sale of Mdse. for another person's note.—3d, Sale of Mdse. on account.—4th, Purchase of Mdse. for cash.—5th, Purchase of Mdse. for your own note.—6th, Purchase of Mdse. on account.—7th, Sale of Mdse. for cash and another person's note.—8th, Sale of Mdse. for cash and on account.—9th, Payment of expenses for the store in cash.—10th, Sale of Mdse. for another person's note and on account.—11th, Purchase of Mdse. for another person's note and on account.—12th, Purchase of Mdse. for cash and on account.—13th, Receipt of cash on account.—14th, Sale of Mdse. for another person's order on you, for cash and on account.—15th, Payment of cash for personal expenses.—16th, Sale of Mdse. for cash, for another person's note and on account.—17th, Payment of an account in cash.—18th, Payment of rent, clerk hire and gas bill in cash.

What is the next thing to be done after journalizing? What is meant by posting?
What is meant by post-marking? How do you post-mark when there is both a debit and a credit on the same line in the Journal?
What test of the Leger is taken when the posting is completed?
Describe the process of taking a Trial Balance, and its use.
Is it usual in business to take it with the difference columns only? How often is it taken?
What is the Inventory-Book? How is the Inventory or Account of Stock taken?
What accounts do you open preparatory to closing the Leger?
What is the next step after opening these accounts?
What class of accounts have the balances of property unsold credited to them?
Define speculating property accounts?
In commencing to close the Leger, what account do you leave open?
What class of accounts are closed into Profit & Loss? What class into Balance?
In closing the Leger, is the first entry made in the account you are closing, or in the account into which you are closing it?
On which side of the account and in what colored ink?
Where is the opposite entry made, and in what colored ink?
In what cases is red ink used in the Leger? How indicated in this work?
When is the Second Trial Balance taken, and of what accounts does it consist?
Is the Second Trial Balance used in a real business?
Which is the first account closed after the taking of the Second Trial Balance?
After the Profit & Loss account has been closed into Stock, what does the difference between the two sides of the Stock account show, and how is it closed?
In what account, and on which side, do you ascertain your gains in business?
In what account, and on which side, do you ascertain your losses in business?
What is shown by deducting total losses from total gains? How is this shown in the Profit & Loss account?
What are your available means at closing styled, and where are they found?
What is your indebtedness at closing styled, and where is it found?
What is shown by deducting total liabilities from total assets? How is this shown in the Balance account?
Where do you find the amount of your effects invested?
Where do you find the amount of your indebtedness at commencing (if any)?
On which side of Stock account are your net gains shown? On which side your net losses?
What is shown by adding the net gains in business to the effects invested at commencing? Where is this seen?
What are your total gains in Set I?* Total losses? Net gains?
What are your total resources or assets at closing Set I? Total liabilities?
What is your net capital or present worth?
What is the amount of your effects invested added to your net gains?
In a gaining business, commencing with net capital, by what two methods can you ascertain your present worth? By what two methods, your net gains?

* The pupil may have his Leger before him in answering this and the following questions.

SET II, DOUBLE ENTRY.

You can write up this Set in the blank books which accompany this treatise. You will perceive that no Journal or Leger is here given, because I wish you now to rely upon your own reasoning powers, aided by such elucidations as are necessary, for applying the principles already learned.

Copy the Day-Book; then journalize it, referring to the elucidations of the different entries for any suggestions required. Having journalized, post from your Journal into the Leger, and take a Trial Balance, which, if correct, will agree in every respect with the one given on page 83. If it does not agree, there is an error, which must be sought and corrected, after the manner described on page 111. When the Trial Balance is right, proceed to close the Leger in the same manner as described for Set I, taking a second Trial Balance when you come to it, as a test of the closures thus far.

You can make out, from your Leger, statements of the net gains and net capital at closing, and compare them with the statements on pages 83 and 84, which will be a still further check upon the correctness of your work.

Set I was a gaining business, and closed with net capital; but this is a losing business, and closes with net insolvency. By comparing carefully the two Sets, and the statements drawn from them, you will acquire clear and definite ideas of both prosperous and adverse business.

NOTE.—The *Key* is designed *solely* for the *teacher*, and the scholar should *in no case* be permitted to use it; or if at all, merely to mpare his books after the teacher has pronounced them correct. He should *hunt his own mistakes*, as this is most excellent practice : him.

DAY-BOOK, SET II.

Philadelphia, February 2d, 1852.

✓	I commence Business with the following Effects:			
	Cash on hand	1,125.00		
	Merchandise, amounting pr. Invoice, to	6,250.00		
	50 Shares Reading Rail-Road Stock @ $25 (Par value $50.)	1,250.00		
	Sundry Notes which I hold against others	2,875.00		
	Joseph B. Lownes owes me on a/c	200.00		
	V. C. Burrell & Co. owe " " "	341.50	12,041	50
✓	I owe as follows:			
	On Notes held by sundry persons against me	7,000.00		
	To Charles T. Mayland on a/c	500.00		
	" Burgess & Pinkerton " "	1,240.56		
	" Levi Williams & Co. " "	960.44		
	" Evans, Peters & Co. " "	1,150.50	10,851	50
	Making my Net Capital $1,190.			
	2d			
✓	Insured Mdse. in the American Fire Ins. Co. to the Am't of $6,000, @ 1½% Prem., for which I have paid Cash		90	00
	"			
✓	Sold to V. C. Burrell & Co., @ 6 mos.,			
	5 Cases, 60 Prs. Men's Stout Boots @ $1.75	105.00		
	2 " 24 " " Kip " " 2.00	48.00		
	2 " 24 " " Calf Pegged " " 2.50	60.00		
	1 " 12 " " " Sewed " " 3.50	42.00	255	00
	3d			
✓	Sold to Walter Stockton & Co.			
	3 Cases, 180 Prs. Boys' Stout Brogans @ 75¢	135.00		
	2 " 120 " " Kip " " 80	96.00		
	2 " 120 " Men's Goat Nullifiers " 80	96.00		
	2 " 24 " " Stitched Boots " $6	144.00	471	00
	Rec'd. in Payment			
	My Note, Philip Beldon's favor, now due, for	320.00		
	Cash for Balance	151.00		
	4th			
✓	Accepted Burgess & Pinkerton's Draft on me, @ 30 days' sight, favor Wm. G. Ashton, for		675	00
	7th			
✓	Bought of Charles T. Mayland,			
	Mdse., amounting pr. Invoice, to		2,000	00
	Paid in part by my Draft on Joseph B. Lownes @ sight	200.00		
	Remainder Bo't. @ 6 mos. credit	1,800.00		

DAY-BOOK, SET II.

Philadelphia, February 9th, 1852.

✓	Paid in Cash my Note, Myers, Claghorn & Co.'s favor, Am't			600 00
	12th			
✓	Exchanged Notes with Isaac McGrath, each drawn @ 30 days, for his Accommodation			1,200 00
	14th			
✓	Bailey & Davis, whose Note I hold for $750.36, have failed, and compounded with their Creditors for 70¢ on the dollar, ½ to be paid in Cash and ½ in Goods.			
	Rec'd in Cash		262.62	
	Mdse., as pr. Invoice, amounting to		262.63	
	Lost the Balance		225.11	750 36
	16th			
✓	Sold to Allen Thompson			
	50 Prs. Children's Calf Brogans @ 37^{2}¢			18 75
	18th			
✓	Bought of Manly & Co. Mdse., as pr. Invoice, Am't			1,200 00
	Paid in part by Note of Lyman Bellamy, my favor		425.00	
	Gave my Note @ 30 days, for		400.00	
	Paid the Balance in Cash		375.00	
	20th			
✓	Sold to Thomas Stotesbury & Co.			
	5 Cases, 300 Prs. Men's Stout Brogans @ $1.10		330.00	
	5 " 300 " " Kip " " 1.00		300.00	
	4 " 240 " Women's " Lace Boots " .60		144.00	
	2 " 120 " " Calf " " .90		108.00	882 00
	Rec'd their Note @ 4 mos. for	441.00		
	Cash for Balance	441.00	882.00	
	21st			
✓	Discounted my Acceptance of the 4th Inst. @ 30 days, favor of Wm. G. Ashton, Am't			675 00
	Paid in Cash		673.20	
	Discount on $675, for 16 days, is		1.80	
	28th			
✓	On the Night of the 22d Inst., my Stock of Goods (with the Store) were almost entirely consumed by Fire.			
	The small portion recovered was yesterday sold at Auction for Cash, netting, after payment of Auctioneer, Drayman, &c.			320 50
	"			
✓	Rec'd in Cash of the American Fire Ins. Co. the Am't for which I was Insured on my Stock of Goods			6,000 00

ELUCIDATIONS FOR JOURNALIZING DAY-BOOK, SET II.

February 2d

This Entry of your effects invested must be commenced in your Journal, "Sundries Dr. To Stock," the same as the opening entry to Set I; and then the different species of property must be debited for the value which you intrust to each, and the different persons for the amount each owes you. Stock (yourself) is Cr. for the whole amount of your investment.

In entering in your Journal this record of your debts at starting, commence it thus: "Stock Dr. To Sundries," extending into the debit column the whole amount of your indebtedness, to show that Stock (yourself) is Dr. for this amount, at commencing business. Then credit Bills Payable for the Am't of notes outstanding against you, and credit the different persons for the sums due each. See remarks on opening the Journal, page 65.

2d

Mdse. is Dr. for the cost of insuring the goods.

Cash is Cr. for producing the means (value) to pay the Insurance.

☞ Commit to memory the general rule for journalizing, page 62, and apply it constantly.

"

V. C. Burrell & Co. have cost you value in the goods which you have furnished them, without immediate remuneration—and must be debited. Mdse. has produced value in the indebtedness of V. C. Burrell & Co.—and must be credited.

3d

Bills Payable and Cash have cost value in Mdse. Mdse. has produced value in your note and the money received. This is one of the notes which were outstanding against you at the commencement of business. It is supposed to have passed from the hands of Philip Beldon to Walter Stockton & Co., and now, coming due, is offered by them in payment for the Mdse.

4th

For definition of *Draft* and *Acceptance*, see the Vocabulary, page 9. *Your accepting* a draft makes it a Bill Payable, and it is the same to you as taking up the draft by giving your promissory note for it: while it is better to the party holding it, as it binds the *drawer* to payment in case you should fail. Whenever you pay a draft on yourself, either by acceptance or in any other way, the drawer must be debited, because value goes out of your possession, at his request and for his benefit.

In this case, Burgess & Pinkerton cost value in Bills Payable.

7th

Mdse. costs value, and is Dr.—J. B. Lownes produces value by permitting you to draw upon him in payment for a portion of the goods bought; and C. T. Mayland produces value by furnishing part of them without immediate payment.

Whenever you draw a draft on another person, that person must be credited, as he produces you value by paying the draft.

9th

Another note, issued by you prior to the commencement of this business, falls due and is paid.

Bills Payable costs value in Cash.

12th

Bills Receivable costs value in my note issued.

Bills Payable produces value in McGrath's note obtained.

14th

Bills Receivable has produced value only to the amount of the Cash and Mdse. received; but it must be credited the *full amount of the note*, \$750.36, in order that the difference of the Bills Receivable account on the Leger may at all times agree with the amount of notes on hand unpaid. Cash is Dr. for what it has cost, \$262.62—Mdse. is Dr. for what it has cost, \$262.63—and *Profit & Loss*, which is the receptacle of all your gains and losses, must be debited for the balance, \$225.11, in order to transfer the loss to that account. This debit to Profit & Loss, and credit to Bills Receivable of \$225.11, is *not* explained on the principle of debiting what costs value, and crediting what produces value, but it is *merely a transfer* entry, to carry the loss into its proper account, instead of permitting it to remain in Bills Receivable.

16th

Mdse. has produced value in the indebtedness of Allen Thompson.

18th

Lyman Bellamy's note is one of those you held against others at commencing business.

Mdse. has cost value—Sundries have produced value.

N. B.—It is proper in recording purchases in the Day-Book to say "as pr. Invoice," and omit the items, since your invoice is preserved on file. But in entering sales, the articles should always be specified in detail.

20th

Sundries have cost value in Mdse., and Mdse. has produced value.

February 21st

A draft which has been accepted by you is styled your "*Acceptance*"—another name for it instead of note. *Discounting* a note means paying it before due, for the sake of the discount.
Bills Payable (your acceptance) has here cost value.
Sundries, viz. Cash and Discount, have produced value.

28th

Cash costs value in Mdse.

"

Mdse. produces value in Cash.
Insurance offices do not generally pay as promptly as here shown: they have usually a proviso in their agreements, allowing from 30 to 60 days' time for payment of losses incurred.

TRIAL BALANCE, LEGER, SET II.

L. F.		Dr.		Cr.	
1	Stock			1,190	00
1	Cash	6,561	92		
1	Merchandise	1,855	38		
1	Reading Rail-Road Stock	1,250	00		
1	Bills Receivable	3,340	64		
2	V. C. Burrell & Co.	596	50		
2	Bills Payable			7,680	00
2	Charles T. Mayland			2,300	00
2	Burgess & Pinkerton			565	56
2	Levi Williams & Co.			960	44
3	Evans, Peters & Co.			1,150	50
3	Profit & Loss	225	11		
3	Allen Thompson	18	75		
3	Discount			1	80
		13,848	30	13,848	30

INVENTORY-BOOK, SET II.

There remains on hand unsold, Feb. 28th, 1852: 50 Shares Reading Rail-Road Stock, which is now selling @ $22 pr. Share	1,100	00

SECOND TRIAL BALANCE, LEGER, SET II.

L. F.		Dr.		Cr.	
1	Stock			1,190	00
3	Profit & Loss	2,228	69		
3	Balance			1,038	69
		2,228	69	2,228	69

STATEMENTS, SET II.

STATEMENT 1ST, SHOWING NET LOSSES.

Losses.			*Gains.*		
Bills Rec., 20 % of B. & D.'s note	225	11	Discount on note paid before due	1	80
Mdse., lost by fire more than gains	1,855	38			
Reading R.-R. Stock, depreciation	150	00			
Total losses	2,230	49			
Deduct gains	1	80			
My net losses are	2,228	69			

STATEMENT 2D, SHOWING NET INSOLVENCY AT CLOSING.

Resources, or Assets.			*Liabilities.*		
Reading R.-R. Stock, Am't unsold	1,100	00	Bills Pay., held by others	7,680	00
Cash on hand	6,561	92	C. T. Mayland, Bal. I owe	2,300	00
Bills Rec., held by me	3,340	64	Burgess & Pinkerton, " " "	565	56
V. C. Burrell & Co., Bal. due me	596	50	L. Williams & Co. " " "	960	44
A. Thompson, " " "	18	75	Evans, Peters & Co. " " "	1,150	50
Total assets	11,617	81	Total liabilities	12,656	50
			Deduct assets	11,617	81
			My net insolvency is	1,038	69

STATEMENT 3D, PROVING STATEMENTS 1ST AND 2D.

My debts at starting were	10,851	50	My net capital at starting was	1,190	00
Add net losses (Statement 1st)	2,228	69	Add net insolvency (Statement 2d)	1,038	69
	13,080	19	Gives net losses (Statement 1st)	2,228	69
Deduct effects invested at starting	12,041	50			
Gives my net insolvency (Statement 2d)	1,038	69			

Therefore :—

In a business commencing with net capital and closing with net insolvency,

To find your Net Insolvency :

1st, Deduct the net capital at starting from the net losses in business.
2d, Deduct the total assets from the total liabilities.

To find your Net Losses in Business :

1st, Deduct the total gains from the total losses.
2d, Add the present net insolvency to the net capital at starting.

QUESTIONS FOR REVIEW, SET II.

With what must the Trial Balance of your Leger agree, to show that you have journalized and posted this Set correctly?
Wherein does the business represented in this Set, differ from that in Set I?
What should be debited and what credited in the following transactions, and why?
1st, Cash paid for insuring Mdse.—2d, Mdse. sold on account.—3d, Mdse. sold for your note outstanding and for cash.—4th, Accepting another person's draft on you.—5th, Buying Mdse. with your draft on another person, and on account.—6th, Taking up your note by paying cash for it.—7th, Exchanging notes with another person.—8th, Failure of a party whose note you hold, payment of part in cash, part in Mdse., and balance lost.—9th, Sale of Mdse. on account.—10th, Purchase of Mdse. for another person's note held by you, your own note, and cash.—11th, Sale of Mdse. for another person's note and for cash.—12th, Discounting your own note.—13th, Sale of Mdse. for cash.—14th, Receipt of cash from an Insurance Co. for Mdse. destroyed by fire.
What are the total losses in Set II? The total gains?
What are the net losses? How ascertained?
What are the total assets? Total liabilities?
What is the net insolvency? How ascertained?
What is the amount of your debts at starting, added to your net losses?
What remains after deducting from this amount your effects invested?
How much was your net capital at starting?
What is found by adding to this your net insolvency?
By what two methods can you ascertain your net insolvency in this Set?
By what two methods can you ascertain your net losses in this Set?

SET III, DOUBLE ENTRY.

In this Set you are supposed to have made a satisfactory arrangement with your creditors, so as to resume and continue your business, which was summarily ended in the last Set, by your stock of goods being consumed by fire.

Philadelphia, March 1*st*, 1852.

I have the following Effects on resuming business.				
Cash on hand		6,561.92		
Sundry Notes of other persons, my favor		3,340.64		
50 Shares Reading Rail-Road Stock, @ $22		1,100.00		
V. C. Burrell & Co. owe me on %		596.50		
Allen Thompson owes " " "		18.75	11,617	81
I owe on sundry Notes outstanding, favor of others		7,680.00		
To Charles T. Mayland on %		2,300.00		
" Burgess & Pinkerton " "		565.56		
" Levi Williams & Co. " "		960.44		
" Evans, Peters & Co. " "		1,150.50	12,656	50
— 1st —				
Bought a new set of % Books, of Murphy & Co., for Cash			20	00
— 2d —				
Bought of Charles T. Mayland Mdse., as pr. Invoice, Am't			3,000	00
Paid him in part by Note of Root, Warden & Co., my favor		1,699.64		
Cash for the Balance		1,300.36		
— " —				
Bought of Burgess & Pinkerton, on %, @ 3 mos.				
Mdse. as pr. Invoice, Am't			2,516	00
— 3d —				
Sold to Allen Thompson,				
6 Cases, 360 Prs. Women's Calf Lace-Boots, @ $1			360	00
— 5th —				
Paid Levi Williams & Co., Cash, in full of %			960	44
— 8th —				
Sold to Bent, Foster & Lewis,				
10 Cases, 120 Prs. Men's Stout Boots, @	$2.00	240.00		
2 " 120 " " Lasting Gaiters, "	1.75	210.00		
6 " 360 " Youth's Stout Brogans "	.62^2	225.00		
8 " 480 " " Kip " "	.50	240.00		
3 " 180 " Children's Calf " "	.37^2	67.50	982	50
Rec'd their Notes, one @ 30 days for	327.50			
" " 60 " "	327.50			
" " 90 " "	327.50	982.50		
— 10th —				
Sold to Blackman & Packard, for Cash,				
2 Cases, 120 Prs. Men's Goat Nullifiers,	@ 80¢	96.00		
2 " 120 " Women's Grain Buskins	" 60	72.00		
2 " 120 " " Lasting ½ Gaiters	" 90	108.00		
2 " 120 " " Col'd " "	" 85	102.00		
2 " 120 " " Kid Slippers R. R.	" 70	84.00		
1 " 60 " Misses' Goat Lace Boots	" 75	45.00		
1 " 60 " " R. R. Paris Ties	" 62^2	37.50	544	50

Philadelphia, March 13*th*, 1852.

Sold to Wilson, Fenner & Welsh,		
6 Cases, 360 Prs. Women's Calf Lace Boots, @ $1.25 450.00		
3 " 180 " " Goat Buskins, " 1.15 207.00		
4 " 240 " " Lasting Gaiter-Boots, " 1.25 300.00		
4 " 240 " " Kid Slippers R. R. " .90 216.00	1,173	00
Rec'd in payment my Note of 19th ult., @ 30 days, favor of Manly & Co. 400.00		
Cash for Bal., including Discount 773.60 1,173.60		
The Discount on my Note, $400, for 9 days, am'ts to		60
16th		
My Note, favor Isaac McGrath, dated 12th ult., @ 30 days, coming due this day, has been taken up by him, and returned to me, for which I have given him his Note, my favor, of same tenor and date	1,200	00
22d		
Bought of Myers, Claghorn & Co., at auction, for Cash, Mdse., amounting, pr. Invoice, to	1,522	36
24th		
Reading Rail-Road Stock having suddenly risen, I have had my 50 Shares sold by a Stock-Broker, @ $30 pr. Share 1,500.00		
Rec'd the Cash, less his Com., @ ½% on $1,500.00, for selling 7.50	1,492	50
27th		
Thomas Stotesbury & Co. have discounted their Note of the 21st ult., @ 4 mos., my favor, for	441	00
Rec'd in Cash 434.53		
Discount on $441, for 88 days, is 6.47		
30th		
Sold to Wm. F. Godwin, for his Note @ 3 mos.,		
10 Cases, 120 Prs. Men's Calf Stitched Boots, @ $5.25 630.00		
5 " 60 " " " Sewed " " 3.50 210.00	840	00
31st		
Rec'd from the Executors of my Aunt Mrs. Whiteman's Estate, Cash in full of her Bequest to me.	500	00

No Ins. has been effected in this Set, because it was not deemed advisable to occupy space with the entry. Many other entries, which, in a real business, would occur, such as paying Rent of Store, &c., have been omitted, in this and the other Sets, for a like reason.

ELUCIDATIONS FOR JOURNALIZING DAY-BOOK, SET III.

March 1st

The opening entries are so nearly like those of Set II, that I think you will need no additional explanation of them.

"

The old books having been badly damaged by fire, you have closed them up, and purchased a new set for use in the Counting-house.

Store Expenses have cost value. Cash has produced value.

2d

Mdse. costs value in Sundries.

Sundries—viz., Bills Receivable and Cash—produce value by paying for the goods.

"

Mdse. costs you value.

Burgess & Pinkerton produce you value by furnishing the goods without payment.

3d

A. Thompson has received value of you to the amount of goods you furnish him—in other words, has cost you value—and is Dr.

Mdse. has produced value in his indebtedness.

5th

Levi Williams & Co. have received value from you in Cash.

Cash has produced value by paying their account.

8th

Bills Receivable costs value in Mdse. Mdse. produces value.

10th

Cash costs value in Mdse.

13th

Bills Payable and Cash have cost value, and Mdse. and Discount have produced value.

As this is the first case in which sundry debtors and sundry creditors occur in the same entry, I will journalize it, to show you the form.

	Sundries Dr. To Sundries.				
2	Bills Payable - - - - - - - - - - - - - -	400	00		
1	Cash - - - - - - - - - - - - - - - -	773	60		
3	To Merchandise - - - - - - - - - - - - -			1,173	00
3	" Discount - - - - - - - - - - - - - -				60

In posting this transaction, the entries in the Leger should be "To Sundries," and "By Sundries;" and neither a post nor a post-mark is required to the word "Sundries."

16th

On the 12th ult. you exchanged notes with Isaac McGrath for his accommodation, because he could use your note, with his endorsement on it, better than he could his own note. He made use of your note, and when it came due to-day, paid it, and now returns it to you and receives his note, which he had given you as security.

Bills Payable has cost you value. Bills Receivable has produced you value.

22d

Mdse. has cost value in Cash.

24th

Cash has cost value in Reading R.-R. Stock. Reading R.-R. Stock has produced value.

NOTE.—Stock-Brokers in Philadelphia and some other cities charge commission on the nominal *par value* of the Stock sold, which, in the Reading R.-R. Stock, is $50 pr. Share, making, in this transaction, $2,500 on which to reckon commission; but as this is a local arrangement, I have preferred to estimate commission only on the real price of sale.

27th

Cash and Discount have cost value.

Bills Receivable has produced value.

30th

Bills Receivable has cost value in Mdse.

31st

This Cash forms a *new investment*, and must be credited to *Stock*, the same as effects invested at the commencement of business. The *general rule* for transactions does not here apply, Cash having been received without value having been given for it.

TRIAL BALANCE, LEGER, SET III.

L. F.		Dr.		Cr.	
1	Stock	538	69		
1	Cash	6,503	89		
1	Bills Receivable	1,822	50		
1	Reading Rail-Road Stock			392	50
1	V. C. Burrell & Co.	596	50		
2	Allen Thompson	378	75		
2	Bills Payable			6,080	00
2	Charles T. Mayland			2,300	00
2	Burgess & Pinkerton			3,081	56
2	Evans, Peters & Co.			1,150	50
3	Store Expenses	20	00		
3	Merchandise	3,138	36		
3	Discount	5	87		
		13,004	56	13,004	56

INVENTORY-BOOK, SET III.

There remains on hand, unsold, Mar. 31st, 1852, Merchandise amounting to*	3,918	51

STATEMENTS, SET III.

The total gains accruing from this business are		$1,172.65
" " losses " " " " "		25.87
Making the net gains		$1,146.78
The total assets at closing the books are	$13,220.15	
" " liabilities " " " "	12,612.06	
Making the net capital, or present worth	$608.09	
I commenced business with a net insolvency of		$1,038.69
From which deduct the bequest of my Aunt Whiteman		500.00
Debit balance of Stock account		$538.69
I have gained sufficiently to cover this indebtedness, and to have a net capital now of		608.09
Making the net gains, as above		$1,146.78
My net gains in business have been	$1,146.78	
The debit balance of Stock account is	538.69	
Making the net capital, as above	$608.09	

Therefore: In a business like the present,

To find your present worth:

1st. Deduct the total liabilities from the total assets.
2d. Deduct the debit balance of Stock account from the net gains in business.

To find your net gains in business:

1st. Deduct the total losses from the total gains.
2d. Add the present worth to the debit balance of Stock account.

* In a real Inventory-Book, of course all the details of the Mdse. or other property unsold would be specified, as this is the very object of the book.

How can you retain cash, notes and other effects in your possession, and commence a new business therewith, as in this Set, when you are really insolvent at the outset? [See page 85.]

What would you debit, and what credit in each of the following transactions—and why?

1st. Purchase of a new set of account books for cash.—2d, Purchase of Mdse. for note of another person, my favor, and for cash.—3d, Purchase of Mdse. on account.—4th, Sale of Mdse. on time.—5th, Payment of cash in full of an account which you owe.—6th, Sale of Mdse. for three notes of another person.—7th, Sale of Mdse. for cash.—8th, Sale of Mdse. for your own note and cash, your note not being yet due, and you being allowed a discount thereon.—9th, Receipt of your note previously exchanged with another, and relinquishment of the other person's note held by you.—10th, Purchase of Mdse. for cash.—11th, Sale of Reading Rail-Road stock for cash.—12, Discount by another person of his note held by you.—13th, Sale of Mdse. for another person's note.—14th, Receipt of a bequest in cash.

What are the total gains accruing from the business in Set III?

What are the total losses? What the net gains?

What are the total assets? The total liabilities? The net capital?

What was the net insolvency at commencing?

What was the amount of Mrs. Whiteman's bequest to you?

What is the debit balance of the Stock account after deducting this bequest?

What amount do you obtain, by adding your present net capital to the debit balance of Stock account? What is this amount called?

What balance remains after deducting the debit balance of Stock account from the net gains in business? and what is this balance called?

In a business like the present, what two methods are there for ascertaining the present worth?

What two methods for ascertaining the net gains?

GENERAL REMARKS.

You have now been presented with three Sets of books by Double Entry:—the first, representing you as commencing business with a snug capital, and without any debts; pursuing it prosperously, and thus increasing your capital. In the second, you commenced with greater means in possession, but owing debts to nearly the same amount:—you were attended with misfortune, in the destruction of your goods by fire, without a full insurance, and probably too for want of experience in the business in which you engaged, neither bought nor sold to the best advantage; thus sustaining a large loss, which swallowed up your net capital, and left you with about an equal insolvency. In the third, you resumed and continued your business so summarily ended in Set II, retaining in your hands all the means left you until such time as you are able to pay your creditors, who are supposed to appreciate your business talents, to confide in your integrity, and to agree to extend the time of payment. Having learned by experience to be more cautious and skilful, you thus make sufficiently large gains to cover your insolvency, and have a small net capital again. A bequest from your Aunt somewhat increases this capital.

I now propose furnishing you with some examples of partnership business, both where the partners share alike in gains and losses, (as in Set IV,) and where their shares and interests are unequal, (as in Set V.)

I shall also now present you with another style of keeping accounts *shorter* than the *old Italian method*, and used by houses engaged in general trading operations, shipping business, and some other mercantile pursuits. It will at first require more thought on your part than the preceding Sets have done, but those you are now supposed to have mastered, and thus to be prepared for a higher step on the road to a thorough knowledge of accounts; and no task should be thought too hard, which care and patience will overcome, and which will lead to knowledge.

SEYMOUR & FITCH.

SET IV.

DAY-BOOK KEPT IN JOURNAL FORM, AND NO JOURNAL USED.

EXPLANATORY REMARKS, SETS IV AND V.

The Sets of books thus far shown in this work have all been conducted upon the *old Italian method.* I now propose to show you a plan which is far more in use at the present time, and by which much useless writing will be saved. It is to entirely dispense with the *Day-Book in History form*, and use instead a *Day-Book in Journal form*, in which the entries are recorded in such a manner as not only to present a complete history of the business transactions, but also to furnish debits and credits under the proper Leger titles, ready for posting; thus rendering it useless to keep a Journal, and doing away with the labor of journalizing. The *general rule for journalizing* becomes now a *general rule* for determining the proper debits and credits *in making original entries.*

I have given a separate history of the business, as it is supposed to have occurred, with elucidations of such transactions as seemed to require elucidating. This *history* you should be careful to distinguish from the historical Day-Books, which you have already passed over, as it is not used in actual business, and is not intended to take the place of any book which is used; but is given solely for the purpose of exhibiting the transactions as they would occur before you in actual commercial operations. The postings are made direct from the Day-Book, which is the book of original entry.

I have omitted, as in the preceding Sets, the Cash-Book, Check-Book, and all other books used *merely as auxiliaries*, because your mind will thus be less burdened, and you will the better understand the primary and more important books of entry. The various auxiliary books are shown in connection with Set VI.

Instructions for Writing up, Set IV.

This Set represents a partnership business, in which the partners invest equal amounts of net capital, and share equally in gains and losses. It is a prosperous business.

After examining the *form* of the Day-Book sufficiently to acquaint yourself with its peculiarities, lay it aside, and turn to the *history* given of the business. Apply carefully the directions previously received for opening books, and the *general rule for determining what to debit and what to credit*, in each case; having decided which, write down the entry in regular Journal form, mingling therewith sufficient explanations to convey to the mind of a stranger a clear idea of the business transaction.

Make out your Day-Book on a loose sheet of paper, and depend upon your own skill in so doing, looking at the Day-Book given as little as possible, until you have completed your own. You can then compare and make any necessary corrections. The next step is to post. Then close up your Leger, make out exhibits, &c., as heretofore shown. In posting, let the partners' accounts be the first accounts opened on the Leger. I have omitted the Index to the Leger; but this you can make out for yourself, as you post.

In closing the Leger, you will observe no Balance account is opened; but instead thereof, the balances (of such accounts as would be closed into it) are "*brought down to new account*," in the same manner as in Single Entry. [See explanation on page 18.] The gains or losses in any account go into Profit & Loss, as heretofore; and Profit & Loss is closed into the accounts of the two partners, half of the net gains to each. When the Leger is *entirely closed*, take your Second Trial Balance—not to be preserved, but as a mere proof of accuracy. It will consist of all the balances brought down to new account, and, if the Leger be correctly closed, the debit balances will be equal in amount to the credit balances, including the partners' net capital.

Instructions for Writing up, Set V.

In this Set, there are three partners, sharing unequally in gains and losses, the capital being invested by two of them. It is a losing business. No Day-Book or Leger is given, but only the *history and elucidations*, from which you can write up your books as explained for Set IV. First prepare your Day-Book on a sheet of paper, and, when corrected, copy it into the blank book designed for it, and post up your Leger also in the accompanying blank book. Draw off statements from your Leger, and compare them with those on pages 109 and 110, with which they should agree.

Teachers will again find use for the Key.

St. Louis, April 1st, 1852.

Bela N. Seymour and Albert Fitch have this day entered into partnership, for five years, under the firm and style of *Seymour & Fitch,* for buying and selling Real Estate, Steamboat Stocks, &c.:—the parties to invest equal amounts of net capital, and to share alike in gains and losses.

B. N. Seymour's Effects invested are as follows:		
Cash on deposit in the State Bank of Missouri	5,000.00	
One-Fourth of Steamboat Sultana, valued at	6,500.00	
One-Eighth of Steamboat Neptune, " "	4,500.00	$16,000.00
He owes a Note, favor of Blackwell & Co., due May 18th, which the Firm assume,		$ 7,500.00
Making his Net Capital $8,500.		

Albert Fitch's Effects are		
Cash on hand	8,000.00	
A Note in his favor, drawn by Thos. Coleman, due May 22d,	3,525.50	$11,525.50
He owes Debts which the Firm assume, to wit:—		
To Coffin & Waite	890.00	
" Silas George & Son	2,135.50	$3,025.50
Making his Net Capital $8,500.		

☞ *There are quite a number of new Leger titles introduced into this Set, and they should be carefully considered.*

In all the preceding Sets, no Bank account has been kept, and all moneys in bank have been counted as cash, the bank being considered as merely another place for keeping money, instead of the safe, and the account with the bank being regulated by the Bank-Book and the Check-Book, (which should always be kept when there are any dealings with bank, and which will be hereafter explained.) This is the usual method; but some houses prefer keeping accounts with the different banks with which they deal, in the same manner as accounts with persons, in their Leger—debiting sums deposited therein, and crediting sums checked out. In this Set the latter method is illustrated.

In the above transactions between the parties at commencing business, observe that—

1st. State Bank of Missouri, Steamboat Sultana Stock and Steamboat Neptune Stock have cost the firm value in their obligation to B. N. Seymour. B. N. Seymour has produced the firm value in his investment.

2d. B. N. Seymour is Dr. because he costs the firm all that they assume to pay for him. Bills Payable is Cr. because it produces the firm value in the indebtedness of B. N. Seymour.

3d. Sundries cost the firm value in their obligation to Albert Fitch. Albert Fitch produces the firm value in his effects invested.

4th. Albert Fitch costs the firm value by their assumption of his debts. Coffin & Waite and Silas George & Son produce the firm value, in the indebtedness of Albert Fitch.

The *general rule for determining what to debit, and what to credit,* (page 62,) is therefore applicable to the opening entries in partnership books.

1st

Deposited Cash in the State Bank of Missouri $8,000.

State Bank of Missouri has cost the firm value in Cash.

3d

Sold $\frac{3}{16}$ of Steamboat Sultana for Cash deposited in State Bank of Missouri $5,250.

State Bank of Missouri has received the value produced by Steamboat Sultana Stock.

When both the debit and credit Leger titles are long, you may place them on separate lines in the Day-Book.

5th

Bought of Greely & Warburton a Farm in Pike Co., of this State, for $3,000. Paid, pr. Check on State Bank of Missouri, $1,000. Gave our two Notes for the Bal., secured by Mortgage on Farm—one @ 1 year, $1,000—one at 2 years, $1,000.

Real Estate, Pike Co., costs the firm the amount paid for the farm. State Bank of Missouri and Bonds & Mortgages Payable produce value. Bonds & Mortgages Payable are a species of Bills Payable, and are sometimes entered to that account; but it is better to keep them distinct.

7th

Drew Cash from State Bank of Missouri, pr. Check, $500.

State Bank of Missouri produces value in Cash.

"

Paid Cash for $\frac{1}{8}$ Repairs of Steamboat Neptune, $75.

Steamboat Neptune Stock costs value in Cash.

St. Louis, April 9th, 1852.

Paid Albert Fitch Cash for private use $50.

Albert Fitch receives value from the firm, for which he must be debited.

"

Bought of Edwin Shippen, Jr., a House & Lot, No. 95 Main St., for $20,000.

Gave in part payment $\frac{1}{16}$ of Steamboat Sultana, for $2,000; Check on State Bank of Missouri, for $9,000; Our Bond, secured by Mortgage on the Property, payable in 2 years, for the Bal.

Real Estate Main St. may be kept in a separate account from the other Real Estate. It has cost value in Sundries.

10th

Checked from State Bank of Missouri, and remitted to Newton Snyder, Pike Co., to be used by him in repairing and fencing Farm, according to directions in our letter of date, $250.

Open an account with *Remittances* instead of N. Snyder. Remittances costs value—State Bank of Missouri produces value.

15th

Rec'd intelligence that the Steamboat Neptune was snagged and sunk in the Mississippi river, above Memphis, on the 9th inst., and has been delivered over to the Underwriters.

The Boat being insured for $34,000, we have received in Cash, (which we have deposited in State Bank of Missouri,) from the Reliance Mutual Ins. Co. of this City, our $\frac{1}{8}$ of same, $4,250, less Expenses $125, = $4,125.

Lost the Bal. of our share of the Cost of said Boat, $450.

Steamboat Neptune Stock must here be credited $4,575 — $4,125 for value produced in cash, and $450 as a *transfer* entry of the loss.

State Bank of Missouri must be debited for its cost, $4,125.

Profit & Loss must be debited $450, to transfer the loss on the steamboat into the Profit & Loss account, which is the receptacle of all gains and losses in business.

The *general rule for transactions* does *not* apply to this transfer of the loss, but the transfer is a regular *closure* of the Steamboat Neptune Stock account, and might be made on the Leger in the same manner as other closing entries. It is usually, however, done through the Day-Book, as here shown.

16th

Bought, at Auction, $\frac{1}{4}$ of Steamboat Sioux, for $6,120.

Paid in part by Note of T. Coleman, favor of A. Fitch and invested by him on commencing Business, due 22d proximo, $3,525.50; Check on State Bank of Missouri, $2,500; Cash for Bal., including Dis. on Note, $115.65.

The Discount on Note, $3,525.50 for 36 days, is $21.15.

Steamboat Sioux Stock and Discount cost value. Bills Receivable and State Bank of Missouri produce value.

"

Passed our Note, @ 30 days, to the St. Louis Ins. Co., for Ins. on our Share of the Steamboat Sioux, for $6,250, @ 2% = $125, & Policy $1.

Steamboat Sioux Stock costs value in Bills Payable.

20th

Loaned Henry Bolton Cash $200.

Open an account with *Loans* instead of Henry Bolton. Loans account costs value in Cash.

23d

Rec'd from Newton Snyder an % of Fencing & Repairs on our Farm, Pike Co., paid from our Remittance of 10th inst.,—Am't, including his Com., $215.

He has sent us the Bal. of the Remittance, in Cash, $35.

Remittances account furnishes the money for repairs, &c., and thus produces the firm value.

Real Estate, Pike Co. and Cash receive this value from the firm.

St. Louis, April 26th, 1852.

Sold our Farm in Pike Co., to Silas George & Son, for $4,000.
Offset, as part payment, the Am't which we owe them on %, $2,135.50; Rec'd Cash in part, $364.50; and their Note for Bal., payable in 2 years, secured by Mortgag on Property.

Silas George & Son, Cash and Bonds & Mortgages Receivable have cost value in Real Estate. Bonds & Mortgages Receivable are a class of Bills Receivable, but should be kept distinct, especially when numerous.

27th

Bought of Lemuel Fraley, pr. Check on State Bank of Missouri,
40 Shares State Bank of Missouri Stock, @ $48 pr. Sh.

State Bank of Missouri Stock has cost value. State Bank of Missouri has produced value. These are two distinct accounts; the Bank Stock being a species of speculating property, like Mdse.

"

Deposited in State Bank of Missouri Cash received for 6 mos. Rent of House and Lot, No. 95 Main St., $600.

Real Estate Main St. has produced value in the indebtedness of the State Bank of Missouri.

28th

Henry Bolton has paid us the Cash loaned him on the 20th, $200.

Loans account has produced value in Cash.

29th

Sold to Coffin & Waite 30 Shares State Bank of Missouri Stock, @ $50 pr. Sh.
Rec'd payment, in part, by the canceling of our indebtedness to them, $890; with Interest allowed by us on same, $6.50; and their Check, which we have deposited in the State Bank of Missouri, for Bal., $603.50.

Coffin & Waite, Interest and State Bank of Missouri have cost value in State Bank of Missouri Stock.

30th

Rec'd in Cash the Dividend on 10 Shares State Bank of Missouri Stock, par value $500, @ 5% = $25.

State Bank of Missouri Stock has produced value in Cash.

"

Rec'd of Clerk of Steamboat Sioux, a Check, which we have deposited in the State Bank of Missouri, for our ¼ Net Proceeds of Trip No. 13, to New Orleans, $309.35.

Steamboat Sioux Stock has produced value in the indebtedness of the Bank.

"

Discounted Note drawn by B. N. Seymour, favor of Blackwell & Co., assumed by the Firm at commencing Business, due the 18th proximo, $7,500.
Paid by Check on State Bank of Missouri, $7,477.50.
Discount on $7,500, for 18 days, is $22.50.

When the firm assumed the payment of a note outstanding against B. N. Seymour at commencing business, Bills Payable received a credit, as cancelling the indebtedness of the firm for the time. This note has now been taken up and has cost the firm value. State Bank of Missouri and Discount have produced value.

DAY-BOOK, SET IV.

St. Louis, April 1st, 1852.

L. F.		Dr.		Cr.	
	Bela N. Seymour and Albert Fitch have this day entered into partnership, as pr. Articles of Agreement.				
1	Sundries — To Bela N. Seymour,				
	For Effects invested			16,000	00
1	State Bank of Missouri, Cash on deposit	5,000	00		
1	Steamboat Sultana Stock, ¼ of said Boat	6,500	00		
1	Steamboat Neptune Stock, ⅛ " " "	4,500	00		
1/2	Bela N. Seymour — To Bills Payable,	7,500	00		
	Note, favor of Blackwell & Co., assumed by the Firm			7,500	00
	1st				
1	Sundries — To Albert Fitch,				
	For Effects invested			11,525	50
2	Cash, On hand	8,000	00		
2	Bills Receivable, Note in his favor, drawn by Thomas Coleman, due May 22d	3,525	50		
1	Albert Fitch — To Sundries,	3,025	50		
2	To Coffin & Waite, Bal. of % assumed			890	00
2	" Silas George & Son, " " " "			2,135	50
	"				
1/2	State Bank of Missouri — To Cash,	8,000	00		
	Deposited			8,000	00
	3d				
1	State Bank of Missouri	5,250	00		
1	To Steamboat Sultana Stock,				
	Sold 3/16 of this Boat for Cash deposited			5,250	00
	5th				
3	Real Estate, Pike Co. — To Sundries,				
	Bo't of Greely & Warburton a Farm, for	3,000	00		
1	To State Bank of Mo., Paid pr. Check			1,000	00
3	" Bonds & Mortgages Payable,				
	Our Notes for Bal., secured by Mortgage on Farm, One @ 1 year, $1,000.00; " " 2 " 1,000.00			2,000	00
	7th				
2/1	Cash — To State Bank of Mo.,	500	00		
	Drew out, pr. Check			500	00
	"				
1/2	Steamboat Neptune Stock, — To Cash,	75	00		
	Paid for ⅛ Repairs of said Boat			75	00
		54,876	00	54,876	00

DAY-BOOK, SET IV.

St. Louis, April 9th, 1852.

L. F.	Account	Particulars	Dr.		Cr.	
1/2	Albert Fitch	To Cash, On %	50	00	50	00
	9th					
3	Real Estate Main St.	To Sundries,				
		Bo't House & Lot, No. 95 Main St., for	20,000	00		
1	To Steamboat Sultana Stock,					
		Gave $\frac{1}{16}$ of this Boat in part Pay't			2,000	00
1	" State Bank of Mo.,	Our Check			9,000	00
3	" Bonds & Mortgages Payable,					
		Our Bond, @ 2 years, secured by Mortgage			9,000	00
	10th					
3/1	Remittances	To State Bank of Mo.,	250	00		
		Checked from Bank, and remitted to Newton Snyder, Pike Co., to be used by him in repairing and fencing Farm, as pr. directions in our letter of date			250	00
	15th					
1	Sundries	To Steamboat Neptune Stock,				
		This Boat was snagged & sunk in the Mississippi river, above Memphis, on the 9th inst., and has been delivered over to the Underwriters			4,575	00
1	State Bank of Mo.,	Rec'd, from the Reliance Mutual Ins. Co., the Am't covered by Ins., ($\frac{1}{8}$ of $34,000,) $4,250, less Expenses, $125,	4,125	00		
3	Profit & Loss,	Lost the Bal.	450	00		
	16th					
	Sundries	To Sundries,				
4	Steamboat Sioux Stock,	$\frac{1}{4}$ of Boat, Bo't at Auction	6,120	00		
4	Discount,	On Note, $3,525.50, for 36 days	21	15		
2	To Bills Receivable,	Paid in part by Note of T. Coleman, favor of A. Fitch, due 22d proximo			3,525	50
1	" State Bank of Mo.,	Our Check			2,500	00
2	" Cash,	For Bal., including Dis. on Note			115	65
	"					
4	Steamboat Sioux Stock		126	00		
2	To Bills Payable,	Our Note @ 30 days, favor St. Louis Ins. Co., for Ins. on $6,250, @ 2 % & Policy			126	00
	20th					
4/2	Loans	To Cash,	200	00		
		Loaned to Henry Bolton			200	00
	23d					
3	Sundries	To Remittances,				
		Rec' of Newton Snyder an % of the use made of our Remittance to him of 10th inst. Amount			250	00
3	Real Estate Pike Co.	Fencing, Repairs, & his Com.	215	00		
2	Cash	Bal. returned	35	00		
			31,592	15	31,592	15

DAY-BOOK, SET IV.

St. Louis, April 26th, 1852.

L. F.		Dr.		Cr.	
3	Sundries To Real Estate Pike Co.,				
	Sold our Farm to Silas George & Son			4,000	00
2	Silas George & Son, Offset the Am't due them	2,135	50		
2	Cash Rec'd in part	364	50		
4	Bonds & Mortgages Receivable,				
	Their Note for Bal., payable in 2 years, and secured by Mortgage on Property	1,500	00		
	27th				
4	State Bank of Missouri Stock	1,920	00		
1	To State Bank of Mo.,				
	Bo't of Lemuel Fraley, pr. Check, 40 Shares Stock @ $48.			1,920	00
	"				
1/3	State Bank of Mo., To Real Estate Main St.,	600	00		
	Rec'd & deposited 6 mos. Rent of House & Lot, No. 95			600	00
	28th				
2/4	Cash To Loans,	200	00		
	Rec'd of Henry Bolton, for Loan of 20th inst.			200	00
	29th				
4	Sundries To State Bank of Mo. Stock,				
	Sold to Coffin & Waite 30 Shares Bank Stock @ $50.			1,500	00
2	Coffin & Waite, Offset Am't we owe them	890	00		
4	Interest, Allowed on their %	6	50		
1	State Bank of Mo., Their Check deposited	603	50		
	30th				
2/4	Cash, To State Bank of Mo. Stock,	25	00		
	Dividend on 10 Shares,—$500 @ 5 %			25	00
	"				
1	State Bank of Mo.	309	35		
4	To Steamboat Sioux Stock,				
	Deposited a Check Rec'd of the Clerk of said Boat, for our ¼ Net Proceeds of Trip No. 13, to N. Orleans			309	35
	"				
2	Bills Payable To Sundries,				
	Disc'd our Note, favor of Blackwell & Co., due 18th prox.	7,500	00		
1	To State Bank of Mo., Our Check			7,477	50
4	" Discount, On $7,500, for 18 days			22	50
		16,054	35	16,054	35

Dr. *Bela N. Seymour.* Cr.

1852.						1852.					
Apr.	1	To Bills Pay.	1	7,500	00	Apr.	1	By Sundries	1	16,000	00
"	30	"*Bal.(Net Cap.)to New %*		10,674	10	"	30	" Profit & Loss	3	2,174	10
				18,174	10					18,174	10
						1852.					
						May	1	By Bal. fr. Old %		10,674	10

Dr. *Albert Fitch.* Cr.

1852.						1852.					
Apr.	1	To Sundries	1	3,025	50	Apr.	1	By Sundries	1	11,525	50
"	9	" Cash 3,075.50	2	50	00	"	30	" Profit & Loss	3	2,174	10
"	30	"*Bal.(Net Cap.)to New %*		10,624	10						
				13,699	60					13,699	60
						1852.					
						May	1	By Bal. fr. Old %		10,624	10

Dr. *State Bank of Missouri.* Cr.

1852.						1852.					
Apr.	1	To B. N. Seymour	1	5,000	00	Apr.	5	By Real Estate	1	1,000	00
"	"	" Cash	1	8,000	00	"	7	" Cash	1	500	00
"	3	" St'b't Stock	1	5,250	00	"	9	" Real Estate	2	9,000	00
"	15	" " "	2	4,125	00	"	10	" Remittances	2	250	00
"	27	" Real Estate	3	600	00	"	16	" Sundries	2	2,500	00
"	29	" State B'k Stock	3	603	50	"	27	" State B'k Stock	3	1,920	00
"	30	" St'b't Stock 23,887.85	3	309	35	"	30	" Bills Pay. 22,647.50	3	7,477	50
						"	"	" *Bal. to New %*		1,240	35
				23,887	85					23,887	85
1852.											
May	1	To Bal. fr. old %		1,240	35						

Dr. *Steamboat Sultana Stock.* Cr.

1852.						1852.					
Apr.	1	To B. N. Seymour	1	6,500	00	Apr.	3	By State B'k Mo.	1	5,250	00
"	30	"*Profit & Loss (gain)*	3	750	00	"	9	" Real Estate 7,250.00	2	2,000	00
				7,250	00					7,250	00

Dr. *Steamboat Neptune Stock.* Cr.

1852.						1852.					
Apr.	1	To B. N. Seymour	1	4,500	00	Apr.	15	By Sundries	2	4,575	00
"	7	" Cash 4,575.00	1	75	00						
				4,575	00					4,575	00

Dr. *Bills Payable.* *Cr.*

Date			Fol.	$	cts.	Date			Fol.	$	cts.
1852.						1852.					
Apr.	30	To Sundries	3	7,500	00	Apr.	1	By B. N. Seymour	1	7,500	00
"	"	" *Bal. to New %*		126	00	"	16	" St'b't Stock 7,626.00	2	126	00
				7,626	00					7,626	00
						1852.					
						May	1	By Bal. fr. Old %		126	00

Dr. *Cash.* *Cr.*

Date			Fol.	$	cts.	Date			Fol.	$	cts.
1852.						1852.					
Apr.	1	To A. Fitch	1	8,000	00	Apr.	1	By State B'k Mo.	1	8,000	00
"	7	" State B'k Mo.	1	500	00	"	7	" St'b't Stock	1	75	00
"	23	" Remittances	2	35	00	"	9	" A. Fitch	2	50	00
"	26	" Real Estate	3	364	50	"	16	" Sundries	2	115	65
"	28	" Loans	3	200	00	"	20	" Loans 8,440.65	2	200	00
"	30	" State B'k Stock 9,124.50	3	25	00	"	30	" *Bal. to New %*		683	85
				9,124	50					9,124	50
1852.											
May	1	To Bal. fr. old %		683	85						

Dr. *Bills Receivable.* *Cr.*

Date			Fol.	$	cts.	Date			Fol.	$	cts.
1852.						1852.					
Apr.	1	To A. Fitch	1	3,525	50	Apr.	16	By Sundries	2	3,525	50

Dr. *Coffin & Waite.* *Cr.*

Date			Fol.	$	cts.	Date			Fol.	$	cts.
1852.						1852.					
Apr.	29	To State B'k Stock	3	890	00	Apr.	1	By A. Fitch	1	890	00

Dr. *Silas George & Son.* *Cr.*

Date			Fol.	$	cts.	Date			Fol.	$	cts.
1852.						1852.					
Apr.	26	To Real Estate	3	2,135	50	Apr.	1	By A. Fitch	1	2,135	50

Dr. *Real Estate Pike Co.* *Cr.*

Date			F.	$	cts	Date			F.	$	cts
1852.						1852.					
Apr.	5	To Sundries	1	3,000	00	Apr.	26	By Sundries	3	4,000	00
"	23	" Remittances (3,215.00)	2	215	00						
"	30	" *Profit & Loss (gain)*	3	785	00						
				4,000	00					4,000	00

Dr. *Bonds & Mortgages Payable.* *Cr.*

Date			F.	$	cts	Date			F.	$	cts
1852.						1852.					
Apr.	30	*To Bal. to New ℀*		11,000	00	Apr.	5	By Real Estate	1	2,000	00
						"	9	" " " (11,000.00)	2	9,000	00
				11,000	00					11,000	00
						1852.					
						May	1	By Bal. fr. Old ℀		11,000	00

Dr. *Real Estate Main St.* *Cr.*

Date			F.	$	cts	Date			F.	$	cts
1852.						1852.					
Apr.	9	To Sundries	2	20,000	00	Apr.	27	By State B'k Mo.	3	600	00
"	30	" *Profit & Loss (gain)*	3	3,100	00	"	30	" *Bal. (Inv't) to New ℀*		22,500	00
				23,100	00					23,100	00
1852.											
May	1	To Bal. fr. Old ℀		22,500	00						

Dr. *Remittances.* *Cr.*

Date			F.	$	cts	Date			F.	$	cts
1852.						1852.					
Apr.	10	To State B'k Mo.	2	250	00	Apr.	23	By Sundries	2	250	00

Dr. *Profit & Loss.* *Cr.*

Date			F.	$	cts	Date			F.	$	cts
1852.						1852.					
Apr.	15	To Neptune Stock	2	450	00	Apr.	30	By Sultana Stock	1	750	00
"	30	" Int. & Dis. (455.15)	4	5	15	"	"	" Estate Pike Co.	3	785	00
"	"	"*B. N. Seymour (½ net gain)*	1	2,174	10	"	"	" " Main St.	3	3,100	00
"	"	"*A. Fitch* " " "	1	2,174	10	"	"	" Sioux Stock	4	63	35
						"	"	" State B'k Stock (4,803.35)	4	105	00
				4,803	35					4,803	35

Steamboat Sioux Stock.

Dr.					Cr.				
1852. Apr.	16	To Sundries	2	6,120 00	1852. Apr.	30	By State B'k Mo.	3	309 35
"	"	" Bills Pay. 6,246.00	2	126 00	"	"	" *Bal.(Inv't) to New a/c*		6,000 00
"	30	" *Profit & Loss (gain)*	3	63 35					
				6,309 35					6,309 35
1852. May	1	To Bal. fr. Old a/c		6,000 00					

Interest & Discount.

Dr.					Cr.				
1852. Apr.	16	To Sundries	2	21 15	1852. Apr.	30	By Bills Pay.	3	22 50
"	29	" State B'k Stock 27.65	3	6 50	"	"	" *Profit & Loss (loss)*	3	5 15
				27 65					27 65

Loans.

Dr.					Cr.				
1852. Apr.	20	To Cash	2	200 00	1852. Apr.	28	By Cash	3	200 00

Bonds & Mortgages Receivable.

Dr.					Cr.				
1852. Apr.	26	To Real Estate	3	1,500 00					

State Bank of Missouri Stock.

Dr.					Cr.				
1852. Apr.	27	To State B'k Mo.	3	1,920 00	1852. Apr.	29	By Sundries	3	1,500 00
"	30	" *Profit & Loss (gain)*	3	105 00	"	30	" Cash 1,525.00	3	25 00
					"	"	" *Bal.(Inv't) to New a/c*		500 00
				2,025 00					2,025 00
1852. May	1	To Bal. fr. Old a/c		500 00					

TRIAL BALANCE, LEGER, SET IV.

L.F.		Dr.		Cr.	
1	Bela N. Seymour			8,500	00
1	Albert Fitch			8,450	00
1	State Bank of Missouri	1,240	35		
1	Steamboat Sultana Stock			750	00
2	Bills Payable			126	00
2	Cash	683	85		
3	Real EstatePike Co.			785	00
3	Bonds & Mortgages Payable			11,000	00
3	Real Estate Main St.	19,400	00		
3	Profit & Loss	450	00		
4	Steamboat Sioux Stock	5,936	65		
4	Interest & Discount	5	15		
4	Bonds & Mortgages Receivable	1,500	00		
4	State Bank of Missouri Stock	395	00		
		29,611	00	29,611	00

INVENTORY-BOOK, SET IV.

Property remaining unsold, April 30th, 1852:		
House & Lot, No. 95 Main St., valued at	22,500	00
One-Fourth Steamboat Sioux, " "	6,000	00
10 Shares State Bank of Missouri Stock, @ $50 pr. Sh.	500	00
	29,000	00

STATEMENTS, SET IV.

The total gains accruing from this business are		$4,803.35
" " losses " " " " "		455.15
Making the firm's net gains		$4,348.20

Each partner's share is ½ of $4,348.20 = $2,174.10.

The total assets* at closing are	$32,424.20	
" " liabilities† " "	11,126.00	
Making the firm's net capital or present worth	$21,298.20	

Net capital of B. N. Seymour at commencing, as pr. credit Bal. of his a/c	$8,500.00
Add his ½ net gains, as above	2,174.10
His net capital is	$10,674.10

Net capital of Albert Fitch at commencing, as pr. credit Bal. of his a/c	$8,500.00
Deduct Am't withdrawn for private use	50.00
Bal. remaining to credit of his a/c	$8,450.00
Add his ½ net gains, as above	2,174.10
His net capital is	$10,624.10

B. N. Seymour's net capital or present worth	$10,674.10
Albert Fitch's " " " " "	10,624.10
Firm's present worth, as above	$21,298.20

* When, as in this Set, no Balance account is opened in the Leger, the *total assets* are ascertained after the Leger is closed, by summing up all the *debit* balances ("brought down to new account") under the various accounts which are kept to show assets and liabilities.

† The *total liabilities* are ascertained by summing up all the *credit* balances under the various accounts kept to show assets and liabilities

Therefore :—

In a partnership business, where the partners invest equal net capital, do a gaining business, and share alike in gains,

Deduct total losses from total gains—to find firm's net gains.

Divide firm's net gains equally—to find each partner's net gains.

Deduct total liabilities from total assets—to find firm's present worth.

Add each partner's ½ net gains to the credit balance of his account—to find his present worth.

The present worth of the two partners, added together, must equal the present worth of the firm.

QUESTIONS FOR REVIEW, SET IV.

Wherein does the plan pursued in Sets IV and V differ from the Italian method?
What does the general rule for journalizing now become?
Which is the book of original entry? From which are all postings made?
Where may the various auxiliary books, omitted in this Set, be found?
Is Set IV an individual or partnership business? Prosperous or adverse?
How do the partners share in gains and losses?
Which are the first accounts to be opened on the Leger, in partnership books?
How does the closure of the Leger differ from the closure in Sets I, II, and III?
How is Profit & Loss account to be closed?
When and for what purpose is the Second Trial Balance to be taken? Of what will it consist?
In the following transactions of a firm, what are the debits and credits—and why?

1st, Investment by one partner of cash deposited in a bank, and of a portion of two steamboats. [Bear in mind that in Set IV a Bank account is kept in the Leger.]—2d, Assumption by the firm of a note which that partner owes.—3d, Investment by the other partner of cash, and a note he holds against another person.—4th, Assumption by the firm of this partner's indebtedness to two different persons.—5th, Deposit of cash in bank.—6th, Sale of portion of a steamboat for cash deposited in bank.—7th, Purchase of a farm in Pike Co., and payment by a check on the bank, and by the firm's notes secured by mortgage on the property.—8th, Drawing cash from the bank, pr. check.—9th, Payment of the firm's portion of repairs of steamboat. —10th, Payment of cash to a partner for private use.—11th, Purchase of a house and lot on Main St., and payment by portion of a steamboat, by check on bank, and by the firm's note secured by mortgage.—12th, Draft of money from bank, and remittance of it abroad, to an agent, to be used by him as directed.—13th, Sinking of a steamboat partly owned by the firm, and receipt of cash for the portion covered by insurance—balance lost.—14th, Purchase of portion of a steamboat, and payment by a note which the firm holds against another person, by check on bank, and by cash—the note not being yet due, and the firm allowing a discount thereon.—15th, Issuing the firm's note for insurance on their portion of a steamboat.—16th, Loan of cash.—17th, Receipt from an agent abroad of a portion of the money previously remitted to him, with information that he has used the balance in making repairs on farm in Pike Co.—18th, Sale of farm in Pike Co., and receipt of payment by offset of an account we owe, by cash, and by another person's note secured by mortgage.—19th, Purchase of stock in bank by check on the bank.—20th, Deposit in bank of money received for rent of house and lot on Main St.—21st, Return of money loaned out.—22d, Sale of bank stock, and receipt of payment by canceling the firm's indebtedness to another person, by interest thereon, and by check of another person deposited in bank.—23d, Receipt of cash for dividend on bank stock.—24th, Receipt, pr. check deposited, of a portion of the net proceeds of steamboat's trip to New Orleans.—25th, Discount of firm's note, and payment of amount (less discount) by check on bank.

What are the total gains of the firm in Set IV? Total losses? Net gains?
What is each partner's share of net gains? How found?
What are the total assets of the firm? Total liabilities? Net capital?
What is the net capital of B. N. Seymour? How ascertained?
What is the net capital of Albert Fitch? How ascertained?
In such a business as Set IV represents, how can you find the firm's net gains? How each partner's? How can you find the firm's present worth? How each partner's? What must the present worth of the two partners, added together, equal?

TIMOTHY H. PORTER & CO.

SET V.

PRODUCE, GROCERY, AND DOMESTIC SHIPPING BUSINESS.

[See page 92 for Instructions for writing up this Set.]

1 # HISTORY AND ELUCIDATIONS, SET V.

Cincinnati, June 1*st*, 1852.

Timothy H. Porter, David Harrington and George Anderson have this day formed a partnership to conduct a *produce*, *grocery* and *domestic shipping* business. Porter and Harrington are to furnish the capital as agreed, and to receive interest thereon; and each is to share two-fifths of the gains or losses. Anderson is to share one-fifth of the gains or losses. Title of firm—"*Timothy H. Porter & Co.*"

T. H. Porter invests in Cash $10,000.

David Harrington invests in Cash $10,000, and in Mdse., pr. Invoice, $3,125.
He owes on Bills Payable, pr. B.-B., which the Firm assume, $2,238.36.
Making his Net Capital $10,886.64.

T. H. Porter produces the firm value in Cash.

David Harrington produces the firm value in the Cash and Mdse. invested; and he costs value in Bills Payable, assumed by the firm.

George Anderson requires neither a debit nor a credit at this time; but, in posting, his account should be the third opened in the Leger, that the partner's accounts may stand together.

☞ *No Bank account is kept in the Leger in this Set.*

2d

Sold to Booth & Plumley 150 Bbls. Mess Pork @ $9.50; and 100 Bbls. Lard, 20,000 lbs. @ 6^1¢—total Am't $2,675.

Rec'd, in payment, 14 Hhds. Sugar, 15,400 lbs. @ 6¢; David Harrington's Note, their favor, assumed by the Firm at commencing business, due 29th inst., for $1,500; and Cash for Bal. of Sale and for Discount on Note, $257.75.

Discount on David Harrington's Note for 27 days is $6.75.

Mdse., Bills Payable and Cash have cost value. Mdse. and Discount have produced value. The entry will be commenced "Sundries To Sundries."

3d

Paid in Cash David Harrington's Note, favor of Charles Elliott & Bro., assumed by the Firm at commencing business, dated Mar. 2d, @ 90 days, with Int. from date. Am't of Note $738.36—Int. 93 days (including Grace).

Reckon the interest on this note first, and then make the proper entry. Bills Payable and Interest have cost value, and Cash has produced value.

"

Bought of Joseph Suydam & Co. 125 Bbls. Superfine Flour @ $4.25; 100 Bbls. Extra Mess Pork @ $9; 600 Bbls. Mess Beef @ $11; 100 Bbls. Prime Beef @ $8.50; 50 Bbls. Beef Hams @ $16; 50 Bbls. Pearl Ashes @ $4.30—total Am't $9,896.25.

Paid in part by 14 Hhds. Sugar, 15,400 lbs. @ 6^2¢; and Cash for the Balance.

Mdse. has cost value in Mdse. and Cash.

In such cases as this, Mdse. *might* be considered as costing only the balance paid for it in Cash—the entry would then be "Mdse. Dr. To Cash $8,895.25;" but the *better* way is to debit Mdse. the full amount $9,896.25, and credit Mdse. and Cash; thus letting the Mdse. account show the entire dealings in Mdse.

4th

Shipped pr. Steamboat Crescent City, Forbes master, and consigned to Goodhue & Co., New Orleans, to be sold on our account and at our risk, 125 Bbls. Superfine Flour @ $4.25; 200 Bbls. Mess Beef @ $11.

Paid Drayage in Cash $10.25.

Passed our Note, @ 30 days, to the Western Insurance Co., for Ins. on $2,777.22 @ 1^1% and for Policy $1.

Goods sent abroad to be sold for your account must not be debited to the consignee, but must have a specific heading or title, under which to keep an account of them; just as goods at home have the title of "Merchandise." The title usually assumed is "*Shipment*" or "*Adventure,*" to such a place or to such a party. You may call this "*Shipment to New Orleans,*" which account has cost value in the amount paid for the goods, and in the expenses attending the shipment of the same.

Sundries:—to wit, Mdse., Cash, and Bills Pay., have produced value.

☞ Explain fully every debit and credit made in the Day-Book.

5th

Paid Cash for sundry Repairs of Store $30.

Cincinnati, June 7th, 1852.

Bought of Claremont, Smith & Co., on %/c, 200 Bbls. Mess Beef @ $11.12½.

7th

Shipped pr. Steamboat Henry Clay, Gaines master, and consigned to Osterhaut & Evans, Mobile, to be sold on our account and risk, 50 Bbls. Pearl Ashes @ $4.30; 200 Bbls. Mess Beef @ $11.12².

Paid Cash for Drayage $8; also to the Ohio Insurance Co., for Ins. on $2,480 @ 1¹% and for Policy $1.

You may term this *"Adventure"* instead of *"Shipment,"* to show variety.
Adventure to Mobile has cost value in Mdse. and Cash.

11th

Rec'd pr. Steamboat Isaac Newton, Manning master, from Van Deursen & Co., N. O., Mdse. previously ordered by us, to wit:—30 Hhds. N. O. Molasses, 3,000 Gals. @ 25¢; 30 Hhds. N. O. Sugar, 30,750 lbs. @ 4²¢.

Paid, in Cash, the Freight, Drayage, &c. on above Mdse. $96.

Mdse. has cost the firm value. Van Deursen & Co., and Cash have produced the firm value, the former by furnishing the goods without pay, the latter by paying freight.

12th

Purchased for Cash, of Bowen & Bros., of this City, their Bill of Exchange on Lafitte & Dalton, N. O., and remitted the same this day to Van Deursen & Co., in payment of Am't due them, $2,133.75. Paid ¼% Prem. for the Bill.

First calculate the premium on $2,133.75 @ ¼%, and then make the entry.
Van Deursen & Co. and Premium have cost the firm value. Cash has produced value.

14th

Bought of Daniel Liebrand & Co., on our Note @ 4 mos., 2,500 Bush. Ohio Wheat, delivered on board the Steamboat Buena Vista, Taylor master, @ $1.03 per Bush., and shipped the same to Austin & Spicer, Galveston, Texas, to be sold for our account and risk.

Issued our Note, @ 15 days, to the Cincinnati Mutual Ins. Co., for Ins. on $2,608.61 @ 1¹% and for Policy $1.

Shipment to Galveston has cost value in Bills Payable.

17th

Sold to Richard Stockton & Co. 20 Hhds. N. O. Molasses, 2,000 Gals. @ 27¢; 100 Bbls. Prime Beef @ $9; 100 Bbls. Mess Beef @ $11.50.

Rec'd Cash in part, $1,295; their Note @ 60 days, for Bal., including Discount, $1,308.74. The Discount on Note ($1,308.74) is for 63 days.

Cash and Bills Receivable have cost the firm value. Mdse. and Discount have produced value.
Reckon this discount in the same manner as interest is calculated, and if right, the amount obtained and the total amount of Mdse. here sold, added together, will equal the gross sum of the money and note received in payment.

18th

Accepted Claremont, Smith & Co.'s Draft on us, @ 30 days' sight, favor of Oakland & Co., for $1,000.

Claremont, Smith & Co. have cost the firm value in Bills Payable.

23d

Shipped, pr. Steamboat Ben Franklin, to T. W. Boswell & Co., Vicksburg, for their %/c, and pursuant to their order, 150 Bbls. Mess Beef @ $11.50.

Paid Drayage in Cash, $4.75.

Here the goods are not shipped for your own account, but for account of another party who ordered them. This is therefore a regular sale; and T. W. Boswell & Co. have cost you value in Mdse. and in Cash.

Cincinnati, June 25th, 1852.

Rec'd intelligence that the Steamboat Buena Vista, on which we made a Shipment on the 14th inst., was wrecked in the Gulf of Mexico on the 20th inst.,—Boat and Cargo total loss.

This is a mere memorandum, to prepare you for the entry of the 29th inst., and showing that in the course of business the firm would now receive this information. *It requires no Day-Book entry.*

26th

Discounted our Acceptance of the 18th inst., @ 30 days' sight, Oakland & Co.'s favor, Am't $1,000.

Discount for 25 days on $1,000 is $4.17—Bal. paid in Cash.

Bills Payable has cost value in Cash and Discount.

28th

Paid George Anderson Cash for private use $200.

29th

The Cincinnati Mutual Ins. Co. has failed, and is able to pay but 10¢ on the dollar, of its indebtedness. Accordingly we have received from the Assignees 10% on the Am't of our Ins. on Ship't to Galveston of 14th inst., pr. Steamboat Buena Vista, which was wrecked in the Gulf of Mexico on the 20th inst.—Boat & Cargo total loss.

Am't insured $2,608.61 @ 10% = $260.86, for which we received our Note of 14th, @ 15 days, $33.61; and Cash for Bal.

The loss of goods belonging to Shipment to Galveston is the means of the firm's receiving $260.86. Shipment to Galveston has therefore produced the firm that amount of value in Bills Payable and Cash.

"

Rec'd an Account-Sales from Osterhaut & Evans, Mobile, of Ashes and Beef sent them on the 7th inst. Net proceeds $2,976.15.

Rec'd also a Draft, remitted by them, on Biddle Brothers, at sight (for part proceeds), which has been paid in Cash, $1,500.00.

An Account-Sales is a detailed statement of the sales of goods, and of the charges attending the same. Adventure to Mobile has here produced value in Cash, and in the indebtedness of Osterhaut & Evans for the portion of proceeds still in their hands.

30th

Rec'd an Account-Sales from Goodhue & Co., New Orleans, of 200 Bbls. Mess Beef, belonging to Ship't to them of 4th inst. Net proceeds $2,380.86.

Shipment to New Orleans has produced value in the indebtedness of Goodhue & Co.

"

Paid Cash for Rent of Store $75; for Clerk hire $100; for Laborers $38.

"

Due to Timothy H. Porter for Int. on Capital invested, $10,000, for one mo., $50.
" " David Harrington " " " " " $10,886.64 " " $54.43.

Interest has cost the firm value in their indebtedness to each of these two partners.
T. H. Porter, and David Harrington have each produced the firm value in the use of capital invested.

TRIAL BALANCE, LEGER, SET V.

L. F.		Dr.		Cr.	
1	Timothy H. Porter			10,050	00
1	David Harrington			10,941	07
1	George Anderson	200	00		
1	Cash	9,906	04		
2	Merchandise	5,237	75		
2	Bills Payable			2,610	72
2	Interest, Discount & Premium	96	54		
2	Shipment to New Orleans	396	36		
3	Store Expenses	243	00		
3	Claremont, Smith & Co.			1,225	00
3	Adventure to Mobile			496	15
3	Shipment to Galveston	2,347	75		
4	Bills Receivable	1,308	74		
4	T. W. Boswell & Co.	1,729	75		
4	Osterhaut & Evans	1,476	15		
4	Goodhue & Co.	2,380	86		
		25,322	94	25,322	94

INVENTORY-BOOK, SET V.

Property remaining unsold June 30th, 1852:			
Merchandise,			
175 Bbls. Mess Pork	@ $9.00	1,575	00
150 " " Beef	" 11.00	1,650	00
50 " Beef Hams	" 16.00	800	00
30 Hhds. N. O. Sugar, 30,750 lbs.	" $.04^3$	1,460	63
10 " " Molasses, 1,000 Gals.	" $.26^1$	262	50
		5,748	13
Ship't to New Orleans,			
125 Bbls. Superfine Flour	" 4.25	531	25
		6,279	38

STATEMENTS, SET V.

The total losses of the firm in this business have been	$2,687.29
" " gains " " " " " " " "	1,141.42
Making the firm's net losses	$1,545.87

Timothy H. Porter's share is $\frac{2}{5}$ = $618.35
David Harrington's " " $\frac{2}{5}$ = $618.35
George Anderson's " " $\frac{1}{5}$ = $309.17

The total assets of the firm at closing are	$23,080.92
" " liabilities " " " " "	3,835.72
Making the firm's net capital or present worth	$19,245.20

Timothy H. Porter invested at commencing - - - -	$10,000.00	
Add interest, as agreed - - - - - -	50.00	
Total credit to his account - - -	$10,050.00	
Deduct his $\frac{2}{5}$ net losses, as before - - - - -	618.35	
His net capital is - - - -	$9,431.65	

David Harrington invested, at commencing, a net capital of - - -	$10,886.64
Add interest, as agreed - - - - - - - - - -	54.43
Credit balance to his account - - - - -	$10,941.07
Deduct his $\frac{2}{5}$ net losses, as before - - - - - - - -	618.35
His net capital is - - - - - -	$10,322.72

George Anderson has drawn out for private use, as pr. total debit to his account - - - - - - - -	$200.00
Add his $\frac{1}{5}$ net losses, as before - - - - - -	309.17
His net insolvency is - - - -	$509.17

Add { Porter's net capital or present worth - - - - - -	$9,431.65
Add { Harrington's " " " " - - - - - - -	10,322.72
	$19,754.37
Deduct Anderson's net insolvency - - - - - - -	509.17
Firm's present worth, as before - - - -	$19,245.20

Therefore :—

In a partnership business with three partners, like the present, in which two of the partners invest the capital, while the other partner invests nothing, but draws out for private use, and they do a losing business,

Deduct total gains from total losses—to find the firm's net losses.

Divide firm's net losses, according to the original agreement—to find each partner's share of net losses.

Deduct total liabilities from total assets—to find the firm's net capital.

Deduct the net losses of each partner who invests capital from the credit total, or balance, of his account—to find his net capital at closing.

Add the net losses of the partner who makes no investment to the debit total (or balance) of his account—to find his net insolvency at closing.

Deduct the net insolvency of one partner from the sum total of the net capitals of the other two—to find the firm's net capital—which must agree with the difference between the firm's assets and liabilities.

NOTE.—It will be seen that the net capital of Porter and of Harrington consists in part of the indebtedness of Anderson to the firm.

DETECTION AND CORRECTION OF ERRORS.

Much has been said and written about the detection of errors in Book-keeping, and many *so-called infallible* schemes have been put forth, by which to discover at a glance whether an error exists, and, if so, to trace it to its origin. But *no* plan has yet come before the public which will bear the test of rigid scrutiny; and the only certainty of accuracy in every respect appears to be an examination of items in detail. The Trial Balance is the best short test of correctness in posting yet discovered, and this is defective, inasmuch as errors may exist while the Trial Balance is apparently entirely correct:—such as posting to the wrong account, although on the right side; omitting to post a debit and a credit of equal amount, &c. But if the Trial Balance is not in equilibrium, there is certainly an error, which must be sought and corrected.

Detection.

1st. See whether the pencil footings on the Leger, made preparatory to taking the Trial Balance, are correct, and whether the balances of the different accounts have been transferred into the Trial Balance rightly.

2d. If there is still an undiscovered error, examine each post separately, checking the entries in both Journal and Leger as you proceed, until you have been over the whole; and then look through again, to see if any amount remains unchecked, and, if so, investigate the cause of the omission.

In this manner, you can scarcely fail to discover the mistake, provided the Journal is correct; but great care should be taken to see that the Journal is in equilibrium before posting, as any discrepancy there will give you much trouble in the Leger.

Correction.

In the Day-Book (or any other book of original entry) erasures are not admissible, since this book is taken as evidence in courts of justice, and any thing obliterated or erased looks suspicious, would probably render invalid the entry with which it is connected, and in some cases might even throw the whole book out of court, as evidence unfit to receive. Errors in it should therefore be corrected by making other entries explaining them; or the erroneous entry, if it has not been journalized, may be marked "Void," and remain without further alteration, a new and correct entry being made of the transaction.

In the Journal, erasures are sometimes admissible, although it is generally advisable to treat errors as directed for the Day-Book.

In the Leger, if an entry be posted to the wrong account, or to the wrong side of the account, make ciphers of the figures, and leave the remainder, so as not to deface the Leger; then post the entry to its proper place. If a wrong amount be posted, alter it to the right. And if a duplicate post be made, make ciphers of the figures in the erroneous one.

QUESTIONS FOR REVIEW, SET V.

How many partners in Set V?
How do they share in gains and losses?
How many of the partners invest capital?
Is it a gaining or losing business?
} For answers to these questions, see page 92.

In the following transactions of a firm, what are the debits and credits—and why?

1st, Investment of cash by one partner.—2d, Investment by another partner of cash and Mdse.—3d, Assumption by the firm of notes outstanding against that partner.—4th, Sale of Mdse., and receipt of payment by Mdse., by a note of the firm outstanding, and by cash—the note not being yet due, and they being allowed a discount thereon.—5th, Payment in cash of the firm's note with interest on same from date.—6th, Purchase of Mdse. for Mdse. and cash.

—7th, Shipment of Mdse. to New Orleans, to be sold for account of the firm, and payment of drayage on same in cash, and of insurance by firm's note.—8th, Purchase of Mdse. on account. —9th, Shipment of Mdse. to Mobile to be sold for account of the firm, and payment of drayage and insurance on same in cash.—10th, Receipt of Mdse. previously ordered from abroad, but not paid for, and payment of freight, drayage, &c. on same in cash.—11th, Purchase for cash, @ $\frac{1}{4}$% premium, of a bill of exchange, and remittance of same to pay an account which the firm owe.—12th, Purchase of wheat by firm's note, and shipment of same to Galveston to be sold for their account, insurance thereon being also paid by their note.—13th, Sale of Mdse. at cash price, receiving part cash, and for the balance a note sufficiently large to cover discount thereon, so as to make it equal to cash.—14th, Acceptance by the firm of a draft on them.—15th, Shipment of Mdse. to another person, pursuant to his order and for his account; and payment of drayage in cash.—16th, Discounting, by the firm, of their acceptance outstanding. —17th, Payment of cash to a partner for private use.—18th, Receipt of the firm's note and cash from an Insurance Co., for 10% on the amount insured on goods shipped to Galveston, which have been wrecked.—19th, Receipt of an account-sales of goods consigned abroad, accompanied by a draft for a portion of the amount, which you immediately convert into cash.—20th, Receipt of an account-sales without any remittance.—21st, Payment of store rent and clerk hire in cash.—22d, Allowance of interest to two partners on capital invested.

What are the total losses of the firm in Set V? The total gains? The net losses?

What is Porter's share of the net losses? What is Harrington's share? What is Anderson's share?

What are the total assets of the firm? The total liabilities? The net capital?

What is the net capital of Timothy H. Porter? How ascertained?

What is the net capital of David Harrington? How ascertained?

What is the net insolvency of George Anderson? How ascertained?

What is the balance resulting, by deducting Anderson's net insolvency from the amount of Porter and Harrington's net capitals added together?

In such a business as Set V represents, how can you find the firm's net losses? How each partner's? How can you find the firm's net capital? How can you find the net capital of each partner who invests capital at starting? How the net insolvency of the partner who makes no investment, but draws out funds for private use? If you deduct the net insolvency of one partner from the sum total of the net capitals of the other two, what will the difference show: —with what must it agree?

QUESTIONS ON DETECTION AND CORRECTION OF ERRORS.

Has any short and infallible method been discovered for detecting errors in books?

What affords the only certainty of accuracy in keeping books?

What is the best short test of correctness in posting yet discovered?

Why is this test defective?

Mention some errors that may exist when the Trial Balance is apparently correct.

If the Trial Balance is not in equilibrium, what may you be certain of?

Explain how to detect errors made in posting, or taking a Trial Balance.

How should an error be corrected in the Day-Book?

How should an error be corrected in the Journal?

How should an error be corrected in the Leger?

BALANCE SHEETS

AND

LEGER ACCOUNTS.

BALANCE SHEETS EXPLAINED.

Take a sheet of unruled foolscap or letter paper, and draw a double red line around it close to the edge, for a border; then draw a pencil line across the sheet lengthwise, about three-quarters of an inch from the border on one side; follow this with two other pencil lines, one-half that distance apart; then draw a double red line under the first and last pencil lines. This serves for a heading.

For "*Stock*" Sheets, commence under this heading, and rule enough lines, with pencil, to receive all the accounts in your Trial Balance, and leave eight extra. Now turn the sheet, so that the heading will be at your left, and commence ruling, with red ink, the money columns, after the pattern shown on the following page, dropping three lines after "Balance," two after "Stock," two after "Profit & Loss," and one after "Face of Leger." Next rule the footing and closing lines at the bottom of the columns.

In "*Partnership*" Sheets, for two partners, rule twelve more pencil lines from the heading than your Trial Balance contains accounts; then, in ruling for the money columns, drop four lines after "Balance," two after the first partner, two after the second partner, three after "Profit & Loss," and one after "Face of Leger." For three partners, rule sixteen extra pencil lines; and, in ruling for the money columns, drop five lines after "Balance," two after the first partner, two after the second, two after the third, four after "Profit & Loss," and one after "Face of Leger."

Having prepared your Sheet thus, and made the proper headings to it, first bring into it the Trial Balance of your Leger, which, you will now observe, is called in the Balance Sheet, "Face of Leger."

Next, enter to each property account the property remaining unsold, as pr. Inventory-Book; placing the amount in small red ink figures in "Face of Leger" column, on the credit side, immediately below the line containing the difference of said account; and making the opposite entry in "Balance" column, on the debit side, in black ink. At this state, the sheet is like the Leger when ready to close.

You will now transfer the difference of Stock, as shown in the "Face of Leger," into the column appropriated for it, headed "Stock;" then follow with the next account in order, taking its difference into "Profit & Loss," or "Balance," agreeably to its nature; and thus continue until all the accounts in the "Face of Leger" have been transferred. In each speculating property account which has a balance of property unsold, as shown by the red ink entry in "Face of Leger" column, this balance must be counted in as a credit to the account, and then the difference must be transferred into "Profit & Loss." After finishing all these transfers, "Stock," "Profit & Loss," and "Balance" only remain open, and the Balance Sheet corresponds to the Leger when ready for taking the Second Trial Balance.

Finally, close "Profit & Loss" into "Stock," when the differences of the "Stock" and "Balance" columns should just equal each other, and should both show your Net Capital, or Net Insolvency.

Footing up these columns completes the Balance Sheet, which will now be found to agree with your Leger when closed.

Balance Sheets are given for Sets I and IV. You may make these out for yourself, and also make those for Sets II, III and V.

NOTE.—When the *personal* accounts are numerous, they may be summed up together, under two heads, "Personal a/cs due me," "Personal a/cs I owe." See page 168 High School edition, or 238 Counting-House edition.

BALANCE SHEET, LEGER, SET I.

*——————————

Philadelphia, January 31st, 1852.	L. Folio.	Face of Leger. Dr.	Face of Leger. Cr.	Profit & Loss. Dr.	Profit & Loss. Cr.	Stock. Dr.	Stock. Cr.	Balance. Dr.	Balance. Cr.
Stock	1		5,815 00				5,815 00		
Merchandise	1	1,320 40	† 2,522 50		1,202 10			2,522 50	
Cash	1	3,079 98						3,079 98	
Bills Receivable	1	1,590 38						1,590 38	
Philip Somers	2	340 00						340 00	
Bills Payable	2		1,990 00						1,990 00
Elihu Barnes	2		547 50						547 50
Thomas Carpenter & Co.	2	856 74						856 74	
Store Expenses	2	205 00		205 00					
Martin Pemberton	2	500 00						500 00	
Samuel W. Fairburn	3	400 00						400 00	
Personal Expenses	3	60 00		60 00					
		8,352 50	8,352 50						
To Stock, for Net Gain				937 10			937 10		
				1,202 10	1,202 10				
Net Capital						6,752 10			
						6,752 10	6,752 10		
Total Resources and Liabilities								9,289 60	2,537 50
Net Capital, as pr. Stock									6,752 10
								9,289 60	9,289 60

* You can here insert your name.

† Bal. of Mdse. remaining unsold, as pr. Inventory.

SEYMOUR & FITCH'S BALANCE SHEET, LEGER, SET IV.

St. Louis, April 30th, 1852.	L. Folio.	Face of Leger. Dr.	Face of Leger. Cr.	Profit & Loss. Dr.	Profit & Loss. Cr.	Bela N. Seymour. Dr.	Bela N. Seymour. Cr.	Albert Fitch. Dr.	Albert Fitch. Cr.	Balance. Dr.	Balance. Cr.
Bela N. Seymour	1		8,500 00				8,500 00				
Albert Fitch	1		8,450 00						8,450 00		
State Bank of Missouri	1	1,240 35								1,240 35	
Steamboat Sultana Stock	1		750 00		750 00						
Bills Payable	2		126 00								126 00
Cash	2	683 85								683 85	
Real Estate Pike Co.	3		785 00		785 00						
Bonds & Mortgages Payable	3		11,000 00								11,000 00
Real Estate Main St.	3	19,400 00	22,500 00		3,100 00					22,500 00	
Profit & Loss	3	450 00		450 00							
Steamboat Sioux Stock	4	5,936 65	6,000 00		63 35					6,000 00	
Interest & Discount	4	5 15		5 15							
Bonds&Mortgages Receivable	4	1,500 00								1,500 00	
State Bank of Missouri Stock	4	395 00	500 00		105 00					500 00	
		29,611 00	29,611 00								
To Seymour, for 1/2 Net Gain				2,174 10			2,174 10				
" Fitch, " " " "				2,174 10					2,174 10		
				4,803 35	4,803						
Nett Capital						10,674 10					
						10,674 10	10,674 10				
Net Capital								10,624 10			
								10,624 10	10,624 10		
Total Assets and Liabilities										32,424 20	11,126 00
B. N. Seymour's Net Capital											10,674 10
Albert Fitch's " "											10,624 10
										32,424 20	32,424 20

LEGER ACCOUNTS.

If you have written up the several preceding Sets of books, individual and partnership, you have been made acquainted with the *main facts* and *principles* which govern the science of Double Entry Book-keeping, in journalizing, posting, opening and closing Legers, and making out exhibits therefrom. Before proceeding further, it will be well to note the application of these principles to the different Leger accounts, tracing out the *reasons* for every debit and credit therein contained, and thereby fixing in the mind such facts as are necessary to guide you in your future progress. I shall, therefore, here furnish a concise explanation of the various accounts which occur in the more simple business operations, omitting such as pertain exclusively to Shipping and Commission business for a subsequent part of the Counting-House edition.

Observe the fact, that the *rule for journalizing* is constantly applied in these explanations; thus showing that it is not only of utility as an assistant in journalizing, but is the *main key* for unlocking *all* the treasures of the science.

Cash.

The Cash account is kept to show the amount of cash received, the amount paid out, and the balance on hand at any time.

Cash costs value, and is debited, when it is received; consequently, the *debit* side shows *the amount received.*

Cash produces value, and is credited, when it is paid out; consequently, the *credit* side shows *the amount paid out.*

The *balance on hand* is ascertained by deducting the total credit from the total debit. The debit side is always the larger as long as there is any cash on hand, since cash must be received before it can be paid out.

This account is closed "By Balance."

Note.—When no *Balance* account is opened in the Leger, the entry in closing Cash is "By Balance to new account,"—and so in similar closures.

Merchandise, and other Speculating Property Accounts.

Merchandise account is kept to know the cost and proceeds of merchandise; and as a consequence, the gains or losses thereon.

Merchandise costs value when it is purchased—it is debited when it costs value—and consequently the *debit* side shows its *cost*, or *purchases.*

Merchandise produces value when it is sold—it is credited when it produces value—and consequently the *credit* side shows its *proceeds*, or *sales.*

When all is sold, the difference between the two sides will be a gain or loss. If a portion of goods remains on hand unsold, this balance must be credited to the account, prior to closing, as an offset thus far against its cost.

If the debit side is the larger, it is closed "By Profit & Loss," if the credit side is the larger, "To Profit & Loss," always into Profit & Loss.

Real Estate, Bank Stock, Rail-Road Stock, Steamboat Stock, Shipment accounts, Adventure accounts, and all other *speculating property* accounts, are kept for the same purpose, and treated in the same manner as Merchandise account.

Personal Accounts.

Accounts are kept with persons to show your business dealings with them. A person is debited when he is the occasion of any outgo or expenditure to you; in other words, whenever he costs you value; and he is credited whenever he produces you value in any way.

The *debit* side shows what the *person owes you.* The *credit* side shows what you *owe the person.*	The difference shows the balance either due you or due him.

These accounts are closed either "To Balance" or "By Balance."

Sundry Debtors. Sundry Creditors.

SUNDRY DEBTORS.—This account is the representative of persons who owe you, and is used to avoid opening numerous petty accounts upon the Leger. It contains entries to persons with whom your dealings are too limited to open a separate account to each. On the debit side of the account, in the Leger, instead of writing "To *Merchandise*," (or "To" whatever other title constitutes the balancing entry,) it is customary to place the name of the person who is debtor, thus—"To John Barbour," "To Samuel Black," &c.,—and by this arrangement you can see in the account who it is that owes you. Then each credit is commonly posted on the same line as the debit which it cancels—leaving a blank space opposite to the names of such persons as have not paid.

The closure is "By Balance."

SUNDRY CREDITORS.—This account is exactly the reverse of Sundry Debtors, in its treatment and the mode of entry to it:—and is kept for the same purpose, viz. to avoid opening numerous petty accounts upon the Leger.

NOTE.—When no Balance account is opened, these accounts would be permitted to remain unclosed, as each line constitutes in fact a separate account, and has its own independent balance.

Bad Debts, or Suspended Debts.

Into this account are transferred such personal accounts as are considered of too doubtful a character to be relied upon as constituting a part of your assets. It is closed "By Balance," but whenever any portion is positively ascertained to be bad, that portion is closed into "Profit & Loss."

Bills Receivable.

The object in keeping this account is that you may know the amount of other persons' notes received, the amount that has been paid, and the balance yet due you.

Whenever you receive a note, it costs you value, and this account is debited; therefore the *debit* side shows the *amount of notes received.* When a note which you hold is paid, it produces you value, and this account is credited; therefore the *credit* side shows the *amount paid.* The *debit* side is always the larger, if either, and the excess shows the balance of notes on hand unpaid.

When all the notes you hold are paid, this account closes itself; but if any remain unpaid, it is closed "By Balance."

Bills Payable.

Bills Payable account is kept that you may know the amount of your own notes issued, the amount taken up, and the balance still outstanding against you.

Whenever you issue a note, it produces you value, and Bills Payable account is credited, hence the *credit* side shows the *amount of notes issued.* When a note which you have issued is taken up by you, it costs value, and Bills Payable account is debited, hence the *debit* side shows the *amount taken up.*

The credit side is always the larger, if either, and the excess shows the balance of notes outstanding unpaid.

When all the notes issued are paid, this account closes itself, but if any remain unpaid, it is closed "To Balance."

Bonds & Mortgages Receivable.

Bonds & Mortgages Receivable are a class of Bills Receivable, and might be kept under that head, but it is usually preferable to open a separate account, which is treated precisely like Bills Receivable.

Bonds & Mortgages Payable.

Bonds & Mortgages Payable are a class of Bills Payable. This account is treated recisely like Bills Payable account.

Bank.

When a Bank account is kept, it is similar in its treatment to Cash and Bills eceivable, the *debit* side showing the amount of value *deposited* in bank, and the *credit* de the amount *checked* out: consequently the difference is a balance in bank—closed By Balance."

Generally no Bank account is kept in the Leger, and sums of money in bank are unted as cash on hand in balancing the Cash account. Your dealings with the bank ould then be regulated by the Bank-Book and Check-Book.

remium, Interest, Discount, Exchange, Commission, Guarantee, Insurance, Expenses, Charges, &c.

These and similar accounts are kept to ascertain what they cost you, what they proce you, and, as a consequence, whether you gain or lose thereon.

Excess of *debit* shows a larger amount of cost than proceeds, and a consequent *loss* on the account; while excess of *credit* shows a larger amount of proceeds than cost, d a consequent *gain.*

These accounts are always closed into "Profit & Loss."

Remittances.

Remittances account is used for preserving a record of sums sent *to agents* to be plied by them for your benefit, according to your direction.

This account costs you value, when you send the money abroad, and is debited; nce the *debit* shows the *amount remitted to your agent.*

It produces you value, when the money previously charged to it is used in transacting ur business, or is remitted to you again; hence the *credit* shows the *amount disbursed your agent.* The difference shows a balance still in the hands of the agent, and is sed "By Balance," the debit being always the larger, if either.

This account may also be used for preserving a record of sums remitted *to you*, to be bursed for others. In this case the *credit* side would receive the first entries, and ıld be the larger so long as any funds remained in your possession; and therefore closure would be "To Balance."

Loans.

This account is used as the representative of persons to whom you loan and of whom borrow money.

The *debit* side contains sums loaned by you to others, and payments by you of ıeys previously borrowed of others, because in these cases the Loans account costs ıe.

The *credit* side contains sums borrowed by you of others, and payments by others of ıeys previously loaned to them, because in such cases the Loans account produces value.

f the debit is larger, it shows you have money due you on loans—if the credit is ger, it shows that you owe borrowed money.

t is closed "To" or "By Balance."

Profit & Loss.

This account is the receptacle of your gains and losses in business. During the business, any outgo or expenditure which has no other appropriate account for its reception, is debited to this account, and any income which cannot properly be classed under another head, is credited to this account. In closing the books, all gains and losses are transferred into this account, losses being placed on the debit, and gains on the credit, as in the accounts from which the transfer is made.

Therefore :—The *debit* side contains *losses.*
The *credit* side contains *gains.*
The *difference* shows net *gains* or *losses.*

This account is *closed into Stock*, or into the *partners accounts.*

Stock.

This is your representative, when conducting business without a partner, and is used instead of your own name.

Debts at starting, sums drawn out during the business, and net losses at closing, are placed upon the *debit* side of Stock :—Effects invested at starting, sums invested during the business, and net gains at closing, are placed upon the *credit* side.

After receiving the gains or losses, if the credit of this account is the larger, the excess is your *net capital ;* if the debit is the larger, the excess is your *net insolvency.*

It is closed into Balance.

Partners' Accounts.

The *debit* side of a Partner's account contains debts assumed by the firm for him, either at starting or during the business, sums received by him from the firm, and his share of the net losses at closing: The *credit* side contains his investment at starting, sums invested during the business, and his share of net gains at closing.

After receiving the gains or losses, an excess of debit shows *net insolvency*, an excess of credit *net capital.* The account is *closed into Balance.*

Balance.

When this account has received all the balances which are closed into it, the *debit* side contains the *available means* of the individual or firm whose business is represented, consisting of property on hand, and balances of accounts due, styled *resources* or *assets.*

The credit side contains the *indebtedness* of the individual or firm, styled *liabilities.*

If the difference be a *debit* excess, it is *net capital ;* if a *credit* excess, it is *net insolvency.*

The balance brought down from Stock account closes this account.

In a partnership, the balances from the several partners' accounts close it.

N. B. THE FINAL PROOF OF DOUBLE ENTRY BOOK-KEEPING consists in the agreement of *Stock* and *Balance* differences; and is the result of an arrangement to bring all the gains or losses of the business through Profit & Loss into the account of *Stock*, thus increasing or diminishing that account just in the same proportion that the assets and liabilities are increased or decreased, as shown in the *Balance* account.

In the closure of the Legers to the first three Sets of books given in this work, a *Balance* account has been used, believing that you would thereby obtain a better knowledge of the agreement between accounts which show gains and losses, and accounts which show assets and liabilities. In actual business, however, this account is seldom, or never, used, and it is therefore omitted in the other Legers given. But the *same principles* apply in closing Legers *without* the Balance account as with it; and the SAME PROOF exists, since the *assets* and *liabilities* are *as really* contained in the Leger, although found under the various accounts usually closed into Balance. (Continued on page 183 Counting-House edition.)

QUESTIONS ON LEGER ACCOUNTS.

For what purpose is the *Cash* account kept?
What does the debit side show, and why?
What does the credit side show, and why?
How is the balance on hand ascertained?
Which side must be the larger, if either? How is the account closed?
Why is *Merchandise* account kept?
What does the debit show, and why? What does the credit show, and why?
When all is sold, what will the difference between the two sides be?
If a portion remains unsold, what is to be done prior to closing?
How is this account closed?
Why are *Real Estate* and other *speculating property* accounts kept, and how treated?
For what object are *personal* accounts kept?
What is shown upon the debit? What upon the credit? What by the difference?
How are these accounts closed?
Of what is the account of Sundry Debtors the representative? Why is it used?
What does it contain? How are entries made therein? How closed?
Explain the account of Sundry Creditors, and its use.
Explain Bad Debts, or Suspended Debts.
For what is the account of *Bills Receivable* kept?
What does the debit show? What does the credit show?
Which side is the larger, if either, and what does the excess show?
How do you close this account?
Explain the object of *Bills Payable.*
Explain the credit—the debit. Which side is the larger, if either?
How is this account closed?
Explain *Bonds & Mortgages Receivable.* Explain *Bonds & Mortgages Payable.*
To what is *Bank* account similar in its treatment?
What does the debit—the credit—and balance of this account show? How closed?
Is a *Bank* account usually kept in the Leger?
Why are accounts kept with *Premium*, *Interest*, *Expenses*, and the like?
What is shown by an excess of debit? What by an excess of credit?
How are such accounts closed?
For what is *Remittances* account used?
When do you debit, and when credit Remittances, and why?
Which side of Remittances is usually the larger and how is the closure made?
For what other purposes may this account be used?
What does the *Loans account* represent?
What does the debit side contain? What does the credit?
What does the difference show, and how is the account closed?
Of what is *Profit & Loss* the receptacle?
During the business, with what is it debited and credited?
In closing the books, what are transferred into it?
What does the debit contain? What does the credit?
What does the difference show? How is the account closed?
Whom does *Stock* represent, and instead of what is it used?
What items are placed upon the debit side? What upon the credit?
How does it show the *net capital*, or *net insolvency?*
How is it closed?
What does the debit, and what the credit of a *Partner's* account contain?
After receiving the gains or losses, what does the difference show? How closed?
What is contained on the debit side of *Balance* account? What on the credit?
What does the difference show? How is the account closed?
Wherein does the final proof of Double Entry Book-keeping consist?
Of what is it the result?
Is Balance account generally used in business?
Does the same proof of correctness exist in closing without a Balance account as with it?

THOMAS HARVEY & CO.

SET VI.

FOREIGN SHIPPING AND GENERAL COMMISSION BUSINESS.

EXPLANATORY REMARKS, SET VI.

In every thing connected with this Set, my endeavor has been to make it pre-eminently *practical.* To accomplish this the better, I visited, in the spring of 1849, some eight or ten of the heaviest shipping-houses in New York and Philadelphia, and conversed at length with the Principals, and with their Book-keepers, on the nature of foreign transactions; the port-charges, duties, and other expenses incidental to trafficking at foreign ports; the method of making payments in, and the currency of different countries, &c. &c. I procured actual foreign Invoices, Account-Sales, and Account-Currents: examined into the method of keeping books adopted by the different Accountants with whom I conversed, and compared their ideas with my own: had interviews also with several gentlemen who were formerly Captains in the East India trade: and have thus striven to embody the experience of many, for the good of all who may take the trouble to investigate the following pages.

There are some details connected with this business which are too extended to be embraced within any limits that could be reasonably appropriated to it, but a little thought will readily supply them. Such details as are given may be relied upon for accuracy, especially in the Adventures to Canton and the West Indies, in which the proportionate expenses, the time required to make the voyages, and the season of year best adapted to them, have been carefully arranged.

The length of the Canton voyage has forced me to occupy about a year's time with this Set, and I have divided this time into three periods of *four months* each, in order to represent, so far as the *closing of the books* and the agreements of the partners are concerned, a *three years'* business—the first two years with two partners, and the last with three partners. At the end of the first year (represented by four months) the accounts are closed in the Leger, by bringing the balances down to new account; and at the end of the second, when another partner enters the Firm, the books are supposed to be full, and new ones to be purchased, into which the business is transferred. The two Day-Books and Legers are distinguished by being lettered "A." and "B."

The Cash-Book, in conformity with the usual practice of Shipping-houses, is made *one of the main books of original entry*, and then, at the end of every month, the entries from it are transferred into the Day-Book, from which all postings are made to the Leger. By this means, the Cash account, to which the debits and credits are very numerous, receives but one debit post and one credit for each month.

Note.—Interest, in this Set, as throughout the work, is calculated at six per centum, although seven per centum is the legal interest in New York State, the rate varying in different States according to special statutes therein enacted.

CASH-BOOK, SET VI.

The Cash-Book is always an important book, for the Cash account is found to be the most difficult to keep correctly of the whole list of accounts, because Cash is the basis of all trade, and is constantly passing out for purchases and expenses, and coming in for debts and sales.

In Double Entry, as well as in single, the debit side of this book contains all cash received, and the credit side all cash paid out, and the difference between the two sides (or the debit excess) should always show the exact amount of cash on hand, counting—if you keep no Bank account in the Leger—the amount in bank, as well as that which is not in bank. This balance should also agree, at all times, with the balance of the Cash account in the Leger, when that account is posted up.

In connection with Sets I to V inclusive, a Cash-Book would be only for the purpose just mentioned, to preserve the Cash account from errors; but, as used in this Set, it has another and still more important office, for it is the exclusive and only book of original entry for cash transactions, and the Leger titles (as well as the explanations) should be carefully ascertained and correctly recorded, otherwise the Day-Book entries therefrom will be erroneous. Although generally the Cash-Book may be balanced daily, or at such times and as often as suits the taste and convenience of the book-keeper, yet, as here used, it will be found more convenient to make a formal balance of it but once a month; in order that the monthly total *debit* footing of this book (less the balance brought down at the commencement of each month) shall agree with the gross amount of the entry "Cash To Sundries" in the Day-Book; and that the total *credit* footing (less the balance at the close of each month) shall agree with the gross amount of the entry "Sundries To Cash" in the Day-Book. But once a week, or as often as it is wished to make trial of the correctness of the Cash account, the debit and credit columns may be footed up on a scrap of paper, and then the amount of cash in bank (as shown by the Check-Book) and the amount in Safe may be added together, and if their sum be equal to the difference of the cash columns, it proves the account correct.

Some transactions require entries on both the debit and credit sides of the Cash-Book at the same time, as, for example, on the 10th Nov., we have Cash Dr. "To Bills Receivable, No. 8, discounted at Phenix Bank, $5,530.42," as if the firm actually received the full amount of the note; and then, on the opposite side, Cash Cr. "By Discount on Bills Rec., No. 8, pr. contra," for the discount on the note.

In making out Account-Sales and Account-Currents, the Cash-Book, which is not posted until the end of the month, must be examined, to see if any items are entered on it which will affect the Account-Sales or Account-Current. So also in the settlement of accounts with individuals.

LEGERS, SET VI.

THE accounts of *Ship Massachusetts* and *Adventure to Canton* are both left open in closing Leger A, because there is no means of ascertaining the value of the property unsold belonging to either of them. As Insurance has been effected thereon, however, it may be considered safe for the firm to estimate each of these accounts as secure for its cost thus far, and to let them remain open, counting nothing gained or lost upon them as yet.

There are various ways of transferring accounts from one Leger to another. Some open a Balance account in the old Leger, closing all the accounts into it, as shown in the first Sets given in this work, and then make a Day-Book entry of the effects and debts on commencing the new business. But the method here shown, of transferring the differences of the accounts direct from one Leger to the other, answers the purpose equally well, when all the accounts are to be transferred, and saves considerable useless writing. Great care should be taken, however, to have equal amounts of debits and credits appear in the new Leger at starting, since, if there is not an equilibrium, the Leger will ever after be out of balance; just as a pair of scales, with one side heavier than the other, if you continually add equal weights to the two sides, will never hang true. To be sure, therefore, that you are in equilibrium, it will be well always to take a Trial Balance of the new Leger immediately after opening all the accounts therein.

INSTRUCTIONS FOR WRITING UP, SET VI.

In the Counting-house edition, the Day-Books, Cash-Book and Legers are given, because Accountants and others who use it as a book of reference will thereby be better accommodated; and where it is adopted as a text-book in Commercial Institutions, the pupils will be of sufficient age and discretion to consult their own best interests by *not* consulting the book until after they have finished the work for themselves. But in the High-School edition, these books are omitted, and are inserted in the Key, for the use of teachers or of private students.

The *history* of the business is given, as in Sets IV and V, and from this the pupil will make out his Day-Books and Cash-Book, first on loose sheets of paper for correction, and then in the blank books which are prepared for them. Transactions in no wise connected with cash are to be entered only in the Day-Book—exclusive cash transactions, only in the Cash-Book—and those of a mixed nature, in both Day-Book and Cash-Book, as elucidated. At the end of each month transfer to the Day-Book all the entries made in the Cash-Book during the month. Commence with the debit side—"Cash To Sundries"—and enter the various receipts to the credit of the proper accounts, and place together the several sums received at different times from the same account, so as to add up and post them in one amount to the Leger. This renders it necessary to look over the whole of the Cash debits carefully for each account entered, to find all the receipts therefrom; and, to avoid omissions and errors, check each sum in the Cash-Book, as soon as journalized. To afford convenient reference from the Day-Book to the Cash-Book at any time, affix to each sum its proper date. Having completed the debits, next journalize the credit side, saying "Sundries To Cash," and debiting all accounts for which payments have been made during the month.

The two columns for dollars and cents are not used to distinguish debits from credits, but the first is for items, and the second for the extension of sums total. In posting the entries transferred from the Cash-Book, the last day of the month may be used for the date in the Leger.

☞ Be particular and make your own additions, extensions, and other calculations, wherever they occur in any of the books. In the Elucidations, "[D.-B.]" signifies "enter in the Day-Book," and "[C.-B.]"—"enter in the Cash-Book."

HISTORY AND ELUCIDATIONS, SET VI.

New York, July 2d, 1852.

Thomas Harvey and Salmon P. Nixon have this day formed a partnership for conducting a *foreign shipping* and *general commission* business; the parties agreeing to furnish equal capital, and to share alike in gains and losses. No Interest account is to be kept. Settlements are to be made yearly, and each partner's share of gains, if any, accruing from the business, to be added to his account, as a new investment. The partners can draw out funds, from time to time, as needed for private use. Title of Firm—"*Thomas Harvey & Co.*"

Thomas Harvey accordingly invests as follows:			
Cash in Phenix Bank		9,000.00	
Ship Massachusetts, valued at		25,000.00	
A Note against Bagley & Thompson, due Aug. 10th, No. 1,		1,000.00	$35,000.00
Salmon P. Nixon invests			
Cash in Bank of Commerce	10,750.00		
Do. on hand in Safe	318.75	11,068.75	
A Note against Wm. Longfellow, due July 20th, No. 2,	4,500.00		
" " " Jonas Savage & Co.," Aug. 30th, " 3,	2,225.50		
" " " Ezra Coe & Co., " Sep. 8th, " 4,	645.00		
" " " John Vanarsdale, " Nov. 2d, " 5,	1,960.75	9,331.25	
Ginseng, amounting, pr. I.-B., fol. 1, to		14,000.00	
Store Fixtures, valued at		600.00	$35,000.00

By agreement, the Notes are to be received by the Firm without Discount.

1. Ship Massachusetts and Bills Rec. cost the firm value. T. Harvey produces the firm value.
2. Bills Rec., Mdse. and Expenses cost the firm value. S. P. Nixon produces the firm value. } [D.-B.]
3. Cash costs the firm value in their indebtedness to T. Harvey.
4. Cash costs the firm value in their indebtedness to S. P. Nixon. } [C.-B.]

9th

We are preparing the Ship Massachusetts for a voyage to Canton, China; and have freighted her in part with Merchandise consigned to Hughes, Miller & Co., of that city, to be sold for our $^a/_c$ and risk, as pr. O.-I.-B., fol. 1, to wit:

Drills, Bo't of A. A. Lawrence & Co., pr. I.-B., fol. 1, on our Notes,			
No. 1 @ 4 mos. for	14,000.00		
" 2 " 6 " "	14,000.00		
" 3 " 8 " "	14,000.00	42,000.00	
Ginseng from Store, invested by S. P. Nixon, as pr. I.-B., fol. 1,		14,000.00	
Lead, Bo't of Haines, Hampton & Co., pr. I.-B., fol. 1, pr. Check on Bank of Commerce, Am't		7,000.00	$63,000.00
Passed our Note No. 4, @ 12 mos., to the Atlantic Insurance Co.,			
for Ins. on $72,000, @ 1^2 %	1,080.00		
And for policy	1.25	1,081.25	
Com. on $63,000, @ 2^2 %		1,575.00	2,656.25
Due, pr. Average, Nov. 12th,			$65,656.25

It matters but little what title you give this voyage, so that whatever name is once assumed be preserved uniformly in making all subsequent debits or credits to it. It might be termed "Adventure No. 1," "Adventure pr. Ship Massachusetts," "Adventure to Canton," or any other title you please to give. I have called it "Adventure to Canton." You will perceive that the sum insured is about 10 per cent. larger than the Am't of the Invoice. This is customary in Marine Ins. This Adventure has now cost value, and Bills Pay., Mdse, Haines, Hampton & Co., and Com. have produced value. [D.-B.] Again, Haines, Hampton & Co. have cost value in Cash. [C.-B.]

"

Agreed with John Hollingshead & Co. to bring home for them, from Canton, in the Ship Massachusetts, Fillmore master, 250 Tons Freight @ $20 pr. Ton, allowing them also the privilege of sending out Freight to Canton, by said Ship, to an amount not exceeding 200 Tons, free of charge.

A Captain, 1st and 2d Mates, Carpenter, Steward, Cook, 10 Seamen, and 2 Boys, compose the crew of the Ship Massachusetts.

No Day-Book entry is required for this history. It is a small piece of information furnished you for use hereafter.

HISTORY AND ELUCIDATIONS, SET VI.

New York, July 12th, 1852.

Bo't of various Persons, as pr. Bills, the following Provisions for Ship Massachusetts:

Pr. Check on Phenix Bank, 20 Bbls. Beef @ $11,		220.00		
" " " " " 20 " Pork " 9,		180.00	400.00	
" " " Bank of Com. 100 " Bread " 3,		300.00		
" " " " " Cabin Stores and Small Stores,		450.00	750.00	
Paid Cash for getting 4,000 Gals. Water on board,			10.00	$1,160.00

Keep an account of the outgoes for, and income from the Ship under its own head, separate from the Adventure. Ship Massachusetts costs value. Cash produces value. [C.-B.]

14th

Rec'd the Passage-money of 6 Passengers to Canton, pr. Ship Massachusetts, (which we have deposited in Bank of Commerce,) @ $300, $1,800.00

Ship Massachusetts produces value in Cash. [C.-B.]

The fact that this Cash was deposited in the Bank of Commerce does not alter the entry, and need not be mentioned in the Cash-Book. It is given here that you may be able the better to understand the Check-Book. You will find minute details of the business frequently given in this history, for the purpose of making the whole transactions clear to your mind; but which need not be written in your books. While omitting them, however, you should be careful to leave out nothing which is important to be recorded.

16th

Paid the New York Ins. Co., by our Note No. 5 @ 12 mos., for Ins. on the Ship Massachusetts, for $27,500, @ 7 % 1,925.00

And for policy 1.25 $1,926.25

Ship Massachusetts costs value in Bills Pay. [D.-B.]

"

Paid Custom House Charges in Cash, for Clearance of Ship Massachusetts, which sails this day for Canton, $5.60

Ship Massachusetts costs value in Cash. [C.-B.]

20th

Bills Rec., No. 2, drawn by Wm. Longfellow, favor of S. P. Nixon, deposited in Phenix Bank on the 10th inst. for Collection, comes due this day, and is paid at the Bank. Am't $4,500.00

Cash costs value in Bills Rec. [C.-B.]

In a real business, the Cash-Book would here require an entry of the Cash received, the Bill-Book a memorandum of the payment of this Note, and the Check-Book a record of the deposit in Bank of the proceeds thereof. You may make the entry in the Cash-Book only for the present, but refer to the Bill-Book and Check-Book given, to see the connection between the entries.

Aug. 2d

Chartered of Hollister, Son & Co., the Bark Phillis, of 200 Tons register, for a voyage to Kingston, Jamaica, and back to New York, by way of Havana, with 25 lay days in the two ports. We are to pay all foreign Port Charges, and $2,000 Charter-money—one-half considered earned at Havanna. Demurrage, $25 pr. day.

No Day-Book entry is here requisite.

Lay days are the days agreed upon for a vessel to remain in port. Demurrage is the forfeiture for each day she is detained beyond the time specified in the Charter-party—which is the agreement drawn up between the parties when a vessel is chartered.

"

Passed our Note, No. 6, @ 12 mos., to the American Mutual Ins. Co., for an open policy of Insurance, to cover all shipments by us or consignments to us, during the year, within the limits of the United States, or the West Indies, until the premium on the same amounts to the Note, $2,000.00

This method of *Marine* Insurance is quite customary. The Ins. Co. takes a Note as security for a certain amount of premium, and furnishes the House insuring with an open policy. Then, at any time, when the House ships goods or receives information of goods being shipped to them, they notify the Ins. Co., and get it entered on this open policy. At the end of the year, if no losses have occurred, settlement is made, and so much of the Note is paid as has been used up by the Prem. on goods insured. A per centage is also charged by the Co. (usually 10 per cent.) on the Bal. of the Note. If goods so insured are lost, the Note is returned in part payment thereof.

Here the American Mutual Ins. Co. has cost value in our Note.
Bills Pay. has produced value in the obligation of the Co. on open policy. } [D.-B.]

HISTORY AND ELUCIDATIONS, SET VI.

New York, August 2d, 1852.

Bought of Morton & Godwin, pr. Check on Phenix Bank, Flour, pr. I.-B.,		$4,540.00	
Bought of Otis & Brother, pr. Check on Bank of Commerce, Meal and Corn,		$3,540.00	
Shipped the above on board Bark Phillis, Bingham, master, bound to the West Indies, and consigned as pr. O.-I.-B., p. 1, to Daniel Starr & Co., Kingston, Jamaica, to be sold for our %c and risk. Am't			8,080.00
Insured for the voyage in American Mutual Ins. Co., on open policy, $9,000, @ 3 %	270.00		
And for policy	1.25	271.25	
Drayage and Labor		71.50	
Commission on $8,080, @ 2^{2}%		202.00	544.75
			$8,624.75

Adventure pr. Bark Phillis costs value.
Morton & Godwin, Otis & Brother, American Mutual Ins. Co., Charges, and Commission have each produced value. [D.-B.]
Charges is an account to which we credit all sums charged for drayage, labor, storage, weighing, &c., on goods consigned to us to be sold, and debit sums paid draymen and laborers, when their bills are rendered, or their month's wages is due.
Again, Morton & Godwin and Otis and Brother have cost the firm value in cash. [C.-B.]

10th

Bagley & Thompson's Note, No. 1, Thomas Harvey's favor, fell due and was paid this day, at the Phenix Bank. Am't	$1,000.00

Bills Rec. produces value in Cash. [C.-B.]

24th

Paid Thomas Harvey Cash on %c	$130.00

30th

Jonas Savage & Co.'s Note, No. 3, favor of S. P. Nixon, fell due and was paid this day, at the Bank of Commerce. Am't	$2,225.50

31st

Paid S. P. Nixon on %c pr. Check on Bank of Commerce	125.00	
" Wages of Clerks to date in Cash	95.00	220.00

Sept. 8th

Note No. 4, favor of S. P. Nixon, Ezra Coe & Co. drawers, was this day paid at the Bank of Commerce. Am't	$645.00

22d

Rec'd from John Gundry & Co., Cincinnati, 500 Bbls. Flour, to be sold for their %c and risk. Am't, pr. Invoice, $1,579.75.

Paid Freight on same, pr. Check on Phenix Bank	425.00	
Drayage	15.75	$440.75

You may keep an account of this Flour under the head of "Sales for account of John Gundry & Co.," which now costs the Firm value to the am't of the Freight and Drayage, $440.75, and must be debited therefor in C.-B. and D.-B.
Cash produces the Firm value by paying Freight. [C.-B.]
Charges produces the Firm value in Drayage. [D.-B.]

Oct. 5th

Having rec'd advice, pr. Mail, (by Steamer to Charleston,) that an Invoice was about to be shipped from Havana, pr. Bark Phillis, of upwards of $14,000, we have effected an additional Ins. on open policy, in the American Mutual Ins. Co., for excess of homeward Cargo over the $9,000 insured thereon.

$6,000, @ 1^{2}%	$90.00

Adventure pr. Bark Phillis here costs value.
American Mutual Ins. Co. produces value.

HISTORY AND ELUCIDATIONS, SET VI.

New York, October 11th, 1852.

'he Bark Phillis arrived in port this day, having reached Kingston, Aug. 27th, and Havana Sept. 10th, and having been detained in the two ports 30 days. At Kingston, the Flour, Meal, and Corn were sold, as pr. the following Account-Sales received.

---

ales of Merchandise, received pr. Bark Phillis, Captain Bingham, from New York, for account and risk of Messrs. Thomas Harvey & Co.

		£	s.	d.	£	s.	d.
BEQUER BROTHERS, Payable @ 60 days,							
500 Bbls. Flour	@ 28*s.*				700	0	0
PREVOST & DELANEY, @ 30 days,							
700 Bbls. Corn Meal	@ 18*s.*	630	0	0			
100 Bags Corn	" 8*s.*	40	0	0	670	0	0
S. W. CATTELL & SON,							
500 Bbls. Flour	@ 28*s.*				700	0	0
MITCHELL, ATTERBY & CO., @ 60 days,							
300 Bags Corn	@ 8*s.*	120	0	0			
300 Bbls. Corn Meal	" 18*s.*	270	0	0	390	0	0
					£2,460	0	0
Charges.							
To Cash paid Duties, 1000 Bbls. Flour	@ 3*s.*	150	0	0			
1000 " Meal	" 7½*d.*	31	5	0			
400 Bags Corn	" 3*d.*	5	0	0			
" " " Port Charges on vessel		65	3	3			
" " " Wharfage		30	17	9			
" " " Lighterage		2	4	0			
" Advertising in Kingston papers			8	0			
" Bank Discount on Sales		23	14	6			
" Prem. & Stamps on Sterling Bills Exchange in favor of Suarez Brother & Co., Havana, @ 60 days		33	17	6			
" Com. on £2,460 @ 5 %		123	0	0			
" *Bal., being Net Proceeds of Sales, carried down*		1,994	10	0			
		£2,460	0	0	£2,460	0	0
By Net Proceeds Bro't down					1,994	10	
To a Set of Colonial Bank Bills, on Court Directors, London, in favor of Daniel Starr & Co., and endorsed by them over to Messrs. Suarez Brothers & Co., Havana,		1,000	0	0			
To a Set do. do. do.		794	10	0			
To a Set of Jamaica Bank Bills, on Baring Brothers & Co., London, in favor of Daniel Starr & Co., and endorsed by them over to Messrs. Suarez Brother & Co., Havana, @ 60 days.		200	0	0			
E. & O. E.		£1,994	10	0	£1,994	10	0

Kingston, Jamaica, Sept. 6th, 1852.

DANIEL STARR & CO.
pr. John Brown.

he Sterling Sets of Exchange obtained for the Net Proceeds of this Sale, were taken to Havana, and there sold, as appears by the Account-Current of Suarez Brother & Co., Com. Merchants, @ 9 % Prem., and the proceeds used by them in purchasing Sugars for our a/c, as pr. the following Invoice.

HISTORY AND ELUCIDATIONS, SET VI.

New York, October 11*th*, 1852.

Invoice of Sugars, shipped by Suarez Brother & Co., pr. Bark Phillis, Captain Bingham, for New York, by order, and for account and risk of Messrs. Thomas Harvey & Co.

			Dols.	Rials.	Dols.	Rials.
P. B. #1 to 300	300 Boxes Sugar, ea. 20 arobes (25 lbs. pr. arobe) 6000 arobes, @ 6 rials		4,500	0		
	300 Boxes @ 26 rials		975	0	5,475	0
P. C. #301 to 500	200 Boxes Sugar, ea. 20 arobes, @ 6 rials		3,000	0		
	200 Boxes @ 26 rials		650	0	3,650	0
P. D. #501 to 600	100 Hhds. Sugar, ea. 60 arobes, @ 5 rials		3,750	0		
	100 Hogsheads @ $5		500	0	4,250	0
					$13,375	0
	Charges.					
	Export Duty, 3 rials pr. Box	$187-4				
	7^2 " " Hhd.	93-6	281	2		
	Cartage & Weighing, 2 " " Box	$125-0				
	4 " " Hhd.	50-0	175	0		
	Brokerage on $13,375, @ ½ %		66	7		
	Consul's Certificate		2	0	525	1
					$13,900	1
	Com. on $13,900 @ 2^2 %				347	4
					$14,247	5
	E. & O. E.	*U. S. Currency*, $14,247.63				
	Havana, Cuba, Sept. 28th, 1852.	SUAREZ BROTHER & Co.				

They also paid the Charter money falling due at Havana, and the Port Charges at that place, remunerating themselves for the excess of outlay over the proceeds of the Sets of Exchange received from Kingston by drawing on us for the balance, charging 1^2 % for negotiating the Draft, and 3 % as the rate of exchange required to convert it into Cash:—all of which appears by the following Account-Current.

Messrs. Thomas Harvey & Co.,
In Account with Suarez Brother & Co.

		Dr.		Cr.	
To One-half Am't Charter Money, paid Captain		1,000	00		
" Invoice of Sugars, purchased for them		14,247	63		
" Cash paid Port Charges		556	00		
By a Set of Colonial Bills for £1,000, sold @ 9 % Prem.	$4,844.44				
" " " " " £794.10s. " 9 " "	3,848.91				
" " Jamaica Bank Bills for £200 " 9 " "	968.89			9,662	24
" Our draft on Thomas Harvey & Co., @ 30 d's sight	$6,430.77				
Less Prem. for negotiating 1^2 % and Exch. 3 %	289.38			6,141	39
		$15,803	63	$15,803	63
Havana, Cuba, Sept. 28th, 1852. E. & O. E.					
SUAREZ BROTHER & Co.					

Balance due Suarez Brother & Co. (including Prem. & Exch.) $6,430.77, for which they have drawn on us.

Adventure pr. Bark Phillis, as shown by the foregoing statements, has cost the firm $16,093.01, and has produced the firm $9,662.24. The total cost *might* be debited, and the total proceeds credited, but the same result is accomplished, and with less writing, by debiting only the excess of cost over proceeds, or the amount for which Suarez Brother and Co. have drawn on the firm—$6,430.77.

Suarez Brother & Co., by advancing the additional outlay required for the Adventure, have produced the firm value, and must be credited the Am't due them—$6,430.77. It might seem, that as they have remunerated themselves by drawing on us, therefore nothing is due them, and they should receive no credit. But the Draft has not yet been presented to the firm for acceptance. When it is accepted, Suarez Brother & Co. will receive a debit which will balance their account. See entry of the 20th inst.

HISTORY AND ELUCIDATIONS, SET VI.

New York, October 11*th*, 1852.

Paid pr. Check on Phenix Bank, Duties on Invoice of Sugar, received pr. Bark Phillis, from Havana (Sales of Sugar, No. 1), Am't, $14,247.63, @ 30 % — $4,274.29

This is an expenditure for Adventure pr. Bark Phillis, and *might* be debited directly to that account, but when Mdse. belonging to an Adventure is taken into the Store to be sold, it is customary to open a Sales Account for it, as you would for a Consignor, debiting thereto all charges and expenses, and crediting all Sales; then, when the Mdse. is all sold, the net proceeds are transferred to the Adventure account.

Sales of Sugar, No. 1, has cost value in Cash. [C.-B.]

12th

Paid Hollister, Son & Co. pr. Check on Phenix Bank, for Bal. of Charter Money, due on the voyage of Bark Phillis to the West Indies.	1,000.00	
5 days' Demurrage @ $25 pr. day	125.00	$1,125.00

Adventure pr. Bark Phillis costs value in Cash.

15th

Sold J. Fallstaff & Co., for their Note @ 6 mos., No. 6, 300 Boxes and 100 Hhds. of Sugar, received pr. Bark Phillis (Sales of Sugar, No 1), Am't, pr. S.-B. — $16,455.00

Sales of Sugar, No. 1, has produced value in Bills Rec.

18th

Sold Lyman F. Bache, for his Note @ 6 mos., No. 7, 200 Boxes Sugar, received pr. Bark Phillis, (Sales of Sugar, No. 1,) Am't. pr. S.-B. — $6,240.00

After writing up your Day-Book to this point, you may post it to the Leger, so as to be able to understand more clearly the closure of Sales of Sugar, No. 1, which occurs in the next entry. And in each closure of a Sales account hereafter occurring in this Set, the Leger should be posted up before making the closing entry.

19th

The Sugar belonging to Sales of Sugar, No. 1, has all been sold.

Total Proceeds	22,695.00	
Less Duties entered 11th inst.	4,274.29	$18,420.71
Cooperage, Storage, and Labor	55.50	
Interest on Duties, $4,274.29, for 8 days	5.70	
Our Commission on $22,695 @ 2^2 %	567.38	
Net Proceeds, due pr. Average June 8th, 1853, to be credited to Adventure pr. Bark Phillis,	17,792.13	$18,420.71

Sales of Sugar, No. 1, has cost value in Charges, Int. and Com., and in our obligation to Adventure pr. Bark Phillis, for Net Proceeds of Sales.

This entry is made with a view to close *Sales of Sugar, No.* 1, and at the end of the month, (after the Cash entries have been transferred from the Cash-Book into the Day-Book, and posted,) you may rule and add up that account upon the Leger. You can trace out the details here stated as follows:—Turn to Sales of Sugar, No. 1, in your Leger, and if it is posted up to this point, you will find two credits amounting to $22,695, which, by reference from the Leger to Day-Book, and from the Day-Book to Sales-Book, you will see are the Total Proceeds of Sugar sold. You will also find, on the credit side of your Cash-Book, one debit (not yet posted) of $4,274.29, which you will see is the charge for Duties paid. Deducting these Duties from the Total Proceeds, you have $18,420.71, the Am't which must be debited to the account to close it. This Am't is made up of the following items:

Cooperage, Storage, & Labor, which are supposed to have been preserved in small memorandum books, kept for the purpose, until this time. Int. on Duties from time of payment, so as to bring the charges all up to the present date, for convenience in averaging. Com. of firm on Sales $22,695, at 2^2 %; and Net Proceeds, due Adventure after paying all charges.

20th

Accepted a Bill of Exchange of Messrs. Suarez Bro. & Co., Havana, on us, @ 30 days sight, for — $6,430.77

Suarez Bro. & Co. have cost the firm value in Bills Pay.

22d

There is Interest to be charged Adventure pr. Bark Phillis, as pr. Account-Current of date, (A.-C.-B., fol 1,)	699.09	
The Net Gains, as shown by the Account-Current, are	822.52	$1,521.61

Adventure pr. Bark Phillis has here cost value, and Int. has produced value, $699.09:—and in order to transfer the Net Gains to Profit and Loss account, you must also debit the Adventure, and credit Profit & Loss with $822.52—thus making the entry "Adventure pr. Bark Phillis To Sundries."

30th

Paid Draymen and Laborers in Cash,		94.75	
" Wages of Clerks to date	95.00		
" Rent of Store " "	400.00	495.00	$589.75

Obtained the requisite amount of funds in hand, by checking on Phenix Bank for $600.

Charges and Store Expenses have cost value in Cash.

End of first year's business.

HISTORY AND ELUCIDATIONS, SET VI.

New York, November 1st, 1852.

We have agreed, pr. correspondence, to enter into a Pork Speculation in Company with Faxon, Field & Co., Cincinnati, sharing equally with them in the expenses and proceeds thereof; they to receive 2² % for purchasing, and we 2² % for selling. They have accordingly purchased 1,000 Bbls. Pork, and shipped to us, as pr. advice this day received, on which we have effected an Ins. in the American Mutual Ins. Co., on open policy, for $10,000, @ 1² %. $150.00

We will call this "Sales of Pork, Co. A."

Sales of Pork, Co. A., has here cost value, and American Mutual Ins. Co. has produced value.

2d

John Vanarsdale's Note, S. P. Nixon's favor, No. 5, deposited in the Bank of Commerce on the 18th ult. for collection, falls due this day. Am't $1,960.75

Cash costs value in Bills Receivable. [C.-B.]

5th

Rec'd, pr. Steamboat, Canal, and Railroad, via Pennsylvania, from Faxon, Field & Co., Cincinnati, 1,000 Bbls. Pork, (marked TH,) to be sold for their and our joint ⁰/c, amounting, pr. Invoice of the 26th ult., to $9,256.25, of which our ½ is

		$4,628.12
Paid Freight, pr. Check on Phenix Bank,	850.00	
The Drayage amounts to	31.25	881.25
		$5,509.37

Sales of Pork, Co. A., has cost the Firm value in their indebtedness to F., F. & Co., and in Freight and Drayage. Enter all except the payment of Freight in the Day-Book, [D.-B.]—but place this payment in the Cash-Book, [C.-B.]

6th

Paid the Saratoga Fire Ins. Co., pr. Check on the Bank of Commerce, for Ins. on Stock of Goods

in Store, for one year, to the Am't of $15,000, @ 1² %,	225.00	
Policy	1.25	$226.25

You may debit Charges with this cost, and let it stand to that account, to cover some credits of Ins. which will hereafter occur. Cash has produced value. [C.-B.]

"

Sold to Jeremiah Brown 500 Bbls. Pork, belonging to Co. A., @ $11	$5,500.00
Took his Note, No. 8, @ 30 days, for $5,530.42.	
The Discount on $5,530.42, for 33 days, (to make it equal to Cash,) is	30.42
	$5,530.42

Sales of Pork, Co. A., and Discount have produced value in Bills Rec.

"

Remitted to Faxon, Field & Co., pr. their Order of 1st inst., a Bill of Exchange on Bacon & Boswell, Cincinnati, purchased at par of Clark, Prime & Co., pr. Check on Bank of Commerce, for $5,000.00

Faxon, Field & Co. have cost value in Cash.

8th

Bo't of Caleb Johnson, on our Note, No. 8, @ 6 mos.,

150 Hhds. Cuba Molasses,	15,360 Gals.,	@	19 ¢	2,918.40	
125 " " Sugar,	157,500 lbs.,	"	4²	7,087.50	
500 Bbls. Lard,	100,000 "	"	5¹	5,250.00	$15,255.90

Mdse. has cost value in Bills Payable.

10th

Sold to H. S. Pierson & Co., for their Check on Phenix Bank, which we have deposited,

500 Bbls. Flour—Sales for ⁰/c John Gundry & Co.	—@ $5.	2,500.00	
500 " Pork —Sales of Pork, Co. A.	—" 10.75	5,375.00	$7,875.00

Sales for account of John Gundry & Co., and Sales of Pork, Co. A., have each produced value in Cash.

"

Had J. Brown's Note, No. 8, due Dec. 9th, discounted at the Phenix Bank.

Am't $5,530.42, netting	5,503.69	
Dis. for 29 days is	26.73	$5,530.42

Bills Rec. has produced value in Cash $5,530.42. } [C.-B., one debit, one credit.]
Discount has cost value in Cash $26.73.

12th

Paid at the Phenix Bank our Note, No. 1, favor of A. A. Lawrence & Co. Am't $14,000.00

Bills Pay. has cost value in Cash.

New York, November 15th, 1852.

Rendered J. Gundry & Co. an Account-Sales of 500 Bbls. Flour, consigned to us, to be sold for their a/c.

Am't of Sales, as pr. S.-B.,			2,500.00
Deduct Charges entered Sept. 22d			440.75
Excess of credit now on Leger			$2,059.25
Additional Charges:			
Int. on $440.75 from Sept. 22d	3.97		
Storage, Labor, Cooperage, &c.	60.25		
Commission, @ 2^2 %, on Total Sales	62.50	126.72	
John Gundry & Co.'s Net proceeds, due 12th inst.		1,932.53	$2,059.25

Sales for account of John Gundry & Co. has cost value in the various Charges, and in the Firm's indebtedness to John Gundry & Co. Interest, Charges, Commission, and John Gundry & Co. have produced value—the latter by permitting the Net Proceeds now due them to remain in the hands of the Firm.

"

Rendered Faxon, Field & Co. an a/c Sales of 1,000 Bbls. Pork, sold for a/c of "Sales of Pork, Co. A."

Total Sales			10,875.00
Deduct Charges entered		1,031.25	
" " and Commission as below		465.19	1,496.44
Net Proceeds			$9,378.56
Interest on Charges to date		1.82	
Storage, Labor, Cooperage, &c.	41.50		
Ins. vs. Fire, 1^2 % on $10,000	150.00	191.50	
Com. on 10,875, @ 2^2 %		271.87	
Faxon, Field & Co.'s ½ Net Proceeds, due 10th inst.		4,689.28	$5,154.47

Sales of Pork, Co. A., has cost value in Int., Charges, and Com., and in the indebtedness of the Firm to Faxon, Field & Co., for their Share of the Net Proceeds.

"

Our Share of the Net Proceeds from "Sales of Pork, Co. A.,"		is	4,689.28
" " " First Cost	Do.	was	4,628.12
Making our Net Gains			$61.16

You here debit Sales of Pork, Co. A., with the Gains thereon, and credit Profit & Loss. This is a mere *transfer* entry, to take the Gains to the proper receptacle for them, and the *Rule* for determining debits and credits in transactions does not apply

16th

Sold to James Maitland & Co., for Cash, (dep. in Bank of Commerce,)

500 Bbls. Lard. Am't, pr. S.-B.,	5,250.00	
50 Hhds. Molasses. " "	1,024.00	$6,274.00

Mdse. has produced value in Cash.

22d

Paid, at the Bank of Com., our Note, No. 7, draft of Suarez Brother & Co., Am't $6,430.77

Dec. 6th

Sold to Stiles & Nesmith, for their Check, which we have dep. in the Bank of Commerce, 125 Hhds. Sugar. Am't, pr. S.-B., $7,875.00

10th

Paid James Buchanan, pr. Check on Bank of Commerce, the Bal. due John Gundry & Co., in accordance with advice received from them, as pr. letter of 1st inst.

Am't due Nov. 12th	1,932.53	
Interest for 28 days on $1,932.53	9.02	$1,941.55

John Gundry & Co. and Int. have cost value in Cash.

Jan. 10th, 1853.

The Phenix Bank has discounted J. Falstaff & Co.'s Note, No. 6, due April 18th /53,

Am't $16,455—netting	16,186.23	
Discount for 98 days, on $16,455, is	268.77	$16,455.00

12th

Paid, at the Phenix Bank, our Note, No. 2, favor of A. A. Lawrence & Co. Am't $14,000.00

HISTORY AND ELUCIDATIONS, SET VI.

New York, January 15*th*, 1853.

Faxon, Field & Co., Cincinnati, and Douglass, Forest & Co., of this City, have agreed to join us in a Company Speculation—the parties to share equally; Douglass, Forest & Co. are to furnish White and Brown Sugars, Molasses, &c., at prices agreed upon, for two-thirds of which we are to give them our Note, payable @ 6 mos. One-third so purchased by us is for a/c of Faxon, Field & Co., and to apply against what we owe them. We are to attend to the Business, receiving 2^2% Commission, and 2^2% Guarantee.

Accordingly, we have received this day from Douglass, Forest & Co. an Invoice of Loaf and Crushed White Sugars, Muscovado Sugar, N. O. Molasses, and Rice, delivered at our Store, free of charge. Amounting to $12,465.36.

Gave them our Note, No. 9, @ 6 mos., for our ⅓ of Invoice	4,155.12	
And for Faxon, Field & Co.'s ⅓ " "	4,155.12	$8,310.24

We will call this "Sales of Mdse., Co. B."

Bills Payable has produced the Firm value, $8,310.24.
"Sales of Mdse., Co. B," and Faxon, Field & Co. have each cost the Firm their ⅓ of the Invoice.

21st

Sold James Maitland & Co., on Note No. 9, @ 4 mos., a Lot of Loaf and Crushed White Sugars, belonging to Sales of Mdse., Co. B., Amounting, pr. S.-B., to $4,657.25

Sales of Mdse., Co. B., has produced value in Bills Receivable.

Feb. 1st

Bo't of Bailey & Welsh, on our Note, No. 10, @ 6 mos., 2,000 Sacks of Coffee, 131,520 lbs., @ 6^2¢ $8,548.80

Mdse. has cost value in Bills Payable.

5th

Shipped, pr. D. Leech & Co.'s Line, via Pennsylvania, and consigned to Faxon, Field & Co., Cincinnati, to be sold for their and our a/c jointly, as pr. Correspondence,

2,000 Sacks of Coffee, pr. O.-I.-B., 131,520 lbs., @ 6^2		8,548.80
Insured in American Mutual Ins. Co., on open policy, $9,500, @ 1^2%		142.50
Drayage, Labor, Weighing, Mending Bags, &c.		61.20
Commission on $8,548.80, @ 2^2%		213.72
½ Invoice for a/c of Faxon, Field & Co.	$4,483.11	$8,966.22
½ " " " Adventure to Cincinnati, Co. C.	4,483.11	

Faxon, Field & Co. and Adventure to Cincinnati, Co. C, have cost value.
Mdse., American Mutual Ins. Co., Charges, and Com. have produced value.

19th

Sold to Watson G. Gaylord, for his Note, No. 10, @ 10 days, 50 Tierces Rice, belonging to Sales of Mdse., Co. B. $2,931.50

28th

Rendered Faxon, Field & Co. and Douglass, Forest & Co., each, an a/c Sales of Sugar and Rice,

belonging to "Sales of Mdse., Co. B." Am't, pr. S.-B.			7,588.75
Deduct Charges and Com., as below			496.56
Net Proceeds			$7,092.19
Insurance vs. Fire on $6,500, (½ Am't insured,) @ 1^2%	97.50		
Cooperage, Weighing, and Labor	19.62	117.12	
Commission and Guarantee on $7,588.75, @ 5%		379.44	
Faxon, Field & Co.'s ⅓ Net Proceeds, due April 27th		2,364.06	
Douglass, Forest & Co.'s ⅓ " " " " "		2,364.06	$5,224.68

Sales of Mdse., Co. B., has cost value in Charges, Com., and in the Firm's indebtedness to Faxon, Field & Co., and Douglass, Forest & Co., for their respective shares of Net Proceeds.

As the Mdse. belonging to this Co. is not all sold, the closing entry, transferring Gains into Profit & Loss, is not now to be made in the Day-Book. The closure will, however, be made in the Leger, and our Share of the Bal. remaining on hand be brought down to the New Year's business.

"

Paid Wages of Clerks, (pr. Check on Bank of Com.,)	110.00		
" Rent of Store " " " "	400.00	510.00	
" Laborers & Draymen, " " " "		195.00	$705.00

End of second year's business.

HISTORY AND ELUCIDATIONS, SET VI.

New York, March 1st, 1853.

James L. Grant has been associated as one of the partners of this concern; the firm still to retain its original title, "Thomas Harvey & Co." The former partners are each to share two-fifths, and James L. Grant one-fifth of the gains or losses in business. The partners to receive interest on their several investments.

James L. Grant invests Cash on deposit in Phenix Bank $15,000.00

Cash costs the firm value. James L. Grant produces value in his investment. [C.-B.]

4th

Watson G. Gaylord's Note, No. 10, deposited in Bank of Commerce on the 1st inst. for collection, was this day protested for non-payment, and returned to us 2,931.50

Paid protest in Cash 1.50 $2,933.00

Bills Rec. have a beginning, a duration, and an end. This Note is at an end, it having matured without being paid. It has also subjected the firm to the expense of protest. They therefore consider the drawers responsible to them for the Note and protest, which they retain as evidence of the obligation.

Bill Rec. has produced value in the indebtedness of W. G. Gaylord, $2,931.50. [D.-B.]

Cash has produced value in the indebtedness of W. G. Gaylord, $1.50. [C.-B.]

12th

Paid at the Phenix Bank, our Note, No. 3, favor of A. A. Lawrence & Co., Am't $14,000.00

25th

Gave our Note, No. 11, @ 6 mos., for Insurance effected in the Atlantic Ins. Co., on Cargo of Ship Massachusetts, now on her homeward trip from Canton, for $75,500 @ 1² %, and policy $1,133.75

Adventure to Canton has cost value in Bills Payable.

April 9th

Sold to Leonard Barber & Co., for their Note, No. 11, @ 6 mos.,
The Bal. of Sugars and Molasses belonging to Sales of Mdse., Co. B, Am't pr. S.-B. $5,525.00

"

Rendered an Account-Sales to Faxon, Field & Co., and to Douglass, Forest & Co., of Sugars and Molasses, belonging to Sales of Mdse., Co. B, Am't pr. S.-B.

		5,525.00
Deduct Charges and Commission, as below		383.60
Net Proceeds		$5,141.40
Ins. vs. Fire on $6,500 @ 1² %	97.50	
Cooperage, Weighing, Labor, &c.	9.85	107.35
Commission and Guarantee on $5,525 @ 5 %		276.25
Faxon, Field & Co.'s ⅓ Net Proceeds, due Oct. 26th		1,713.80
Douglass, Forest & Co.'s " " " " " "		1,713.80
		$3,811.20

"

We find, on examination, a Loss on the last Sales effected for % of Mdse., Co. B, of $166.45

When this account was closed in the old books, the Firm's share of Mdse. remaining unsold was estimated at its cost, $1,880.25, while their share of the Net Proceeds now is only $1,713.80. A sudden depreciation in the price of Sugar and Molasses, owing to the market being overstocked, has caused this Loss. Debit Profit & Loss, and credit Sales of Mdse, Co. B, to close it. [D.-B.]

21st

Note No. 7, our favor, Lyman F. Bache drawer, deposited in Phenix Bank on 13th inst., falls due this day, and is paid, Am't $6,240.00

26th

Watson G. Gaylord has paid us Cash for his Note, No. 10, which was protested at the Bank of Commerce on the 4th ult., and charged to his %.

Note and protest 2,933.00

Int. on $2,933, for 53 days 25.91 $2,958.91

Deposited $2,500 in Phenix Bank.

Watson G. Gaylord and Int. have produced value in Cash. [C.-B.]

30th

Sold to Peter Parker, for Check on Phenix Bank, deposited,
100 Hhds. Cuba Molasses, 10,240 Gals. @ 19¢ $1,945,60

Mdse. has produced value in Cash.

HISTORY AND ELUCIDATIONS, SET VI.

New York, May 6th, 1853.

The Ship Massachusetts arrived in port this day, direct from Canton, and we have received from Captain Fillmore the following Account-Sales, Invoices, and Account-Current, rendered by Hughes, Miller & Co., Commission Merchants of that City.

Account-Sales of Merchandise received pr. Ship Massachusetts, Capt. Fillmore, from New York, for account of Thomas Harvey & Co., owners of said Ship.

G. T. C.			
#1 to 500	500 Bales Drills, ea. 40 Pieces=20,000 ps. @ $2.30	46,000	00
#501 to 600	100 Casks Ginseng, Net 270 Piculs ($133\frac{1}{3}$ lbs. ea.) " 50.00	13,500	00
	2,000 Pigs Lead, 1,050 " " 6.50	6,825	00
		66,325	00
	Charges.		
	Labor, Landing, Weighing, &c. $237.00		
	Commission, 2^2 % on $66,325 1,658.12	1,895	12
	Net Proceeds	$64,429	88
	Canton, Dec. 10th, 1852.		
	HUGHES, MILLER & Co.		

Invoice of Tea, shipped by Hughes, Miller & Co., pr. Ship Massachusetts, Captain Fillmore, for New York, by order, and for account of Messrs. Thomas Harvey & Co., owners of said Ship.

Mark.	No.	Chests.	Chops.	Kind.	Bo't of	Gross lbs.	Tare lbs.	Net lbs.	Piculs—Taels.	Taels.	Mace	Can.
G. T.	#1	500h'f Chests	Moi Chun	Pouchong	Yengua	25,500	6,508	18,992	$142\frac{44}{100}$ @ 14	1,994	1	6
	2	1,000 " "	Wo Chun	Y'ngHyson	Eshing	79,974	14,978	64,996	$487\frac{47}{100}$ " 50	24,373	5	0
	3	200 Chests	Yoing	Hyson	"	19,890	3,954	15,936	$119\frac{52}{100}$ " 42	5,019	8	4
	4	500 "	SamChun	HysonSkin	Sungua	50,120	10,040	40,080	$300\frac{60}{100}$ " 11	3,306	6	0
	5	1,000 "	How Tal	Souchong	Eshing	101,256	21,256	80,000	600 " 15	9,000	0	0
										43,694	1	0

@ 72 candarines pr. dollar		$60,686	25
Paid for Matting	80.00		
" " Papers	20.00		
Com. on $60,786.25, @ 2 %	1,215.73	1,315	73
E.E. *Canton, Jan. 1st*, 1853.	Dollars	$62,001	98
HUGHES, MILLER & Co.			

Invoice of Matting, shipped by Hughes, Miller & Co., pr. Ship Massachusetts, Captain Fillmore, for New York, by order, and for account of Messrs. Thomas Harvey & Co., owners of said Ship.

G. T. #6	1,000 Rolls $\frac{4}{4}$ White Matting, ea. 40 Yards, 40,000 Yds., @ 14¢	5,600	00
	Commission on $5,600, @ 2 %	112	00
	Canton, Jan. 1st, 1853. E. E.	$5,712	00
	HUGHES, MILLER & Co.		

Messrs. Thomas Harvey & Co., in Account with Hughes, Miller & Co.

	Dr.		Cr.	
To Invoice of Tea, pr. Massachusetts	62,001	98		
" Do. Matting, Do.	5,712	00		
" Port Charges, Piloting, Wharfage, &c., of Ship Massachusetts	816	20		
" Refitting, Repairs, and Sea Stores for Do.	1,150	00		
By Net Proceeds of Drills, Ginseng, and Lead, pr Do.			64,429	88
" Drafts, @ 6 mos., on Baring, Brothers & Co., London, under Letters of credit dated July 9th /52, for £1,500, @ 4*s.* 4*d.* pr. dollar $6,923.08				
Less Com. for negotiating, 1 % 69.23				
Shroffage, &c. 5.31 74.54			6,848	54
	69,680	18	71,278	42
E. E. Balance due Thomas Harvey & Co.	1,598	24		
Canton, Jan. 1st, 1853.	71,278	42	71,278	42

(Entry continued.)

New York, May 6th, 1853.

(*Entry continued.*)

By the foregoing Account-Current, it appears that Hughes, Miller & Co. have overdrawn their a/c, leaving a balance in our favor, payable in Canton, of 1,598.24
Dis. on $1,682.36 @ 5 %, to convert it into Canton funds 84.12 $1,682.36

It is considered generally to cost about 5 pr. ct. to carry our coin to Canton, or to convert our money, in any way, into funds useable in Canton; therefore the Adventure to Canton has here produced value, $1,682.36, that being the amount in the hands of Hughes, Miller & Co., with the exchange on the same added. Hughes, Miller & Co. and Discount have cost the firm value.

The Adventure to Canton has cost the firm, as shown by Hughes, Miller & Co.'s Account-Current, the amount of their Drafts on Baring Brothers & Co., London. But this will appear in a subsequent entry, where the firm purchase Bills on London to meet them, and therefore no account need now be made of it.

The money in Canton is reckoned in taels, mace, and candarines—10 candarines make a mace, and 10 mace a tael. The weights are piculs, catties, and tales—16 tales to a catty, and 100 catties to a picul. A picul is 133⅓ lbs. avoirdupois weight. Shroffage is the charge made by Shroffs or Bankers.

"

The Account-Current of Hughes, Miller & Co., and Statements of details accompanying it, show that a portion of the proceeds of Adventure to Canton were appropriated to payment of expenses of Ship Massachusetts at Canton, to wit:

Port Charges, Piloting, Wharfage, &c.	816.20		
Refitting, Repairs, and Sea Stores	1,150.00	1,966.20	
To which add 5 % Discount on $2,069.68		103.48	$2,069.68

Ship Massachusetts has cost value, and Adventure to Canton has produced value to the full amount of expenses with the exchange on money.

9th

Rec'd of John Hollingshead & Co., their Check on Bank of Commerce, for Freight on 250 Tons, pr. Ship Massachusetts, from Canton, @ $20 per Ton $5,000.00

Ship Massachusetts has produced value in Cash.

"

Paid, pr. Check on Bank of Commerce, Duties on Matting, received pr. Ship Massachusetts, from Canton (Sales of Matting, No. 2), Am't of Invoice $5,712, @ 25 % $1,428.00

"

There is due the Ship Massachusetts for Freight

On Matting (Sales of Matting, No. 2), 125 Tons, @ $20	2,500.00	
" Tea (Sales of Tea, No. 3), 300 " " 20	6,000.00	$8,500.00

Sales of Matting, No. 2, and Sales of Tea, No. 3, have cost value. Ship Massachusetts has produced value.

"

Checked on Bank of Commerce for $3,500, and paid Wages of Crew of Ship Massachusetts in Cash, as follows:

Captain,	10 mos.		@ $120	1,200.00	
1st Mate,	10 "		" 45	450.00	
2d Mate,	10 "		" 25	250.00	
Carpenter,	9 "	20 days	" 25	241.67	
Steward,	9 "	20 "	" 15	145.00	
Cook,	10 "		" 13	130.00	
10 Seamen,	9 "	20 "	" 13 ea.	1,256.67	
2 Boys,	9 "	20 "	" 7 "	135.33	$3,808.67

Ship Massachusetts has cost value in Cash.

11th

Our Note, No. 8, favor of Caleb Johnson, was paid this day at Phenix Bank, Am't $15,255.90

18th

Myers & Wolbert, Auctioneers, have sold at Auction the Teas belonging to

Sales of Tea, No. 3, Amounting pr. their Ac't-Sales, to	95,441.05	
Less Auction Duty, and Commission 2¼ %	2,147.42	$93,293.63

Received of them Notes, No. 12, 13, 14, and 15, as pr. B.-B., drawn payable @ 6 mos., and endorsed by them.

Sales of Tea, No. 3, have produced value in Bills Receivable.

24th

J. Maitland & Co.'s Note, No. 9, our favor, fell due and was paid at the Bank of Commerce this day. Am't $4,657.25

HISTORY AND ELUCIDATIONS, SET VI.

New York, June 1st, 1853.

The Total Proceeds of Sales of Tea, No. 3, Am't to	93,293.63	
Deduct Charges entered	6,000.00	$87,293.63
Additional Charges, Cartage	110.00	
Labor, receiving and delivering	82.00	
1 mos. Storage	64.00	256.00
Interest on Charges to date		23.00
Com. and Guar. on $93,293.63 @ 5 %		4,664.68
Net Proceeds, due Adventure to Canton, pr. average, Dec. 14th		82,349.95
		$87,293.63

10th

Sold to Fithian & Morris, for their Note, No. 16, @ 4 mos.	
1000 Rolls 4/4 White Matting, 40,000 Yds., @ 21¢	$8,400.00

Sales of Matting, No. 2, has produced value in Bills Receivable.

11th

Rec'd an Account-Sales from Faxon, Field & Co., Cincinnati, of Coffee belonging to Adventure to Cincinnati, Co. C.	
Net Proceeds $9,422.72, due pr. average Aug. 10th. Our ½ is	$4,711.36

Adventure to Cincinnati, Co. C, has produced value in the indebtedness of Faxon, Field & Co.

"

Paid S. P. Nixon, on %c pr. Check on Bank of Commerce	500.00	
" Thos. Harvey, " " " " " " " "	450.00	$950.00

15th

The Total Proceeds of Sales of Matting, No. 2, Am't as pr. S.-B. to	8,400.00	
Deduct Charges entered	3,928.00	$4,472.00
Additional Charges, Cartage	15.00	
Labor, receiving and delivering	30.00	45.00
Interest on Charges to date		24.22
Com. and Guar. on $8,400, @ 5 %		420.00
Net Proceeds, due Adventure to Canton, pr. average Feb. 23d, 1854		3,982.78
		$4,472.00

18th

Bo't of Brown & Co., pr. Check on Bank of Commerce, a Set of Exchange, @ 90 days' sight, on Baring Brothers & Co., London, and remitted the same to cover Hughes, Miller & Co.'s Drafts from Canton, Jan. 1st, @ 6 mos. sight, due in London, Oct. 3d,	£1,500	
London Bankers Com. 2 %	30	£1,530.
£1,530, @ 8 % Prem.		$7,344.00

20th

Bal. of Int. to be debited Adventure to Canton, pr. Account-Current of date	4,167.21
Net Gains, as shown by the Account-Current	11,783.56
	$15,950.77

30th

Checked on Bank of Commerce for $900, and paid in Cash,		
Wages of Clerks	265.50	
Rent of Store	400.00	665.50
Draymen and Laborers		237.00
		$902.50

"

The debit Bal. of Interest on the %c of Ship Massachusetts, reckoned to July 1st, is	$1,431.84

Ship Massachusetts has cost value. Interest has produced value.

"

Due Thos. Harvey,	Int. on Capital to July 1st	735.06
" S. P. Nixon	" " " " " "	735.00
" James L. Grant,	" " " " " "	300.00
		$1,770.06

Interest has cost the firm value. Each partner has produced the firm value.

THOMAS HARVEY & CO.

DAY-BOOK A, SET VI.

DAY-BOOK A, SET VI.

New-York, July 2d, 1852.

L. F.						
	Thomas Harvey and Salmon P. Nixon have this day entered into partnership, as pr. articles of agreement.					
1	Sundries	To Thomas Harvey,				
1	Ship Massachusetts,	Valued at	25,000	00		
1	Bills Receivable,	No. 1, due Aug. 10th, pr. B.-B.	1,000	00	26,000	00
1	Sundries	To Salmon P. Nixon,				
1	Bills Receivable,	No. 2, due July 20th, pr. B.-B. 4,500.00				
		No. 3, " Aug. 30th, " " 2,225.50				
		No. 4, " Sept. 8th, " " 645.00				
		No. 5, " Nov. 2d, " " 1,960.75	9,331	25		
2	Merchandise,	Ginseng, pr. I.-B., fol. 1, Am't	14,000	00		
2	Expenses,	Store Fixtures, valued at	600	00	23,931	25
	9th					
1	Adventure to Canton	To Sundries,				
		For Mdse., as pr. O.-I.-B., fol. 1, shipped on board Ship Massachusetts, and consigned to Hughes, Miller & Co., Canton, China, to be sold for our % and risk, and for Expenses attending Shipment. Due pr. Average, Nov. 12th.				
2	To Bills Payable,	Paid A. A. Lawrence & Co., for Drills, as pr. I.-B. fol. 1, by our Notes, No. 1, @ 4 mos., 14,000.00				
		No. 2, " 6 " 14,000.00				
		No. 3, " 8 " 14,000.00				
		Also gave our Note, No. 4, @ 12 mos., to the Atlantic Ins. Co. for Ins. on $72,000 @ 1½ % and Policy 1,081.25	43,081	25		
2	" Merchandise,	Ginseng, from Store, pr. I.-B., fol. 1	14,000	00		
2	" Haines, Hampton & Co.,	Bill of Lead " " " "	7,000	00		
3	" Commission,	On $63,000 @ 2½%	1,575	00	65,656	25
	16th					
1/2	Ship Massachusetts	To Bills Payable,				
		Our Note, No. 5, @ 12 mos., favor of New York Ins. Co., for Ins. on this Ship for $27,500 @ 7% and Policy			1,926	25
	31st					
2	Cash	To Sundries, pr. C.-B.				
1	To Thomas Harvey,	2d			9,000	00
1	" Salmon P. Nixon,	"			11,068	75
1	" Ship Massachusetts,	14th			1,800	00
1	" Bills Receivable,	20th			4,500	00
					26,368	75
	"					
2	Sundries	To Cash, pr. C.-B.				
2	Haines, Hampton & Co.,	9th			7,000	00
1	Ship Massachusetts,	12th	1,160	00		
	" "	16th	5	60	1,165	60
					8,165	60
	Aug. 2d					
3/2	American Mutual Ins. Co.	To Bills Payable,				
		Issued our Note, No. 6, @ 12 mos., for an open policy of Ins. on all Shipments by us, or Consignments to us, during the year, within the limits of the United States or West Indies, until the Prem. on the same amounts to the Note.			2,000	00

DAY-BOOK A, SET VI.

New York, August 2d, 1852.

L. F.					
3	Adventure pr. Bark Phillis To Sundries,				
	For Mdse. shipped pr. Bark Phillis, Bingham master, as pr. O.-I.-B., fol. 1, and consigned to Daniel Starr & Co., Kingston, Jamaica, to be sold for our % and risk, and for Expenses of Shipment.				
4	To Morton & Godwin, Flour, pr. I.-B.	4,540	00		
4	" Otis & Brother, Meal and Corn, pr. I.-B.	3,540	00		
3	" American Mutual Ins. Co.,				
	For Ins. on $9,000 @ 3% and Policy	271	25		
3	" Charges, Drayage and Labor	71	50		
3	" Commission, On $8,080 @ 2½%	202	00	8,624	75
	31st				
2/1	Cash To Bills Receivable, pr. C.-B., 10th	1,000	00		
	" " " " " 30th	2,225	50	3,225	50
	"				
2	Sundries To Cash, pr. C.-B.				
4	Morton & Godwin, 2d			4,540	00
4	Otis & Brother, "			3,540	00
1	Thomas Harvey, 24th			130	00
1	S. P. Nixon, 31st			125	00
2	Expenses, "			95	00
				8,430	00
	Sept. 22d				
3/3	Sales for a/c of John Gundry & Co. To Charges,				
	Drayage on 500 Bbls. Flour, to be sold for % and risk of J. Gundry & Co., Cincinnati, Am't pr. Invoice, $1,579.75			15	75
	30th				
2/1	Cash To Bills Receivable, pr. C.-B., 8th			645	00
	"				
3/2	Sales for a/c of John Gundry & Co. To Cash, pr. C.-B., 22d			425	00
	Oct. 5th				
3/3	Adventure pr. Bark Phillis To American Mutual Ins. Co.				
	Ins. on Excess of homeward Cargo from Havana, $6,000 @ 1½%			90	00
	11th				
3/4	Adventure pr. Bark Phillis To Suarez, Brother & Co.,				
	For Excess of Expenditures by Suarez, Bro. & Co., Havana, for % of this Adventure, over the proceeds resulting to them from same, as pr. their Ac't-Current, and other Papers, Rec'd pr. Bark Phillis.			6,430	77
	15th				
1/4	Bills Receivable To Sales of Sugar, No. 1,				
	J. Fallstaff & Co.'s Note, No. 6, @ 6 mos., for Sugar pr. S.-B.			16,455	00
	18th				
1/4	Bills Receivable To Sales of Sugar, No. 1,				
	Lyman F. Bache's Note, No. 7, @ 6 mos., for Sugar pr. S.-B.			6,240	00

DAY-BOOK A, SET VI.

New York, October 19th, 1852.

L. F.	Particulars	Details				
4	Sales of Sugar, No. 1 To Sundries,					
	The total sales for this % Am't to	22,695.00				
	Deduct Duties entered 11th inst.	4,274.29 $18,420.71				
3	To Charges,	Cooperage, Storage and Labor	55	50		
4	" Interest,	On Duties, $4,274.29, for 8 d's	5	70		
3	" Commission,	On $22,695 @ 2 1/2 %	567	38		
3	" Adv. pr. Bark Phillis,	Net proceeds, due June 8th, /53	17,792	13	18,420	71
	20th					
4/2	Suarez, Brother & Co. To Bills Payable,					
	Accepted their Bill of Exchange on us, @ 30 days' sight				6,430	77
	22d					
3	Adventure pr. Bark Phillis To Sundries,					
4	To Interest,	As pr. Ac't-Current, A.-C.-B. fol. 1	699	09		
4	" Profit & Loss,	Net Gains, pr. Ac't-Current	822	52	1,521	61
	30th					
2	Sundries To Cash,	pr. C.-B.				
4	Sales of Sugar, No. 1,	11th			4,274	29
3	Adventure pr. Bark Phillis,	12th			1,125	00
3	Charges,	30th			94	75
2	Expenses,	"			495	00
					5,989	04

End of first year.

L. F.	Particulars	Details				
	November 1st, 1852.					
5	Sales of Pork, Co. A					
3	To American Mutual Ins. Co.,					
	Ins. on Pork shipped to us by Faxon, Field & Co., Cincinnati, as pr. Advice, $10,000 @ 1 1/2 %				150	00
	5th					
5	Sales of Pork, Co. A To Sundries,					
	Rec'd from Faxon, Field & Co., Cincinnati, 1,000 Bbls. Pork, Am't pr. Invoice $9,256.25, to be sold on joint %.					
5	To Faxon, Field & Co.,	Our 1/2 Invoice	4,628	12		
3	" Charges,	Drayage	31	25	4,659	37
	6th					
1	Bills Receivable To Sundries,					
	Rec'd of Jeremiah Brown his Note, No. 8, @ 30 days, in Pay't of Pork sold to him, and for Discount.					
5	To Sales of Pork, Co. A,	500 Bbls. Pork @ $11.	5,500	00		
4	" Discount,	On $5,530.42 for 33 days.	30	42	5,530	42
	8th					
2/2	Merchandise To Bills Payable,					
	Bo't of Caleb Johnson, on our Note @ 6 mos., No. 8, Molasses, Sugar and Lard, pr. Invoice				15,255	90
	15th					
3	Sales for a/c of John Gundry & Co. To Sundries,					
	Rendered J. Gundry & Co. an Ac't-Sales of 500 Bbls. Flour,					
	Total Sales,	2,500.00				
	Deduct Charges entered	440.75 $2,059.25				

Entry continued

DAY-BOOK A, SET VI.

New York, November 15*th*, 1852.

L. F.						
√	Sales for a/c of J. Gundry & Co. To Sundries (*continued*).					
4	To Interest,	On $440.75 from Sept. 22d	3	97		
3	" Charges,	Storage, Labor, Cooperage, &c.	60	25		
3	" Commission,	On $2,500 @ 2½%	62	50		
5	" John Gundry & Co.,	Net Proceeds, due 12th inst.	1,932	53	2,059	25
	15th					
5	Sales of Pork, Co. A To Sundries,					
	Rendered Faxon, Field & Co., an Ac't-Sales of 1,000 Bbls. Pork,					
	Total Sales 10,875.00					
	Deduct Charges entered 1,031.25					
	" do. and Com. as below 465.19 1,496.44					
	Net Proceeds $9,378.56					
4	To Interest,	On Charges to date	1	82		
3	" Charges,	Storage, Labor, Cooperage, &c. 41.50				
		Ins. vs. Fire, $10,000 @ 1½% 150.00	191	50		
3	" Commission,	On $10,875 @ 2½%	271	87		
5	" Faxon, Field & Co.,	Their ½ Net Proceeds, due 10th inst.	4,689	28	5,154	47
	"					
5/4	Sales of Pork, Co. A To Profit & Loss,					
	Our ½ Net Proceeds $4,689.28					
	Our ½ First Cost 4,628.12 therefore we have gained				61	16
	30th					
2	Cash To Sundries,	pr. C.-B.				
1	To Bills Receivable,	2d	1,960	75		
	" " "	10th	5,530	42	7,491	17
3	" Sales for a/c of John Gundry & Co.,	"			2,500	00
5	" Sales of Pork, Co. A,	"			5,375	00
2	" Merchandise,	16th			6,274	00
					21,640	17
	"					
2	Sundries To Cash,	pr. C.-B.				
5	Sales of Pork, Co. A,	5th			850	00
3	Charges,	6th			226	25
5	Faxon, Field & Co.,	"			5,000	00
4	Discount,	10th			26	73
2	Bills Payable,	12th	14,000	00		
	"	22d	6,430	77	20,430	77
					26,533	75
	Dec. 31st					
2/2	Cash To Merchandise,	pr. C.-B., 6th			7,875	00
	"					
2	Sundries To Cash,	pr. C.-B.				
5	John Gundry & Co.,	10th			1,932	53
4	Interest,	"			9	02
					1,941	55
	Jan. 15th, 1853					
2	Sundries To Bills Payable,					
	Our Note, No. 9, @ 6 mos., favor of Douglass, Forest & Co., for two-thirds Invoice of Sugars, Molasses and Rice, to be sold for the joint a/c of Douglass, Forest & Co., Faxon, Field & Co., and ourselves:—Am't pr. Invoice $12,465.36.					
5	Sales of Mdse., Co. B,	Our ⅓ of Speculation	4,155	12		
5	Faxon, Field & Co.,	Their ⅓ " "	4,155	12	8,310	24

DAY-BOOK A, SET VI.

New York, January 21st, 1853.

L. F.						
1/5	Bills Receivable	To Sales of Mdse., Co. B,				
	Rec'd of James Maitland & Co. their Note, No. 9, @ 4 mos., for a Lot of Loaf & Crushed White Sugars. Am't pr. S.-B.				4,657	25
	31st					
2/1	Cash	To Bills Receivable, pr. C.-B., 10th			16,455	00
	"					
2	Sundries	To Cash, pr. C.-B.				
4	Discount,	10th			268	77
2	Bills Payable,	12th			14,000	00
					14,268	77
	Feb. 1st					
2/2	Merchandise	To Bills Payable,				
	No. 10, @ 6 mos., favor of Baily & Welsh, for Coffee, pr. Invoice				8,548	80
	5th					
	Sundries	To Sundries,				
	Consigned to Faxon, Field & Co., Cin'i, an Invoice of Coffee, as pr. O.-I.-B., to be sold for their and our joint %.					
5	Faxon, Field & Co.,	Their ½ Adv.	4,483	11		
5	Adv. to Cincinnati, Co. C,	Our ½ "	4,483	11		
2	To Merchandise,	2000 Sacks Coffee			8,548	80
3	" American Mutual Ins. Co.,	Ins. on $9,500 @ 1½%			142	50
3	" Charges,	Drayage, Labor, Weighing, &c.			61	20
3	" Commission,	On $8,548.80 @ 2½%			213	72
	19th					
1/5	Bills Receivable	To Sales of Mdse., Co. B,				
	Note of W. G. Gaylord, No. 10, @ 10 d's, for Rice, as pr. S.-B.				2,931	50
	28th					
5	Sales of Mdse., Co. B	To Sundries,				
	Rendered Faxon, Field & Co. and Douglass, Forest & Co. each an Account-Sales. Am't, as pr. S.-B.	7,588.75				
	Deduct Charges & Com. as below	496.56				
	Net Proceeds	$7,092.19				
3	To Charges,	Ins. vs. Fire on $6,500 @ 1½% 97.50				
		Cooperage, Weighing & Labor 19.62	117	12		
3	" Commission,	Com. & Guar. on $7,588.75 @ 5%	379	44		
5	" Faxon, Field & Co.,	Their ½ Net Proceeds, due Apr. 27th	2,364	06		
5	" Douglass, Forest & Co.,	" " " " " " "	2,364	06	5,224	68
	"					
2	Sundries	To Cash, pr. C.-B.				
2	Expenses,	28th			510	00
3	Charges,	"			195	00
					705	00

THOMAS HARVEY & CO.

DAY-BOOK B, SET VI.

DAY-BOOK B, SET VI.

New York, March 4th, 1853.

L. F.	Particulars				
4/2	Watson G. Gaylord — To Bills Receivable,				
	Note No. 10 protested at Bank of Commerce			2,931	50
	25th				
2/2	Adventure to Canton — To Bills Payable,				
	For Note No. 11, @ 6 mos., to the Atlantic Ins. Co., for Ins. on Cargo homeward from Canton, $75,000 @ 1^2 % and Policy			1,133	75
	31st				
1/1	Cash — To James L. Grant, pr. C.-B., 1st			15,000	00
	"				
1	Sundries — To Cash, pr. C.-B.				
4	Watson G. Gaylord, 4th			1	50
2	Bills Payable, 12th			14,000	00
				14,001	50
	Apr. 9th				
2/3	Bills Receivable — To Sales of Mdse., Co. B.,				
	Rec'd of Leonard Barber & Co. their Note, No. 11, @ 6 mos., for Sugars and Molasses, Am't pr. S.-B.			5,525	00
	"				
3	Sales of Mdse., Co. B — To Sundries,				
	Rendered to Faxon, Field & Co. and Douglass, Forest & Co., Account-Sales of Sugars and Molasses, belonging to this Co., Am't pr. S.-B., 5,525.00				
	Deduct Charges and Com. as below 383.60				
	Net Proceeds $5,141.40				
3	To Charges, Ins. vs. Fire on $6,500 @ 1^2 % 97.50; Cooperage, Weighing, Labor, &c. 9.85	107	35		
3	" Commission, Com. & Guar. on $5,525 @ 5 %	276	25		
2	" Faxon, Field & Co., Their ½ Net Proceeds, due Oct. 26th	1,713	80		
3	" Douglass, Forest & Co., " " " " " " "	1,713	80	3,811	20
	"				
3/3	Profit & Loss — To Sales of Mdse., Co. B.,				
	For our Net Loss on Sales effected for Co.			166	45
	30th				
1	Cash — To Sundries, pr. C.-B.				
2	To Bills Receivable, 21st			6,240	00
4	" Watson G. Gaylord, 26th			2,933	00
4	" Interest, "			25	91
2	" Merchandise, 30th			1,945	60
				11,144	51
	May 6th				
2	Sundries — To Adventure to Canton,				
4	Hughes, Miller & Co., Bal. in our favor, payable in Canton. as pr. their Ac't-Current, and other Papers Rec'd pr. Ship Mass.	1,598	24		
4	Discount, On $1,682.36 @ 5 %	84	12	1,682	36
	"				
1/2	Ship Massachusetts — To Adventure to Canton,				
	Expenses of the Ship at Canton, as pr. Account-Current of Hughes, Miller & Co., $1,966.20, with 5 % Dis. added			2,069	68

New York, May 9th, 1853.

L. F.	Account	Particulars				
1	Sundries	To Ship Massachusetts,				
4	Sales of Matting, No. 2,	Freight on 125 Tons @ $20.	2,500	00		
4	Sales of Tea, No. 3,	" " 300 " " 20.	6,000	00	8,500	00
	18th					
2/4	Bills Receivable	To Sales of Tea, No. 3,				
		Rec'd of Myers & Wolbert, Auctioneers, Notes No. 12, 13, 14 and 15, @ 6 mos., as pr. B.-B., endorsed by them, in Pay't of Teas sold, Am't pr. their Ac't-Sales 95,441.05				
		Less Auction Duty and Com. 2¹ % 2,147.42			93,293	63
	31st					
1	Cash	To Sundries, pr. C.-B.				
1	To Ship Massachusetts,	9th			5,000	00
2	" Bills Receivable,	24th			4,657	25
					9,657	25
	"					
1	Sundries	To Cash, pr. C.-B.				
4	Sales of Matting, No. 2,	9th			1,428	00
1	Ship Massachusetts	"			3,808	67
2	Bills Payable,	11th			15,255	90
					20,492	57
	June 1st					
4	Sales of Tea, No. 3	To Sundries,				
		Total Proceeds of Sales of Tea 93,293.63				
		Deduct Duties entered 6,000.00 $87,293.63				
3	To Charges,	Cartage 110.00				
		Labor receiving & delivering 82.00				
		1 mo. Storage 64.00	256	00		
4	" Interest,	On Charges to date	23	00		
3	" Commission,	Com. & Guar. on $93,293.63 @ 5 %	4,664	68		
2	" Adventure to Canton,	Net Proceeds, due Dec. 14th	82,349	95	87,293	63
	10th					
2/4	Bills Receivable	To Sales of Matting, No. 2,				
		Rec'd of Fithian & Morris their Note, No. 16, @ 4 mos., for 1,000 Rolls $\frac{4}{4}$ White Matting, 40,000 Yds. @ 21¢			8,400	00
	11th					
2/3	Faxon, Field & Co.	To Adventure to Cincinnati, Co. C,				
		Rec'd from them an Account-Sales of Coffee belonging to this Adventure. Net Proceeds $9,422.72 due, pr. average, Aug. 10th. Our ½ is			4,711	36
	15th					
4	Sales of Matting, No. 2	To Sundries,				
		Total Sales of Matting, pr. S.-B., 8,400.00				
		Deduct Charges entered 3,928.00 $4,472.00				
3	To Charges,	Cartage 15.00				
		Labor receiving & delivering 30.00	45	00		
4	" Interest,	On Charges to date	24	22		
3	" Commission,	Com. & Guar. on $8,400 @ 5 %	420	00		
2	" Adventure to Canton,	Net Proceeds, due Feb. 23d /54	3,982	78	4,472	00
	20th					
2	Adventure to Canton	To Sundries,				
4	To Interest,	Debit Bal., pr. Ac't-Current of date	4,167	21		
3	" Profit & Loss	Net Gains, " " " " "	11,783	56	15,950	77

DAY-BOOK B, SET VI.

New York, June 30th, 1853.

L. F.				
1/4	Ship Massachusetts To Interest,			
	Debit Bal. of Int. on the Ship's %, to July 1st			1,431 84
	30th			
4	Interest To Sundries,			
1	To Thos. Harvey, Int. on Capital to July 1st		735 06	
1	" S. P. Nixon, " " " " " "		735 00	
1	" Jas. L. Grant, " " " " " "		300 00	1,770 06
	"			
1	Sundries To Cash,	pr. C.-B.		
1	S. P. Nixon,	12th		500 00
1	Thos. Harvey,	"		450 00
2	Adventure to Canton,	18th		7,344 00
4	Expenses,	30th		665 50
3	Charges,	"		237 00
				9,196 50

THOMAS HARVEY & CO.

CASH-BOOK, SET VI.

CASH-BOOK, SET VI.

Dr. *Cash.*

1852.					
July	2	To Thomas Harvey,	Amount invested	9,000	00
"	"	" Salmon P. Nixon,	" "	11,068	75
"	14	" Ship Massachusetts,	Passage money of 6 Passengers to Canton	1,800	00
"	20	" Bills Receivable,	No. 2, collected at Phenix Bank	4,500	00
				26,368	75
Aug.	2	To Balance,	Brought down from July 31st	18,203	15
"	10	" Bills Receivable,	No. 1 collected at Phenix Bank	1,000	00
"	30	" Do.	No. 3, " " Bank of Commerce	2,225	50
				21,428	65
Sept.	1	To Balance,	From Aug. 31st	12,998	65
"	8	" Bills Receivable,	No. 4, collected at Bank of Commerce	645	00
				13,643	65
Oct.	1	To Balance,	From Sept. 30th	13,218	65
				13,218	65
Nov.	1	To Balance,	From Oct. 30th	7,229	61
"	2	" Bills Receivable,	No. 5, collected at Bank of Commerce	1,960	75
"	10	" Sales for a/c of John Gundry & Co.,			
			500 Bbls. Flour, sold H. S. Pierson & Co., @ $5.	2,500	00
"	"	" Sales of Pork, Co. A.,	500 " " " " " $10.75	5,375	00
"	"	" Bills Receivable,	No. 8, discounted at Phenix Bank	5,530	42
"	16	" Merchandise,	Sale to J. Maitland & Co., Am't pr. S.-B.	6,274	00
				28,869	78
Dec.	1	To Balance,	From Nov. 30th	2,336	03
"	6	" Merchandise,	Sale to Stiles & Nesmith, Am't pr. S.-B.	7,875	00
				10,211	03

Cash. *Cr.*

Date		Account	Particulars		Amount
1852. July	9	By Haines, Hampton & Co.,	Paid for Bill of Lead		7,000 00
"	12	" Ship Massachusetts,	" various Bills for Provisions and Water		1,160 00
"	16	" Do.	" Custom House charges for Clearance		5 60
"	31	" *Balance,*	*In Bank of Commerce*	$4,800.00	
			" Phenix Bank	13,100.00	
			" Safe	303.15	18,203 15
					26,368 75
Aug.	2	By Morton & Godwin,	For Flour, pr. I.-B.		4,540 00
"	"	" Otis & Brother,	" Meal and Corn, pr. I.-B.		3,540 00
"	24	" Thomas Harvey,	On %		130 00
"	31	" S. P. Nixon,	" "		125 00
"	"	" Expenses,	Wages of Clerks		95 00
"	"	" *Balance,*	*In Bank of Commerce*	$3,360.50	
			" Phenix Bank	9,560.00	
			" Safe	78.15	12,998 65
					21,428 65
Sept.	22	By Sales for a/c of John Gundry & Co.,	Freight on 500 Bbls. Flour from Cincinnati, on consignment		425 00
"	30	" *Balance,*	*In Bank of Commerce*	$4,005.50	
			" Phenix Bank	9,135.00	
			" Safe	78.15	13,218 65
					13,643 65
Oct.	11	By Sales of Sugar, No. 1,	Duties on Invoice of Sugar from Havana, Am't $14,247.63 @ 30 %		4,274 29
"	12	" Adventure pr. Bark Phillis,	Paid Hollister, Son & Co., Bal. of Charter money $1,000, and 5 days' Demurrage $125.		1,125 00
"	30	" Charges,	Paid Draymen & Laborers		94 75
"	"	" Expenses,	Wages of Clerks $95, Rent of Store $400.		495 00
"	"	" *Balance,*	*In Bank of Commerce*	$4,005.50	
			" Phenix Bank	3,135.71	
			" Safe	88.40	7,229 61
					13,218 65
Nov.	5	By Sales of Pork, Co. A.,	Freight on 1,000 Bbls. Pork, from Cincinnati		850 00
"	6	" Charges,	Effected Ins. in the Saratoga Fire Ins. Co., on Stock of Goods in Store, for one year, to the Am't of $15,000 @ 1½ %, & Policy		226 25
"	"	" Faxon, Field & Co.,	Remitted, as pr. their Order of 1st inst., a Bill of Exchange on Bacon & Boswell, Cin'i, purchased @ par of Clark, Prime & Co.		5,000 00
"	10	" Discount,	On Bills Rec. No. 8, pr. contra, for 29 days		26 73
"	12	" Bills Payable,	No. 1, paid at Phenix Bank		14,000 00
"	22	" Do.	No. 7, " " Bank of Commerce		6,430 77
"	30	" *Balance,*	*In Bank of Commerce*	$583.23	
			" Phenix Bank	1,664.40	
			" Safe	88.40	2,336 03
					28,869 78
Dec.	10	By John Gundry & Co.,	Paid to J. Buchanan, pr. their Order		1,932 53
"	"	" Interest,	On the above from Nov. 12th		9 02
"	31	" *Balance,*	*In Bank of Commerce*	$6,516.68	
			" Phenix Bank	1,664.40	
			" Safe	88.40	8,269 48
					10,211 03

CASH-BOOK, SET VI.

Dr. *Cash.*

1853.					
Jan.	1	To Balance,	From fol. 1, Dec. 31st /52	8,269	48
"	10	" Bills Receivable,	No. 6, discounted at Phenix Bank	16,455	00
				24,724	48
Feb.	1	To Balance,	From Jan. 31st	10,455	71
				10,455	71
Mar.	1	To Balance,	From Feb. 28th	9,750	71
"	"	" James L. Grant,	Am't invested on entering the Firm	15,000	00
				24,750	71
Apr.	1	To Balance,	From Mar. 31st	10,749	21
"	21	" Bills Receivable,	No. 7, collected at Phenix Bank	6,240	00
"	26	" Watson G. Gaylord,	Rec'd in full for Note No. 10, protested at Bank of Commerce on the 4th ult., and charged to his %—Note $2,931.50, Protest $1.50	2,933	00
"	"	" Interest,	On $2,933, for 53 days	25	91
"	30	" Merchandise,	Sale to Peter Parker, pr. S.-B.	1,945	60
				21,893	72
May	2	To Balance,	From Apr. 30th	21,893	72
"	9	" Ship Massachusetts,	Rec'd of John Hollingshead & Co. for Freight from Canton, 250 Tons @ $20 pr. Ton	5,000	00
"	24	" Bills Receivable,	No. 9, collected at Bank of Commerce	4,657	25
				31,550	97
June	1	To Balance,	From May 31st	11,058	40
				11,058	40
1853.					
July	1	To Balance,	From June 30th	1,861	90

CASH-BOOK, SET VI.

Cash. *Cr.*

1853.						
Jan.	10	By Discount,	On Bills Rec. No. 6, pr. contra, for 98 days		268	77
"	12	" Bills Payable	No. 2, paid at Phenix Bank		14,000	00
"	31	" *Balance,*	*In Bank of Commerce*	$6,516.68		
			" *Phenix Bank*	3,850.63		
			" *Safe*	88.40	10,455	71
					24,724	48
Feb.	28	By Expenses,	Wages of Clerks $110, Rent of Store $400.		510	00
"	"	" Charges,	Paid Laborers & Draymen		195	00
"	"	" *Balance,*	*In Bank of Commerce*	$5,811.68		
			" *Phenix Bank*	3,850.63		
			" *Safe*	88.40	9,750	71
					10,455	71
Mar.	4	By Watson G. Gaylord,	Paid Protest of his Note, No. 10		1	50
"	12	" Bills Payable,	No. 3, paid at Phenix Bank		14,000	00
"	31	" *Balance,*	*In Bank of Commerce*	$5,811.68		
			" *Phenix Bank*	4,850.63		
			" *Safe*	86.90	10,749	21
					24,750	71
Apr.	30	*By Balance,*	*In Bank of Commerce*	$5,811.68		
			" *Phenix Bank*	15,536.23		
			" *Safe*	545.81	21,893	72
					21,893	72
May	9	By Sales of Matting, No. 2,	Duties on Invoice from Canton, $5,712 @ 25 %		1,428	00
"	"	" Ship Massachusetts,	Wages of Crew		3,808	67
"	11	" Bills Payable,	No. 8, paid at Phenix Bank		15,255	90
"	31	" *Balance,*	*In Bank of Commerce*	$10,540.93		
			" *Phenix Bank*	280.33		
			" *Safe*	237.14	11,058	40
					31,550	97
June	12	By S. P. Nixon,	On %		500	00
"	"	" Thomas Harvey,	" "		450	00
"	18	" Adventure to Canton,	Bo't of Brown & Co. a Set of Exchange, @ 90 days' sight, on Baring, Brothers & Co., London, and remitted the same to cover Hughes, Miller & Co.'s Drafts from Canton, Jan. 1st, @ 6 mos.' sight, due in London Oct. 3d, £1,500, and for London Banker's Com. 2 % £30. Total £1,530, @ 8 % Prem.		7,344	00
"	30	" Expenses,	Wages of Clerks $265.50, Rent of Store $400		665	50
"	"	" Charges,	Paid Draymen & Laborers		237	00
"	"	" *Balance,*	*In Bank of Commerce*	$1,346.93		
			" *Phenix Bank*	280.33		
			" *Safe*	234.64	1,861	90
					11,058	40

THOMAS HARVEY & CO.

LEGER A.

SET VI.

INDEX.

LEGER A, SET VI.

Thomas Harvey.

Dr.											Cr.
1852. Aug.	31	To Cash	2	130	00	1852. July	2	By Sundries	1	26,000	00
Oct.	30	"*Bal. (Net Cap.) to New a/c*		36,234	85	"	31	" Cash	1	9,000	00
						Oct.	30	" Profit & Loss 35,000.00	4	1,364	85
				36,364	85					36,364	85
853. *Feb.*	28	*To Bal. to Leger B, fol.*	1	36,824	02	1852. Nov.	1	By Bal. fr. Old a/c		36,234	85
						1853. Feb.	28	" Profit & Loss	4	589	17

Salmon P. Nixon.

Dr.											Cr.
1852. Aug.	31	To Cash	2	125	00	1852. July	2	By Sundries	1	23,931	25
Oct.	30	"*Bal. (Net Cap.) to New a/c*		36,239	84	"	31	" Cash	1	11,068	75
						Oct.	30	" Profit & Loss 35,000.00	4	1,364	84
				36,364	84					36,364	84
1853. *Feb.*	28	*To Bal. to Leger B, fol.*	1	36,829	02	1852. Nov.	1	By Bal. fr. Old a/c		36,239	84
						1853. Feb.	28	" Profit & Loss	4	589	18

Ship Massachusetts.

Dr.											Cr.
1852. July	2	To Thomas Harvey	1	25,000	00	1852. July	31	By Cash	1	1,800	00
"	16	" Bills Pay.	1	1,926	25	1853. *Feb.*	28	" *Bal. to Leger B, fol.*	1	26,291	85
"	31	" Cash 28,091.85	1	1,165	60						
				28,091	85					28,091	85

Bills Receivable.

Dr.											Cr.
1852. July	2	To Thomas Harvey	1	1,000	00	1852. July	31	By Cash	1	4,500	00
"	"	" S. P. Nixon	1	9,331	25	Aug.	"	" "	2	3,225	50
Oct.	15	" Sales No. 1	2	16,455	00	Sept.	30	" "	2	645	00
"	18	" " 33,026.25	2	6,240	00	*Oct.*	"	" *Bal. to New a/c* 8,370.50		24,655	75
				33,026	25					33,026	25
1852. Nov.	1	To Bal. fr. Old a/c		24,655	75	1852. Nov.	30	By Cash	4	7,491	17
"	6	" Sundries	3	5,530	42	1853. Jan.	31	" " 23,946.17	5	16,455	00
1853. Jan.	21	" Sales Co. B	5	4,657	25	*Feb.*	28	" *Bal. to Leger B, fol.*	2	13,828	75
Feb.	19	" " 37,774.92	5	2,931	50						
				37,774	92					37,774	92

Adventure to Canton.

Dr.											Cr.
1852. July	9	To Sundries	1	65,656	25	1853. *Feb.*	28	*By Bal. to Leger B, fol.*	2	65,656	25

LEGER A, SET VI.

Dr. — *Cash.* — *Cr.*

Date	Day	Particulars	Fol.	$	c.	Date	Day	Particulars	Fol.	$	c.
852.						1852.					
uly	31	To Sundries	1	26,368	75	July	31	By Sundries	1	8,165	60
ug.	"	" Bills Rec.	2	3,225	50	Aug.	"	" "	2	8,430	00
ept.	30	" " 30,239.25	2	645	00	Sept.	30	" Sales for J. G. & Co.	2	425	00
						Oct.	"	" Sundries	3	5,989	04
						"	"	" *Bal. to New a/c* 23.009.64		7,229	61
				30,239	25					30,239	25
852.						1852.					
ov.	1	To Bal. fr. Old a/c		7,229	61	Nov.	30	By Sundries	4	26,533	75
"	30	" Sundries	4	21,640	17	Dec.	31	" "	4	1,941	55
ec.	31	" Mdse.	4	7,875	00	1853.					
853.						Jan.	"	" "	5	14,268	77
an.	"	" Bills Rec. 53,199.78	5	16,455	00	Feb.	28	" " 43,449.07	5	705	00
						"	"	" *Bal. to Leger B, fol.*	1	9,750	71
				53,199	78					53,199	78

Dr. — *Merchandise.* — *Cr.*

Date	Day	Particulars	Fol.	$	c.	Date	Day	Particulars	Fol.	$	c.
852.						1852.					
uly	2	To S. P. Nixon	1	14,000	00	July	9	By Adv. to Canton	1	14,000	00
852.						1852.					
ov.	8	To Bills Pay.	3	15,255	90	Nov.	30	By Cash	4	6,274	00
853.						Dec.	31	" "	4	7,875	00
eb.	1	" " 23,804.70	5	8,548	80	1853.					
"	28	" *Profit & Loss (gain)*	4	838	70	Feb.	5	" Sundries 22,697.80	5	8,548	80
						"	28	" *Bal. to Leger B, fol.*	2	1,945	60
				24,643	40					24,643	40

Dr. — *Bills Payable.* — *Cr.*

Date	Day	Particulars	Fol.	$	c.	Date	Day	Particulars	Fol.	$	c.
52.						1852.					
ct.	30	*To Bal. to New a/c*		53,438	27	July	9	By Adv. to Canton	1	43,081	25
						"	16	" Ship Mass.	1	1,926	25
						Aug.	2	" Amer. Mut. Ins. Co.	1	2,000	00
						Oct.	20	" Suarez, Bro. & Co. 53,438.27	3	6,430	77
				53,438	27					53,438	27
52.						1852.					
ov.	30	To Cash	4	20,430	77	Nov.	1	By Bal. fr. Old a/c		53,438	27
53.						"	8	" Mdse.	3	15,255	90
an.	31	" " 34,430.77	5	14,000	00	1853.					
eb.	28	" *Bal. to Leger B, fol.*	2	51,122	44	Jan.	15	" Sundries	4	8,310	24
						Feb.	1	" Mdse. 85,553.21	5	8,548	80
				85,553	21					85,553	21

Dr. — *Expenses.* — *Cr.*

Date	Day	Particulars	Fol.	$	c.	Date	Day	Particulars	Fol.	$	c.
352.						1852.					
ıly	2	To S. P. Nixon	1	600	00	*Oct.*	30	*By Profit & Loss (loss)*	4	1,190	00
ug.	31	" Cash	2	95	00						
ct.	30	" " 1,190.00	3	495	00						
353.						1853.					
eb.	28	To Cash	5	510	00	*Feb.*	28	*By Profit & Loss (loss)*	4	510	00

Dr. — *Haines, Hampton & Co.* — *Cr.*

Date	Day	Particulars	Fol.	$	c.	Date	Day	Particulars	Fol.	$	c.
352.						1852.					
ıly	31	To Cash	1	7,000	00	July	9	By Adv. to Canton	1	7,000	00

LEGER A, SET VI.

Commission.

Dr.						Cr.					
1852. Oct.	30	*To Profit & Loss (gain)*	4	2,344	38	1852. July	9	By Adv. to Canton	1	1,575	00
						Aug.	2	" Adv. pr. Phillis	2	202	00
						Oct.	19	" Sales No. 1 2,344.38	3	567	38
1853. *Feb.*	28	*To Profit & Loss (gain)*	4	927	53	1852. Nov.	15	By Sales for J. G. & Co.	4	62	50
						"	"	" Sales Co. A	4	271	87
						1853. Feb.	5	" Sundries	5	213	72
						"	28	" Sales Co. B 927.53	5	379	44
				927	53					927	53

Charges.

Dr.						Cr.					
1852. Oct.	30	To Cash	3	94	75	1852. Aug.	2	By Adv. pr. Phillis	2	71	50
"	"	" *Profit & Loss (gain)*	4	48	00	Sept.	22	" Sales for J. G. & Co.	2	15	75
						Oct.	19	" Sales No. 1 142.75	3	55	50
				142	75					142	75
1852. Nov.	30	To Cash	4	226	25	1852. Nov.	5	By Sales Co. A	3	31	25
1853. Feb.	28	" " 421.25	5	195	00	"	15	" Sales for J. G. & Co.	4	60	25
"	"	" *Profit & Loss (gain)*	4	40	07	"	"	" Sales Co. A	4	191	50
						1853. Feb.	5	" Sundries	5	61	20
						"	28	" Sales Co. B 461.32	5	117	12
				461	32					461	32

American Mutual Insurance Co.

Dr.						Cr.					
1852. Aug.	2	To Bills Pay.	1	2,000	00	1852. Aug.	2	By Adv. pr. Phillis	2	271	25
						Oct.	5	" "	2	90	00
						"	30	" *Bal. to New a/c* 361.25		1,638	75
1852. Nov.	1	To Bal. fr. Old a/c		1,638	75	1852. Nov.	1	By Sales Co. A	3	150	00
						1853. Feb.	5	" Sundries 292.50	5	142	50
						"	28	" *Bal. to Leger B, fol.*	2	1,346	25

Adventure pr. Bark Phillis.

Dr.						Cr.					
1852. Aug.	2	To Sundries	2	8,624	75	1852. Oct.	19	By Sales No. 1	3	17,792	13
Oct.	5	" Amer. Mut. Ins. Co.	2	90	00						
"	11	" Suarez, Bro. & Co.	2	6,430	77						
"	22	" Sundries	3	1,521	61						
"	30	" Cash 17,792.13	3	1,125	00						
				17,792	13					17,792	13

Sales for Account of John Gundry & Co.

Dr.						Cr.					
1852. Sept.	22	To Charges	2	15	75	1852. Nov.	30	By Cash	4	2,500	00
"	30	" Cash 440.75	2	425	00						
Nov.	15	" Sundries 2,500.00	3	2,059	25						

Sales of Sugar, No. 1.

Dr.						Cr.				
1852.					1852.					
Oct.	19	To Sundries	3	18,420 71	Oct.	15	By Bills Rec.		2	16,455 00
"	30	" Cash 22,695.00	3	4,274 29	"	18	" " 22,695.00		2	6,240 00
				22,695 00						22,695 00

Interest.

Dr.						Cr.			
1852.					1852.				
Oct.	30	*To Profit & Loss (gain)*	4	704 79	Oct.	19	By Sales No. 1	3	5 70
					"	22	" Adv. pr. Phillis 704.79	3	699 09
1852.					1852.				
Nov.	30	To Cash	4	26 73	Nov.	6	By Bills Rec.	3	30 42
Dec.	31	" "	4	9 02	"	15	" Sales for J. G. & Co.	4	3 97
1853.					"	"	" Sales Co. A 36.21	4	1 82
Jan.	31	" " 304.52	5	268 77	1853. Feb.	28	" *Profit & Loss (loss)*	4	268 31
				304 52					304 52

Profit & Loss.

Dr.						Cr.			
1852.					1852.				
Oct.	30	To Expenses	2	1,190 00	Oct.	22	By Adv. pr. Phillis	3	822 52
"	"	" *T. Harvey, ½ net gains*	1	1,364 85	"	30	" Commission	3	2,344 38
"	"	" *S. P. Nixon, ½ " "*	1	1,364 84	"	"	" Charges	3	48 00
					"	"	" Interest	4	704 79
				3,919 69					3,919 69
1853.					1852.				
Feb.	28	To Expenses	2	510 00	Nov.	15	By Sales Co. A	4	61 16
"	"	" Interest	4	268 31	1853.				
"	"	" *T. Harvey, ½ net gains*	1	589 17	Feb.	28	" Mdse.	2	838 70
"	"	" *S. P. Nixon, ½ " "*	1	589 18	"	"	" Commission	3	927 53
					"	"	" Charges	3	40 07
					"	"	" Sales Co. B	5	89 20
				1,956 66					1,956 66

Morton & Godwin.

Dr.						Cr.			
1852.					1852.				
Aug.	31	To Cash	2	4,540 00	Aug.	2	By Adv. pr. Phillis	2	4,540 00

Otis & Brother.

Dr.						Cr.			
1852.					1852.				
Aug.	31	To Cash	2	3,540 00	Aug.	2	By Adv. pr. Phillis	2	3,540 00

Suarez, Brother & Co.

Dr.						Cr.			
1852.					1852.				
Oct.	20	To Bills Pay.	3	6,430 77	Oct.	11	By Adv. pr. Phillis	2	6,430 77

Sales of Pork, Co. A.

Dr. | Cr.

Date		Particulars	Fol.	$	cts.	Date		Particulars	Fol.	$	cts.
1852. Nov.	1	To Amer. Mut. Ins. Co.	3	150	00	1852. Nov.	6	By Bills Rec.	3	5,500	00
"	5	" Sundries	3	4,659	37	"	30	" Cash 10,875.00	4	5,375	00
"	15	" "	4	5,154	47						
"	"	" Profit & Loss	4	61	16						
"	30	" Cash 10,875.00	4	850	00						
				10,875	00					10,875	00

Faxon, Field & Co.

Dr. | Cr.

Date		Particulars	Fol.	$	cts.	Date		Particulars	Fol.	$	cts.
1852. Nov.	30	To Cash	4	5,000	00	1852. Nov.	5	By Sales Co. A	3	4,628	12
						"	15	" "	4	4,689	28
1853. Jan.	15	" Bills Pay.	4	4,155	12	1853. Feb.	28	" Sales Co. B 11,681.46	5	2,364	06
Feb.	5	" Sundries 13,638.23	5	4,483	11	"	"	" *Bal. to Leger B, fol.*	2	1,956	77
				13,638	23					13,638	23

John Gundry & Co.

Dr. | Cr.

Date		Particulars	Fol.	$	cts.	Date		Particulars	Fol.	$	cts.
1852. Dec.	31	To Cash	4	1,932	53	1852. Nov.	15	By Sales for J. G. & Co.	4	1,932	53

Sales of Merchandise, Co. B.

Dr. | Cr.

Date		Particulars	Fol.	$	cts.	Date		Particulars	Fol.	$	cts.
1853. Jan.	15	To Bills Payable	4	4,155	12	1853. Jan.	21	By Bills Rec.	5	4,657	25
Feb.	28	" Sundries 9,379.80	5	5,224	68	Feb.	19	" " 7,588.75	5	2,931	50
"	"	" *Profit & Loss (gain)*	4	89	20	"	28	" *Bal. to Leger B, fol.*	3	1,880	25
				9,469	00					9,469	00

Adventure to Cincinnati, Co. C.

Dr. | Cr.

Date		Particulars	Fol.	$	cts.	Date		Particulars	Fol.	$	cts.
1853. Feb.	5	To Sundries	5	4,483	11	1853. *Feb.*	28	*By Bal. to Leger B, fol.*	3	4,483	11

Douglass, Forest & Co.

Dr. | Cr.

Date		Particulars	Fol.	$	cts.	Date		Particulars	Fol.	$	cts.
1853. *Feb.*	28	*To Bal. to Leger B, fol.*	3	2,364	06	1853. Feb.	28	By Sales Co. B	5	2,364	06

THOMAS HARVEY & CO.

LEGER B.

SET VI.

INDEX.

LEGER B, SET VI.

Dr. *Thomas Harvey.* *Cr.*

1853.						1853.					
June	30	To Cash	3	450	00	Mar.	1	By Bal. fr. Leger A, fol.	1	36,824	02
"	"	" *Bal. (Net Cap.) to New %*		46,280	32	June	30	" Interest	3	735	06
						"	"	" Profit & Loss 37,559.08	4	9,171	24
				46,730	32					46,730	32
						1853. July	1	By Bal. fr. Old %		46,280	32

Dr. *Salmon P. Nixon.* *Cr.*

1853.						1853.					
June	30	To Cash	3	500	00	Mar.	1	By Bal. fr. Leger A, fol.	1	36,829	02
"	"	" *Bal. (Net. Cap.) to New %*		46,235	26	June	30	" Interest	3	735	00
						"	"	" Profit & Loss 37,564.02	4	9,171	24
				46,735	26					46,735	26
						1853. July	1	By Bal. fr. Old %		46,235	26

Dr. *James L. Grant.* *Cr.*

1853.						1853.					
June	30	*To Bal. (Net. Cap.) to New %*		19,885	62	Mar.	31	By Cash	1	15,000	00
						June	30	" Interest	3	300	00
						"	"	" Profit & Loss 15,300.00	4	4,585	62
				19,885	62					19,885	62
						1853. July	1	By Bal. fr. Old %		19,885	62

Dr. *Cash.* *Cr.*

1853.						1853.					
Mar.	1	To Bal. fr. Leger A, fol.	2	9,750	71	Mar.	31	By Sundries	1	14,001	50
"	31	" Jas. L. Grant	1	15,000	00	May	"	" "	2	20,492	57
Apr.	30	" Sundries	1	11,144	51	June	30	" " 43,690.57	3	9,196	50
May	31	" " 45,552.47	2	9,657	25	"	"	" *Bal. to New %*		1,861	90
				45,552	47					45,552	47
1853. July	1	To Bal. fr. Old %		1 861	90						

Dr. *Ship Massachusetts.* *Cr.*

1853.						1853.					
Mar.	1	To Bal. fr. Leger A, fol.	1	26,291	85	May	9	By Sundries	2	8,500	00
May	6	" Adv. to Canton	1	2,069	68	"	31	" Cash 13,500.00	2	5,000	00
"	31	" Cash	2	3,808	67	*June*	30	" *Bal. (Inv't.) to New %*		22,500	00
June	30	" Interest 33,602.04	3	1,431	84						
"	"	" *Profit & Loss (gain)*	3	2,397	96						
				36,000	00					36,000	00
1853. July	1	To Bal. fr. Old %		22,500	00						

LEGER B, SET VI.

Dr. *Bills Receivable.* *Cr.*

1853.						1853.					
Mar.	1	To Bal. fr. Leger A, fol.	1	13,828	75	Mar.	4	By W. G. Gaylord	1	2,931	50
Apr.	9	" Sales Co. B	1	5,525	00	Apr.	30	" Cash	1	6,240	00
May	18	" Sales No. 3	2	93,293	63	May	31	" "	2	4,657	25
June	10	" Sales No. 2 121,047.38	2	8,400	00	*June*	30	" *Bal. to New a/c* 13,828.75		107,218	63
				121,047	38					121,047	38
1853.											
July	1	To Bal. fr. Old a/c		107,218	63						

Dr. *Merchandise.* *Cr.*

1853.						1853.					
Mar.	1	To Bal. fr. Leger A, fol.	2	1,945	60	Apr.	30	By Cash	1	1,945	60

Dr. *Adventure to Canton.* *Cr.*

1853.						1853.					
Mar.	1	To Bal. fr. Leger A, fol.	1	65,656	25	May	6	By Sundries	1	1,682	36
"	25	" Bills Pay.	1	1,133	75	"	"	" Ship Mass.	1	2,069	68
June	20	" Sundries	2	15,950	77	June	1	" Sales No. 3	2	82,349	95
"	30	" Cash 90,084.77	3	7,344	00	"	15	" Sales No. 2 90,084.77	2	3,982	78
				90,084	77					90,084	77

Dr. *Bills Payable.* *Cr.*

1853.						1853.					
Mar.	31	To Cash	1	14,000	00	Mar.	1	By Bal. fr. Leger A, fol.	2	51,122	44
May	"	" "	2	15,255	90	"	25	" Adv. to Canton 52,256.19	1	1,133	75
June	30	" *Bal. to New a/c* 29,255.90		23,000	29						
				52,256	19					52,256	19
						1853.					
						July	1	By Bal. fr. Old a/c		23,000	29

Dr. *American Mutual Insurance Co.* *Cr.*

1853.											
Mar.	1	To Bal. fr. Leger A, fol.	3	1,346	25						

Dr. *Faxon, Field & Co.* *Cr.*

1853.						1853.					
Mar.	1	To Bal. fr. Leger A, fol.	5	1,956	77	Apr.	9	By Sales Co. B	1	1,713	80
June	11	" Adv. Co. C 6,668.13	2	4,711	36	*June*	30	" *Bal. to New a/c*		4,954	33
				6,668	13					6,668	13
1853.											
July	1	To Bal. fr. Old a/c		4,954	33						

Sales of Merchandise, Co. B.

Dr.			Fol.	$	cts.			Cr.	Fol.	$	cts.
1853.						1853.					
Mar.	1	To Bal. fr. Leger A, fol.	5	1,880	25	Apr.	9	By Bills Rec.	1	5,525	00
Apr.	9	" Sundries 5,691.45	1	3,811	20	"	"	" Profit & Loss 5,691.45	1	166	45
				5,691	45					5,691	45

Adventure to Cincinnati, Co. C.

Dr.			Fol.	$	cts.			Cr.	Fol.	$	cts.
1853.						1853.					
Mar.	1	To Bal. fr. Leger A, fol.	5	4,483	11	June	11	By Faxon, Field & Co.	2	4,711	36
June	30	" *Profit & Loss (gain)*	3	228	25						

Douglass, Forest & Co.

Dr.			Fol.	$	cts.			Cr.	Fol.	$	cts.
1853.						1853.					
June	30	*To Bal. to New %*		4,077	86	Mar.	1	By Bal. fr. Leger A, fol.	5	2,364	06
						Apr.	9	" Sales Co. B 4,077.86	1	1,713	80
										4,077	86
						1853.					
						July	1	By Bal. fr. Old %		4,077	86

Charges.

Dr.			Fol.	$	cts.			Cr.	Fol.	$	cts.
1853.						1853.					
June	30	To Cash	3	237	00	Apr.	9	By Sales Co. B	1	107	35
"	"	" *Profit & Loss (gain)*	3	171	35	June	1	" Sales No. 3	2	256	00
						"	15	" Sales No. 2 408.35	2	45	00
				408	35					408	35

Commission.

Dr.			Fol.	$	cts.			Cr.	Fol.	$	cts.
1853.						1853.					
June	30	*To Profit & Loss (gain)*	3	5,360	93	Apr.	9	By Sales Co. B	1	276	25
						June	1	" Sales No. 3	2	4,664	68
						"	15	" Sales No. 2 5,360.93	2	420	00
				5,360	93					5,360	93

Profit & Loss.

Dr.			Fol.	$	cts.			Cr.	Fol.	$	cts.
1853.						1853.					
Apr.	9	To Sales Co. B	1	166	45	June	20	By Adv. to Canton	2	11,783	56
June	30	" Expenses	4	665	50	"	30	" Ship Mass.	1	2,397	96
"	"	" *T. Harvey, $\frac{2}{5}$ net gains*	1	9,171	24	"	"	" Adv. Co. C	3	228	25
"	"	" *S. P. Nixon, $\frac{2}{5}$ " "*	1	9,171	24	"	"	" Charges	3	171	35
"	"	" *J. L. Grant, $\frac{1}{5}$ " "*	1	4,585	62	"	"	" Commission	3	5,360	93
						"	"	" Interest	4	3,818	00
				23,760	05					23,760	05

Interest.

Dr.						Cr.					
1853.						1853.					
May	6	To Adv. to Canton	1	84	12	Apr.	30	By Cash	1	25	91
June	30	" Sundries 1,854.18	3	1,770	06	June	1	" Sales No. 3	2	23	00
"	"	" *Profit & Loss (gain)*	3	3,818	00	"	15	" Sales No. 2	2	24	22
						"	20	" Adv. to Canton	2	4,167	21
						"	30	" Ship Mass. 5,672.18	3	1,431	84
				5,672	18					5,672	18

Watson G. Gaylord.

Dr.						Cr.					
1853.						1853.					
Mar.	4	To Bills Rec.	1	2,931	50	Apr.	30	By Cash	1	2,933	00
"	31	" Cash 2,933.00	1	1	50						

Hughes, Miller & Co.

Dr.						Cr.					
1853.											
May	6	To Adv. to Canton	1	1,598	24						

Sales of Matting, No. 2.

Dr.						Cr.					
1853.						1853.					
May	9	To Ship Mass.	2	2,500	00	June	10	By Bills Rec.	2	8,400	00
"	31	" Cash	2	1,428	00						
June	15	" Sundries 8,400.00	2	4,472	00						
				8,400	00					8,400	00

Sales of Tea, No. 3.

Dr.						Cr.					
1853.						1853.					
May	9	To Ship Mass.	2	6,000	00	May	18	By Bills Rec.	2	93,293	63
June	1	" Sundries 93,293.63	2	87,293	63						

Expenses.

Dr.						Cr.					
1853.						1853.					
June	30	To Cash	3	665	50	*June*	30	*By Profit & Loss (loss)*	3	665	50

Property remaining unsold February 28th, 1853:			
Merchandise.			
100 Hhds. Cuba Molasses, 10,240 Gals. @ 19 ¢ - - - - -		1,945	60
Merchandise, Co. B.			
74 Hhds. Muscovado Sugar, 88,066 lbs. @ 4^3 ¢ - -	4,183.14		
75 Hhds. N. O. Molasses, 7,879 Gals. @ 18^2 ¢ - -	1,457.61		
	$5,640.75		
Our one-third of which is - - - - - -		1,880	25
Adv. to Cincinnati, Co. C.			
Our one-half of Invoice of February 5th - - - - - -		4,483	11
		8,308	96
Property remaining unsold June 30th, 1853:			
Ship Massachusetts valued at - - - - - - - - -		22,500	00

TRIAL BALANCE, LEGER A, SET VI. *Oct. 30th,* 1852.

L.F.		Dr.		Cr.	
1	Thomas Harvey - - - - - - - - - - - - -			34,870	00
1	Salmon P. Nixon - - - - - - - - - - -			34,875	00
1	Ship Massachusetts - - - - - - - - - - -	26,291	85		
1	Bills Receivable - - - - - - - - - - -	24,655	75		
1	Adventure to Canton - - - - - - - - - - -	65,656	25		
2	Cash - - - - - - - - - - - - -	7,229	61		
2	Bills Payable - - - - - - - - - - - -			53,438	27
2	Expenses - - - - - - - - - - - - - -	1,190	00		
3	Commission - - - - - - - - - - - - - -			2,344	38
3	Charges - - - - - - - - - - - - - -			48	00
3	American Mutual Insurance Co. - - - - - - - -	1,638	75		
3	Sales for a/c of John Gundry & Co. - - - - - - -	440	75		
4	Interest - - - - - - - - - - - - - -			704	79
4	Profit & Loss - - - - - - - - - - - - -			822	52
		127,102	96	127,102	96

TRIAL BALANCE, LEGER A, SET VI. *Feb. 28th,* 1853.

L.F.		Dr.		Cr.	
1	Thomas Harvey - - - - - - - - - - - - -			36,234	85
1	Salmon P. Nixon - - - - - - - - - - -			36,239	84
1	Ship Massachusetts - - - - - - - - - - -	26,291	85		
1	Bills Receivable - - - - - - - - - - -	13,828	75		
1	Adventure to Canton - - - - - - - - - - -	65,656	25		
2	Cash - - - - - - - - - - - - -	9,750	71		
2	Merchandise - - - - - - - - -	1,106	90		
	Am'ts carried forward	116,634	46	72,474	69

TRIAL BALANCE (*continued*).

L. F.		Dr.		Cr.	
	Am't Bro't forward	116,634	46	72,474	69
2	Bills Payable			51,122	44
2	Expenses	510	00		
3	Commission			927	53
3	Charges			40	07
3	American Mutual Insurance Co.	1,346	25		
4	Interest	268	31		
4	Profit & Loss			61	16
5	Faxon, Field & Co.	1,956	77		
5	Sales of Merchandise, Co. B	1,791	05		
5	Adventure to Cincinnati, Co. C	4,483	11		
5	Douglass, Forest & Co.			2,364	06
		126,989	95	126,989	95

TRIAL BALANCE, LEGER B, SET VI. *March 1st*, 1853.

L. F.		Dr.		Cr.	
1	Thomas Harvey			36,824	02
1	Salmon P. Nixon			36,829	02
1	Cash	9,750	71		
1	Ship Massachusetts	26,291	85		
2	Bills Receivable	13,828	75		
2	Merchandise	1,945	60		
2	Adventure to Canton	65,656	25		
2	Bills Payable			51,122	44
2	American Mutual Insurance Co.	1,346	25		
2	Faxon, Field & Co.	1,956	77		
3	Sales of Merchandise, Co. B	1,880	25		
3	Adventure to Cincinnati, Co. C	4,483	11		
3	Douglass, Forest & Co.			2,364	06
		127,139	54	127,139	54

TRIAL BALANCE, LEGER B, SET VI. *June 30th*, 1853.

L. F.		Dr.		Cr.	
1	Thomas Harvey			37,109	08
1	Salmon P. Nixon			37,064	02
1	James L. Grant			15,300	00
1	Cash	1,861	90		
1	Ship Massachusetts	20,102	04		
2	Bills Receivable	107,218	63		
2	Bills Payable			23,000	29
2	American Mutual Insurance Co.	1,346	25		
2	Faxon, Field & Co.	4,954	33		
3	Adventure to Cincinnati, Co. C			228	25
3	Douglass, Forest & Co.			4,077	86
3	Charges			171	35
3	Commission			5,360	93
3	Profit & Loss			11,617	11
4	Interest			3,818	00
4	Hughes, Miller & Co.	1,598	24		
4	Expenses	665	50		
		137,746	89	137,746	89

AUXILIARY BOOKS

FOR SET VI.

BANK-BOOK.
CHECK-BOOK.
BILL-BOOK.
INVOICE-BOOK.
SALES-BOOK.
OUTWARD-INVOICE-BOOK.
ACCOUNT-SALES-BOOK.
ACCOUNT-CURRENT-BOOK.
LETTER-BOOK.

BANK-BOOK AND CHECK-BOOK.

BANK-BOOK.

This is a small memorandum book given by Banks to individuals who deposit funds with them. The deposits made in Bank are entered in it by the receiving clerk, at the time of deposit; and about once a month a clerk of the Bank enters the amounts that have been checked out, and balances the book. This is called writing up and balancing.

Notes and Drafts lodged with the Bank for collection are noted inside the money column, but not extended. When collected they form a deposit in Bank, and are extended; but if protested for non-payment, a stroke of the pen is made through the figures, and they are not extended. If the Note or Draft does not fall due before the time of writing up and balancing, instead of an extension a new entry must be made when collected.

No Bank-Book is given with Set VI, since the form is so simple as not to require it.

CHECK-BOOK.

This is a printed book of blank checks, with a broad margin, in which is noted deposits made in Bank. Whenever it is wished to draw out funds from the Bank, one of these blank checks is filled and torn off, and a memorandum of it also made in the margin.

By adding all sums deposited, and subtracting all sums withdrawn or checked out, the amount remaining in Bank is always readily seen, and must agree with the balance of the Bank-Book when that book is written up and balanced.

Notes and Drafts deposited for collection are entered in this book when they are collected. Some make a memorandum of them at the time of deposit, but this is unnecessary, as the Bank-Book is the voucher for their having been left with the Bank, and they do not form a real deposit upon which to draw until they are collected.

Houses doing business with more than one Bank have a separate Check-Book for each.

In Set VI, the Firm has dealings with the Phenix Bank and the Bank of Commerce; but I have given a portion only of the Check-Book of one of these Banks, this being sufficient to show the form. It will be a good exercise for you to fill up the remainder of this book, and also to make out a Check-Book for the Bank of Commerce from the history of the business.

Phenix

1852.		
July 2d.		
Dep. by T. Harvey	9,000	00
July 12th.		
Check No. 1	400	00
	8,600	00
July 20th.		
Note No. 2 collected	4,500	00
	13,100	00
Aug. 2d.		
Check No. 2	4,540	00
	8,560	00
Aug. 10th.		
Note No. 1 collected	1,000	00
	9,560	00
Sep. 22d.		
Check No. 3	425	00
	9,135	00
Oct. 11th.		
Check No. 4	4,274	29
	4,860	71
Oct. 12th.		
Check No. 5	1,125	00
	3,735	71

NOTE.—The portion of this page occupied with the explanation of the Bank-Book and Check-Book constitutes properly a part of the Check-Book, being the back or blank side of the checks. When the checks are torn off, nothing remains in this book but the inner marginal memorandums.

CHECK-BOOK, SET VI.

Bank.

Stub	Dollars	Cents	Check
No. 1. Date. July 12th, 1852. *Favor of* Joseph Kelsey & Bro. for Beef and Pork.	400	00	No. 1. New York, July 12th, 1852. **PHENIX BANK,** *Pay to* Joseph Kelsey & Brother, *or Bearer,* Four Hundred ——— ~/100 *Dollars.* 400 *Dolls.* ~ *cts.* Thomas Harvey & Co.
No. 2. Date. Aug. 2d, 1852. *Favor of* Morton & Godwin, for Flour.	4,540	00	No. 2. New York, August 2d, 1852. **PHENIX BANK,** *Pay to* Morton & Godwin, *or Bearer,* Four Thousand Five Hundred and Forty ~/100 *Dollars.* 4,540 *Dolls.* ~ *cts.* Thomas Harvey & Co.
No. 3. Date. Sep. 22d, 1852. *Favor of* D. Leech & Co., for Freight.	425	00	No. New York, ———— 18— **PHENIX BANK,** *Pay to* ———— *or Bearer,* ———— /100 *Dollars.* *Dolls. cts.*
No. 4. Date. Oct. 11th, 1852. *Favor of* No. 4, for Duties.	4,274	29	No. — New York, ———— 18— **PHENIX BANK,** *Pay to* ———— *or Bearer,* ———— /100 *Dollars.* *Dolls. cts.*
No. 5. Date. Oct. 12th, 1852. *Favor of* Hollister, Son & Co., for Charter Money and Demurrage.	1,125	00	No. — New York, ———— 18— **PHENIX BANK,** *Pay to* ———— *or Bearer,* ———— /100 *Dollars* *Dolls. cts.*

BILL-BOOK, SET VI.

Bills

No.	When Received.		Drawers.	In whose favor.	For what received.	Where payable.	Date of Note.	
	1852.						1852.	
1	July	2	Bagley & Thompson	Thomas Harvey	For % of T. Harvey	Phenix Bank	May	7
2	"	"	Wm. Longfellow	Salmon P. Nixon	" " S. P. Nixon	New York	May	18
3	"	"	Jonas Savage & Co.	" "	" " "	Bank of Com.	Apr.	27
4	"	"	Ezra Coe & Co.	" "	" " "	" "	Mar.	5
5	"	"	John Vanarsdale	" "	" " "	New York	Apr.	30
6	Oct.	15	J. Falstaff & Co.	Ourselves	Sales of Sugar, No. 1	" "	Oct.	15
7	"	18	Lyman F. Bache	"	" " "	" "	Oct.	18
8	Nov.	6	Jeremiah Brown	"	Sales of Pork, Co. A	Phenix Bank	Nov.	6
	1853.						1853.	
9	Jan.	21	James Maitland & Co.	"	Sales of Mdse., Co. B.	Bank of Com.	Jan.	21
10	Feb.	19	Watson G. Gaylord	"	" " "	New York	Feb.	19
11	Apr.	9	Leonard Barber & Co.	"	" " "	" "	Apr.	9
12	May	18	Carrigan & Allen	Myers & Wolbert	Sales of Tea, No. 3	Bank of Com.	May	18
13	"	"	Brooks & Monteith	" "	" " "	" "	May	18
14	"	"	Burrill & Webb	" "	" " "	Phènix Bank	May	18
15	"	"	J. Dugan & Co.	" "	" " "	" "	May	18
16	June	10	Fithian & Morris	Ourselves	Sales of Matting, No. 2	" "	June	10

Bills

No.	When Issued.		Drawers.	In whose favor.	On whom drawn.	For what given.	Where payable.
	1852.						
1	July	9	Ourselves	A. A. Lawrence & Co.		Drills	Phenix Bank
2	"	"	"	" " "		"	" "
3	"	"	"	" " "		"	" "
4	"	"	"	Atlantic Ins. Co.		Insurance	New York
5	"	16	"	New York Ins. Co.		"	" "
6	Aug.	2	"	Amer. Mutual Ins. Co.		"	" "
7	Oct.	20	Suarez, Brother & Co.	Hart & Cushing	Ourselves	Adv. pr. Phillis	" "
8	Nov.	8	Ourselves	Caleb Johnson		Mdse.	Phenix Bank
	1853.						
9	Jan.	15	"	Douglass, Forest & Co.		Mdse. Co. B. & F.F. & Co.	Bank of Com.
10	Feb.	1	"	Bailey & Welsh		Coffee	" "
11	Mar.	25	"	Atlantic Ins. Co.		Insurance	New York

Bills Receivable and Bills Payable are usually bound in opposite ends of the same book, styled Bill-Book. This book is so simple, that the student will see, by inspection, its utility; and all necessary explanations are made by the headings of the different columns. By comparing the "Amount" and "When paid" columns with the Leger accounts of Bills Receivable and Bills Payable, they will be found to agree at all times, if correct. The column, "On whom drawn," in Bills Payable, (in the formula above,)

Receivable.

Time to run.	When due. Jan.	Feb.	Mar.	Apr.	May	June	July	Aug.	Sep.	Oct.	Nov.	Dec.	Amount.		When paid.		Remarks and Endorsements.
3 mos.								10					1,000	00	Aug.	10	
60 d's							20						4,500	00	July	20	Deposited in Phenix Bank July 10th.
4 mos.								30					2,225	50	Aug.	30	
6 mos.									8				645	00	Sep.	8	
6 mos.											2		1,960	75	Nov.	2	Deposited in Bank of Commerce Oct. 18th
6 mos.				18									16,455	00	Apr.	18	Discounted at Phenix Bank Jan. 10th.
6 mos.				21									6,240	00	Apr.	21	Deposited in Phenix Bank April 13th.
30 d's												9	5,530	42	Dec.	9	Discounted at Phenix Bank Nov. 10th.
4 mos.					24								4,657	25	May	24	
10 d's			4										2,931	50	Apr.	26	{ Dep. Mar. 1st, and protested Mar. 4th { Paid with Int. & Charges April 26th.
6 mos.										12			5,525	00			
6 mos.											21		14,256	25			Endors'd to our order by Myers & Wolbert.
6 mos.											21		29,434	33			" " "
6 mos.											21		35,620	20			" " "
6 mos.											21		13,982	85			" " "
4 mos.										13			8,400	00			

Payable.

Date of Note.		Time to run.	When due.		Amount.		When paid.		Remarks and Endorsements.
1852.			1852.						
July	9	4 mos.	Nov.	9/12	14,000	00	Nov.	12	
			1853.						
"	"	6 mos.	Jan.	9/12	14,000	00	Jan.	12	
"	"	8 mos.	Mar.	9/12	14,000	00	Mar.	12	
"	"	12 mos.	July	9/12	1,081	25			
"	16	12 mos.	July	16/19	1,926	25			
Aug.	2	12 mos.	Aug.	2/5	2,000	00			
			1852.						
Oct.	20	30 d's	Nov.	19/22	6,430	77	Nov.	22	
			1853.						
Nov.	8	6 mos.	May	8/11	15,255	90	May	11	
1853.									
Jan.	15	6 mos.	July	15/18	8,310	24			
Feb.	1	6 mos.	Aug.	1/4	8,548	80			
Mar.	25	6 mos.	Sep.	25/28	1,133	75			

nay also be inserted in Bills Receivable, if desired. The column, "When due," will be found convenient for a small business, as seen in the latter form; but where many Notes are received and issued, the former will be preferable, as by it can be more readily seen what Notes fall due on a certain month or day.

N. B. Notes falling due on Sunday must be paid on the Saturday preceding.

INVOICE-BOOK, SET VI.

Messrs. Thomas Harvey & Co.

To Salmon P. Nixon Dr.

	To 100 Casks Ginseng, 48,120 lbs., gross, 8,120 " tare, 40,000 " net, @ 35¢ *New York, July 2d,* 1852.	$14,000	00

Messrs. Thomas Harvey & Co.

Bo't of A. A. Lawrence & Co.

G. T. C. #1 to 500	500 Bales Drills, ea. 40 Pieces, ea. 30 Yds. = 600,000 Yds., @ 7¢ Delivered on Ship Massachusetts free of charge. Received in payment their Notes, @ 4, 6, & 8 mos. A. A. LAWRENCE & Co. *New York, July 9th,* 1852.	$42,000	00

Messrs. Thomas Harvey & Co.

Bo't of Haines, Hampton & Co.

G. T. C.	2,000 Pigs Lead, 140,000 lbs., @ 5¢ Delivered on Ship Massachusetts free of charge. Received payment. HAINES, HAMPTON & Co. *New York, July 9th,* 1852.	$7,000	00

Invoice of Flour, shipped by John Gundry & Co., pr. Steamboat Boston, Robinson master, via Pittsburg, and consigned to Messrs. Thomas Harvey & Co., New York, to be sold for account of Shippers.

M.	500 Bbls. Flour, @ $3,		1,500	00
	Drayage, Cooperage, Labor, &c.,	42.25		
	Commission on $1,500, @ 2½%,	37.50	79	75
	E. E. JOHN GUNDRY & Co.		$1,579	75
	Cincinnati, September 13th, 1852.			

An *Invoice* is a statement in detail of goods sold, shipped abroad, or consigned to another to be sold. When applied to goods sold, it is frequently called a *Bill* or *Bill of sale.*

The Invoice-Book is used for taking copies of the Invoices which accompany goods purchased or received on consignment. Some houses, instead of copying, *paste* their Invoices in a blank Invoice-Book, prepared for the purpose.

In order to save room, I have given above only a few of the Invoices which occur in this Set; but those given are sufficient to show the different methods of making out Invoices; and you can see by the history the instances in which other Invoices are required, and, imagining the details, fill them up for yourself.

Invoices of goods to be sold on commission may be kept in a separate book, if preferred.

New York, October 15th, 1852.

P. B. #1 to 300	Sold to J. Falstaff & Co., Note @ 6 mos.,				
	300 Boxes Sugar—Sales of Sugar, No. 1—ea. 480 lbs., @ 6^1¢	9,000	00		
P. D. #501to600	100 Hhds. " — " " " —ea. 1420 " " 5^1¢	7,455	00	16,455	00
	18th				
P. C. #301to500	Sold to Lyman F. Bache, Note @ 6 mos.,				
	200 Boxes Sugar—Sales of Sugar, No. 1—ea. 480 lbs., @ 6^2¢			6,240	00
	Nov. 6th				
	Sold Jeremiah Brown,				
T H	500 Bbls. Pork—Sales of Pork, Co. A— @ $11			5,500	00
	Took Note, @ 30 days, for $5,530.42				
	Dis. on Note for 33 days, to make it equal to Cash			30	42
	10th				
	Sold H. S. Pierson & Co., Cash,				
M	500 Bbls. Flour—Sales for % J. Gundry & Co.—@ $5.	2,500	00		
T H	500 " Pork—Sales of Pork, Co. A— " 10.75	5,375	00	7,875	00
	16th				
	Sold James Maitland & Co., Cash,				
	500 Bbls. Lard, 100,000 lbs., @ 5^1¢	5,250	00		
	50 Hhds. Molasses, 5,120 Gals., " 20	1,024	00	6,274	00
	Dec. 6th				
	Sold Stiles & Nesmith, Cash,				
	125 Hhds. Sugar, 157,500 lbs., @ 5¢			7,875	00
	Jan. 21st, 1853				
	Sold James Maitland & Co., Note @ 4 mos.,				
◇D	25,909 lbs., Loaf Sugar—Sales of Mdse., Co. B—@ 9¢	2,331	81		
◇E	29,068 " Crushed " — " " " — " 8	2,325	44	4,657	25
	Feb. 19th				
	Sold Watson G. Gaylord, Note @ 10 d's,				
◇H	50 Tierces Rice—Sales of Mdse., Co. B—90,200 lbs., @ 3^1¢			2,931	50
	April 9th				
	Sold Leonard Barber & Co., Note @ 6 mos.,				
◇F	74 Hhds. Mus'do Sugar—Sales Mdse., Co. B—87,943^{2}lbs. @ $4\frac{5}{8}$¢	4,067	39		
◇G	75 " N. O. Molasses, " " " 7,879 Gals. " 18^2	1,457	61	5,525	00
	30th				
	Sold Peter Parker, Check,				
	100 Hhds. Cuba Molasses, 10,240 Gals., @ 19¢			1,945	60
	June 10th				
	Sold Fithian & Morris, Note @ 4 mos.,				
.. T. # 6	1,000 Rolls 4/4 White Matting—Sales of Matting, No. 2—40,000 Yds., @ 21¢			8,400	00

This book is used for recording, in detail, all sales.

In houses doing a mixed business, the Sales-Book and Commission-Sales-Book can, ith equal propriety, be kept together or separate, as convenience may dictate. They re here blended in one.

In actual business, the sale is first recorded here, and subsequently the entry is made om this book to the Day-Book.

1 OUTWARD-INVOICE-BOOK, SET VI.

Invoice of Merchandise, shipped by Thomas Harvey & Co., pr. Ship Massachusetts, Captain Fillmore, for Canton, and consigned to Hughes, Miller & Co., to be sold for account and risk of Shippers.

G. T. C.				
#1 to 500	500 Bales Drills, ea. 40 Pieces, ea. 30 Yds. = 600,000 Yds., @ 7¢		42,000	00
#501to600	100 Casks Ginseng, 48,120 lbs., gross,			
	8,120 " tare,			
	40,000 " net, @ 35¢		14,000	00
	2,000 Pigs Lead, 140,000 lbs., @ 5¢		7,000	00
	Charges.			
	Ins. on $72,000, @ 1½%, and policy	1,081.25		
	Com. on $63,000, @ 2½%	1,575.00	2,656	25
	E. E.		$ 65,656	25
	New York, July 9th, 1852.			
	THOMAS HARVEY & Co.			

Invoice of Merchandise, shipped by Thomas Harvey & Co., pr. Bark Phillis, Bingham master, and consigned to Daniel Starr & Co., Kingston, Jamaica; Sales and returns for account of Shippers.

◇O◇ D.	1,000 Bbls. Flour, @ $4,50	4,500.00		
	Inspection 1¢, Lining 3¢ pr. Bbl.	40.00	4,540	00
◇O◇ E.	1,000 Bbls. Corn Meal, @ $3	3,000.00		
	Inspection 1¢, Lining 3¢ pr. Bbl.	40.00	3,040	00
◇O◇ F.	400 Bags Corn, (ea. 2 Bushels,) @ $1.25		500	00
			8,080	00
	Com. on $8,080, @ 2½%	202.00		
	Porterage & Labor	71.50	273	50
	Ins. on $9,000, for the voyage, @ 3%	270.00		
	Policy	1.25	271	25
	New York, Aug. 2d, 1852. E. E.		$8,624	75
	THOMAS HARVEY & Co.			

Invoice of Merchandise, shipped pr. D. Leech & Co.'s line, via Pennsylvania, and consigned to Faxon, Field & Co., Cincinnati, to be sold for joint account of Shippers and Consignees.

WA	2,000 Sacks Coffee, 131,520 lbs., @ 6½¢		8,548	80
	Charges.			
	Ins. on $9,500, @ 1½%	142.50		
	Drayage, Labor, Weighing, Mending Bags, &c.	61.20		
	Com. on $8,548.80, @ 2½%	213.72	417	42
			$8,966	22
	E. E. *New York, Feb. 5th,* 1853.			
	THOMAS HARVEY & Co.			

In the Outward-Invoice-Book, copies are taken of Invoices shipped abroad, or consigned to others to be sold for your account.

ACCOUNT-SALES-BOOK, SET VI.

Sales of Sugar (No. 1), for account of Adventure pr. Bark Phillis.

	1852.				
P. B.	Oct. 15th.	Sold J. Fallstaff & Co., @ 6 mos.,			
#1 to 300		300 Boxes Sugar, ea. 480 lbs., @ 6¼¢	9,000.00		
P. D. #501to600		100 Hhds. " " 1,420 " " 5¼	7,455.00	16,455	00
P. C.	Oct. 18th.	Sold Lyman F. Bache, @ 6 mos.,			
#301to500		200 Boxes Sugar, ea. 480 lbs., @ 6½¢		6,240	00
				22,695	00
		Charges.			
		Duties paid Oct. 11th	4,274.29		
		Int. on $4,274.29 for 8 days	5.70		
		Cooperage, Stor. & Lab.	55.50		
		Com. on $22,695, @ 2½%	567.38	4,902	87
		E. E. Net Proceeds due June 8th /53		$17,792	13
	New York, Oct. 19th, 1852.				
		THOMAS HARVEY & Co.			

Account-Sales of Flour, received, pr. D. Leech & Co.'s line, from Cincinnati, for account and risk of J. Gundry & Co.

1852.					
Nov.	10	By H. S. Pierson & Co.,			
		M. 500 Bbls. Flour, @ $5		2,500	00
		Charges.			
		To Freight & Drayage	440.75		
		" Int. on $440.75, from Sept. 22d	3.97		
		" Stor., Lab., Cooperage, &c.	30.25		
		" Com. on $2,500, @ 2½%	62.50	567	47
		E. E. Net Proceeds due Nov. 12th		$1,932	53
		New York, Nov. 15th, 1852.			
		THOMAS HARVEY & Co.			

When goods received on commission are sold, the agent makes out, for the inspection of the consignor, a detailed account of the sales of said goods, together with such charges as have been made on account of the same. In making out an Account-Sales, the mode of procedure is, to turn to the proper account in the Leger, and from thence refer to the necessary details, as found in the books of original entry. For the details of the sale, reference must be had to the Sales-Book; the charges, commission, &c., will be found in the Day-Book.

A variety of forms are here given, of which the first and last are the most common in business. Thinking it unnecessary to occupy space with them, I have omitted

ACCOUNT-SALES-BOOK, SET VI.

Faxon, Field & Co. and Thomas Harvey & Co.,

Dr. *In Account-Sales with Thomas Harvey & Co.* *Cr.*

1852.					1852.				
Nov.	1	To Ins. on $10,000, @ 1½%	150	00	Nov.	6	By J. Brown, TH 500 Bbls. Pork, @ $11	5,500	00
"	5	" Freight	850	00					
"	"	" Drayage	31	25					
"	15	" Int. on Charges to date	1	82	"	10	" H. S. Pierson & Co., TH 500 Bbls. Pork, @ $10.75	5,375	00
"	"	" Stor., Lab., Cooperage, &c.	41	50					
"	"	" Ins. vs. Fire, on $10,000, @ 1½%	150	00					
"	"	" Com. on $10,875, @ 2½%	271	87					
"	"	" Faxon, Field & Co.'s ½ Net Proceeds, due 10th inst.	4,689	28					
"	"	" Thos. Harvey & Co.'s ½ Net Proceeds, due 10th inst.	4,689	28					
			$10,875	00				$10,875	00

E. E. *New York, Nov. 15th*, 1852.

THOMAS HARVEY & CO.

Sales of Merchandise, for joint account of Faxon, Field & Co., Douglass, Forest & Co., and Ourselves.

1853.					
Jan.	21	Sold James Maitland & Co., @ 4 mos.,			
		◇D 25,909 lbs. Loaf Sugar, @ 9 ¢	2,331.81		
		◇E 29,068 " Crushed " " 8	2,325.44	4,657	25
Feb.	19	Sold Watson G. Gaylord, @ 10 days,			
		◇H 50 Tierces Rice, 90,200 lbs., @ 3¼¢		2,931	50
				7,588	75
		Charges.			
		Ins. vs. Fire on $6,500, (½ Am't Ins.,) @ 1½%	97.50		
		Cooperage, Weigh., & Lab.	19.62		
		Com. & Guar. on $7,588.75, @ 5%	379.44	496	56
		Net Proceeds, due Apr. 27th		$7,092	19
		Faxon, Field & Co.'s ⅓ net proceeds	2,364.06		
		Douglass, Forest & Co.'s ⅓ " "	2,364.06		
		Thomas Harvey & Co.'s ⅓ " "	2,364.07		
		E. E. *New York, Feb. 28th*, 1853.			
		THOMAS HARVEY & CO.			

several of the Account-Sales rendered in Set VII, and you can test your knowledge obtained of the ones given by making out those omitted.

The object of the Account-Sales-Book is to preserve a copy of the Account-Sales rendered to consignors.

ACCOUNT-CURRENT-BOOK, SET VI.

Account-Current of Adventure pr. Bark Phillis, with Interest to June 8th, 1853.

Date.		Description.	Time.	Interest.		Amount.	
1852.		Dr.					
Aug.	2	To Invoice of Flour, Corn Meal, and Corn, Shipped to Kingston, Ja., as pr. O.-I.-B.	10 m. 6 d's	439	86	8,624	75
Oct.	5	" Ins. in American Mutual Ins. Co., on $6,000, @ 1½%	8 " 3 "	3	65	90	00
"	11	" Bal. due Suarez, Brother & Co., Havana, as pr. their Account-Current				6,430	77
		Int. on $6,430.77, from Nov. 22d, the date when their Draft on us falls due	6 " 17 "	211	14		
"	12	" Balance of Charter money 1,000.00					
"	"	" Demurrage, 5 days, @ $25 125.00	7 " 27 "	44	44	1,125	00
		Total Interest		699	09	699	09
		Net Gains, due June 8 /53				822	52
						17,792	13
1852.		Cr.					
Oct.	19	By Net Proceeds of Sales of Sugars, due, pr. average, June 8 /53				17,792	13

E. E. *New York, Oct. 22d,* 1852.

Adventure to Canton in Account-Current with Thomas Harvey & Co. Interest calculated to Feb. 23d, 1854.

Date.		Description.	Time.	Interest.		Amount.	
1852.		Dr.					
July	9	To Invoice of Cargo, as pr. O.-I.-B., due Nov. 12th	15 m.11 d's	5,044	59	65,656	25
1853.							
Mar.	25	" Our Note @ 6 mos., to the Atlantic Ins. Co., for Ins. on Cargo homeward	4 " 25 "	27	40	1,133	75
June	18	" Set of Exchange, @ 90 days' sight, on Baring Brothers & Co., London, Bo't pr. Check, and remitted to cover Hughes, Miller & Co.'s Drafts from Canton, due in London, Oct. 3d. Am't £1,530, @ 8% Prem.	8 " 5 "	299	88	7,344	00
		Debit Bal. of Interest				4,167	21
		Net Gains, due Feb. 23 /54				11,783	56
				5,371	87	90,084	77
1853.		Cr.					
May	6	By Bal. in Hughes, Miller & Co.'s hands, Due Jan. 1 /53 1,598.24; 5% Dis., to convert to Canton funds 84.12	13 m.22 d's	115	52	1,682	36
"	"	" Port Charges, Piloting, Repairs, Sea Stores, &c., for Ship Massachusetts, due Jan. 1 /53 1,966.20; 5% Dis., to convert to Canton funds 103.48	13 " 22 "	142	12	2,069	68
June	1	" Sales of Tea No. 3, due Dec. 14 /53	2 " 9 "	947	02	82,349	95
"	15	" Sales of Matting No. 2, due Feb. 23 /54				3,982	78
		Debit Bal. of Interest		4,167	21		
				5,371	87	90,084	77

E. E. *New York, June 20th,* 1853.

ACCOUNT-CURRENT-BOOK, SET VI.

Messrs. Faxon, Field & Co., Cincinnati, in Account-Current and Interest-account with Thomas Harvey & Co., to July 1*st*, 1853.

Dr. *Cr.*

Date.	When due.	Description of Debits.	Amount.	Mos.	Days.	Interest.	Date.	When due.	Description of Credits.	Amount	Mos.	Days.	Interest
1852. Nov. 6	1852. Nov. 6	To Bill of Exchange, on Bacon & Boswell, Cincinnati, at par	5,000 00	7	25	195 83	1852. Nov. 5	1852. Oct. 26	By our ½ Invoice of Pork, furnished by you to be sold, for your and our joint %	4,628 12	8	5	188 98
1853. Jan. 15	1853. July 18	To our Note, @ 6 mos., favor of Douglass, Forest & Co., in Pay't of your ⅓ Invoice furnished by them, to be sold for your, their, and our joint %	4,155 12				" 15	Nov. 10	By your ½ Net Proceeds of Sales of Pork, for your and our joint %, pr. Ac't-Sales rendered	4,689 28	7	21	180 54
Feb. 5	Feb. 5	To your ½ Invoice of Coffee, furnished by us, to be sold for your and our joint %	4,483 11	4	26	109 09	1853. Feb. 28	1853. April 27	By your ½ Net Proceeds of Sales of Sugar and Rice, for your, Douglass, Forest & Co.'s, and our joint %, as pr. Ac't-Sales rendered	2,364 06	2	4	25 22
June 11	Aug. 10	To our ½ Net Proceeds of Sales of Coffee, for your and our joint %, pr. your Ac't-Sales	4,711 36				April 9	Oct. 26	By your ⅓ Net Proceeds of Sales of Sugars and Molasses, for your, D., F. & Co.'s, and our joint %, pr. Ac't-Sales Ren'd	1,713 80			
July 1		To Dis. on $1,713.80, pr. contra		3	25	32 85	July 1		By Dis. on $4,155.12, pr. contra			17	11 77
		Credit Bal. of Interest				99 36	" 1		By " " $4,711.36, " "		1	9	30 62
			18,349 59			437 13				13,395 26			437 13
									Add Bal. of Interest	99 36			
							" 1		*By Bal. carried down*	4,854 97			
			18,349 59							18,349 59			
1853. July 1		To Bal. due us, E. E.	4,854 97										

New York, July 1*st*, 1853.

THOMAS HARVEY & Co.

The Account-Current-Book is used for copying Ac't-Currents. An Ac't-Current, as will be seen by the formulas given, is a detailed statement of business transactions, and may be made out with or without interest. Between houses of extensive dealing, an Ac't-Current is usually made out before settlement, by one of the parties, and frequently by both, for the adjustment of differences in interest, &c.

LETTER-BOOK, SET VI.

New York, September 22nd, 1852.

Messrs. John Gundry & Co.,
Cincinnati:

GENTLEMEN,—We have this day received, pr. D. Leech Co.'s line, 500 Bbls. Flour, in good order, consigned to us to be sold for your ℅ and sk, as pr. your Invoice of the 13th inst.

As prices are rising, we think it advisable not to push it upon the market at present, but shall endeavor to seize the most favorable opportunity for effecting sales to dvantage.

Very respectfully,
Your ob't servants,
THOMAS HARVEY & Co.

New York, February 5th, 1853.

GENTLEMEN,

Your reply to our proposition to unite in a Company speculation of Mdse., be sold at Cincinnati, came to hand on the 1st inst., and in accordance therewith, e have this day shipped 2,000 Sacks Coffee, as pr. Invoice enclosed, and consigned em to you to be sold for your and our ℅, jointly. One-half of the Invoice we have arged to your ℅, in accordance with the terms of our agreement.—Am't $4,483.11.

A portion of the Sugars consigned to us for joint ℅ of yourselves, Douglass, Forest Co., and ourselves, have been advantageously sold, and there is prospect of another le soon.

Hoping this new adventure may prove for our mutual benefit,

We remain, gentlemen,
Very respectfully, yours,
THOMAS HARVEY & Co.

Messrs. Faxon, Field & Co.,
Cincinnati.

This book is used for taking copies of all business letters of importance, written to hers. Letters received are usually filed away. A business letter should be written brief terms and yet explicitly. To be well skilled in mercantile correspondence is small acquirement.

ADDITIONAL AUXILIARIES.

In addition to the auxiliary books already given, there are several others of less importance, but still convenient in some branches of business; among which are the following—

ORDER-BOOK, for taking copies of all orders received for merchandise.

MEMORANDUM-BOOK, for noting down mercantile affairs of importance, that have occurred or are likely to occur.

EXPENSE BOOK, for keeping an account in detail of those smaller expenses which are constantly occurring about an establishment.

POSTAGE-BOOK, for keeping an account of postages paid.

TIME-BOOK, for keeping the time of hands employed. See Form below.

FORM OF TIME-BOOK.

September.	Monday	Tuesday	Wednesday	Thursday	Friday	Saturday		1852.		Monday	Tuesday	Wednesday	Thursday	Friday	Saturday		Spinning room No. 1.		
Names.	6	7	8	9	10	11	Tot'l	Wag's	Am't.	13	14	15	16	17	18	Tot'l	Wag's	Am't.	Remarks.
Ann Robins	1	1	1	1	1	1	6	4,00	4 00	1	1	1	1	1	1	6	4,00	4 00	Good h'd.
Mary J. Linn	1	1	–	1	1	½	4½	3,00	2 25	1	1	1	1	1	1	6	3,00	3 00	" "
Anne Bowen	1	1	1	½	½	1	5	3,00	2 50	1	–	–	–	–	–	1	3,00	50	Sick.
Bet. S. Collins	1	1	1	1	½	½	5	3,50	2 92	1	1	1	1	1	1	6	3,50	3 50	Good h'd.
Susan Holt	1	½	1	–	1	1	4½	3,50	2 62	½	1	½	1	1	1	5	3,50	2 92	" "
Phebe Martin	1	1	1	1	1	1	6	2,50	2 50	1	½	1	1	1	1	5½	2,50	2 29	Slow

Manufacturers generally make use of this book.

When hands are employed by the month, the columns for days may be increased in number to twenty-six, the number of working days in a month.

LEGER ACCOUNTS.

(*Continued from Page* 120)

Sales Accounts, or Consignment Accounts.

THESE accounts show the charges on goods consigned to you to be sold for others, and the total sales or proceeds of the same.

The *debtor* exhibits all charges against them, the *creditor* all sales of goods con signed, and the *difference* the net proceeds due the consignors.

An account of this kind is closed by a Day-Book entry, debiting it and crediting the consignor with the amount of net proceeds. Or if payment be made immediately, the account which furnishes the means of payment may be credited instead of the consignor.

Merchandise in Co., and other Co. Speculating Accounts.

These accounts are kept to ascertain what you make or lose in each Co. Speculation of which you have the management; also the amount of net proceeds due each individual of the Co.

The *debit* side contains all that the Co. costs you, viz.: the amount of your investment, the charges and expenses paid by you, your commission for selling, and the amount of net proceeds due the other individuals of the Co.

The *credit* side contains all that the Co. produces you, viz.: the total proceeds of Co. goods sold, and, at closing, your portion of the balance unsold, if any.

The *difference* will be your gain or loss on the Co., which is usually carried to the Profit & Loss account by a Day-Book entry, although it may be transferred upon the Leger.

Adventure, or Shipment Accounts.

The *debit* side of an account of this kind shows the cost of goods consigned by you to another, to be sold for you.

The *credit* side shows the net proceeds of sales as rendered by the party abroad, or the net proceeds of sales, by you, of goods received in return for those sent abroad.

The *difference* will be a gain or loss, which is carried to the Profit & Loss account, usually by a Day-Book entry.

There are frequently other items of debit and credit, especially in foreign adventures, but the general rule of *debiting what costs you value* and *crediting what produces you value*, will enable you always to make the correct entries.

Adventure in Co., or Shipment in Co.

The *debit* side is to show what the adventure costs you, or your share of the Invoice of goods consigned; and the *credit* side the amount it produces you, or your share of the net proceeds of sales, as rendered by the party abroad.

The *difference* is always a gain or loss, and is closed into Profit & Loss, usually by a Day-Book entry. If all the Ac't-Sales have not been received at the time of closing, the account may be credited "By Balance," for the amount remaining unsold.

QUESTIONS FOR REVIEW, SET VI.

What kind of business is represented in Set VI?

How many years' business, and with how many partners for each year?

Explain the object and treatment of a Cash-Book, as used with Sets I to V inclusive.

What other and still more important office has it, as used with Set VI?

How often should it be balanced?

In making out account-sales and account-currents, and in settling accounts with individuals, what must be done with the Cash-Book?

Why are the accounts of *Ship Massachusetts* and *Adventure to Canton* left open in closing Leger A?

Explain how to transfer accounts from one Leger to another.

What test of the new Leger should be taken immediately after opening all the accounts in it?

In this Set what are the proper entries to be made by the firm, in both Day-Book and Cash-Book, for each of the following transactions—and why?

1st, Shipment of a cargo to Canton, pr. Ship Massachusetts, part of which was bought on their notes, part for cash, and part furnished from store; their note being also given for insurance, and they charging a commission for doing the business.—2d, Giving their note to an Insurance Co. for marine insurance on open policy.—3d, Purchase of a cargo for cash, and shipment of same pr. Bark Phillis, to the West Indies, to be sold for their account; insurance being effected on open policy, and a charge being made for drayage, labor and commission.—4th, Receipt of flour on consignment, to be sold for account of another person, and payment of freight thereon in cash; the drayage being performed by their drays.—5th, Insurance, on open policy, upon homeward cargo of Bark Phillis from the West Indies.—6th, Receipt of statements in detail of proceeds and expenditures on account of Adventure pr. Bark Phillis, by which it appears there is a balance owing by the firm to the commission merchants at Havana.—7th, Payment of duties on invoice of sugar received pr. Bark Phillis.—8th, Payment of charter money and demurrage on voyage of Bark Phillis.—9th, Sale of sugar received pr. Phillis, for another person's note.—10th, Closure of the Sales-account of sugar received pr. Bark Phillis, debiting it with the proper charges, and transferring the net proceeds to the Adventure account.—11th, Debit excess of interest on the Adventure account, and net gains as shown by the account-current.—12th, Effecting insurance on open policy on pork to be sold for joint account of firm and another person.—13th, Receipt of pork from a person abroad, furnished by that person to be sold on his and their joint account, and payment of freight on same in cash—drayage done by their drays.—14th, Sale, for a person's note, of pork received to be sold on joint account.—15th, Sale, for cash, of flour received to be sold for account of another person.—16th, Closure of the Sales account of flour sold for another person, and transfer of the net proceeds to his account.—17th, Debiting the Sales account of pork sold on joint account with the proper charges, and transfer of a share of the net proceeds to account of the person interested with the firm in the company speculation.—18th, Entry of gains accruing on the joint pork speculation.—19th, Shipment of coffee to another person, to be sold by him on his and their joint account, with insurance on open policy, charges and commission thereon.—20th, Protest of another person's note at bank.—21st, Payment by another of his note which has been protested, with interest.—22d, Receipt of statements of voyage to Canton, showing a balance against the commission merchants there, 5 % discount being required to convert United States currency into Canton funds.—23d, Receipt of statements showing that a portion of the proceeds of Adventure to Canton were appropriated to the payment of expenses of Ship Massachusetts at Canton.—24th, Closure of Sales of Tea, No. 3.—25th, Receipt of an account-sales for a joint adventure abroad.—26th, Closure of Sales of Matting, No. 2.—27th, Purchase for cash of a set of exchange, and remittance of same to cover drafts from Canton on account of the voyage.—28th, Closure of Adventure to Canton, by entry of debit balance of interest, and the net gains.

Describe the form and use of the Bank-Book;—Check-Book;—Bill-Book;—Invoice-Book;—Sales-Book;—Outward-Invoice-Book;—Ac't-Sales-Book;—Ac't-Current-Book;—Letter-Book.

What other Auxiliaries are sometimes used, and for what?

What do Sales accounts or Consignment accounts show?

What does the *debtor* exhibit?—What the *creditor?*—What the difference?—How closed?

For what are Merchandise in Co. and other Co. Speculating accounts kept?

What does the *debit* side contain?—What the *credit?*—What will the difference be and how closed?

What does the *debit* side of Adventure or Shipment accounts show?

What does the *credit* side show?—What will the *difference* be and how closed?

What does the *debit* side of an Adventure in Co. or Shipment in Co. show?

What does the *credit* side show?—What is the *difference* and how closed?

SET OF STEAMBOAT BOOKS.

This set of books is adapted to the *western river* business, and will be found particularly serviceable to clerks on board western boats, but may also be applied to other boating operations.

The books given are a Freight-Book, Passage-Book, Cash-Book, Leger, and Crews' Leger, which are all described under their several heads. There are, besides, several smaller books, used for taking memorandums; as, the Deck-Passage-Book, for entering sums received from deck passengers; the Fuel-Book, which contains printed blank receipts, to be filled up, when fuel is purchased, and signed by the person to whom payment is made; and a memorandum book for taking an account of goods when received on board or delivered, from which the record is made in the Freight-Book. A Bill-Book is sometimes kept, although it is generally unnecessary, on account of the small number of notes taken, the business being principally cash.

INSTRUCTIONS FOR THE STUDENT.

In order the more readily to comprehend these books, it will be well to imagine yourself on board the Steamboat Sultana, acting in the capacity of clerk.

After ruling, according to the forms given, enough paper for the several books, enter in the Cash-Book the amount of cash advanced by Simonds & Morrison, the owners of the boat, for its use. Next set down in the Crews' Leger the name of each of the hands, and the agreement made with him: after which, record in the Freight-Book all the goods taken on board at Cincinnati. Then enter in the Journal the note given for charges on Bill Lading No. 1; and in the C.-B. the cash paid on B. L. No. 2, and the cash received on B. L. No. 3: also enter in the C.-B. the sums paid for groceries, marketing, and wharfage. Next record in the Passage-Book the passengers from Cincinnati; after which make the entry, in the C.-B., of cash received for freight on goods landed at Louisville, and record in the Freight-Book the goods taken on board at that place. Then enter the following items in the order mentioned, putting them in the Cash, Freight, and Passage books alternately, as indicated by the nature of the entries, viz.: wharfage and canal tollage paid at Louisville; passengers from Louisville; Do. from Smithland; wharfage paid at Cairo; cash received for freight on goods landed at Memphis; goods taken on board at Do.; passengers from Do.; marketing and wharfage at Do.; passengers from Vicksburg; cash for freight on goods landed at Natches; passengers from and wharfage at Do. Now foot up the Passage-Book, and enter on the C.-B. the total amount received for fare. Next in order comes the amount paid for fuel—marketing at New Orleans—cash received for freight on the different bills—freight paid Brig Adelaide on goods reshipped—and lastly the wages paid the hands, which are to be entered both in the C.-B and Crews' Leger.

You may now close up the C.-B. after the manner described under that head, and journalize it; then post the Journal.

Proceed in the same manner with the next trip; and, having completed it, close up the Leger, and make a Balance Sheet.

Steamboat Sultana's Trip No. 1, *from*

Shipper.	Embarkation.	Consignee.	Destination.	No. of B. Lading.	Mark.
Joseph S. Smith	Cincinnati	O. A. Ogden	N. Orleans	1	AA
"	"	"	"	"	"
"	"	Townsend & Williamson	Memphis	2	O
"	"	"	"	"	"
John Farlan	"	James Morris	N. York	3	N
"	"	"	"	"	"
H. Jennings	"	J. Moore & Co.	N. Orleans	4	H
"	"	"	"	"	"
"	"	"	"	"	"
Anson Avery	"	J. C. Buckles	Louisville	5	G
"	"	"	"	"	"
P. Arbuckle & Co.	"	Pease & Co.	N. Orleans	6	B
"	"	"	"	"	"
Fellows & Co.	Louisville	E. C. Stockton	Natches	7	X
"	"	"	"	"	"
Armour Lake & Co.	Memphis	Pervis & Wood	N. Orleans	8	P

This book is used for recording all goods received on shipment. The headings of the different columns will show the manner of entry.

It frequently happens that the boat pays previous charges on goods for freight, storage, &c., or that she pays freight on goods reshipped by her. Sums so paid are entered in the "Freight and Charges paid" column, at the time of payment. The amount paid for *previous* charges, as shown by this column, is added to the boat's charges for freight as shown

FREIGHT-BOOK. 1

Cincinnati to New Orleans, June 1st, 1853.

Description of Freight.	Weight.	Rate.	Amount.	Freight and charges paid.	Freight and charges received.	Remarks.
200 Bbls. Whiskey		44	88 00	75 00		Gave note for charges on this bill $75
500 " Flour		30	150 00			
			238 00		313 00	
700 Bbls. Pork		44	308 00	25 00		
300 Firkins Butter		25	75 00			
			383 00		408 00	
700 Bbls. Flour		75	525 00			Shipper paid freight to New York.
900 " Pork		1,00	900 00			
			1,425 00	700 00	1,425 00	Shipped on Brig Adelaide at N. Orleans, and p'd her freight, $700.
10 Bbls. Eggs		30	3 00			
20 " Apples		30	6 00			
75 " Potatoes		30	22 50			
			31 50		31 50	
45 Bbls. Flour		15	6 75			
50 Boxes Cheese	2,500	12½	3 13			
			9 88		9 88	
40 Boxes Candles	1,600	25	4 00			
35 " Soap	2,100	25	5 25			
			9 25		9 25	
50 Pieces Bagging		10	5 00			
50 Coils Rope		10	5 00			
			10 00		10 00	
250 Bales Cotton		1,00	250 00		250 00	
				800,00		
					2,456,63	

by the "Amount" column, and their sum is extended into the "Freight and Charges received" column; which gives the total amount to be received. This may be done at any time when convenient during the trip.

When the trip is posted, the *debit* side of Freight account in the Leger should agree with the "Freight and Charges paid" column, and the *credit* side of the same account with the "Freight and Charges received" column.

Steamboat Sultana's Trip No. 2, from

Shipper.	Embarkation.	Consignee.	Destination.	No. of B. Lading.	Mark.
T. Saunders	N. Orleans	L. & G. Farwell & Co.	St. Louis	9	L
"	"	"	"	"	M
"	"	"	"	"	"
"	"	"	"	"	"
O. A. Ogden	"	Pratt & Co.	"	10	S
"	"	"	"	"	
"	"	"	"	"	W
Pervis & Wood	"	W. B. Morris & Co.	Louisville	11	D D
J. Newgate & Co.	"	Samuel Ewing	Memphis	12	E
"	"	"	"	"	"
"	"	"	"	"	"
"	"	"	"	"	"
J. McIntire	"	Stacker, Wood & Co.	St. Louis	13	V
"	"	"	"	"	"
P. W. Morrison	"	O. B. Batewell	"	14	Y
"	"	"	"	"	"
A. H. Hawley	Vicksburg	A. H. Hawley (on board.)	"	15	H
J. T. Lanphier	Memphis	Joseph Charles & Co.	"	16	C
"	"	"	"	"	"

New Orleans to St. Louis, June 13th, 1853.

Description of Freight.	Weight.	Rate.	Amount.	Freight and charges paid.	Freight and charges received.	Remarks.
40 Boxes Mdse.	9,000	30	27 00			
36 " "	12,600	30	37 80	25 00		
45 Bbls. Molasses		30	13 50			
30 Hhds. Sugar	33,750	25	84 38			
			162 68		187 68	
100 Sacks Salt		20	20 00			
150 " Coffee		20	30 00			
25 Hhds. Molasses	25,500	25	63 75			
			113 75		113 75	
40 Hhds. Sugar	44,200	25	110 50		66 30	Shipped on steamer Boston, at Cairo, and transferred B. L. to her, she paying our charges, $66,30.
30 Boxes Mdse.	9,000	20	18 00			
2 Crates Crockery		1,25	2 50			
5 Bbls. Sundries		20	1 00			
10 Cases Shoes		15	1 50			
			23 00		23 00	
Scotch Pig Iron	60,000	20	120 00	40 00		Rec'd. Note at 10 days for $185. (Jour. p. 1.)
400 Blocks French Burr Stone	80,000	20	160 00	65 00		
			280 00		385 00	Cash for Bal. $200. (C. B. p. 2.)
3 Boxes Pianos	1,500	40	6 00	12 00		
15 " Furniture	3,000	40	12 00			
			18 00		30 00	
10 Boxes Sundries	2,500	25	6 25		6 25	
20 Bbls. Castor Beans		12½	2 50			
8 Casks Sundries		12½	1 00			
			3 50		3 50	
				142,00		
					815,48	

1

STEAMBOAT SULTANA'S PASSAGE-BOOK.

Trip No. 1, *from Cincinnati to New Orleans.*

Date.		Names.	Embarkation.	Destination.	Fare.	
1853.						
June	1	Wm. H. Gorin	Cincinnati	New Orleans	15	00
"	"	Thos. Cobart	"	Louisville	3	00
"	"	Nathan Ives	"	New Orleans	15	00
"	"	Saml. Miller	"	Vicksburg	12	00
"	"	Norman Bliss	"	New Orleans	15	00
"	"	R. A. Butler	"	"	15	00
"	"	S. H. Hartly and lady	"	"	30	00
"	"	James Benson	"	"	15	00
"	"	J. N. Norton Miss Norton " Bates	Louisville	Memphis	24	00
"	"	I. Peterson	"	New Orleans	15	00
"	3	D. C. Budd	Smithland	"	11	00
"	4	R. Buttles	Memphis	"	9	00
"	"	Miss Stanley	"	Natchez	6	00
"	6	B. Burton	Vicksburg	New Orleans	6	00
"	"	Peter Quinn	"	"	6	00
"	"	J. G. Carlton	"	"	6	00
"	7	Benj. Black	Natchez	"	4	00
"	"	Philip Frazer	"	"	4	00
				Amt. from Deck-Passage-Book	38	00
				C.-B. page 1.	$249	00

In this book are registered the names of the cabin passengers, with the place of their embarkation and destination, and the fare.

At or near the end of the trip, the amount from the Deck-Passage-Book is brought into it, and it is then footed and the total entered in the Cash-Book.

Trip No. 2, from New Orleans to St. Louis.

Date.		Names.	Embarkation.	Destination.	Fare.	
1853.						
June	13	J. B. Stackhouse	New Orleans	St. Louis	12	00
"	"	R. D. Dewey	"	"	12	00
"	"	Peter Vanderlip	"	"	12	00
"	"	Francis Guerlain	"	Memphis	8	00
"	"	Marcus Snow	"	Vicksburg	5	00
"	"	Matthew White	"	St. Louis	12	00
"	"	M. E. Brown	"	"	12	00
"	"	S. N. Green	"	"	12	00
"	"	D. V. Black	"	Natchez	4	00
"	"	J. B. Jerome, wife, and 2 daughters	"	St. Louis	45	00
"	"	David Cross and lady	"	"	24	00
"	"	S. B. Beekman	"	"	12	00
"	"	J. Andrews	"	"	12	00
"	"	John Armour	"	Cairo	11	00
"	"	Madame Shawl and servant	"	St. Louis	18	00
"	"	D. Parks	"	"	12	00
"	"	Silas Buck	"	"	12	00
"	"	Seth Stone, wife, and sister	"	"	35	00
"	14	John Peacock	Natchez	"	10	00
"	"	C. Loffland	"	"	10	00
"	"	C. B. Bowes	"	"	10	00
"	15	A. H. Hawley and lady	Vicksburg	"	10	00
"	"	S. Birdseye	"	"	9	00
"	16	S. W. Lewelling	Memphis	"	5	00
"	"	Miss Simpson	"	"	5	00
"	"	Wm. Roberts	"	"	5	00
"	"	Jas. Raflin	"	"	5	00
"	"	Dr. McDowell	"	"	5	00
"	"	T. B. Withers	"	"	5	00
"	"	C. B. Payne	"	"	5	00
			Am't. from Deck-Passage-Book		685	00
				C.-B. page 2	$1,039	00

STEAMBOAT SULTANA'S

Dr *Cash.*

	Jour. page.		Freight.	Passage	Sundries.	Amount.
Trip No. 1.	1	To Simonds & Morrison, for cash advanced Boat -			500 00	
		" Freight, on Bill Lading, No. 3 - -	1,425 00			
		" " " " " " 5 - -	9 88			
		" " " " " " 2 - -	408 00			
		" " " " " " 7 - -	10 00			
		" Passage as pr. Passage-Book - -		249 00		
		" Freight, on Bill Lading, No. 1 - -	313 00			
		" " " " " " 4 - -	31 50			
		" " " " " " 6 - -	9 25			
		" " " " " " 8 - -	250 00			
	1	Rec'd for Freight this trip	2,456 63		2,456 63	
	1	" " Passage " "		249 00	249 00	
	1	Total cash receipts			3,205 63	3,205 63

This book is prepared with sundry columns on both the debit and credit side. When entries are made in it, the sums are placed in one or other of the columns, according as the headings indicate. Time is kept by trips, no dates being given.

At the end of a trip the different columns are footed up, and the totals extended into

Cash. *Cr.*

Trip No. 1.

Jour. page.		Expenses.	Wages.	Freight.	Sundries.
	By Charges paid on Bill Lading, No. 2			25 00	
	" Groceries at Cincinnati - - -	30 00			
	" Marketing " " - - -	20 00			
	" Butter and Eggs " " - - - -	15 00			
	" Wharfage " " - - - -	5 00			
	" Wharfage " Louisville - - -	1 00			
	" Canal Tollage " " - - - -	75 00			
	" Wharfage " Cairo - - - -	1 00			
	" Marketing " Memphis - - -	10 00			
	" Wharfage " " - - - -	1 00			
	" " " Natchez - - -	1 00			
	" Fuel, as pr. Fuel-Book - - - -	200 00			
	" Marketing at New Orleans - - -	6 00			
	" Freight paid Brig Adelaide on Bill Lading No. 3 - - - - - - -			700 00	
	" M. B. Butler on a/c - - -		5 00		
	" Benj. Stockton " " - - - -		4 00		
	" Peter Lawrence " " - - - -		1 50		
	" David Lyndes " " - - - -		10 00		
	" Samuel Johnson " " - - - -		20 00		
	" J. C. Allen " " - - - -		3 00		
	" R. E. Patterson " " - - - -		12 00		
	" Caleb Woolson " " - - - -		5 00		
	" Sarah Williams " " - - - -		3 00		
	" Ralph Brown " " - - - -		15 00		
	" Henry Webb " " - - - -		5 00		
	" Nathan Hatch " " - - - -		3 00		
	" James Manning " " - - - -		10 00		
	" Thos. J. Bates " " - - - -		10 00		
1	Paid for Expenses this trip	365 00			365 00
1	" " Wages " "		106 50		106 50
1	" " Freight " "			725 00	725 00
1	Total cash payments				1,196 50
	" *Balance on hand carried to Trip 2*				2,009 13
					3,205 63

he "Sundries" columns, which are also footed, and the closing is made after the manner hown—the final amount on the debit side, and the balance brought down, being exended into the "Amount" column.

The items in the "Sundries" columns are then journalized.

Dr. *Cash.*

Trip No. 2.

Jour. page.		Freight.		Passage.		Sundries.		Amount.	
	To Balance from Trip No. 1 - - -							2,009	13
	" Freight, on Bill Lading, No. 12 - -	23	00						
	" " " " " " 11 -	66	30						
	" Passage as pr. Passage-Book - - -			1,039	00				
	" Freight, on Bill Lading, No. 9 -	187	68						
	" " " " " " 10 - -	113	75						
	" " " " " " 13 -	200	00						
	" " " " " " 14 - -	30	00						
	" " " " " " 15 -	6	25						
	" " " " " " 16 - -	3	50						
1	Rec'd for Freight this trip	630	48			630	48		
1	" " Passage " "			1,039	00	1,039	00		
1	Total cash receipts					1,669	48	1,669	48
								3,678	61
	To Bal. on hand Bro't down - - -							2,926	97

CASH-BOOK.

Cash. Cr.

	Jour. page.		Expenses.		Wages.		Freight.		Sundries.	
Trip No. 2.		By Charges on Bill Lading, No. 9 -					25	00		
		" " " " " " 13 - -					105	00		
		" " " " " " 14 -					12	00		
		" Groceries at New Orleans - -	100	00						
		" Marketing " " - - - -	35	00						
		" Wharfage " " - - - - -	5	00						
		" Marketing " Vicksburg - - -	15	00						
		" Wharfage " " - - - - -	1	00						
		" Marketing " Memphis - - -	20	00						
		" Wharfage " " - - - - -	1	00						
		" Fuel, pr. Fuel-Book - - - - - -	150	00						
		" D. Lyndes in full - - -			50	00				
		" S. Johnson " " - - - - -			40	00				
		" J. C. Allen " " - - - - -			6	00				
		" R. E. Patterson " " - - - - -			15	00				
		" C. Woolson " " - - - - -			7	00				
		" Sarah Williams " " - - - - -			4	20				
		" Ralph Brown " " - - - - -			21	00				
		" Henry Webb " " - - - - -			5	80				
		" N. Hatch " " - - - - -			9	00				
		" M. B. Butler " " - - - - -			5	80				
		" Benj. Stockton " " - - - - -			11	00				
		" Peter Lawrence " " - - - - -			4	50				
		" James Manning " " - - - - -			73	34				
		" Thos. J. Bates " " - - - - -			30	00				
	1	Paid for Expenses this trip	327	00					327	00
	1	" " Wages " "			282	64			282	64
	1	" " Freight " "					142	00	142	00
	1	Total cash payments							751	64
		" *Balance on hand carried down* - -							2,926	97
									3,678	61

STEAMBOAT SULTANA'S JOURNAL.

Trip No. 1, *from Cincinnati to New Orleans, June* 1*st*, 1853.

1/1	Freight Dr. To Bills Payable for charges on B. Lading, No. 1	75 00	75 00
1 2 1 1	Cash Dr. To Sundries To Simonds & Morrison " Freight " Passage	3,205 63	 500 00 2,456 63 249 00
1 2 2 1	Sundries Dr. To Cash Expenses Wages Freight	 365 00 106 50 725 00	1,196 50
	Trip 2, *from N. O. to St. Louis, June* 13*th*, 1853.		
1/1	Bills Receivable Dr. To Freight for part pay't B. L. No. 13	185 00	185 00
1 1 1	Cash Dr. To Sundries To Freight " Passage	1,669 48	 630 48 1,039 00
1 2 2 1	Sundries Dr. To Cash Expenses Wages Freight	 327 00 282 64 142 00	751 64

The cash items in this book come from the Cash-Book. All other entries are made here directly from the transactions. Time is kept by trips, and posts made to the Leger in the same manner.

STEAMBOAT SULTANA'S LEGER.

INDEX.

LEGER.

Dr. *Freight.* **Cr.**

1853.						1853.					
Trip	1	To Bills Pay.	1	75	00	Trip	1	By Cash	1	2,456	63
"	"	" Cash	1	725	00	"	2	" Bills Rec.	1	185	00
"	2	" Do.	1	142	00	"	"	" Cash	1	630	48
"	"	" *Profit & Loss*	2	2,330	11						
				3,272	11					3,272	11

Dr. *Bills Payable.* **Cr.**

1853.						1853.					
Trip	2	*To Balance*	2	75	00	Trip	1	By Freight	1	75	00

Dr. *Bills Receivable.* **Cr.**

1853.						1853.					
Trip	2	To Freight	1	185	00	*Trip*	2	*By Balance*	2	185	00

Dr. *Cash.* **Cr.**

1853.						1853.					
Trip	1	To Sundries	1	3,205	63	Trip	1	By Sundries	1	1,196	50
"	2	" Do.	1	1,669	48	"	2	" Do.	1	751	64
						"	2	" *Balance*	2	2,926	97
				4,875	11					4,875	11

Dr. *Passage.* **Cr.**

1853.						1853.					
Trip	2	*To Profit & Loss*	2	1,288	00	Trip	1	By Cash	1	249	00
						"	2	" Do.	1	1,039	00

Dr. *Wages.* **Cr.**

1853.						1853.					
Trip	1	To Cash	1	106	50	*Trip*	2	*By Profit & Loss*	2	389	14
"	2	" Do.	1	282	64						

Dr. *Simonds & Morrison.* **Cr.**

1853.						1853.					
Trip	2	*To Balance*	2	3,036	97	Trip	1	By Cash	1	500	00
						"	2	" Profit & Loss	2	2,536	97

Dr. *Expenses.* **Cr.**

1853.						1853.					
Trip	1	To Cash	1	365	00	*Trip*	2	*By Profit & Loss*	2	692	00
"	2	" Do.	1	327	00						

Dr. *Profit & Loss.* **Cr.**

1853.						1853.					
Trip	2	To Wages	2	389	14	Trip	2	By Freight	1	2,330	11
"	"	" Expenses	2	692	00	"	"	" Passage	1	1,288	00
"	"	" *Simonds & Morrison*	2	2,536	97						
				3,618	11					3,618	11

Dr. *Balance.* **Cr.**

1853.						1853.					
Trip	2	To Bills Rec.	1	185	00	Trip	2	By Bills Pay.	1	75	00
"	"	" Cash	1	2,926	97	"	"	" *Simonds & Morrison*	2	3,036	97
				3,111	97					3,111	97

STEAMBOAT SULTANA'S CREW'S LEGER.

This is used for keeping the accounts of the hands. It is a book of original entry, and n fact entirely independent of any of the other books. Its form is so simple as scarcely o need any description. The names of the hands are recorded in it similarly to the titles 1 the main Leger, and if needed for convenience, an alphabet may be used for referring to hem.

Under the name of each person, the time when he commenced, and the agreement with im for wages, &c., is stated. Amounts paid him from time to time are entered to his lebit, and, as often as is desirable, a settlement is made and credit given for wages.

☞ This book is an exemplification of a short and easy mode of SINGLE ENTRY Book-Keeping, which may be used to advantage by a farmer, or mechanic, whose accounts are few and small, in preserving his business relations with his neighbors. See pages 55—57.

It will also be found very convenient for keeping the accounts of the hands in a manufacturing business.

James Manning, (*Capt.*) *Dr.* *Cr.*

			Dr.	Cr.
1853.		*Commenced June 1st, 1853, at $125 pr. mo.*		
June	10	To Cash on a/c	10 00	
"	20	" Do. in full	73 34	
"	"	By ⅔ month's Wages		83 34
			83 34	83 34

Thomas J. Bates, (*Clerk.*) *Dr.* *Cr.*

			Dr.	Cr.
1853.		*Commenced June 1st, 1853, at $60 pr. mo.*		
June	10	To Cash on a/c	10 00	
"	20	" Do. in full	30 00	
"	"	By ⅔ month's Wages		40 00
			40 00	40 00

David Lyndes. (*Pilot.*) *Dr.* *Cr.*

			Dr.	Cr.
1853.		*Commenced June 1st, 1853, at $100 pr. mo.*		
June	10	To Cash on a/c	10 00	
"	18	" Do. in full	50 00	
"	"	By ⅗ month's Wages		60 00
			60 00	60 00

Samuel Johnson, (*Engineer.*) *Dr.* *Cr.*

			Dr.	Cr.
1853.		*Commenced June 1st, 1853, at $100 pr. mo.*		
June	10	To Cash on a/c	20 00	
"	18	" Do. in full	40 00	
"	"	By ⅗ month's Wages		60 00
			60 00	60 00

Ralph Brown, (*Mate.*) *Dr.* *Cr.*

			Dr.	Cr.
1853.		*Commenced June 1st, 1853, at $60 pr. mo.*		
June	10	To Cash on a/c	15 00	
"	18	" Do. in full	21 00	
"	"	By ⅗ month's Wages		36 00
			36 00	36 00

Benj. Stockton, (Steward.)

			Dr.	Cr.
1853.		*Commenced June 1st, 1853, at $25 pr. mo.*		
June	10	To Cash on a/c	4 00	
"	18	" Do. in full	11 00	
"	"	By 3/5 month's Wages		15 00
			15 00	15 00

R. E. Patterson, (Carpenter.)

			Dr.	Cr.
1853.		*Commenced June 1st, 1853, at $45 pr. mo.*		
June	10	To Cash on a/c	12 00	
"	18	" Do. in full	15 00	
"	"	By 3/5 month's Wages		27 00
			27 00	27 00

Morris B. Butler, (Deck hand.)

			Dr.	Cr.
1853.		*Commenced June 1st, 1853, at $18 pr. mo.*		
June	10	To Cash on a/c	5 00	
"	18	" Do. in full	5 80	
"	"	By 3/5 month's Wages		10 80
			10 80	10 80

J. C. Allen, (Deck hand.)

			Dr.	Cr.
1853.		*Commenced June 1st, 1853, at $15 pr. mo.*		
June	10	To Cash on a/c	3 00	
"	18	" Do. in full	6 00	
"	"	By 3/5 month's Wages		9 00

Henry Webb, (Deck hand.)

			Dr.	Cr.
1853.		*Commenced June 1st, 1853, at $18 pr. mo.*		
June	10	To Cash on a/c	5 00	
"	18	" Do. in full	5 80	
"	"	By 3/5 month's Wages		10 80

Nathan Hatch, (*Fireman.*)

			Dr.		Cr.	
1853.		*Commenced June 1st, 1853, at $20 pr. mo.*				
June	10	To Cash on a/c	3	00		
"	18	" Do. in full	9	00		
"	"	By 3/5 month's Wages			12	00

Caleb Woolson, (*Fireman.*)

			Dr.		Cr.	
1853.		*Commenced June 1st, 1853, at $20 pr. mo.*				
June	10	To Cash on a/c	5	00		
"	18	" Do. in full	7	00		
"	"	By 3/5 month's Wages			12	00

Sarah Williams, (*Chambermaid.*)

			Dr.		Cr.	
1853.		*Commenced June 1st, 1853, at $12 pr. mo.*				
June	10	To Cash on a/c	3	00		
"	18	" Do. in full	4	20		
"	"	By 3/5 month's Wages			7	20

Peter Lawrence, (*Cabin boy.*)

			Dr.		Cr.	
1853.		*Commenced June 1st, 1853, at $10 pr. mo.*				
June	10	To Cash on a/c	1	50		
"	18	" Do. in full	4	50		
"	"	By 3/5 month's Wages			6	00

STEAMBOAT SULTANA'S BALANCE SHEET.

St. Louis, June 20th, 1853.	Folio.	Face of Leger. Dr.	Face of Leger. Cr.	Profit & Loss. Dr.	Profit & Loss. Cr.	Simonds & Morrison. Dr.	Simonds & Morrison. Cr.	Balance. Dr.	Balance. Cr.
Freight	1		2,330 11	...	2,330 11				
Bills Pay.	1	...	75 00	...	...	...	...	...	75 00
Bills Rec.	1	185 00	...	...	...	...	...	185 00	
Cash	1	2,926 97		...	...	...	...	2,926 97	
Passage	1	...	1,288 00	...	1,288 00				
Wages	2	389 14	...	389 14					
Simonds & Morrison	2	...	500 00	...	...	...	500 00		
Expenses	2	692 00	...	692 00					
		4,193 11	4,193 11						
To Simonds & Morrison, for Net proceeds				2,536 97	...	...	2,536 97		
				3,618 11	3,618 11				
To Balance, for Am't due them						3,036 97	...	...	3,036 97
						3,036 97	3,036 97	3,111 97	3,111 97

MANIFEST.

Steamer Sultana's Trip No. 2, from N. O. to St. Louis, June 17th, 1853.

Mark.	Articles.	Consignee.	Destination.
L	40 Boxes Mdse.	L. & G. Farwell & Co.	St. Louis.
M	36 " Do.	"	"
"	45 Bbls. Molasses	"	"
"	30 Hhds. Sugar	"	"
S	100 Sacks Salt	Pratt & Co.	"
"	150 " Coffee	"	"
W	25 Hhds. Mols.	"	"
V	Scotch Pig Iron	Stacker, Wood & Co.	"
"	400 Blocks French Burr Stone	"	"
Y	3 Boxes Pianos	O. B. Batewell	"
"	15 " Furniture	"	"
H	10 " Sundries	A.H.Hawley (on board)	"
C	20 Bbls. Castor Beans.	Jos. Charles & Co.	"
"	8 Casks Sundries	"	"
DD	40 Hhds. Sugar	W. B. Morris & Co.	Louisville.
B	30 Boxes Mdse.	Samuel Ewing	Memphis.
"	2 Crates Crockery	"	"
"	5 Bbls. Sundries	"	"
"	10 Cases Shoes	"	"

Thos. J. Bates, Clerk.

A manifest, as will be readily seen by the above illustration, is an exhibit of a vessel's Cargo; to which is frequently added a list of the passengers on board.

It is made out by the Clerk, and suspended in a prominent part of the vessel, so that any person interested may readily ascertain what goods are on board, and to whom they are consigned.

STEAMBOAT REPORT.

Steamer Sultana's Trip No. 1, *from Cin'i to N. Orleans, June* 10*th*, 1853.

Receipts.			
Cash for Freight, as pr. Freight-Book - - - - - - - -		2,456	63
" " Fare of 22 Cabin passengers - - - - - -		211	00
" " " " 15 Deck Do. - - - - - - - -		38	00
		2,705	63
Expenditures.			
Charges on B. L. No. 1, paid by Note to J. S. Smith -	75,00		
" " " " 2, " in Cash " " - -	25,00		
Freight " " " 3, " " " " Brig Adelaide -	700,00		
Marketing, Tollage, and Wharfage - - - - - -	165,00		
Fuel, as pr. Fuel-Book, - - - - - - - - -	200,00		
Am't paid Hands - - - - - - - - - - -	106,50		
" due Do. - - - - - - - - - - -	102,83	1,374	33
Net proceeds		$1,331	30

To Messrs. Simonds & Morrison. T. J. Bates, Clerk.

BILL OF LADING.

SHIPPED, by *T. Saunders*, on board Steamboat *Sultana*, whereof *James Manning* is master, now in the port of *N. Orleans*, and bound for *St. Louis*, viz.: 76 *Boxes Merchandise*, 45 *Bbls. Molasses, and* 30 *Hhds. Sugar*, being in good order and well conditioned, marked and numbered as in the margin, and to be delivered in like good order and condition (dangers of the river excepted), unto *L. & G. Farwell & Co.*, or to *their* assigns, he or they paying freight on the said *Merchandise*. In witness whereof, the Master of said Steamboat hath affirmed to *three* Bills of Lading, all of this tenor and date; one of which being accomplished, the others to stand void.

L 40 *Boxes.*
M 36 "
" 45 *Bbls.*
" 30 *Hhds.*

To L. & G. Farwell & Co., St. Louis.

Dated in N. Orleans, the 13*th* day of *June*, 1853.

James Manning.

This is an instrument used as cognisance of Merchandise or other property having been shipped for transportation. It is customary to have three of the same tenor and date. One is retained by the master of the vessel on which the goods are shipped, another is kept by the shipper, and the third is forwarded to the consignee. These instruments are printed blanks. In the above, the words in *italics* are the filling up of a shipment.

BILL FOR FREIGHT.

Messrs. L. & G. Farwell & Co.,

To Steamer Sultana, Dr.

For Freight on 76 Boxes Mdse. 21,600 lbs. @ 30 c.	64,80
" " " 45 Bbls. Molasses @ 30 c.	13,50
" " " 30 Hhds. Sugar, 33,750 lbs. @ 25 c.	84,38
St. Louis, June 18th, 1853.	$162,68

Rec'd. payment,

Thos. J. Bates, Clerk.

FORMS OF NOTES, DRAFTS, RECEIPTS, &c.

PROMISSORY NOTES.

225\frac{35}{100}$. *Cincinnati, November 5th*, 1852.

On demand, I promise to pay A. Farnum, or bearer, two hundred and twenty-five $\frac{35}{100}$ dollars, with interest. Value received.

No. 16. PETER LAMBERT.

$1,200. *New Orleans, November 2d*, 1852.

Sixty days from date, we promise to pay Blank & Boynton, at the City Bank, one thousand two hundred dollars, value received.

No. 80. J. C. SMITHSON & Co.

No. 1, 125. *Philadelphia, January 1st*, 1853.

Eight months after date, we severally and jointly promise to pay to the order of J. Durant six hundred and seventy-five and $\frac{50}{100}$ dollars, without defalcation, for value received.

675\frac{50}{100}$. NATHAN PETERSON.
J. W. MORRIS.

$500. *Philadelphia, January 15th*, 1853.

Four months from date, I promise to pay to Charles Johnson, or order, five hundred dollars, in Flour, at the market value when due, for value received.

JOHN TAYLOR.

REMARKS. 1st. If interest be not mentioned in a note, it is now generally conceded that it cannot be collected thereon. But if the time when the bill falls due pass without its being paid, Int. is recoverable from that date, and sometimes even damages.

2d. Custom allows *three days grace* on all notes; but Int. or discount is reckoned for *these three days*, the same as for any other time.

3d. Notes drawn "On demand" are not *legally* due until a formal demand, in presence of witnesses, has been made. To avoid this inconvenience, it is better to write them payable "One day after date."

4th. Notes made payable at a particular place must be demanded, or held in readiness, *there*,-when due, before the maker can be held responsible at any other place. For example, a note payable at a particular bank must be deposited in said bank for collection.

5th. Some states require the words "Without defalcation" to be inserted in all bills to render them negotiable; others "Without defalcation or discount;" others, only the words "Or bearer," "Or order," or "To the order of."

DUE BILLS.

Due, Cincinnati, January 4th, 1853, to S. P. Long, or order, thirty-five dollars, in goods from our store, value received.

BOYLE & BENEDICT.

$35.

413\frac{25}{100}$

Due, on demand, to Messrs. Laflin & Stephens, four hundred and thirteen $\frac{25}{100}$ dollars, with interest.

JOHN LUCAS.

Memphis, July 5th, 1853.

NOTE.—Due bills draw no interest unless specified.

DRAFTS.

$5,000. *St. Louis, June 20th*, 1853.

At thirty days' sight, pay to the order of F. H. Cossitt five thousand dollars, without defalcation or discount, value received, (payable at maturity in Missouri Bank funds,) and charge to account of

To *Wm. Akin*, Boonville, Mo. — WM. ROGERS.

$2,000. *Memphis, Sept. 12th*, 1853.

Sixty days from date, pay to Messrs. Parker & Co., at the City Bank, two thousand dollars, value received, and place the same to account of Messrs. Pervis & Wood, as per advice.

To Messrs. *Brander & Williams*, New Orleans. — JOHN S. MARTIN & CO.

REMARKS. 1st. When a draft is accepted, it becomes a promissory note, and can afterwards, with safety, be passed from hand to hand. For mode of acceptance see Vocabulary.

2d. Drafts drawn payable at a certain bank, must be deposited in said bank for collection. See remark 4th, under forms of notes.

3d. Drafts drawn "At sight" are usually paid at the time they are presented. All other drafts have *three days grace* allowed on them.

BILL OF EXCHANGE.

Exch. $3,000. *New Orleans, Nov. 14th*, 1853.

At ten days' sight, pay to the order of Messrs. Blank & Boynton, in Philadelphia, three thousand dollars, value received, and place the same to our account, with or without further advice.

To Mr. *J. Conly*, Philadelphia. — F. & R. E. TITUS.

SET OF EXCHANGE.

Exch. £900 Sterling. *Philadelphia, March 5th*, 1853.

Sixty days after sight of this, our *first* of exchange, (second and third of the same tenor and date unpaid,) pay to the order of Lovering & Bache, in London, nine hundred pounds sterling, for value received, as per advice, for the account of

To Messrs. *Barings & Co.*, London. — CLARK & CO.

Exch. £900 Sterling. *Philadelphia, March 5th*, 1853.

Sixty days after sight of this, our *second* of exchange, (first and third of the same tenor and date unpaid,) pay to the order of Lovering & Bache, in London, nine hundred pounds sterling, for value received, as per advice, for the account of

To Messrs. *Barings & Co.*, London. — CLARK & CO.

Exch. £900 Sterling. *Philadelphia, March 5th*, 1853.

Sixty days after sight of this, our *third* of exchange, (first and second of the same tenor and date unpaid,) pay to the order of Lovering & Bache, in London, nine hundred pounds sterling, for value received, as per advice, for the account of

To Messrs. *Barings & Co.*, London. — CLARK & CO.

BILLS AND SETS OF EXCHANGE.

Remarks. 1st. A *bill of exchange* has nearly the same phraseology as a *draft*. But the former name is generally applied to a bill drawn payable in a foreign country or state, while the latter is restricted chiefly to a bill payable in some part of the country in which it is drawn. The remarks on drafts apply also to bills of exchange.

2d. *Set of exchange* is a term applied to several *bills* of exchange, each drawn payable *provided the others remain unpaid;* so that whichever is first presented is paid, and the others are then void. The date of each is the same, and the phraseology also, with this exception—"*First* of exchange (second and third of the same tenor and date unpaid)"—"*Second* of exchange (first and third of the same tenor and date unpaid)," &c. Each bill of the set is sent by a different conveyance, as security against loss or inconvenience by miscarriage.

3d. Most foreign bills are now drawn through bankers, or brokers, and a "*Set* of exchange" is commonly spoken of as a "*Bill* of exchange," without regard to the distinction between a single bill and a set.

4th. When a bill of exchange is protested for non-acceptance or non-payment, and returned, the holder can recover the amount of the bill, and damages "consisting, besides interest, of the exchange or re-exchange, commission, postage, and expenses of protest, and interest on those expenses," from either the drawer or endorser, or if accepted, the acceptor. Several of the states have special enactments upon the subject, allowing a certain per-centage in addition to, or in lieu of, these damages.

5th. When an acceptance is *partial*, as to pay a part instead of the whole bill, or *qualified*, as to pay provided some future event occurs, notice of such partial or qualified acceptance should be given by the holder to the other parties to the bill, if he mean to resort to them in case of non-payment.

6th. A bill is sometimes drawn *at usance*, which means the usual time for payment allowed by the custom or law of the place where it is payable. The *usance* of Amsterdam, Rotterdam, Antwerp, Hamburg and Bremen, is 1 mo. after date; of Madrid and Gibraltar, 2 mos. after sight; of Leghorn, Genoa, Venice, and Naples, 3 mos. after date; of London, 60 days after sight; of Paris, Bordeaux, Malta, and Rio Janeiro, 30 days after date; of Dublin, 21 days after sight; of Dantzic, 14 days after date; of Leipsic, 14 days after acceptance.

7th. In most foreign countries, as in the United States, *days of grace* beyond the time when a bill becomes due are allowed for its payment. The *days of grace* in Great Britain are 3, except on bills drawn payable at sight, which must be paid as soon as presented. In Geneva they are 5; in Lisbon, Amsterdam, Antwerp, Rotterdam, Cadiz, Venice, Oporto, and Rio Janeiro, 6; in Bremen 8; in Dantzic, Paris, and Bordeaux, 10; in Altona and Hamburg, 12; in Malta, 13; in Madrid, Gibraltar, Barcelona, and Bilboa, 14; in Genoa, 30.

ORDERS.

Mr. James Park will please pay to S. Ely, or bearer, eighty dollars, in merchandise, on our account.

Wm. Hughes & Co.

Memphis, May 22d, 1852.

New Orleans, November 23d, 1852.

Messrs. Blank & Boynton:

Gentlemen—Please pay Messrs. Rogers & Co., or order, the fifty dollars due me for repairs of your store, and oblige

Yours, &c., S. Bridges.

RECEIPTS.

Received of Mr. J. S. Brown, three hundred dollars, in part of his account. Philadelphia, January 18th, 1853.

J. M. Reynolds.

$300.

Received, St. Louis, December 4, 1852, of Messrs. Sifert & Philips, seventy-five dollars, in full for all demands.

R. M. Gibbs.

$75.

Received from Mr. A. C. Keyes, two hundred dollars, which is endorsed on his Note of June 5th, 1852.

A. G. Martin.

$200.

Cincinnati, January 1st, 1853.

Practical Forms

To save Labor in

Keeping Books,

In Wholesale, Retail, Professional, Mechanical, Jobbing, Importing, Manufacturing, & Commission Business.

PRACTICAL FORMS.

PRELIMINARY REMARKS.

In the former part of this work, the nature of transactions; the philosophy, object, and utility of the various accounts; the manner of treating diversified operations, both simple and complex, which arise among every class of the trading community; in short, all those general principles, which are the foundation of the science of Book-keeping, have been fully discussed and elucidated.

A variety of Forms for practical purposes will now be given, which, while they will so abbreviate the operations as to lessen materially the amount of labor requisite, will not in the least depart from the fundamental principles of the science, but will rather require a previous knowledge of them, in order to be understood and appreciated. These Forms will be found adapted to almost every variety of business,* from the most simple to the most complicated; requiring only such slight alterations as the taste of the Book-keeper or the circumstances of the case may suggest.

Much might be said of the utility and real practical adaptedness of the following Forms; but, it is believed, they will commend themselves to all who will give them a careful examination.

The Legers to the Forms following are omitted, thinking it unnecessary to occupy room with them. Any new features in them are explained. But, lest there should be any difficulty in fully comprehending them, from the explanations, I have caused the Legers to Forms 3, 4, and 6, to be inserted in the Key, which those who find it necessary can procure.

Several of the minor auxiliary books, necessary for each of the Forms, are also omitted.

* It may be well to suggest that the Form of books appropriate to *Shipping* business is shown in Set VI. The Form for *Steamboat* books has also been given.

PRACTICAL FORM,

No. 1.

This Form is intended for professional gentlemen, mechanics, teachers, and others, whose accounts are limited. It will be found to embrace all the essential features and advantages of Double Entry, with little, if any, more writing than is required in Single Entry books. To make this clear to all, by comparison of the two systems, the same entries are used in illustrating this Form as were given in Set I, Single Entry.

The only books necessary in Form 1 are a Day-Book and Leger, the latter of which is here omitted.

The Day-Book is the first book of entry for all transactions, the left hand page being occupied with the date, the record of transactions which occur, and columns for Leger folios; and the right hand page being divided into six columns for dollars and cents. Two of these columns (one debit and one credit) are for Cash, two for Shop, and two for Sundries. Into the Cash debit column are extended all receipts of Cash;* into the credit, all payments out of the same:—into the Shop debit column, all outgoes and expenditures which may be properly considered as incurred for that account; into the credit, all proceeds resulting from the same:—and into the Sundries columns, debits and credits to accounts of persons, or to any other accounts, except Cash and Shop. The right and left hand pages of the blank book used constitute, together, one page or folio in the Day-Book.

No Cash-Book is required; and whenever it is wished to balance the Cash account, the debits and credits are added up, and opposite their totals, the amount in bank and in safe, being the balance on hand, is entered in red ink, which, if the account be correct, will agree with the difference between the debit and credit footings. In each subsequent balance of Cash, the last preceding footings of the columns are included in the additions made; thus the gross amount of Cash received and paid out is carried forward, until such time as it is desirable to post it.

At the bottom of each folio, the several columns are footed up, and the amounts taken forward to the folio following.

Those items extended into the Sundries columns are posted from day to day, at convenience, to the debit and credit of their proper accounts; but items extended into the columns appropriated to Cash and Shop accounts are not posted until the close of the week, month, or three months, according to the taste and convenience of the accountant. It is well to check the items so omitted in posting, to avoid errors. When the periodical time selected arrives, the gross amounts are posted to the Cash and Shop accounts respectively, as indicated by the headings of the different columns. The final footing of each column shows the amount to be posted in each case, except the debit side of Cash; from which the Balance on hand, if any, at former posting, must be deducted, to give the proper debit post to this account. The balance of Cash on hand, which is placed in the Cash debit column on commencing again, must also be placed in the Sundries credit column to produce the equilibrium.

The "Proof" is obtained by adding all the debit and all the credit footings together, to see if they are equal.

NOTE.—In a *printed* book of this Form it is somewhat difficult to trace the figures on the right-hand page; but in a blank book for the counting-house, this difficulty is obviated by the faint ruled lines on which to write.

N. B. The columns headed "Shop," may have any other heading, such as "Professional Services," "Institute," Daguerreotyping," &c., to suit the business; and additional columns may be introduced for any account having sufficiently numerous entries to make it desirable.

---

* Because, when Cash is received, it costs value, and is debtor.

☞ Please mark particularly the application of the *general rule* for journalizing in all the entries made in each different Form. This is the *grand test of correctness* in making debits and credits, and, if violated, it is a certain sign of error.

DAY-BOOK, FORM 1.

Philadelphia, September 1*st*, 1852.

Date.		Description.			L. F. Dr.	L. F. Cr.
1852.						
Sep.	1	Sundries To Stock,	For Effects invested			1
		Cash,	On hand		✓	
		Shop,	Stock of Tools, pr. Inventory		✓	
"	"	Shop To Cash,			✓	✓
		Paid for Paints, Oils, Glass, Brushes, &c., pr. Adams' Bill				
"	"	Bailey T. Stokes To Shop,	Lettering Tin Sign	1.75	2	✓
		1 Light Stained Glass		5.00		
"	2	Shop To Cash,			✓	✓
		2 Books Gold Leaf, 75¢, making Step Ladder, $5.00				
"	"	Mayland, Morris & Co. To Shop,	Bronzing Candelabra		3	✓
"	"	Shop To Cash,	Muslin		✓	✓
"	3	Thomas Templeton To Shop,	Bronzing Valve	.50	3	✓
		6 lbs. Blue Paint, @ 25¢		1.50		
		18 " White " " 12^2		2.25		
"	"	Cash To Shop,			✓	✓
		Glazing 27 Lights for S. Lambert, 10 by 12, @ 25¢				
"	4	Camden & Amboy R.-R. Co. To Shop,			3	✓
		Lettering Sign, 60 feet, @ 20¢ pr. foot		12.00		
		Gilding Border of Sign		2.00		
		Putting up Sign		2.50		
"	"	Shop To Geo. L. Searles,	4 days' labor, @ $1.50		✓	4
"	"	Geo. L. Searles To Cash,	On %		4	✓
"	"	Shop To Cash,	Paid Wages, pr. Time-Book		✓	✓
		In Bank, $345.00, *in Safe*, $41.31=*Bal. on hand*, $386.31				
"	6	Camden & Amboy R.-R. Co. To Shop,			3	✓
		Lettering Sign, 15 feet, @ 20¢		3.00		
		Making Board and putting up		4.25		
"	"	Shop To Henry Talbott,			✓	4
		Making Sign for Camden & Amboy R.-R. Co.				
"	"	Cash To Shop			✓	✓
		Rec'd of John Payson, for painting Sign, pr. agreement				
"	7	Cash To Bailey T. Stokes,	In full of %		✓	2
"	8	Shop To Jonathan Long & Co.,	Paints, Oils, &c., pr. Bill		✓	4
"	"	Jonathan Long & Co. To Cash,	In part of above Bill		4	✓
"	"	Shop To Wm. G. Bradbury,	Bill of Paints, Glass, &c.		✓	5
"	9	Thomas Templeton To Shop,	Glazing 1 Light, 11 by 18		3	✓
"	11	Jonathan Long & Co. To Sundries,			4	
		To Cash, Paid on %				✓
		To Shop, Glazing 10 Lights, 10 by 18, @ 25¢				✓
"	"	Shop To Geo. L. Searles,	5^2 days' labor, @ $1.50		✓	4
"	"	Geo. L. Searles To Cash,	On %		4	✓
"	"	Shop To Cash,	Smith, Wages in full		✓	✓
		In Bank, $364.93, *in Safe*, $10.00=*Bal. on hand*, $374.93				
"	13	Philadelphia Exchange To Shop,			5	✓
		Glazing 4 Lights, 10 by 16, @ 25¢		1.00		
		Painting 3 Rooms, 2 Coats, pr. agreement,		15.00		
			Amounts forward			

Cash Dr.	Cash Cr.	Shop Dr.	Shop Cr.	Sundries Dr.	Sundries Cr.
					575 00
500 00					
		75 00			
	105 32				
		105 32			
			6 75		
				6 75	
	5 75				
		5 75			
			2 00	2 00	
	37	37			
			4 25		
				4 25	
6 75					
			6 75		
			16 50		
				16 50	
		6 00			6 00
	3 00			3 00	
	6 00	6 00			
506 75	120 44				
			7 25		
				7 25	
		3 00			
					3 00
30 00					
			30 00		
6 75					6 75
		52 64			52 64
	25 00			25 00	
		140 00			140 00
			37	37	
				12 50	
	10 00				
			2 50		
		8 25			8 25
	9 00			9 00	
	4 13	4 13			
543 50	168 57				
			16 00		
				16 00	
543 50	168 57	406 46	92 37	102 62	791 64
Bal.	374 93		*Proof*	1,052 58	1,052 58

Philadelphia, September 15*th*, 1852.

Date.		Description.		L. F. Dr.	L. F. Cr.
1852.					
		Amounts Bro't forward			
Sep.	15	J. Long & Co. To Camden & Amboy R.-R. Co.,		4	3
"		My order on C. & A. R.-R. Co., favor of J. Long & Co.			
	17	Cash To Shop,	37 lbs. Blue Paint, @ 25¢	✓	✓
"	18	Shop To Geo. L. Searles,	3^2 days' labor, @ $1.50	✓	4
"	"	Geo. L. Searles. To Cash,	In full (discharged)	4	✓
"	"	Cash To Shop,		✓	✓
"		2 Lights, 10 by 20, Stained Glass, @ $4.50			
"	"	Shop To Cash,	Smith, Wages in full	✓	✓
				1/2	1/2
		In Bank, $374.43, *in Safe*, $5.25			
1852.					
Sep.	20	Balance Cash on hand, from Sept. 18th,			
"	"	Cash To Shop,		✓	✓
		Sold to T. Stone 120 lbs. White Paint, @ 11¢			
"	"	Shop To Cash,	Repairs of Shop	✓	✓
		Making Transparency Frame			
"	22	Sargeant & Willis To Shop		5	✓
		Stained Glass Transparency, Frame, and putting up, as agreed			
"	24	Cash To Shop,		✓	✓
		Rec'd of J. F. Godwin, for Stained Glass, pr. agreement			
		" " Harry Biddle, for painting Church, "			
"	25	Bailey T. Stokes To Shop,	Glazing New Sash at Manu-	2	✓
		factory, as pr. agreement, to wit:			
		56 Lights, 11 by 15, @ 9¢	5.04		
		139 " 10 " 12, " 7	9.73		
		1920 " 8 " 10, " 3	57.60		
		20 " Old Glazing, 11 by 17, @ 35¢	7.00		
		Painting 110 Window Frames, @ 45¢	49.50		
		" Reception Room	5.25		
"	"	Shop To Cash,	Paid Wages, pr. Time-Book	✓	✓
		In Bank, $541,75, *in Safe*, $54.00=*Bal. on hand*, $595.75			
"	27	Personal Expenses To Thomas Templeton,		2	3
		1 Blk. Cloth Dress Coat	15.00		
		1 Pr. Blk. Cass. Pants	6.00		
"	"	Shop To Cash,		✓	✓
		Paid P. Lee for Sundry Jobs Carpentering, as pr. Bill			
"	28	" for 10 Gals. Linseed Oil, @ 1.62^2			
"	29	Cash To Shop,	Rec'd for Tin Sign	✓	✓
"	"	Shop To Cash,	Tin and Japanning	✓	✓
"	30	Sargeant & Willis To Shop,	Painting Office, as agreed	5	✓
"	"	Shop To Cash,		✓	✓
		Paid H. Smith Wages in full			
		" Rent of Shop, one month, to date			
		Cash debits, $637.88, *less former Bal.*, $379.68=$258.20 *Cash Receipts*		1/2	1/2
		In Bank, $521.43, *in Safe*, $18.65			
1852.					
Oct.	1	Balance Cash on hand, from Sept. 30th			

Dr. Cash	Cash Cr.	Dr. Shop	Shop Cr.	Dr. Sundries	Sundries Cr.
543 50	168 57	406 46	92 37	102 62	791 64
				15 14	
					15 14
9 25			9 25		
		5 25			5 25
	7 50			7 50	
9 00					
			9 00		
	6 00	6 00			
561 75	182 07	417 71	110 62	125 26	812 03
Bal.	379 68		*Proof*	1,104 72	1,104 72
379 68					379 68
13 20					
			13 20		
	2 12	2 12			
	4 38	4 38			
			40 00		
				40 00	
25 00			25 00		
210 00			210 00		
			134 12		
				134 12	
	25 63	25 63			
627 88	32 13				
				21 00	
					21 00
	22 50				
		22 50			
	16 25	16 25			
10 00			10 00		
	4 25	4 25			
			30 00	30 00	
	6 00	6 00			
	16 67	16 67			
637 88	97 80	97 80	462 32	225 12	400 68
Bal.	540 08		*Proof*	960 80	960 80
540 08					540 08

BALANCE SHEET, LEGER, FORM 1.

Philadelphia, September 30th, 1852.	L. Folio.	Face of Leger. Dr.	Face of Leger. Cr.	Profit & Loss. Dr.	Profit & Loss. Cr.	Stock. Dr.	Stock. Cr.	Balance. Dr.	Balance. Cr.
Stock	1		575 00				575 00		
Cash	1	540 08						540 08	
Shop	2		57 43 *140 50		197 93			140 50	
Personal Expenses	2	21 00		21 00					
Bailey T. Stokes	2	134 12						134 12	
Mayland, Morris & Co.	3	2 00						2 00	
Thomas Templeton	3		16 38						16 38
Camden & Amboy R.-R. Co.	3	8 61						8 61	
Henry Talbot	4		3 00						3 00
Wm. G. Bradbury	5		140 00						140 00
Philadelphia Exchange	5	16 00						16 00	
Sargeant & Willis	5	70 00						70 00	
		791 81	791 81						
To Stock, for Net Gain				176 93			176 93		
				197 93	197 93				
Net Capital						751 93			
						751 93	751 93		
Total Resources and Liabilities								911 31	159 38
Net Capital, as pr. Stock									751 93
								911 31	911 31

**Inventory.*

Stock of tools	75.00
" " paints	65.50
	$140.50

This Balance Sheet is given that it may be compared with Statements to Set I, Single Entry, page 24.

PRACTICAL FORM,

No. 2.

This Form is intended for a *retail* merchandising business, in which the *purchases* are made periodically, or in large amounts. It is so arranged as to post to the credit of Merchandise monthly, and thereby save much labor. The books of original entry are a Day-Book, Cash-Book, and Petty-Cash-Book. Posts are made from the Day-Book only.

DIRECTIONS FOR WRITING UP.

Prepare the necessary blank books, by ruling, heading, &c., after the formulas given.

Enter in your Day-Book the effects invested on 1st inst., as shown in the Day-Book given; also, in your Cash-Book, on the debit side, the Cash entry of 1st inst.

Next enter, on the debit side of the Cash-Book, the receipt of Cash for Bills Receivable on the 7th inst.; then, on the credit side, the payments of Cash for Expenses and Merchandise on the 8th.

Follow with the entries of 9th inst., in both Day-Book and Cash-Book, then of 11th, and so on, in order of date, until the 16th inst.

Now transfer all the entries from your Cash-Book to your Day-Book, as follows:—Say in Day-Book "Cash To Sundries"—seek the first debit to Cash (after the amount invested), and place it down underneath, with the date, to the account of Bills Receivable, checking opposite the amount in the Cash-Book, to show it is entered in the Day-Book;—examine to see if there be any other receipts from the same source, and, if so, place them down also, with the date, checking, as before, in the Cash-Book;—after finding all that comes under the head of Bills Receivable, take the next account in order in the Cash-Book, and so on, till all the debits are transferred. Write up the credits in the same manner, heading them, "Sundries To Cash."

After this, continue the Cash-Book and Day-Book connectedly, until the end of the month.

For convenience, all the postings may be omitted until the end of the month, although it will be seen that the arrangement is such, that, in actual business, the accounts of persons might be posted from day to day, so as to be always ready for settlement.

DAY-BOOK.

All transactions are entered in this book as they occur, except receipts and payments of Cash, which are first entered in the Cash-Book, and then brought into this once a month, or oftener. This book has an extra credit column, into which all the credits (sales) of Merchandise are extended. This column is footed, and the amount carried forward from folio to folio, until the close of the month, when the sum total is posted to the credit of Merchandise. The items entered in the other two columns are posted from day to day, as convenient.

By examining the formula given, the manner of entry and extension in the different columns will be readily comprehended. It will also be seen that the two credit columns are, together, equal to the debit; thus at the close of the month, when all are posted, we have carried out strictly the principle, that "In amount every debit must have a credit," with very little more writing than *Single Entry* books would have required for the same business, and with much more satisfactory results.

In order to have a proof of each page, an amount equal to the footing of the Merchandise column must also be carried forward into the Sundries debit column.

CASH-BOOK, FORM 2.

Dr. *Cash.*

Date.				Mdse.		Sundries.	
1852.							
Oct.	1	To Stock,	Amount invested			910	50
"	7	" Bills Receivable,	Rec'd for D. Mann's Note, No. 3			525	00✓
"	11	" Merchandise,	Sales pr. P.-C.-B.	25	37		
"	12	" Do.	" " "	123	44		
"	13	" Do.	" " "	62	31		
"	14	" Bills Receivable,	John Allen's Note, No. 2			125	50✓
"	"	" Merchandise,	Sales pr. P.-C.-B.	10	15		
"	15	" Do.	" " "	2	16		
"	16	" Do.	" " "	217	42		
			D.-B., folio 1,	440	85	440	85✓
						2,001	85
1852.							
Oct.	18	To Balance from Old %c				566	09
"	"	" Wm. Bates,	In full of %			30	50✓
"	"	" Bills Receivable, Jan. 18th /53, less Dis., pr. Contra	Slade & Co.'s Note, No. 4, due			51	60✓
"	"	" Merchandise,	Sales pr. P.-C.-B.	76	50		
"	19	" Do.	" " "	110	00		
"	20	" Do.	" " "	31	00		
"	21	" Do.	" " "	60	78		
"	22	" Do.	" " "	26	10		
"	23	" Do.	" " "	356	05		
"	25	" Do.	" " "	91	10		
"	26	" Do.	" " "	46	13		
"	27	" Bills Receivable, 12th, less Dis., pr. Contra	J. Bailey's Note, No. 6, due Apr.			100	00✓
"	"	" Merchandise,	Sales pr. P.-C.-B.	77	77		
"	28	" Isaac Norris,	On %			10	00✓
"	"	" Merchandise,	Sales pr. P.-C.-B.	81	29		
"	29	" Interest,	Dis. on Note, No. 1, pr. Contra			8	76✓
"	"	" Merchandise,	Sales pr. P.-C.-B.	106	10		
"	30	" Do.	" " "	251	66		
			D.-B., folio 3,	1,314	48	1,314	48✓
						2,081	43
1852.							
Nov.	1	To Balance from Oct. 30th /52.				965	96

The above *Cash-Book* is believed to be the most convenient form for a business like that to which it is intended to apply.

The additional columns introduced are merely as a matter of convenience, to facilitate in transferring the entries into the Day-Book.

The Merchandise column, on the debit side, is for all sales effected for Cash, and receives an entry at the close of each day from the Petty-Cash-Book. At the end of the month, or whenever you choose to transfer your Cash entries to the Day-Book, this column is added up, and the amount extended into the Sundries column. All receipts of Cash during the month, except for sales made, are entered at the time in the Sundries column, so that, whenever the sales are extended into it, the footing shows the total Cash debits.

The Expenses column, on the credit side, is the recipient of sums paid for expenses from

CASH-BOOK, FORM 2.

Cash. *Cr.*

Date.				Expenses.		Sundries.	
1852.							
Oct.	8	By Expenses,	Travelling Fare, Board at Boston, and other Incidental Expenses, as pr. Memorandum	31	25		
"	"	" Merchandise,	Paid Freight			12	50✓
"	9	" Do.	Purchases, pr. Invoices			1,353	26✓
"	11	" Expenses,	Blank Books, pr. Bill	11	75		
"	12	" Do.	1 Ton Coal	4	50		
"	16	" Barber T. Lee,	On %			6	00✓
"	"	" Expenses,	Wages of Clerks	16	50		
			D.-B., folio 2,	64	00	64	00✓
"	"	" *Bal. on hand to New %*				566	09
						2,001	85
1852.							
Oct.	18	By Interest,	Dis. on Note No. 4, pr. Contra				77✓
"	"	" Barber T. Lee,	On %			2	00✓
"	22	" Expenses,	Paid for Store Fixtures	13	00		
"	"	" Do.	" Bill of Stoves	22	50		
"	23	" Do.	" Wages	8	75		
"	25	" Do.	" Porterage	1	13		
"	27	" Merchandise,	Bo't of Philip Trent, Agent of Abbott Lawrence, Boston, pr. Invoice			510	28✓
"	"	" Interest,	Dis. on Note No. 6, pr. Contra			1	77✓
"	29	" Bills Payable,	Note No. 1, favor of Draper & Warren, Boston, due April 9th, having been sent, by my request, to the Quincy Bank for collection, I have paid the same, less Dis., pr. Contra, Am't			520	40✓
"	30	" Expenses,	Paid Wages	9	12		
		Do.	" Rent of Store, 1 mo.	15	00		
"	"	" Barber T. Lee,	" In full			10	75✓
			D.-B., folio 3,	69	50	69	50✓
"	"	" *Bal. on hand, to Nov. 1st /52*				965	96
						2,081	43

time to time. Prior to entering in the Day-Book, it is added up, and the amount extended into the Sundries column, which then contains all Cash credits.

In transferring either debits or credits from the Cash-Book to the Day-Book, only those items which are embraced in the Sundries column are taken; thus the credit to Merchandise, and debit to Expenses are in sums total in the Day-Book.

When Bills Receivable are paid before due, as in the entry of 18th inst., the whole face of the note is first entered, as if money was really received to that amount; and then on the opposite side Interest is debited for the amount of discount on the note; this gives the right credit to Bills Receivable.

The same remarks apply to Bills Payable, when paid before due.

As it would not be convenient in this arrangement of Cash-Book to make a formal balance of it nightly, this is done in the Petty-Cash-Book.

PETTY-CASH-BOOK, FORM 2.

North Adams, Mass., October 11*th*, 1852.

EXPLANATION.

The Petty-Cash-Book here given is a small memorandum book, which lies in the money drawer where the receipts for sales during the day are placed.

Each salesman or saleswoman, coming to the drawer to make change, or to place therein sums received, enters in this book the items sold. Then, at night, the footing must agree with the amount of money in drawer; and this sum is entered in the Cash-Book, as the day's sales.

The left hand marginal column is used for the initials of the persons by whom the goods were sold.

This book is also used for balancing the Cash account, nightly, which should always be done in a retail business, to avoid errors.

NOTE.—The sales of only two days are here given. This will be sufficient to serve as a sample.

When the business is sufficiently large to require it, a Petty-Cash-Book may be arranged and used, as described under Form 5.

L. W.	Sewing Silk 6¢, Thread 4¢			10
B. T. L.	8 Yds. Fig'd Lawn, @ 30¢		2	40
S. A. J.	1 Pr. Kid Gloves		1	37
L. W.	Tapes & Ribbons			35
B. T. L.	25 Yds. Eng. Thread Lace, @ 28¢	7.00		
"	10 " Lisle Edging " 30¢	3.00		
"	1 " Bobbin Lace	.15		
"	12 " Emb'd Muslin, " 55¢	6.60	16	75
"	¼ lb. Sewing Silk, " 8.00		2	00
S. A. J.	Lace 10¢, Sewing Silk 4¢, Cord 7¢			21
"	2 Prs. Lisle Thread Gloves, @ 31½¢			63
"	1 " Col'd Kid "			87
L. W.	1 " " " "			69
	Oct. 11th /52. C.-B.		25	37
	Cash debits, pr. C.-B.,			
	Mdse. column	25.37		
	Sundries "	1,435.50	1,460	87
	Cash credits, pr. C.-B.,			
	Expenses column	43.00		
	Sundries "	1,365.76	1,408	76
	Balance Cash on hand		52	11
S. A. J.	1 Velvet Mantilla	35.00		
"	2 Yds. White Illusion, @ 32¢	.64	35	64
B. T. L.	Blk. Twist 13¢, Edging 22¢			35
L. W.	1 Box Artificial Flowers		1	50
"	Floss 25¢, Twist 15¢			40
S. A. J.	1 Changeable Silk Mantilla		18	00
B. T. L.	3 Lace Capes, @ 4.75		14	25
"	Artificial Flowers			25
"	Inserting 30¢, Gloves 56¢			86
L. W.	½ Doz. Italian Cravats @ 12.00		6	00
S. A. J.	Trimmings			33
B. T. L.	1 Emb'd Robe	5.50		
"	12 Yds. White Satin, @ 1.25	15.00		
"	5 " Col'd Velvet, " 3.00	15.00	35	50
L. W.	½ Doz. Neck Ties, " 4.75		2	37
"	Twist			09
B. T. L.	2 Lace Capes, @ 3.50	7.00		
"	2 Prs. Linen Gloves, " 45	90	7	90
	Oct. 12th /52. C.-B.		123	44
	Cash debits, pr. C.-B.,			
	Mdse. column	148.81		
	Sundries "	1.435.50	1,584	31
	Cash credits, pr. C.-B.,			
	Expenses column	47.50		
	Sundries "	1,365.76	1,413	26
	Balance Cash on hand		171	05

DAY-BOOK, FORM 2.

North Adams, Mass., October 1*st*, 1852.

L. F.			Sundries Dr.		Sundries Cr.		Mdse. Cr.	
1	Sundries To Stock,				2,500	00		
	For Effects invested							
1	Cash,	In Quincy Bank	910	50				
2	Bills Receivable,	Sundry Notes, pr. B.-B.	1,200	00				
1	Merchandise,	Stock on hand, pr. Inventory	389	50				
	9th							
1	Merchandise To Sundries,		3,696	25				
	For Goods purchased by me, in Boston, pr. Invoices							
2	To Bills Payable,	Notes issued, pr. B.-B.			2,230	00		
3	" Abbott Lawrence,	Invoice @ 6 mos.			845	50		
4	" Daniel Webster,	" " "			620	75		
	11th							
4	James Peabody To Mdse.,							
	½ Doz. Linen Cambric Hdkfs.	@ 3.50	1	75				
	1 Blk. Italian Cravat		1	50			3	25
	12th							
4	Mrs. Eliza Anderson To Mdse.,							
	12 Yds. Mull Muslin	@ 31^1	3	75			3	75
	"							
5	Wm. Bates To Mdse., pr. wife,							
	2 Yds. Linen Lawn	@ 65	1	30				
	10 " Cambric Edging	" 25	2	50				
	16 " " Inserting	" 34	5	44				
	8 " Swiss "	" 22	1	76				
	1 Velvet Mantilla		25	00				
	1 Lace Cape		4	50			40	50
	14th							
2/5	Expenses To Wm. Bates,							
	For his Bill of Repairs		10	00	10	00		
	16th							
4	Mrs. Eliza Anderson To Mdse.,							
	1 Pr. Blk. Kid Gloves			69				69
	"							
5	Isaac Norris To Mdse., pr. daughter,							
	1 Blk. Silk Mantilla		15	00				
	2 Embroidered Collars	@ 1.12^2	2	25			17	25
	"							
1	Cash To Sundries, pr. C.-B.,		1,091	35				
2	To Bills Rec.,	7th 525.00						
	Do.	14th 125.50			650	50		
✓	" Merchandise,	Cash Sales					440	85
	Mdse. carried forward				506	29	506	29
			7,363	04	7,363	04		

North Adams, Mass., October 16*th*, 1852.

L. F.		Sundries Dr.	Sundries Cr.	Mdse. Cr.
	Mdse. brought forward	506 29		506 29
1	Sundries, To Cash pr. C.-B.,		1,435 76	
1	Merchandise, 8th 12.50			
	Do. 9th 1,353.26	1,365 76		
5	Barber T. Lee, 16th	6 00		
2	Expenses, For the mo.	64 00		
	18th			
5	Barber T. Lee To Mdse.,			
	1 Blk. Italian Cravat	1 25		1 25
	20th			
6	Hiram T. Owens To Mdse., pr. son,			
	1 Yd. Col'd Silk Velvet	3 25		
	1 Pr. Blk. Kid Gloves	1 13		
	2 " Lisle Thread " @ 31¹	62		5 00
	21st			
5	Isaac Norris To Mdse., pr. wife,			
	5 Yds. Swiss Muslin @ 25	1 25		
	1 " Green Barege	30		
	1 White Demi Veil	1 50		
	1 Blk. " "	1 75		
	1 Fancy Silk Scarf	1 88		6 68
	"			
4	Mrs. Eliza Anderson To Mdse.,			
	1 Embroidered Robe	5 00		5 00
	25th			
6	Misses T. & M. Williams To Mdse.,			
	1 Ps. Blk. Crape	3 00		
	3 " Col'd " @ 3.25	9 75		12 75
	26th			
3/2	Profit & Loss To Bills Receivable, Note No. 1 is lost, the drawer, P. T. Lamb, having failed.	25 00	25 00	
	"			
4	James Peabody To Mdse.,			
	1 Pr. Silk Thread Gloves	63		
	2 Pongee Silk Hdkfs. @ 1.00	2 00		2 63
	29th			
Entry continued.	Hiram T. Owens To Mdse., pr. wife,			
	2 Yds. Bonnet Ribbon @ 30	60		
	3 " Cap " " 15	45		
	1 Muslin Cape	3 50	4 55	
	Mdse. carried forward		539 60	539 60
		2,004 91	2,004 91	

DAY-BOOK, FORM 2.

North Adams, Mass., October 29th 1852.

L. F.				Sundries Dr.		Sundries Cr.		Mdse. Cr.	
		Mdse. brought forward		539	60			539	60
6	Hiram T. Owens	To Mdse., (*continued*)		4	55				
	3 Neck Ties		@ 31[1]		94				
	2 Prs. Embroidered Cuffs		" 56[1]	1	12				
	1 Box Artificial Flowers			1	38				
	4 Linen Cambric Hdk'fs		" 45	1	80			9	79
		30th							
2/5	Expenses	To Barber T. Lee,							
	1 month's Wages to date			20	00	20	00		
		"							
1	Cash	To Sundries, pr. C.-B.,		1,515	34				
5	To Wm. Bates,	18th				30	50		
2	" Bills Rec.,	"	51.60						
	" Do.	27th	100.00			151	60		
5	" Isaac Norris,	28th				10	00		
3	" Interest,	29th				8	76		
✓	" Merchandise,		Cash Sales					1,314	48
		"							
1	Sundries	To Cash	pr. C.-B.,			1,115	47		
3	Interest,	18th	.77						
	Do.	27th	1.77	2	54				
5	Barber T. Lee,	18th	2.00						
	Do.	30th	10.75	12	75				
1	Merchandise,	27th		510	28				
2	Bills Payable,	29th		520	40				
2	Expenses,		For the mo.,	69	50				
1		Total Merchandise Credits				1,863	87	1,863	87
				3,200	20	3,200	20		

TRIAL BALANCE, LEGER, FORM 2.

L. F.		Dr.		Cr.	
1	Stock - - - - - - - -			2,500	00
1	Cash - - - - - - - -	965	96		
1	Merchandise - - - - - -	4,097	92		
2	Bills Receivable - - - - -	372	90		
2	Bills Payable - - - - - -			1,709	60
2	Expenses - - - - - - -	163	50		
3	Interest - - - - - - -			6	22
3	Profit & Loss - - - - - -	25	00		
3	Abbott Lawrence - - - - -			845	50
4	Daniel Webster - - - -			620	75
4	James Peabody - - - - -	5	88		
4	Mrs. Eliza Anderson - - - -	9	44		
5	Isaac Norris - - - - - -	13	93		
6	Hiram T. Owens - - - - -	14	79		
6	Misses T. & M. Williams - -	12	75		
		5,682	07	5,682	07

In closing this Leger, the *Mdse. remaining unsold,* as pr. Inventory, may be called $4,563.89.

BALANCE SHEET, LEGER, FORM 2.

North Adams, Mass., November 1st, 1852.	L. Folio.	Face of Leger. Dr.	Face of Leger. Cr	Profit & Loss. Dr.	Profit & Loss. Cr.	Stock. Dr.	Stock. Cr.	Balance. Dr.	Balance. Cr.
Stock	1		2,500 00				2,500 00		
Cash	1	965 96						965 96	
Merchandise	1	4,097 92	4,563 89		465 97			4,563 89	
Bills Receivable	2	372 90						372 90	
Bills Payable	2		1,709 60						1,709 60
Expenses	2	163 50		163 50					
Interest	3		6 22		6 22				
Profit & Loss	3	25 00		25 00					
Abbott Lawrence	3		845 50						845 50
Daniel Webster	4		620 75						620 75
James Peabody	4	5 88						5 88	
Mrs. Eliza Anderson	4	9 44						9 44	
Isaac Norris	5	13 93						13 93	
Hiram T. Owens	6	14 79						14 79	
Misses T. & M. Williams	6	12 75						12 75	
		5,682 07	5,682 07						
To Stock, for Net Gains				283 69			283 69		
				472 19	472 19				
Net Capital						2,783 69			
						2,783 69	2,783 69		
Total Assets and Liabilities								5,959 54	3,175 85
Net Capital, as pr. Stock									2,783 69
								5,959 54	5,959 54

If you write up this Form, you will be able to judge of the correctness of your Leger, by comparison with this Balance Sheet.

E. M. LAFOURCADE, SON & CO.

PRACTICAL FORM, NO. 3.

PLAN FOR JOURNALIZING MONTHLY.

EXPLANATORY REMARKS, FORM 3.

THIS Set exhibits a method of keeping books known to almost every experienced accountant as the plan of "journalizing monthly." It is designed for a *wholesale, jobbing* business; but a similar form of accounts may be used to advantage in many other kinds of business, by varying the books of original entry slightly, as occasion may demand. In *manufactories*, in large *retail* stores, and in houses doing a *general trading* business, such a form is often used.

The important books of original entry are Cash-Book, Bill-Book, Sales-Book, and part of the Journal—which is used during the month for making such entries as would otherwise require a separate Day-Book. The first three mentioned are journalized monthly, by which process the various entries in each to any given account are summed up together in the Journal, and the postings are made in monthly totals, instead of a separate post for every separate entry. These four books (including the Journal only so far as it is so used) are in fact all Day-Books, *i. e.* they all contain the daily original records of transactions, and are the books which must be relied upon for evidence in courts of justice. Therefore, the remarks made on page 111, as to corrections of errors in the Day-Book, are equally applicable to each of these books as used in this Set, which should be so kept as to be above suspicion of fraudulent intent or erroneous result.

Besides these, there are various *auxiliary books* needed, examples of which have been given, with explanations accompanying them, on pages 170–182.

CASH-BOOK.

The explanation of Cash-Book, Set VI, pages 124 and 125, may be taken almost entire as the explanation of this Cash-Book, substituting the word "Journal" wherever the word "Day-Book" occurs. Once a week, or as often as it is wished to make trial of the correctness of the Cash account, the debit and credit columns may be footed up, and then the amount of cash in bank (as shown by the Check-Book) and the amount in Safe may be placed in red ink a little to the left of the credit footing, and if their sum be equal to the difference of the cash columns, it proves the account correct. In each subsequent testing of the account, the last preceding footings of the columns should be included in the additions made; thus the gross amounts are carried forward until the end of the month.

BILL-BOOK.

Bills Receivable and Bills Payable are usually bound in opposite ends of the same book, styled Bill-Book. This book is so simple, that you will see by inspection its utility; and all necessary explanations are made by the headings of the different columns. The entries extend across two opposite pages of the blank book, which together constitute but one page, or folio, of the Bill-Book. Other persons' notes to you are entered in this book at the time of their reception, and your own notes to others are entered at the time they are issued.

The amount of unpaid notes held by you against others, as shown by this book, must agree at all times with the balance of Bills Receivable account in the Leger; and the amount of unpaid notes outstanding against you, as here shown, must agree with the balance of Bills Payable account in the Leger.

This, like the Cash-Book, may be a mere memorandum book, for keeping a correct record of notes received and issued, or it may be, as it is in this Set, an important book of original entry from which to journalize. The total of the Journal entry "Bills Receivable To Sundries" must correspond with the gross amount of notes received; and the total of the entry "Sundries To Bills Payable" must agree with the gross amount of notes issued.

SALES-BOOK.

The Sales-Book, like the books already spoken of, is often used as a mere auxiliary. But, in this Set, it is one of the main books of original entry, and one from which Journal entries are made. All sales, both for cash and on credit, are entered in it, at the time the sale is made. At the close of each day, the sales for cash are transferred to the Cash-Book—first noting on a slip of paper the amounts of the several cash sales, adding them up, and comparing the total with the money actually received during the day for sales, which receipts should be kept separate from the other moneys on hand for the purpose of this comparison. If any portion of such receipts are deposited in bank, a memorandum can be kept thereof, and counted in as so much cash; so also with any other sums added to or taken from the same. The credit sales are supposed to be at six months, when no mention is made of the time.

Credit sales are extended into the outer or right-hand column, but cash-sales are kept in the left-hand column, or if the amount of an entry has been extended, and subsequently, but before the entry is journalized, it is paid, the figures in the outer column should have lines drawn through them, so that they will not be included in the footings of the Sales-Book. The credit sales are added up, and the amount carried forward from page to page till the end of the month. This book is journalized under the heading of "Sundries To Merchandise," and the total credit to Merchandise under this head must agree with the final footing of the Sales-Book.

NOTE.—Houses doing a different kind of business, can vary the books of original entry, adopting such as are most convenient, and still journalize monthly, if desirable.

☞ The *disadvantage* of this Form, compared with Form 4, is, that accounts of persons are seldom posted up ready for settlement, but are generally nearly, or quite, a month behindhand.

JOURNAL

Transactions oftentimes occur in the course of business which cannot appropriately be entered in the Cash-Book, or Bill-Book, or Sales-Book; and for these some have a separate Day-Book, and journalize it monthly like the other books. But I prefer using the Journal as a Day-Book during the month, and placing such entries in it; and then posting them directly from this first entry to the Leger. Purchases of goods on credit, and such cash purchases as you wish to have appear on the Leger, in the account of the person from whom you buy, are entered also originally in the Journal. The invoices are kept on file until the end of the month, when they are arranged in order, and entered "Merchandise To Sundries," all the purchases of any one man being brought together in one total in making the entry, so as to save labor in posting. The remaining and legitimate use of the Journal (that from which it takes its name) is to receive the entries transferred into it monthly from the other books.

Directions for Writing up.

Blank books are prepared for this Set, and accompany the treatise.

Commence with the *first* day of the month, and by examining you will find one entry in the Journal, four in the Cash-Book, one in the Sales-Book, and three in the Bill-Book on that day, which you will enter in the same manner in your Journal, Cash-Book, Sales-Book, and Bill-Book—leaving the Leger folio columns blank, to be filled when you post. Next examine the different books of original entry, to see what transactions occur on the *second* day, and enter the same in your books. After completing them, proceed with the *third* day in like manner. And so on with each succeeding date, recording, in the proper books, all transactions that take place on any particular day, before making any entry of the day following it. This will give an idea of the exact process of entry in the counting-house.

At the close of the month, journalize one of the books of original entry entire, then a second, and so on, until all are journalized. It makes no material difference which book is journalized first, but the Cash-Book is the one here selected. Commence with the debit side—"Cash To Sundries"—and enter the various receipts to the credit of the proper accounts, and place together the several sums received at different times from the same account, so as to add up and post them in one amount to the Leger. This renders it necessary to look over the whole of the Cash debits carefully for each account entered, to find all the receipts therefrom; and, to avoid omissions and errors, check each sum in the Cash-Book, as soon as journalized. To afford convenient reference from the Journal to the Cash-Book at any time, affix to each sum its proper date. Having completed the debits, next journalize the credit side, saying "Sundries To Cash," and debiting all accounts for which payments have been made during the month.

Journalize the Bill-Book under the headings "Bills Receivable To Sundries," and "Sundries To Bills Payable," checking the items as you proceed.

"Sundries To Merchandise" is the proper heading for the Sales-Book.

The two columns for dollars and cents are not used to distinguish debits from credits, but the first is for items, and the second for the extension of sums total.

In posting the entries journalized, the last day of the month may be used for the date in the Leger. In opening the accounts in this Leger, you may observe the usual counting-house arrangement of them, which is to open the accounts of partners, property accounts, and all the general business accounts, in the first part of the Leger, by themselves; and to let all the personal accounts follow them. This renders convenient the taking of Trial Balances and other exhibits from the Leger.

☞ Be particular to make your own additions, extensions, and other calculations, wherever they occur in any of the books.

CASH-BOOK, FORM 3.

Dr. *Cash.*

1852.					
Nov.	1	To Edwin M. Lafourcade,	Am't invested	10,000	00 √
"	"	" Louis P. Lafourcade,	" "	5,000	00 √
"	"	" Chas. Boutelier, Jun.,	" "	5,000	00 √
"	2	" Merchandise,	Sales this day	37	50 √
"	3	" Do.	Of Grayson & Co., less Dis. pr. contra	357	40 √
"	4	" Do.	Sales this day	319	80 √
"	5	" Do.	" " "	25	00 √
"	6	" Do.	" " "	37	88 √
				20,777	58
"	8	" Samuel Tillotson,	On %	500	00 √
"	9	" Merchandise,	Sales this day	339	00 √
"	10	" Interest,	Dis. on Bills Pay. No. 3, pr. contra, $2,806.84 @ 5 %	140	34 √
"	11	" Bills Receivable,	No. 1, discounted by Durbin, Payson & Co.	562	50 √
"	12	" Merchandise,	Of Jacob Lukens, Jun., less Dis. pr. contra	216	00 √
"	13	" Do.	Sales this day	6	30 √
				22,541	72
"	16	" Interest,	Dis. on Bills Pay. No. 4, pr. contra, $492.50, for 52 days	4	27 √
"	20	" Merchandise,	Sales this day	75	00 √
				22,620	99
"	23	" Merchandise,	Net Sale to Peter Phelps, 19th inst.	180	00 √
"	25	" Bills Receivable,	No. 7, discounted by Julius & George Lee	398	67 √
"	27	" Merchandise,	Sales this day	10	00 √
				23,209	66
"	29	" Merchandise,	Of Benj. Loper & Co., less Dis. pr. contra	408	00 √
"	"	" Samuel Tillotson,	On %	500	00 √
"	"	" Merchandise,	Sales this day	40	50 √
"	30	" Mrs. Mary Green,	In full	7	81 √
				24,165	97
1852.					
Dec.	1	To Balance,	From Nov. 30th	10,787	02

Cash. *Cr.*

1852.					
Nov.	1	By Merchandise,	Bo't of Isler & Co., pr. Invoice	643	50 √
"	2	" Expenses	Store Fixtures	30	00 √
"	"	" Do.	Drayage & Labor	12	25 √
"	3	" Interest,	Dis. 5 % on $357.40, pr. contra	17	87 √
"	5	" Merchandise,	Bo't of T. Lathrop, pr. Invoice	162	94 √
"	"	" Do.	Hoops for strapping boxes	15	00 √
"	6	" Expenses,	Cooperage	3	50 √
			In Bank 19,874.13 / *In Safe* 18.39 } $19 892.52	885	06
"	8	" Joseph Ralston,	On %	5	00 √
"	9	" Merchandise,	Bo't of Le Brun & Bro., pr. Invoice	82	10 √
"	"	" Expenses,	Blank Books and Stationery	14	25 √
"	10	" Bills Payable,	No. 3, discounted by us, pr. contra	2,806	84 √
"	11	" Interest	Dis. on Bills Rec. No. 1, pr. contra, $562.50 @ 5 %	28	12 √
"	12	Do.	Dis. on Sale to Jacob Lukens, Jun., 5th inst., pr. contra, $216 @ 5 %	10	80 √
"	13	" Webster & Shaw, Boston,	Paid their Draft on us @ sight, favor of Ludlow & Co., dated 3d inst	725	00 √
			In Bank 17,863.40 / *In Safe* 121.15 } $17,984.55	4,557	17
"	15	" Merchandise,	Bo't of Lind & Beers, pr. Invoice	562	00 √
"	16	" Bills Payable,	No. 4, discounted by us, pr. contra	492	50 √
"	18	" Expenses,	Cooperage, Labor, &c.	2	75 √
"	"	" Louis P. Lafourcade,	On %	500	00 √
"	20	" Joseph Ralston,	" "	10	00 √
"	"	" Merchandise,	Rec'd pr. "City of Glasgow," from Robertson & Howell, Luton, Bedfordshire, Eng., an Invoice of Bonnets, dated 1st inst., Am't £160 8*s.* 6*d.*, for which we have remitted them a Bill of Exchange, @ 3 mos. from date of Invoice, purchased of Ledoux & Cornelle, on Brown, Shipley & Co., Liverpool, @ 9² % Prem.	780	74 √
"	"	" Merchandise,	Freight on above, and Shipping Expenses in Eng.	56	75 √
"	"	" Do.	Duties on £160 8*s.* 6*d.* (@ $4.84 pr. £) @ 30 %	232	94 √
			In Bank 15,420.50 / *In Safe* 5.64 } $15,426.14	7,194	85
"	22	" Expenses,	Paper & Ink		75 √
"	25	" Interest,	Dis. on Bills Rec. No. 7, pr. contra, $398.67 @ 5 %	19	93 √
"	26	" Bouvier Brothers,	On %	1,000	00 √
"	27	" Merchandise,	Geo. Parr & Co.'s Bill of Exchange on Brown, Shipley & Co., Liverpool, for £320 17*s.*, @ 3 mos. from 8th inst., purchased @ 9 % Prem., and remitted to Robertson & Howell, Luton, Eng., for Invoice of Bonnets, Plaits, &c., of same date and time, Rec'd pr. "Niagara"	1,554	34 √
"	"	" Merchandise,	Shipping Expenses in Eng., and Freight	113	50 √
"	"	" Do.	Duties on £320 17*s.* (@ $4.84 pr. £) @ 30 %	465	87 √
			In Bank 12,625.18 / *In Safe* 235.24 } $12,860.42	10,349	24
"	29	" Interest,	Dis. on Sale to Benj. Loper & Co., 26th inst., pr. contra, $408 @ 5 %	20	40 √
"	30	" Merchandise,	Rec'd pr. "Crescent City" from Havre, an Invoice of Swiss Straw Plaits, Laces, &c., dated Nov. 2d, Am't 10,176 francs, forwarded to our Order by Surbridge, Bro. & Co., Wohlen, Switzerland, for which they have drawn on our %, @ 3 mos., as pr. instructions, on Delacroix & Co., Paris. We have purchased a Bill of Exchange of Ledoux & Cornelle, on Delacroix & Co., and remitted to them to cover the Am't of their acceptance f.10,176, and their Com. for accepting 1 %, f.101.76 = f.10,277.76—Exchange @ f.4.89 to the dollar.	2,101	79 √
"	"	" Merchandise,	Transportation from Wohlen, Shipping Charges and Com. of Agent at Havre, and Freight on above Mdse.	186	40 √
"	"	" Merchandise,	Duties on f.10,176 (@ $18\frac{708}{1000}$¢ pr. f.) @ 30 %	571	12 √
"	"	" Expenses,	Rent of Store $75, Wages of Clerks $75	150	00 √
"	"	" *Balance,*	*In Bank* $10,719.10, *In Safe* $67.92	10,787	02
				24,165	97

Bills

No. of Note.	When Received.		Drawer	In whose favor.	Date of Note.		Time.
	1852.				1852.		
1	Nov.	2	Durbin, Payson & Co.	Ourselves	Nov.	2	6 mos.
2	"	3	Willard, Brady & Co.	"	"	3	6 "
3	"	8	Ourselves	Accepted by Ferree & Bro. in our fav.	Oct.	28	6 "
4	"	"	"	" "	Nov.	8	6 "
5	"	11	Decoursey & Wise	Drawer	"	11	6 "
6	"	18	Julius & George Lee	"	"	18	4 "
7	"	"	"	"	"	"	6 "
8	"	"	"	"	"	"	8 "
9	"	25	"	Ourselves	"	25	5 "
10	"	"	"	"	"	"	7 "

Bills

No. of Note.	When Issued.		Drawer.	In whose favor.	Date of Note.		Time.
	1852.				1852.		
1	Nov.	1	Ourselves	Drawer (% of Dufour, N. & Co.)	Nov.	1	2 mos.
2	"	"	"	"	"	"	4 "
3	"	"	"	"	"	"	6 "
4	"	5	"	Margot & Haines	"	5	60 days
5	"	10	"	Drawer (% of Dufour, N. & Co.)	"	10	3 mos.
6	"	16	"	"	"	16	6 "
7	"	23	"	"	"	23	4 "
8	"	29	"	Margot & Haines	"	29	90 days
9	"	"	"	E. B. Bolton	"	29	4 mos.
10	"	30	Dufour, Nephew & Co.	Accepted by us in fav. of Drawers	"	30	3 "

BILL-BOOK, FORM 3.

Receivable.

Where due.	Jan.	Feb.	Mar.	Apr.	May	June	July	Aug.	Sept.	Oct.	Nov.	Dec.	Amount.		Remarks.
Bank of Louisiana					5								562	50	✓ Discounted Nov. 11th
New Orleans					6								102	97	✓
"					1								377	25	✓
"					10								377	25	✓
Bank of Louisiana					14								259	65	✓
"			21										398	67	✓
"					21								398	67	✓ Discounted Nov. 25th
"							21						398	66	✓
Planters' Bank				28									297	00	✓
"						28							297	00	✓
													3,469	62	✓

Payable.

Where due.	Jan.	Feb.	Mar.	Apr.	May	June	July	Aug.	Sept.	Oct.	Nov.	Dec.	Amount.		Remarks.
Bank of Louisiana	4												2,806	83	✓
"			4										2,806	83	✓
"					4								2,806	84	✓ Discounted Nov. 10th
Planters' Bank	7												492	50	✓ " " 16th
"		13											652	36	✓
"					19								422	10	✓
"			26										210	28	✓
"			2										910	35	✓
New Orleans				1									712	00	✓
Bank of Louisiana			3										165	75	✓
													11,985	84	✓

SALES-BOOK, FORM 3.

New Orleans, November 1*st*, 1852.

√	Ferree & Brother,	Natchez.				
	15 Cases, 180 Prs. Men's Stout Boots	@ 2.00	360	00		
	3 " 180 " " Lasting Gaiters	1.75	315	00		
	18 Cooperages	25	4	50	679	50
	2d					
√	Durbin, Payson & Co., (Note pr. B.-B.)	Vicksburg.				
	1 Case, 60 Prs. Men's Goat Nullifiers	@ 80	48	00		
	3 " 180 " Women's Grain Buskins	80	144	00		
	2 " 120 " " Lasting ½ Gaiters	90	108	00		
	1 " 60 " " Col'd " "	80	48	00		
	2 " 120 " " Kid Slippers R. R.	70	84	00		
	2 " 120 " Misses' Goat Lace Boots	75	90	00		
	1 " 60 " " R. R. Paris Ties	62^2	37	50		
	12 Cooperages	25	3	00	562	50
	"					
√	Dolbear & Reikert,	Memphis, Tenn.				
	128 Ps. Straw Trimmings	@ 50	64	00		
	24 " French Straw Lace	1.25	30	00		
	12 " " Inserting "	1.50	18	00		
	Box & Cooperage			75	112	75
	"					
Paid	Cash Sales,					
	50 Scores Sacramento Plait	@ 27^2	13	75		
	50 " " "	47^2	23	75		
			37	50		
	3d					
√	Willard Brady & Co., (Note pr. B.-B.)	Orange St.				
	75 Scores Rock Luton Plait, No. 4	@ 45	33	75		
	100 " " " " " 5	50	50	00		
	8 Maids' Coburg Bonnets " 2	25	2	00		
	18 " China Pearl " " 1	33	5	94		
	12 Women's " " "	37^2	4	50		
	16 " Goffer'd Edge "	33	5	28		
	2 Cases	50	1	00		
	Cooperage			50	102	97
	"					
Paid less Dis.	Grayson & Co.,	Natchez.				
	3 Cases, 180 Prs. Women's Calf Lace Boots	@ 1.25	225	00		
	119 Maids' Feather Edge Bonnets	1.10	130	90		
	4 Cooperages	25	1	00		
	1 Case			50	~~357~~	~~40~~
	4th					
Paid	Cash Sales,					
	10 Prs. Men's Stout Boots	@ 1.98	19	80		
	"					
√	Dolbear & Reikert,	Memphis.				
	48 Women's Cap'd Bonnets	@ 1.12^2	54	00		
	48 " Tulip "	1.20	57	60		
	50 " Eng. Straw "	37^2	18	75		
	Box & Cooperage			75	131	10
	"					
Paid	Jones, Brother & Co., (Net)	Canal St.				
	4 Cases, 240 Prs. Women's Lasting Gaiter Boots	@ 1.25	300	00		
	Am't forward				1,588	82

SALES-BOOK, FORM 3.

New Orleans, November 5th, 1852.

				1,588
√	Samuel Tillotson,	Gravier St.		
	10 Cases, 600 Prs. Women's Goat Buskins	@ 1.15	690 00	
	30 Ladies' Open Fancy Bonnets	38^2	11 55	701 55
	"			
Paid	Cash Sales,			
	100 Infants' China Pearl Bonnets	@ 25	25 00	
	"			
Paid 12th	Jacob Lukens, Jun.,	St. Louis St.		
	4 Cases, 240 Prs. Women's Kid Slippers R. R.	@ 90		~~216 00~~
	6th			
√	Morris L. Halsey,	Camp St.		
	6 Prs. Youths' Stout Brogans	@ 62^2		3 75
	"			
Paid	Caleb Jarden & Nephew,	Jackson St.		
	30 Infants' Diamond Satin Bonnets	@ 26^1	7 88	
	40 Prs. Misses' Goat Lace Ties	75	30 00	
			37 88	
	8th			
√	Ferree & Brother,	Natchez.		
	10 Ps. Swiss Straw Cord	@ 4.50	45 00	
	20 Doz. Tassels	1.50	30 00	75 00
	9th			
Paid	Cash Sales,	Carson & Co.		
	5 Cases, 300 Prs. Men's Stout Brogans	@ 1.10	330 00	
	"			
Paid	Cash Sales,			
	20 Scores Rock Luton Plait	@ 45	9 00	
	"			
√	Mrs. Mary Green,	Calliope St.		
	25 Women's Rock Luton Bonnets	@ 31^1		7 81
	11th			
√	Decoursey & Wise, (Note pr. B.-B.)	Jackson, Miss.		
	120 Scores China Pearl Plait	@ 15	18 00	
	160 " " " "	25	40 00	
	19 " California "	17	3 23	
	15 " " "	35	5 25	
	12 " Sacramento "	47^2	5 70	
	112 " Tulip "	26	29 12	
	180 " Alboni "	31^1	56 25	
	130 " Bedford "	37	48 10	
	50 " Fancy Coburg "	50	25 00	
	10 " Patent "	90	9 00	
	10 " " "	.25	12 50	
	10 " Split Straw "	60	6 00	
	2 Boxes & Cooperage		1 50	259 65
	13th			
Paid	Cash Sales,			
	18 Maids' Triplar Bonnets	@ 35	6 30	
	15th			
√	William P. Lewis,	Market St.		
	2 Doz. Fr. Straw Lace, Emb'd	@ 6.00		12 00
	Am't forward			2,648 58

SALES-BOOK, FORM 3.

New Orleans, November 18*th*, 1852.

					2,648	58
√	Julius & George Lee, (Notes pr. B.-B.) Baton Rouge.					
	4 Cases, 48 Prs. Men's Stout Boots	@ 1.75	84	00		
	4 " 48 " " Kip "	2.00	96	00		
	4 " 48 " " Calf Pegged	2.50	120	00		
	4 " 48 " " " Sewed "	3.25	156	00		
	4 " 240 " Boys' Stout Brogans	75	180	00		
	4 " 240 " " Kip "	80	192	00		
	4 " 240 " Women's Kip Lace Boots	60	144	00		
	4 " 240 " " Calf " "	90	216	00		
	32 Cooperages	25	8	00	1,196	00
	19th					
Paid 23d	Peter Phelps, (Net) Market St.					
	20 Doz. Blond Straw Lace	@ 4.50	90	00		
	20 Ps. Swiss " Cord	4.50	90	00	~~180~~	~~00~~
	20th					
Paid	Cash Sales,					
	50 Doz. Tassels	@ 1.50	75	00		
	22d					
√	Ferree & Brother, Natchez.					
	12 Maids' Feather Edge Bonnets	@ 1.03	12	36		
	50 " Plain Straw "	62^2	31	25		
	62 Paper Boxes	3	1	86	45	47
	25th					
√	Julius & George Lee, (Notes pr. B.-B.) Baton Rouge.					
	6 Cases, 72 Prs. Men's Calf Stitched Boots	@ 5.00	360	00		
	6 " 72 " " " Sewed "	3.25	234	00	594	00
	26th					
Paid 29th	Benjamin Loper & Co., Poydras St.					
	8 Cases, 480 Prs. Women's Kid Slippers, R. R.	@ 85			~~408~~	~~00~~
	27th					
Paid	Cash Sales,					
	12 Prs. Children's Calf Brogans	@ 37^2	4	50		
	"					
√	Samuel Tillotson, Gravier St.					
	15 Cases, 900 Prs. Misses' Goat Lace Boots	@ 75	675	00		
	15 " 900 " " R. R. Paris Ties	60	540	00	1,215	00
	"					
Paid	Cash Sales,					
	20 Girls' Diamond Satin Bonnets	@ 27^2	5	50		
	29th					
Paid	Cash Sales,					
	18 Maids' China Pearl Bonnets	@ 33⅓	6	00		
	30 Women's Tulip "	1.15	34	50		
			40	50		
	30th					
√	Benjamin Loper & Co., Poydras St.					
	5 Cases, 300 Prs. Youths' Stout Brogans	@ 62^2	187	50		
	5 " 300 " " Kip "	50	150	00		
	5 " 300 " Children's Calf "	37^2	112	50		
	2 " 120 " Women's " Lace Boots	1.25	150	00	600	00
	Total Sales on time for the month				6,299	05

New Orleans, November 1*st,* 1852.

Folio	Account	Particulars	Date	$	¢	$	¢
1/1	Merchandise To Edwin M. Lafourcade,						
	Invested, as pr. Invoice					13,628	34
	15th						
3/3	Joseph Ralston To Dolbear & Reikert,						
	Order of J. Ralston on us, favor of Dolbear & Reikert,					25	00
	30th						
2/3	Expenses To Joseph Ralston,						
	Wages for one month					65	00
	"						
1	Merchandise To Sundries,						
	Purchases this month, pr. Invoices.						
3	To Dufour, Nephew & Co.,	Notes @ 2, 4 & 6 mos.,	1st	8,420	50		
	" "	" " 3 mos.,	10th	652	36		
	" "	" " 6 "	16th	422	10		
	" "	" " 4 "	23d	210	28		
	" "	" " 3 "	30th	165	75	9,870	99
3	" Webster & Shaw, Boston, Mass.,	Draft,	3d	725	00		
	" "	" " 4 mos.,	17th	556	50		
	" "	" " 4 "	25th	1,342	64	2,624	14
3	" Margot & Haines,	Note @ 60 days,	5th	492	50		
	" "	" " 90 "	29th	910	35	1,402	85
3	" Bouvier Brothers,	2 mos.,	13th	840	60		
	" "	4 "	26th	610	18	1,450	78
4	" Lewis Davis & Co.,	3 "	18th			2,133	90
4	" Jones & Riggs, Lynn, Mass.,	6 "	22d			1,840	00
4	" Brainerd & Son,	4 "	29th			1,445	80
4	" E. B. Bolton,	Note @ 4 mos.,	"			712	00
	"					21,480	46
1	Cash To Sundries,	Receipts pr. C.-B.					
1	To Edwin M. Lafourcade,		1st			10,000	00
1	" Louis P. Lafourcade,		"			5,000	00
1	" Charles Boutelier, Jun.,		"			5,000	00
1	" Merchandise,		2d	37	50		
	" "		3d	357	40		
	" "		4th	319	80		
	" "		5th	25	00		
	" "		6th	37	88		
	" "		9th	339	00		
	" "		12th	216	00		
	" "		13th	6	30		
	" "		20th	75	00		
	" "		23d	180	00		
	" "		27th	10	00		
	" "		29th	408	00		
	" "		"	40	50	2,052	38
4	" Samuel Tillotson,		8th	500	00		
	" "		29th	500	00	1,000	00
2	" Interest,		10th	140	34		
	" "		16th	4	27	144	61
2	" Bills Receivable,		11th	562	50		
	" "		25th	398	67	961	17
5	" Mrs. Mary Green, (Sundry Debtors)		30th			7	81
						24,165	97

JOURNAL, FORM 3.

New Orleans, November 30th, 1852.

1	Sundries	To Cash,	Payments pr. C.-B.				
1	Merchandise,		1st	643	50		
	"		5th	162	94		
	"		"	15	00		
	"		9th	82	10		
	"		15th	562	00		
	"		20th	780	74		
	"		"	56	75		
	"		"	232	94		
	"		27th	1,554	34		
	"		"	113	50		
	"		"	465	87		
	"		30th	2,101	79		
	"		"	186	40		
	"		"	571	12	7,528	99
2	Expenses,		2d	30	00		
	"		"	12	25		
	"		6th	8	50		
	"		9th	14	25		
	"		18th	2	75		
	"		22d		75		
	"		30th	150	00	213	50
3	Joseph Ralston,		8th	5	00		
	"		20th	10	00	15	00
2	Bills Payable,		10th	2,806	84		
	"		16th	492	50	3,299	34
2	Interest,		3d	17	87		
	"		11th	28	12		
	"		12th	10	80		
	"		25th	19	93		
	"		29th	20	40	97	12
3	Webster & Shaw,		13th			725	00
1	Louis P. Lafourcade,		18th			500	00
3	Bouvier Brothers,		26th			1,000	00
		30th				13,378	95
2	Bills Receivable	To Sundries,	Rec'd pr. B.-B.				
4	To Durbin, Payson & Co.,		2d			562	50
5	" Willard, Brady & Co.,		3d			102	97
5	" Ferree & Brother,		8th	377	25		
	" "		"	377	25	754	50
5	" Decoursey & Wise,		11th			259	65
5	" Julius & George Lee,		18th	398	67		
	" "		"	398	67		
	" "		"	398	66		
	" "		25th	297	00		
	" "		"	297	00	1,790	00
		"				3,469	62
2	Sundries	To Bills Payable,	Issued pr. B.-B.				
3	Dufour, Nephew & Co.,		1st	2,806	83		
	"		"	2,806	83		
	"		"	2,806	84		
	"		10th	652	36		
		(Entry continued)		9,072	86		

JOURNAL, FORM 3.

New Orleans, November 30th, 1852.

L. F.				Amount	¢	Total	¢
	Sundries	To Bills Payable, (continued)		9,072	86		
	Dufour, Nephew & Co.,		16th	422	10		
	"		23d	210	28		
	"		30th	165	75	9,870	99
3	Margot & Haines,		5th	492	50		
	"		29th	910	35	1,402	85
4	E. B. Bolton,		"			712	00
						11,985	84
	30th						
1	Sundries	To Merchandise,	Sales pr. S.-B.				
5	Ferree & Brother,		1st	679	50		
	"		8th	75	00		
	"		22d	45	47	799	97
4	Durbin, Payson & Co.,		2d			562	50
3	Dolbear & Reikert,		"	112	75		
	"		4th	131	10	243	85
5	Willard Brady & Co.,		3d			102	97
4	Samuel Tillotson,		5th	701	55		
	"		27th	1,215	00	1,916	55
5	Morris L. Halsey,	(Sundry Debtors)	6th			3	75
5	Mrs. Mary Green,	" "	9th			7	81
5	Decoursey & Wise,		11th			259	65
5	William P. Lewis,	(Sundry Debtors)	15th			12	00
5	Julius & George Lee,		18th	1,196	00		
	"		25th	594	00	1,790	00
5	Benjamin Loper & Co.,		30th			600	00
						6,299	05
	"						
2	Interest	To Sundries,					
1	To Edwin M. Lafourcade,	On Capital to Dec. 1st		118	14		
1	" Louis P. Lafourcade,	" " " " "		23	92		
1	" Chas. Boutelier, Jun.,	" " " " "		25	00	167	06

RIAL BALANCE, LEGER, FORM 3. *Nov. 30th,* 1852.

L.F.		Dr.	¢	Cr.	¢
3	Dolbear & Reikert	218	85		
4	Samuel Tillotson	916	55		
5	Ferree & Brother	45	47		
5	Sundry Debtors	15	75		
5	Benjamin Loper & Co.	600	00		
	Personal %s having balances due firm	1,796	62		
3	Joseph Ralston			25	00
3	Webster & Shaw			1,899	14
3	Bouvier Brothers			450	78
4	Lewis Davis & Co.			2,133	90
4	Jones & Riggs			1,840	00
4	Brainerd & Son			1,445	80
	Personal %s having balances firm owe			7,794	62
1	Edwin M. Lafourcade			23,746	48
1	Louis P. Lafourcade			4,523	92
1	Charles Boutelier, Jun.			5,025	00
1	Cash	10,787	02		
1	Merchandise	34,286	30		
2	Bills Receivable	2,508	45		
2	Bills Payable			8,686	50
2	Interest	119	57		
2	Expenses	278	50		
	Personal %s due firm	1,796	62		
	Personal %s firm owe			7,794	62
		49,776	52	49.776	52

This Trial Balance, it will be seen, is made out in a different manner from the preceding ones. It is so done to show how personal accounts, which in real business are almost always numerous, may be brought within a sufficiently small space, so that Balance Sheets and similar exhibits can be easily made.

The third division, commencing with the partners' names, is all that will be required in making out a Balance Sheet. See next page.

In closing this Leger, the *Merchandise remaining unsold,* as pr. Inventory, may be called $36,637.11.

The Leger is given in the Key.

BALANCE SHEET, LEGER, FORM 3.

New Orleans, December 1st, 1852.	L. Folio.	Face of Leger. Dr.	Face of Leger. Cr.	Profit & Loss. Dr.	Profit & Loss. Cr.	E. M. Lafourcade. Dr.	E. M. Lafourcade. Cr.	L. P. Lafourcade. Dr.	L. P. Lafourcade. Cr.	Chas. Boutelier, Jun. Dr.	Chas. Boutelier, Jun. Cr.	Balance. Dr.	Balance. Cr.
E. M. Lafourcade	1		23,746 48				23,746 48						
L. P. Lafourcade	1		4,523 92						4,523 92				
Chas. Boutelier, Jun.	1		5,025 00								5,025 00		
Cash	1	10,787 02										10,787 02	
Merchandise	1	34,286 36	36,637 11		2,350 75							36,637 11	
Bills Receivable	2	2,508 45										2,508 45	
Bills Payable	2		8,686 50										8,686 50
Interest	2	119 57		119 57									
Expenses	2	278 50		278 50									
Personal %s due firm		1,796 62										1,796 62	
Personal %s firm owe			7,794 62										7,794 62
		49,776 52	49,776 52										
To E. M. Lafourcade, ½ *Net Gains*				976 34			976 34						
" Louis P. Lafourcade, ¼ *" "*				488 17					488 17				
" Chas. Boutelier, Jun., ¼ *" "*				488 17							488 17		
				2,350 75	2,350 75								
Net Capital						24,722 82							
						24,722 82	24,722 82						
Net Capital								5,012 09					
								5,012 09	5,012 09				
Net Capital										5,513 17			
										5,513 17	5,513 17		
Total Assets and Liabilities												51,729 20	16,481 12
E. M. Lafourcade's Net Capital													24,722 82
L. P. Lafourcade's " "													5,012 09
C. Boutelier, Jun.'s " "													5,513 17
												51,729 20	51,729 20

PRINGLE & FIELD.

PRACTICAL FORM, NO. 4.

POSTING DIRECT FROM VARIOUS BOOKS OF ORIGINAL ENTRY.

EXPLANATORY REMARKS, FORM 4.

This Form is intended for *wholesale, jobbing, importing,* or *manufacturing* houses, and will be found a labor-saving and accurate method of keeping their accounts.

The books of original entry are Day-Book, Cash-Book, Expense-Cash-Book, Sales-Book, and Bill-Book. No Journal is used, and posts are made directly from each of the books of original entry, except the Expense-Cash-Book. The books are so arranged that entries to the accounts of individuals may be posted daily, while most of the property and profit and loss accounts, which require numerous entries, are posted monthly, or at other stated periods.

A particular description follows each book given, except the description of the Sales-Book, which will be seen below.

Sufficient illustrations of Letter-Book, Check-Book, Time-Book, or other auxiliaries needed, have been given in tho preceding portions of the work.

DIRECTIONS FOR WRITING UP.

You will find it of great advantage to write up this Form, which should be done in tho following order, in the blank books which have been prepared for the purpose.

On the *first* day of the month by examining you will find one entry in the Day-Book, and two in the Cash-Book, which you will enter in the same manner in your Day-Book and Cash-Book—leaving the Leger folio columns blank, to be filled when you post. Next examine the different books of original entry, to see what transactions occur on the *second* day, and enter the same in your books. After completing them, proceed with the *third* day in like manner. And so on with each succeeding date, recording, in the proper books, all transactions that take place on any particular day, before making any entry of the day following it. This will give an idea of the exact process of entry in the counting-house.

After writing up the month's business, post from the several books to the Leger in the same *order* as above described, that is, in *order of date.* To distinguish to which book of original entry the folio in the Leger refers, all posts (except monthly total postings to the property accounts) should be entered as follows, viz., those from the Cash-Book, "To" or "By Cash;" from the Sales-Book, "To Sales;" from the Bill-Book, "To Bills Pay." or "By Bills Rec.;" and those from the Day-Book should be marked "D.-B." before the folio.

In opening the accounts in this Leger, you may observe the usual counting-house arrangement of them, which is to open the accounts of partners, property accounts, and all the general business accounts, in the first part of the Leger, by themselves; and let all the personal accounts follow them. This renders convenient the taking of Trial Balances, and other exhibits from the Leger.

☞ Be particular and make your own additions, extensions and other calculations, wherever they occur in any of the books.

SALES-BOOK.

This book is a record in detail of *all sales,* cash and credit. We have supposed the *credit* sales to be all at six months, and have therefore not mentioned the time, which should be done if sales are made at different terms of credit. Posts may be made daily, or at convenience, to the debit of the parties purchasing.

The sales for *cash,* as entered in this book for any given day, must be summed up at night, on a slip of paper, and entered in total in the Cash-Book as "*Cash Sales,* This day," which total must also agree (in business) with the actual amount of cash received for sales during the day. These "*Cash Sales*" must then be marked "C.-B." in the Sales-Book, to indicate they are transferred to the Cash-Book, and "S.-B." in the Cash-Book, to show they come from the Sales-Book; and must receive *no debit* post from this book. They should be summed up, however, in the amount taken forward from page to page, and posted in total with the other sales, at the close of the month, to the *credit* of *merchandise.* Thus the credit post from this book exceeds the several debit posts by the amount sold for cash during the month. But this is offset, and an equilibrium produced by the postings from the Cash-Book, where the monthly *debit* post to *cash* exceeds the several *credits* by just the same amount.

If a *credit* sale be *paid* before it has been posted, it can be noted in the margin as paid on such a date, marked "C.-B.," and entered in the Cash-Book as "Cash Sales."—See entry of 4th inst.

When a sale is made for *cash,* the entry can be brought through the account of the individual on Leger, if preferred, as in case of S. C. Atkinson, 24th inst. Sales for notes must be debited the individual to whom sold in this book, and the note credited to his account in the Bill-Book.

Houses of extensive business frequently have two Sales-Books, called *odd* and *even* Sales-Books, which are alternately used on the days indicated by their titles. The object of this is to give the book-keeper an opportunity to post up the books.

Note. It is the practice with many jobbing houses to take notes of all their customers. Many of these notes are not negotiable, but are taken merely as evidence of debt. For them a separate Bill-Book is kept, and they are not posted to the account of Bills Rec. in the Leger, but the sale remains to the debit of the individual as if he had given no note, and when any payments are made, they are passed to the credit of his account, being endorsed on the note as usual.

DAY-BOOK, FORM 4.

Philadelphia, January 1st, 1853.

L. F.	Particulars					
1	Merchandise To Sundries,					
1	To J. S. Pringle,	Invested pr. Invoice,	565	15		
1	" R. N. Field,	" "	436	24	1,001	39
	——— 13th ———					
2/4	Interest To Laflin and Stephens, For Int. on H. C. Corbit's Note, No. 3, Rec'd of them this day, as pr. B.-B., in part for Sales pr. S.-B.				4	83
	——— 18th ———					
2	H. C. Corbit To Sundries,					
1	To Bills Receivable,	For No. 3, now due,	500	00		
2	" Interest,	On the above,	5	25	505	25
	——— 20th ———					
5	Sundries To Brown, Shipley & Co.					
5	Leaf & Morrison, Manchester, For their Draft on B., S. & Co., Liverpool, in payment for Mdse., as pr. invoice of Jan. 2d, rec'd this day, Amt. £606, 13s. 8d. (@ 4 mos.)		2,696	37		
1	Merchandise,	B., S. & Co.'s Com. @ 1½ % 9 2 0				
	Shipping Charges at Liverpool,	. . . . . . 1 2 4				
	Int. on Com. and Charges, 3 mos.	. . . . . . 3 1				
		£10 7s. 5d.	46	09	2,742	46
	——— 31st ———					
2	Expenses To Sundries,					
3	To P. C. Mortley,	One month's wages,	60	00		
6	" Sam'l Bartlett,	" " "	30	00	90	00
	——— " ———					
1	Merchandise To Sundries, Purchases this month, as pr. Invoices and Cash-Book.					
2	To Henry C. Corbit,	Part Cash, Bal. Note, @ 3 mos., 2d.	11,245	65		
	" Do. Do.	@ 3 mos., 13th.	543	30	11,788	95
4	" See, Brother & Co.,	Note @ 4 mos., 6th.	1,545	25		
	" Do. Do.	Cash, 25th.	850	00	2,395	25
5	" Leaf & Morrison, Invoice of Jan. 2d, pr. "Thomas P. Cope," £606, 13s. 8d.	Manchester, 20th.			2,696	37
5	" Downer & Stewart,	New York—Draft, 21st.			1,341	50
6	" C. W. Churchman,	@ 4 mos., 27th.			2,563	75
6	" S. B. Rawley,	Note @ 3 mos., 29th.			1,260	75
C.-B.	" Cash Purchases,	Walsh & Co., 3d.	225	00		
C.-B.	" Do. Do.	Walsh & Co., 11th.	53	34		
C.-B.	" Do. Do.	A. Clark, 13th.	545	50		
C.-B.	" Do. Do.	Walsh & Co., 15th.	454	25		
C.-B.	" Do. Do.	Duties pr. "Cope," 20th.	825	26		
C.-B.	" Do. Do.	A. Clark, 25th.	150	25		
C.-B.	" Do. Do.	Walters & Co., "	125	50		
C.-B.	" Do. Do.	Exch. on Note No. 3, for goods pr. "Cope," 27th.	246	82	2,625	92
					24,672	49

The Day-Book is used for recording such transactions as cannot properly be entered in either of the other oks of original entry. Its form is simple, and will be readily comprehended by those who have familiarized emselves with previous portions of the work.

At the close of the month, it is also made the receptacle of purchases, which are treated as follows. The ceiving clerk examines the Invoice as the goods are received, and if he finds it correct, marks it "Ex'd," signing s initials to show who is responsible for its correctness. This being done, it is placed on file, or pasted in a ank book prepared for the purpose, called an Invoice-Book.

Purchases on time are supposed to be entered in the Day-Book from the original invoices, either as filed or pre-rved in the Invoice-Book, taking care to collect together all purchases from the same person, that one post y need be made to each individual's account for the month.

" *Cash Purchases*" are taken from the Cash-Book, where they have been previously entered at the date of the currence of the transaction. They will be found in the Cash-Book, marked "D.-B." by looking along the ger folio column. They must be marked "C.-B." in the Day-Book, and no other post made of them, save debit in total to Merchandise.

CASH-BOOK, FORM 4.

Dr. *Cash.*

Date.	L. F.			Int. Cr.		B. Rec. Cr.		Cash Dr.	
1853.									
Jan. 1	1	To J. S. Pringle,	Amt. invested,					8,000	00
" 1	1	" R. N. Field,	" "					8,000	00
" 2	S.-B.	" Cash Sales,	This day,					28	00
" 3	S.-B.	" Do. Do.	" "					16	25
								16,044	25
" 6	S.-B.	" Cash Sales,	This day,					171	65
" 7	3	" S. C. Atkinson,	Rec'd on a/c					400	00
" 7	S.-B.	" Cash Sales,	Rec'd of P. G. Collins & Co. for Sales made them 4th inst., less Dis. pr. contra,					119	00
" 9	S.-B.	" Cash Sales,	This day,					639	35
" 9	✓	" Interest,	Dis. on Bills Pay. No. 2, pr. contra,	30	90			30	90
" 10	S.-B.	" Cash Sales,	This day,					14	00
" 11	4	" Burgess & Walker,	In part for Sales, pr. S.-B.,					100	00
" 11	✓	" Bills Receivable,	In full for Elliot & Burnap's Note, No. 1, due July 5th, less Dis. pr. contra,			601	28	601	28
								18,120	43
" 14	S.-B.	" Cash Sales,	This day,					310	75
" 15	S.-B.	" Do. Do.	" "					9	00
" 16	S.-B.	" Do. Do.	" "					65	00
" 17	4	" Burgess & Walker,	In full for Bal. of a/c due pr. Average, Mar. 29th, 1850.*					71	24
" 18	S.-B.	" Cash Sales,	This day,					257	25
								18,833	67
" 20	4	" T. W. Lakeman & Co.	On a/c					50	00
" 20	4	" Turner, Wheelwright & Co.	Rec'd pr. mail on a/c					300	00
" 21	S.-B.	" Cash Sales,	This day,					150	63
" 23	S.-B.	" Do. Do.	" "					37	12
" 24	3	" S. C. Atkinson,	Rec'd for Sales pr. S.-B.					536	29
" 25	✓	" Interest,	Discount on Bill of See, Bro. & Co., as pr. contra,	25	50			25	50
								19,933	21
" 27	✓	" Interest,	Discount on Bills Pay. No. 3—Am't as pr. Contra, including Exch., $2,989.28—from April 14th (time when our Pay't is considered Cash in England) to May 5th, (when Leaf & Morrison's Draft on Brown, Shipley & Co. matures,)	10	46			10	46
" 27	5	" Cushing & Brother,	In full for a/c due July 20th,					117	10
" 27	S.-B.	" Cash Sales,	This day,					244	50
" 28	✓	" Bills Receivable,	Rec'd pr. mail on Miles & Ransford's Note, No. 4,			400	00	400	00
" 29	S.-B.	" Cash Sales,	This day,					1,036	44
" 30	4	" T. W. Lakeman & Co.,	In full for Bal. of their a/c, due pr. Average, Oct. 21st,*					91	50
" 31	S.-B.	" Cash Sales,	This day,					40	20
	2		Interest Credits this month,	66	86				
	1		Bills Rec. " " "			1,001	28		
	1		Cash Debits " "					21,873	41
Feb. 1		To Balance	Bro't down,					4,614	05

* In these averages grace is added to the sale, but not to the Cash payment.

CASH-BOOK, FORM 4.

Cash. *Cr.*

Date.	L. F.			Int. Dr.		B. Pay. Dr.		Cash Cr.	
1853.									
Jan. 2	2	By Henry C. Corbit,	Paid in part for Purchases,					7,500	00
" 3	D.-B.	" Cash Purchases,	Walsh & Co.,					225	00
" 4	✓	" Expenses,	Paid pr. Exp. C.-B. this week,					28	63
			In Bank, 8,275.50 *In Safe,* 15.12 } 8,290.62					7,753	63
" 7	3	" P. C. Mortley,	On %,					12	00
" 7	✓	" Interest,	Discount 5 % on P. G. Collins & Co.'s Bill of 4th, as pr. contra,	5	95			5	95
" 9	✓	" Bills Payable,	In full for our Note No. 2, favor See, Brother & Co., due May 9th, less Discount pr. contra,			1,545	25	1,545	25
" 11	D.-B.	" Cash Purchases,	Walsh & Co.,					53	34
" 11	✓	" Interest,	Discount on Bills Rec. No. 1, pr. contra,*	17	54			17	54
" 11	✓	" Expenses,	Paid pr. Exp. C.-B. this week,					36	50
			In Bank, 8,642.01 *In Safe,* 54.21 } 8,696.22					9,424	21
" 13	D.-B.	" Cash Purchases,	A. Clark,					545	50
" 14	1	" J. S. Pringle,	On %,					175	00
" 15	D.-B.	" Cash Purchases,	Walsh & Co.,					454	25
" 16	3	" P. C. Mortley,	On %,					25	00
" 17	✓	" Interest,	Discount on B. & W.'s %, as pr. contra,	5	12			5	12
" 18	✓	" Expenses,	Paid pr. Exp. C.-B. this week,					33	25
			In Bank, 8,110.50 *In Safe,* 60.84 } 8,171.34					10,662	33
" 20	D.-B.	" Cash Purchases,	Paid Duties, $805.70, and Freight, $19.56 on Mdse., pr. ship "T. P. Cope," from Liverpool,					825	26
" 21	5	" Downer & Stewart,	Sent them this day, Benson & Co.'s Draft on Bicknell & Co., New York,					1,341	50
" 21	✓	" Interest,	Paid ⅛ % Prem. on above Draft,	1	68			1	68
" 25	D.-B.	" Cash Purchases,	A. Clark,					150	25
" 25	D.-B.	" Do. Do.	Walters & Co.,					125	50
" 25	4	" See, Brother & Co.	Paid in full for Purchases this day, they allowing 3 % Discount,					850	00
" 25	✓	" Expenses,	Paid pr. Exp. C.-B. this week,					54	62
			In Bank, 5,886.21 *In Safe,* 35.86 } 5,922.07					14,011	14
" 27	✓	" Bills Payable,	In full for our Note No. 3, favor Brown & Bowen, due April 5th, £617, 1s. 1d.,			2,742	46	2,742	46
" 27	D.-B.	" Cash Purchases,	Exchange @ 9 % Prem. on above Note,					246	82
" 27	6	" Samuel Bartlett,	On %,					16	50
" 27	✓	" Interest,	Discount on C. & B.'s %, pr. contra,	3	40			3	40
" 29	1	" R. N. Field,	On %,					95	45
" 30	✓	" Interest,	Discount on T. W. L. & Co.'s %, pr. contra,	4	03			4	03
" 31	✓	" Expenses,	Paid pr. Exp. C.-B. this week,					139	56
	2		Expenses this month, pr. Exp. C.-B. $292.56,						
	2		Interest Debits this month,	37	72				
	2		Bills Pay. " " "			4,287	71		
	1		Cash Credits " "					17,259	36
" 31		*By Balance,*	*In Bank,* $4,517.70, *In Safe,* $96.35.					4,614	05
								21,873	41

* In calculating Int. and Dis. in Forms 4 and 6, the time is reckoned in days.

EXPENSE-CASH-BOOK, FORM 4.

Philadelphia, January 2d, 1853.

1853. Jan.	2	Paid Store Fixtures,	G. Sims,	25	00		
"	4	" 1 Ream Paper,	J. Elliot,	2	13		
"	"	" Drayman,	. .	1	50	28	63
"	10	" Stove Bill,	R. Simpson,	25	00		
"	"	" Labor,	E. Patrick,	1	50		
"	11	" Advertising,	U. S. Gazette,	10	00	36	50
"	13	" 2 Reams Letter Paper,	J. Elliot,	5	00		
"	17	" Stationery Bill,	"	10	50		
"	"	" 1 Ton Coal,	Peterson,	4	50		
"	18	" Painting,	Thomas,	13	25	33	25
"	20	" Gas Light Bill,	. . .	21	25		
"	21	" Freight pr. "Ocean," from N. Y.	. . .	3	12		
"	23	" Carpentering,	G. Sims,	12	50		
"	"	" Sundry Bills for Labor,	. . .	11	25		
"	"	" McCleary's Bill for Drayage,	. . .	6	50	54	62
"	27	" Circulars,	U. S. Gazette,	5	00		
"	31	" Postage, pr. Postage-Book,	. . .	7	56		
"	"	" Rent of Store to Feb. 1st,	. . .	60	00		
"	"	" John Thomas for wages,	. . .	20	00		
"	"	" Peter Baker " "	. . .	15	00		
"	"	" S. C. Martin " "	. . .	12	00	139	56
		Ent'd on Cash-Book, folio 1,				292	56

CASH-BOOK.

In this Book are entered, either directly or through the medium of the Sales-Book and the Expense-Cash-Book, all *cash* transactions. In posting from it, all entries on the *debit* side (except the total Cash debit) are posted to the *credit* of the different accounts affected, and vice versâ.

In order to save posts, two additional columns have been introduced on each side of the Cash-Book. On the *debit* side, one column is for *Interest credits* and one for *Bills Receivable credits.* On the *credit* side one is for *Interest debits* and one for *Bills Payable debits.* A glance at the book will show that entries, affecting either of these accounts for which separate columns are introduced, have their amounts extended into *two* columns—the cash column and one other. No posts are made daily to Interest, Bills Rec., Bills Pay. or Cash, but the amounts extended to each of these accounts must be carried forward in the columns provided for them, and posted in total at the close of the month. Items to the debit of *Expenses*, as brought in weekly from the Expense-Cash-Book, for the balancing of the Cash account, may also be passed over in posting, and the total expenses, as shown by the footing of the outer column of the Expense-Cash-Book, may be entered in the margin of this Book at the close of the month, for the purpose of posting.

"*Cash-Sales*," as explained in remarks on the Sales-Book, are marked "S.-B.," and receive no post except in monthly total to the debit of Cash.

When *Cash* is paid out for *goods bought*—or for *duties, exchange, freight*, &c., where these items of expense are properly a part of the cost of purchase—the entry must be made "By *Cash Purchases*," in this book, and marked "D.-B." At the close of the month, these must be written up in the Day-Book with other purchases, and marked "C.-B." to show they are taken from the Cash-Book. No post is made to the debit or credit of "*Cash Purchases*," but an equilibrium is produced by including the amount in the monthly *debit* post to Mdse. from the Day-Book, and in the monthly *credit* post to Cash, from the Cash-Book; the process being precisely similar to that described in the treatment of "Cash-Sales."

Purchases for cash may, if preferred, be brought through the account of the individual in the Leger. See Ent. to See, Bro. & Co., 25th inst.

Once a week, or as often as it is wished to make trial of the correctness of the Cash account, after bringing in the amount from the Expense-Cash-Book, the debit and credit cash columns may be footed up, and then the amount of cash in bank (as shown by the Check-Book) and the amount in safe may be placed a little to the left of the credit footing, and if their sum be equal to the difference of the cash columns, it proves the account correct. The entries may then be continued on without closing the book till the end of the month.

When a Bal. of Cash on hand is brought down from a preceding month, this balance must be deducted from the footing of the debit column, to obtain the right amount for posting to the debit of Cash. This may be done in the margin.

Note. In this Form no Bank account is kept in the Leger. Deposits in Bank are treated as Cash.

EXPENSE-CASH-BOOK.

This needs no explanation. It is a small book of expenses kept after the formula shown, and having its footings taken to the Cash-Book as often as desirable.

SALES-BOOK, FORM 4.

Philadelphia, January 2d, 1853.

L. F.				
3	N. L. Lippincott & Co.	Second St.		
	5 Ps. Italian Lustring	132, 129^2, 128^1, 127, 131^1 } 648 Braces, 405 Yds. @ 80		324 00
	2d			
C.-B.	Cash Sales,	J. Milton.		
	1 Doz. Cashmere Scarfs			28 00
	"			
3	Elliot & Burnap, (Note pr. B.-B.)	Walnut St.		
	5 Ps. Cashmere d'Ecose	98 Aunes, 122^2 Yds. @ 60	73 50	
	8 " Mouseline de Laine	195 " 243^3 " 50	121 88	
	6 " Super Gros d'Afric	396 " 495 " 82	405 90	601 28
	3d			
C.-B.	Cash Sales,	F. Bates.		
	1 Doz. Ladies' Kid Gloves			7 25
	"			
3	Samuel C. Atkinson,	Chestnut St.		
	2 Ps. Col'd Gros de Levant	118 Aunes, 147^2 Yds. @ 90	132 75	
	10 " Blk. Alpacca	320 " 47^2	152 00	
	20 " Col'd Do.	610 " 45	274 50	
	6 " Olive French Merino	200 Aunes, 250 " 75	187 50	
	6 " Blk. Paris Crape	72 " 40	28 80	775 55
	"			
C.-B.	Cash Sales,	F. Bates.		
	1 Light Silk Shawl			9 00
	4th			
C.-B. Paid 7th.	P. G. Collins & Co.,	Market St.		
	8 Ps. Fig'd Alpacca	248 Yds. @ 30	74 40	
	2 " Plaid Do.	60 " 41	24 60	
	4 Barege Shawls	5,00	20 00	119 00
	6th			
C.-B.	Cash Sales,	S. Burke.		
	12 Ps. Irish Linen	144 Yds. @ 80	115 20	
	4 " Mull Muslin	48 " 30	14 40	129 60
	"			
3	Jos. Roberts & Co., (Note pr. B.-B.)	Harrisburg.		
	5 Ps. White Paris Crape	60 Yds. @ 45	27 00	
	8 " Blue Do. Do.	96 " 50	48 00	
	10 " Super Balzarine	555 " 55	305 25	
	20 " Barege	885 " 37^2	331 88	712 13
	"			
C.-B.	Cash Sales,	R. Bacon.		
	1 Ps. Blk. French Merino	42 Aunes, 52^2 Yds. @ 72		37 80
	"			
C.-B.	Cash Sales,	J. Myers.		
	1 Doz. Elastic Mitts			4 25
	8th			
4	Turner, Wheelwright & Co.	Pittsburg.		
	10 Light Silk Shawls	@ 10,00	100 00	
	14 Barege Do.	4,50	63 00	
	16 Cashmere Do.	7,50	120 00	
	10 Brochea Do.	12,00	120 00	
	12 Embroidered Thibet Shawls	10,50	126 00	
	8 Plain Do. Do.	7,50	60 00	
	6 Do. Do. Do. wool fringe	4,00	24 00	
	7 Do. Blk. Do. Do. " "	3,75	26 25	639 25
		Am't forward		3,387 11

SALES-BOOK, FORM 4.

Philadelphia, January 9th, 1853.

L. F.						
					3,387	11
C.-B.	Cash Sales,	Bryan & Co.				
	8 Brochea Shawls	@ 10,00	80	00		
	16 Embroidered Thibet Shawls	9,00	144	00	224	00
	9th					
C.-B.	Cash Sales,	Turner & Bates.				
	30 Ps. Assorted Alpacca	923 Yds. @ 45			415	35
	10th					
C.-B.	Cash Sales,	T. Walker.				
	1 Ps. Linen Cambric				14	00
	11th					
4	Burgess & Walker,	Lancaster.				
	4 Ps. Swiss Muslin	48 Yds. @ 38	18	24		
	10 " Jaconet Do.	120 " 40	48	00		
	10 " French Lawn	300 " 35	105	00	171	24
	13th					
4	Laflin & Stephens (Corbit's Note in part pr. B.-B.)	Cincinnati.				
	20 Ps. Col'd. Florence	1482 Aunes, 1852^{2} Yds. @ 32	592	80		
	50 " Assorted Persians	1650 Braces, 1031^{1} " 20	206	25	799	05
	"					
4	T. W. Lakeman & Co.	Spruce St.				
	12 Cashmere Scarfs	@ 2,50	30	00		
	20 Barege Do.	2,00	40	00		
	6 Doz. Prs. Black Kid Gloves	7,25	43	50		
	4 " " Light Do. Do.	7,00	28	00	141	50
	14th					
C.-B.	Cash Sales,					
	5 Ps. Black Lustring	578 Braces, 361^{1} Yds. @ 80			289	00
	"					
C.-B.	Cash Sales,	S. Burton.				
	3 Ps. Bandana H'dk'fs.	@ 7,25			21	75
	15th					
C.-B.	Cash Sales,					
	2 Doz. Prs. Light Net Gloves				9	00
	16th					
C.-B.	Cash Sales,	G. Murray.				
	1 Ps. Blk. French Satin	52 Aunes, 65 Yds. @ 1,00			65	00
	17th					
5	Cushing & Brother,	Chestnut St.				
	6 Ps. Linen Cambric	72 Yds. @ 1,30	93	60		
	4 Doz. Prs. ½ Fing'd Mitts	3,75	15	00		
	2 " " Elastic Do.	4,25	8	50	117	10
	18th					
C.-B.	Cash Sales,	S. Evans.				
	3 Ps. Poult de Soie	180 Aunes, 225 Yds. @ 75			168	75
	"					
C.-B.	Cash Sales,	Clark & Co.				
	6 Ps. Pongee H'dk'fs.	@ 3,50	21	00		
	1 " Blk. Silk Velvet	18 Aunes, 22^{2} Yds. @ 3,00	67	50	88	50
	20th					
5	Miles & Ransford, (Note pr. B.-B.)	Columbus, O.				
	10 Ps. Shusan	330 Yds. @ 20	66	00		
	10 " Crape de Laine	270 Aunes, 337^{2} " 28	94	50		
	6 " Green French Merino	236 " 295 " 65	191	75		
	5 " Drab Do. Do.	176 " 220 " 72^{2}	159	50		
	5 " Blk. English Do.	164 " 205 " 50	102	50	614	25
		Am't forward			6,525	60

SALES-BOOK, FORM 4.

Philadelphia, January 21st, 1853.

L. F.						
					6,525	60
C.-B.	Cash Sales,	T. Walker.				
	3 Ps. Fig'd Gros de Nap.	189 Yds. @ 67	126	63		
	1 Doz. Barege Scarfs		24	00	150	3
	22d					
5	Wm. Chapman, (Note pr. B.-B.	Canton, O.				
	2 Ps. Col'd Poult de Soie	124 Aunes, 155 Yds. @ 75	116	25		
	15 " Pongee H'dk'fs.	3,50	52	50		
	10 " Choppas Do.	6,00	60	00	228	75
	23d					
C.-B.	Cash Sales,					
	4 Ps. Crape de Laine	114^1 Aunes, 142^3 Yds. @ 26			37	12
	24th					
3	Samuel C. Atkinson,	Chestnut St.				
	4 Ps. Blk. Satin Vesting	112^1 Metres, 121^2 Yds. @ 2,75	334	12		
	4 " Fig'd Gros de Nap.	256 Aunes, 320 " 72	230	40		
			564	52		
		Discounted 5 % for cash	28	23	536	29
	27th					
C.-B.	Cash Sales,	L. M. Oviatt.				
	4 Ps. Col'd Marcelline	240 Aunes, 300 Yds. @ 48	144	00		
	3 " Blk. Bombazine	62 " 77^2 " 1,00	77	50	221	50
	"					
C.-B.	Cash Sales,	B. Wesley.				
	4 Ps. Blk. Crape				23	00
	28th					
3	N. L. Lippincott & Co.,	Second St.				
	3 Ps. Blk. Silk Velvet	56 Aunes, 70 Yds. @ 3,15	220	50		
	2 " " " Serge	204 " 255 " 1,00	255	00	475	50
	29th					
C.-B.	Cash Sales,	E. Ely.				
	3 Ps. German Merino	133^3 Yds. @ 80	107	00		
	4 " Col'd Fig'd Gros de Levant	248 Aunes, 310 " 1,00	310	00		
	7 " " Marcelline	576 " 44	253	44	670	44
	"					
6	Aiken & Ransford,	Seventh St.				
	2 Ps. Blk. French Satin	112 Aunes, 140 Yds. @ 1,10			154	00
	"					
C.-B.	Cash Sales,	Binney & Co.				
	6 Ps. Col'd Fig'd Alpacca	165 Yds. @ 40	66	00		
	1 " " Gros de Levant	60 Aunes, 75 " 1,00	75	00	141	00
	"					
C.-B.	Cash Sales,	J. Emm.				
	5 Ps. Blk. Silk Vesting	90 Aunes, 112^2 Yds. @ 2,00			225	00
	31st					
6	Welty & Martin,	Broad St.				
	15 Doz. Blk. Italian Cravats	Doz. 5. @ $12, 5. 15, 5. 18,	225	00		
	2 lbs. Blue Blk. Italian Sewings	@ $12	24	00	249	00
	"					
C.-B.	Cash Sales,					
	6 Thibet Shawls	@ 6,70			40	20
1	Total month's Sales posted to Credit of Mdse.				9,678	03

Bills

No. of Note.	When Rec'd.		To *Credit* of whom.	L. F.	Drawer.	In whose favor.	For what rec'd.	Date of Note.	
	1853.							1853.	
1	Jan.	2	Elliot & Burnap	3	Elliot & Burnap	Ourselves	Mdse.	Jan.	2
2	"	6	J. Roberts & Co.	3	Ourselves on J. R. & Co.	Ourselves	"	"	6
								1852.	
3	"	13	Laflin & Stephens	4	H. C. Corbit	Laflin & Stephens	"	Nov.	16
								1853.	
4	"	20	Miles & Ransford	5	Miles and Ransford	Ourselves	"	Jan.	20
5	"	22	Wm. Chapman	5	Wm. Chapman	Ourselves	"	"	22
				1	Debit total Bills Rec'd	this month . .	. . . .	.	.

Bills

No. of Note.	When Issued.		To *Debit* of whom.	L. F.	Drawer.	In whose favor.	For what given.	Date of Note.	
	1853.							1853.	
1	Jan.	2	H. C. Corbit	2	Ourselves	H. C. Corbit	Mdse.	Jan.	2
2	"	6	See, Bro. & Co.	4	Ourselves	See, Bro. & Co.	"	"	6
3	"	20	Brown, Shipley & Co., Liverpool	5	Brown, Shipley & Co. on ourselves	Brown & Bowen	Account of B. Shipley & Co.	"	2
4	"	29	S. B. Rawley	6	Ourselves	S. B. Rawley	Mdse.	"	29
				2	Credit total Bills Issued	this month . .	. . . .	.	.

BILL-BOOK.

A moment's inspection will show that the entries in this book extend across two opposite pages, which together constitute but *one* page, or folio, of the Bill-Book. When the note to be entered is an accepted draft, both the *drawer* and *drawee* may be mentioned in the column headed "Drawer," as in Bills Rec entry of 6th inst., and Bills Pay. of 20th inst.

Bills Rec. are entered in the Bill-Book at the time of their reception. They are posted to the credit of individuals daily, or at convenience, and to the debit of Bills Receivable account in monthly totals. Bills Pay. are entered in the Bill-Book when issued. They are posted to the debit of individuals daily, and to the credit of Bills Payable account in monthly totals.

Bills Payable and Bills Receivable usually occupy opposite ends of the same book.

REMARKS ON THE PRIVATE LEGER.

Houses frequently find it desirable to keep from public observation the amount of their capital and by whom invested, their gains and losses in business, &c. For this purpose some have a *Private Leger*, in which they keep the partners' accounts, Merchandise, Profit and Loss, Interest, and such other gaining and losing accounts as they think proper, and sometimes, also, the accounts of the different clerks employed.

In connection with this Leger, a Private Day-Book is usually kept, in which entries on opening the books, entries for interest on capital invested, for salaries, &c., are made.

Those who wish to make use of this Leger will find the plan of posting from the books of original entry, pursued in Form 3, very convenient for so doing. Entries in any of the books of original entry, (Private Day-Book included,) either to the debit or credit of accounts kept in the *Private* Leger, must be posted to this Leger, and all other entries must be posted to their proper accounts in the *main* Leger. Thus the *two* Legers contain the same matter usually embraced in *one*, and may be considered as constituting strictly but *one*, although bound in two covers; and Trial Balances, Balance Sheets, and other Leger exhibits, must contain the accounts in both.

BILL-BOOK, FORM 4.

Receivable.

Time.	Where due.	Jan.	Feb.	Mar.	Apr.	May	June	July	Aug.	Sep.	Oct.	Nov.	Dec.	Amount.		Remarks.
6 mos.	Philadelphia							5						601	28	Discounted Jan. 11th.
6 mos.	Bank of N. America							9						712	13	
60 d's.	Philadelphia	18												500	00	Int. from date, Charged Corbit on the 18th.
6 mos.	"							23						614	25	Rec'd Jan. 28th, $400.
6 mos.	"							25						228	75	
. .	. . . . . .													2,656	41	

Payable.

Time.	Where due.	Jan.	Feb.	Mar.	Apr.	May	June	July	Aug.	Sep.	Oct.	Nov.	Dec.	Amount.		Remarks.
3 mos.	Bank of N. America				5									3,745	65	Purchases $11,245 65 Cash 7,500 00
4 mos.	Philadelphia					9								1,545	25	Discounted Jan. 9th.
3 mos.	Philadelphia				5									2,742	46	£617 1s. 1d. Discounted Jan. 27th.
3 mos.	Philadelphia Bank					2								1,260	75	
. .	. . . . . .													9,294	11	

TRIAL BALANCE, LEGER, FORM 4.

3	N. L. Lippincott & Co.	799	50		
3	S. C. Atkinson	375	55		
4	Turner, Wheelwright & Co. .	339	25		
4	Laflin & Stephens	294	22		
6	Aiken & Ransford	154	00		
6	Welty & Martin	249	00		
	Personal %s having balances due firm	2,211	52		
2	H. C. Corbit			38	05
3	P. C. Mortley			23	00
6	Samuel Bartlett			13	50
6	C. W. Churchman			2,563	75
	Personal %s having balances firm owe			2,638	30
1	J. S. Pringle			8,390	15
1	R. N. Field			8,340	79
1	Cash	4,614	05		
1	Merchandise	16,041	94		
1	Bills Receivable	1,155	13		
2	Bills Payable			5,006	40
2	Interest			29	56
2	Expenses	382	56		
	Personal %s due firm	2,211	52		
	Personal %s firm owe			2,638	30
		24,405	20	24,405	20

This Trial Balance is made out in the same manner as the Trial Balance to Form 3, and for the reasons there given.

In closing this Leger, the *Mdse. remaining unsold*, as pr. Inventory, may be called $18,250.25.

The Leger and Balance Sheet are given in the Key.

PRACTICAL FORM, No. 5.

By making a few changes in the preceding Form, (No. 4,) a Form may be obtained which will be found very convenient for houses doing a *wholesale* and *retail* business, or for those engaged in *extensive retail* trade.

1st. In place of the Expense-Cash-Book, a Petty-Cash-Book, (or as some call it, a Cash-Sales-Book,) may be substituted, arranged after the formula given below. The debit side of this book is ruled with two more money columns than there are hands employed in the store, and is a record of cash sales. The credit side is used for entering the various expenses of the store. In houses of this kind, it is common to have a cashier, who sits at the desk to make change. Each salesman or saleswoman is provided with paper and pencil, and whenever a sale is effected, memorandums it upon a slip of paper, signing his or her initials. This, with the money received, is handed to the cashier, who sticks the paper upon a file and returns the required change. Each hand has his or her separate column in the Petty-Cash-Book, in which the cashier places at night the several sales effected during the day, as taken from the slips of paper placed by him on file. In order to balance his cash account at night, the cashier can preserve a memorandum in his drawer of the amount placed in it from the safe each morning for making change during the day.

The amount received for each day's sales may be taken from this book to the Cash-Book, and entered "*Cash Sales*, This day." The daily expenses, as here shown, may also be transferred and entered "*Expenses*, This day." A check mark, as shown below, is the sign of this transfer. The *total* columns may be footed and the amounts taken forward till the close of the month; when the *debit* total footing must be transferred to the Sales-Book, saying "*Cash Sales*, This month, pr. Petty-Cash-Book." Thus the Sales-Book will show the entire sales, cash and credit, and an equilibrium will be produced in the Leger, as explained in Form 4, without making any post to "Cash Sales." The footing of the *credit* total column may be entered monthly in the margin of the Cash-Book, for posting; the *daily* entries of "Expenses" in that book being checked and passed over in posting.

2d. When there are but few transactions in Notes, the Bill-Book may be used merely as a memorandum for reference, without posting from it. Bills Rec. taken, and Bills Pay. issued, will then be entered in the Day-Book. The Bills columns in the Cash-Book may also be dispensed with, and separate posts made for any entries occurring therein.

These will be the main changes requisite. The book-keeper can make such others as the particular business demands.

PETTY-CASH-BOOK.

Dr. *Cash.*

Jno. R. B.	Wm. S. T.	Lucy W. L.	Mary S.	Margaret T.	Betsy B. W.	Louisa C. C.	Alvira M.	Recapitulation.	TOTALS.
14 45	1 40	10	2 50	6 98	37½	25 00	4 60	24 15	
1 00	25	19	1 25	1 03	1 12½	25	30	29 51	
56	38	6 75	87½	04	4 67		2 20	18 54	
2 26	96	12½	3 17	19	3 33		1 87½	12 42	
06	4 52	1 37½	4 62½		45		5 00	8 24	
5 40	20 50	10 00			1 20			12 59	
27	10				1 05			25 25	
15	1 40				39			13 97½	✓ 144 67
24 15	29 51	18 54	12 42	8 24	12 59	25 25	13 97½		
1 25	26 75	13 25	14	11 30	1 12½	70	9 00		
5 16	1 11	4 62½	11 40	75	60½	42	26 75	53 63½	
12½	46	25	76	9 90	45	33	1 20	84 89½	
7 62½	03	94	6 92	12½	3 34	1 44		50 81½	
9 87½	14 40	10 40	14 20	62½	7 72	67		42 43½	
35	36 77	21 35	8 14	37½	4 87½	3 20		44 60	
29 25	4 25		87½	21 12½	16 50	12½		34 61½	
	1 12½			40		1 86		10 74½	
						2 00		36 95	✓ 358 69
53 63½	84 89½	50 81½	42 43½	44 60	34 61½	10 74½	36 95		

Cash, *Cr.*

	Expenses.	TOTALS.
Wednesday, Jan. 1st, 1853.		
Porterage,	37½	
Stationery,	1 50	
1 Ton Coal,	5 00	
Fixing Door Lock,	75	
Advertising in Bulletin,	2 50	
	10 12	✓ 10 12
Bal. in Drawer,	134 55	
	144 67	
Thursday, Jan. 2d, 1853.		
New Desk, J. Ward,	10 00	
Fixtures to Gas Pipe,	1 75	
Drayage,	25	
Errand Boy,	50	
Advertising in N. American,	6 00	
	18 50	✓ 18 50
Bal. in Drawer,	340 19	
	358 69	

JAMES DUNLAP & CO.

PRACTICAL FORM,

No. 6.

THE main features of this form are taken from the practice of one of the largest *commission* houses in the city of Philadelphia.

Great care has been bestowed upon its arrangement, to make it acceptable and useful to those for whom it is particularly intended, and it is confidently believed that commission and company speculating houses will find it better adapted in its general arrangement, and more accurate in detail, for their business, than any thing before in print.

A mode of connecting wholesale merchandising with commission operations, is also illustrated, by which *Sales for account of Merchandise* are treated the same as Sales for account of a *Consignor*.

A particular description of each book will be found immediately following it.

Posts are made from the Cash-Book, Sales-Book, and Journal.

DIRECTIONS FOR WRITING UP.

Blank books have been prepared for this Form also.

In writing up this Form, first take the Cash-Book, Sales-Book, Journal, Receiving-Book and Expense-Cash-Book, and make entries in them severally and successively *in order of date*, as explained in directions to Form 4.

Having completed them all, (except the entry of 31st, "By Charges," on the credit side of Cash-Book, and the last entry in Journal—which you will leave for the present,) transfer the sales, as shown in your Sales-Book, to the different "Sales for account of" consignors in the Account-Sales-Book. This process is entirely similar to posting. Next enter, underneath each Account-Sales, the charges as found in the Receiving-Book—also the postage as supposed to come from the Postage-Book—and calculate for yourself the interest, commission, and guarantee.

Then journalize the Account-Sales-Book, which will complete the Journal. Lastly, add together the items of interest in the several Account-Sales, and enter the total in the Cash-Book "By Charges"—also bring in the expenses from the Expense-Cash-Book.

When the books have all been prepared, post the Sales-Book to the Sales-Leger;* and then post all other entries from the Cash-Book and Journal, *in order of date*.

NOTE.—Some prefer to have the Bill-Book prepared with twelve divisions, one for each month in the year, and marked upon the outer edge of the leaves, similar to the Alphabet of a Leger. Then, whenever a bill is to be entered, place it in that division marked with the month in which it falls due. By this arrangement, a ready reference can at all times be had for ascertaining what bills fall due in any month. If more bills usually fall due in one month than another, let the division for that month be the largest.

---

* See remarks on Legers, page 261.

CASH-BOOK, FORM 6.

Dr. *Cash, Notes and Interest.*

Date.		L.F.		Int. Dr.	B. Rec. Dr.	B. Pay. Dr.	Cash Dr.
1853.							
Mar.	1	1	To J. Dunlap, Capital invested				3,000 00
"	"	1	" S. Robinson, " "				3,000 00
"	"	1	" T. W. Welch, " "				3,000 00
"	10	4	" B. Warner & Co., Their note for sales, due July 13th, No. 1,		1,420 00		
"	11	4	" E. Jones, His check on Phila. B'k for sales				1,535 75
"	14	4	" J. Thompson, Rec'd for sales				2,061 75
"	17	5	" J. Lapsley & Co., " " "				1,895 25
"	24	✓	" Bills Receivable, Rec'd in full for note No. 1, due July 13th, Am't $1420	26 27			1,393 73
"	"	4	" J. Thompson, His note for sales, due Sept. 27th, No. 2,		607 00		
"	"	4	" Shepherd & Co., In full for %, due July 15th, Am't 3,068	57 78			3,010 22
"	29	✓	" Cash, Paid note No. 1 and Int., pr. contra,	14 49		3,621 69	
"	"	✓	" Do., " " " 2 " "	4 66		1,866 04	
"	30	4	" J. Smith, For note in full for %, due July 18th, No. 3,		2,474 72		
"	31	4	" B. Warner & Co., Their note for sales, due Aug. 3d, No. 4,		219 83		
"	"	2	Interest debits this month	103 20			
"	"	2	Bills Rec., " "		4,721 55		
"	"	2	Bills Pay., " "			5,487 73	
"	"	1	Cash " "				18,896 70
Apr.	1		To Bal. from Old %				5,518 52

The object of entering notes and interest in this book, in preference to the Journal, is twofold,—first, they are most frequently connected with cash entries, and second, in this book we are enabled, by appropriating a set of columns for all cash, bills and interest entries, to post in weekly or monthly totals to these accounts, while the other accounts which balance these columns are posted daily, or as often as we choose.

When either Cash, Bills Payable, Bills Receivable, or Interest are debtor, and some of them also creditor in the same transaction, the entry may be made on *both* sides of the book, for the purpose of bringing into columns all the sums entered to these accounts—as seen in entries of 24th and 29th. Then, in posting the individual items of the book, those accounts found debited or credited, which have columns appropriated for them, must be checked and passed over.

The footing of each of the several columns this month is the amount to be posted to

CASH-BOOK, FORM 6.

Cash, Notes and Interest. *Cr.*

Date.		L.F.			Int. Cr.		B. Rec. Cr.		B. Pay. Cr.		Cash Cr.	
1853.												
Mar.	5	1	By Charges,	* Our bond for duties on Mdse., due Apr. 7th, with Int., No. 1,					3,621	69		
"	"	2	" Lovering & Bache,	Bill of exchange on Barings & Co., London, for £900, Bo't of Clark & Co., and sent them this day							4,000	00
"	"	1	" Merchandise,	† Premium on the above bill @ 9¼ %							370	00
"	14	1	" Charges	* Our bond for duties on Sharpless & Co.'s cons't., due Apr. 16th, with Int., No. 2,					1,866	04		
"	24	✓	" Cash and Int.,	Rec'd on note No. 1, pr. contra			1,420	00				
"	25	2	" Sharpless & Co.,	Paid at sight their bill of exchange on us at 10 days' sight, S. C. Morton's favor, for $3,000	6	50					2,993	50
"	29	✓	" Bills Pay. and Int.,	Paid note No. 1, dated 5th inst.							3,636	18
"	"	✓	" Do.	Do. " " " 2, " 14th							1,870	70
"	31	1	" Charges,	For am't of Int. credited charges in Ac't-Sales rendered this day, pr. Ac't S.-B.	5	89						
"	"	1	" Do.	Paid as pr. Expense C.-B., this month							345	30
"	"	3	" Store Expenses,	" " " "							162	50
"	"	2		Interest credits this month	12	39						
"	"	2		Bills Rec. " "			1,420	00				
"	"	2		Bills Pay. " "					5,487	73		
"	"	1		Cash " "							13,378	18
"	"		*By Balance on hand, to New %*								5,518	52
											18,896	70

the debit or credit of the account shown by the heading; but the footing of the "Cash debit" column of the next month will be too large by the amount of the balance brought down, which sum will need to be deducted from it to obtain the amount for posting.

The entries from the Expense-Cash-Book may be made at any time; and the cash account then proved by footing up the cash columns, and minuting opposite the footings their difference, or the balance on hand, after the manner shown in Cash-Book, Form 4.

Those who prefer to do so, can substitute the Cash-Book of Form 4, instead of this; or may use a simple one column Cash-Book, and enter bills and interest in the Journal.

---

* By law of August, 1842, duties are required to be paid in cash, but these bonds with interest are introduced here to show a variety of entries.

† This premium is passed to the debit of *Merchandise*, because the sum paid is strictly a part of the cost of goods purchased of Lovering & Bache.

SALES-BOOK, FORM 6.

Philadelphia, March 3d, 1853.

S. L. F.	Consignor.									
4		John Smith,		Market St.		8 m.				
✓	C. D.	B 476	1 Case	Prints,	1,000 Yds. @	10	100	00		
✓	"	B 466 and 468.	2 Bales	Drillings,	900 " "	12	108	00		
✓	P. K.	C 111 and 112.	2 "	Tickings,	900 " "	17	153	00		
✓	"	C 113 and 114.	2 "	Extra Do.,	850 " "	20	170	00	531	00
				4th						
4		E. Jones,		Coates St.		6 m.				
✓	E.D.&O.	E 210	1 Case	Satinets,	600 Yds. @	70	420	00		
✓	"	E 208	1 "	Do.,	720 " "	65	468	00		
✓	"	E 211	1 "	Cassimeres,	500 " "	1,00	500	00		
✓	"	E 212	1 "	Ribb'd Do.,	500 " "	1,25	625	00		
✓	P. K.	C 115 and 116.	2 Bales	Tickings,	900 " "	15	135	00		
✓	"	C 117 and 120.	2 "	Do.,	800 " "	16	128	00		
✓	C. D.	B 467	1 "	Check Cottons,	600 " "	12	72	00	2,348	00
				6th						
4		A. Edwards & Co.,		Race St.		6 m.				
✓	E.D.&O.	E 209	1 Case	Satinets,	550 Yds. @	70	385	00		
✓	C. D.	D 532 and 533.	2 Bales	Check Cottons,	900 " "	10	90	00		
✓	"	D 526 and 529.	2 "	Drillings,	950 " "	10	95	00		
✓	M.	◇A 81	2 Ps.	Fine Blk. Cassimeres,	80 " "	2,50	200	00		
✓	"	"	2 "	Extra Fine Bl'k. Do.,	80 " "	2,75	220	00		
✓	"	◇A 84	4 "	Super W. D. Blk. Cloths,	92 " "	9,25	851	00		
✓	"	"	5 "	Fine Blue Blk. Do.,	120 " "	7,50	900	00	2,741	00
				8th						
4		John Smith,		Market St.		3 m.				
✓	M.	◇A 86	7 Ps.	Assorted Brown Cloths,	175 Yds. @	4,75	831	25		
✓	"	◇A 81	4 "	Extra Blk. Cassimeres,	160 " "	2,75	440	00		
✓	"	◇A 82	4 "	Oxford Mill'd Do.,	152 " "	2,32	352	64		
✓	"	◇A 83	2 "	Mill'd Drab Do.,	84 " "	2,30	193	20	1,817	09
				10th						
4		B. Warner & Co.,		Arch St.		Note @ 4 m.				
✓	C. D.	B 469 and 470.	2 Cases	Extra Fine Prints,	2,000 Yds. @	14	280	00		
✓	"	D 525 and 528.	2 "	Ginghams,	1,800 " "	20	360	00		
✓	E.D.&O.	E 201 and 202.	2 "	Satinets,	1,200 " "	65	780	00	1,420	00
				11th						
4		E. Jones,		Coates St.		Check on Bank.				
✓	M.	◇A 87	5 Ps.	Blue Cloths,	125 Yds. @	5,25	656	25		
✓	"	"	2 "	Extra Blue Cloths,	50 " "	6,00	300	00		
✓	"	"	2 "	Light Mix'd Do.,	50 " "	4,75	237	50		
✓	"	"	3 "	Dark " Do.,	72 " "	4,75	342	00	1,535	75
					Am't. forward				10,392	84

SALES-BOOK, FORM 6.

Philadelphia, March 12*th*, 1853.

S. L. F.	Consignor.							
							10,392	84
4		Shepherd & Co.,	Chestnut St.	4 m.				
✓	E.D.&O.	E 204 and 205.	2 Cases Cassimeres,	800 Yds. @ 1,50	1200	00		
✓	"	E 203	1 " Do.,	400 " " 1,25	500	00		
✓	M.	◇A 85	4 Ps. Blk. Cloths,	100 " " 6,00	600	00		
✓	"	◇A 88	8 " Victoria Do.,	192 " " 4,00	768	00	3,068	00
			14th					
4		J. Thompson,	Fourth St.	Cash.				
✓	S. & Co.	□ 26	6 Ps. Assorted Green Cloths,	150 Yds. @ 4,75	712	50		
✓	"	"	6 " " Brown Do.,	126 " " 5,50	693	00		
✓	"	"	5 " " Blue Do.,	125 " " 5,25	656	25	2,061	75
			15th					
5		Bonnard & Bates,	Filbert St.	6 m.				
✓	E.D.&O.	E 206	1 Case Satinets,	425 Yds. @ 72	306	00		
✓	"	E 207	1 " Do.	450 " " 50	225	00	531	00
			17th					
5		J. Lapsley & Co.,	Second St.					
✓	M.	◇A 89	3 Ps. Superfine Inv. Green Cloths,	75 Yds. @ 7,50	562	50		
✓	S. & Co.	□ 28	2 " " Olive Brown Do.,	48 " " 7,50	360	00		
✓	"	"	2 " " Blue Do.,	48 " " 7,50	360	00		
✓	"	"	6 " Victoria Do.,	150 " " 4,75	712	50		
					1995	00		
			Discount 5 % for cash		99	75	1,895	25
			19th					
5		Smith & Williams,	Broad St.	6 m.				
✓	M.	◇A 89	6 Ps. Fine Drab Cloths,	150 Yds. @ 3,75			562	50
			20th					
4		A. Edwards & Co.,	Race St.	6 m.				
✓	S. & Co.	□ 27	5 Ps. Black Cloths,	125 Yds. @ 6,75	843	75		
	"	"	4 " Extra Fine Blk. Cloths,	96 " " 9,25	888	00	1,731	75
			24th					
4		J. Thompson,	Fourth St.	Note @ 6 m.				
✓	C. D.	D 521 and 522.	2 Bales Drillings,	950 Yds. @ 10	95	00		
✓	"	D 534	1 Case Ginghams,	925 " " 16	148	00		
✓	"	B 475	1 " Fine Prints,	1,025 " " 12	123	00		
✓	P. K.	C 125	1 Bale Tickings,	475 " " 16	76	00		
✓	"	C 119	1 " Do.,	500 " " 15	75	00		
✓	"	C 124	1 " Extra Do.,	450 " " 20	90	00	607	00
			"					
4		Bonnard & Bates,	Filbert St.	6 m.				
✓	S. & Co.	□ 28	2 Ps. Superfine Inv. Green Cloths,	48 Yds. @ 7,50	360	00		
✓	"	"	3 " Victoria Do.,	75 " " 4,75	356	25		
✓	"	□ 29	6 " Extra F. Blk. Cassimeres,	236 " " 2,50	590	00		
✓	"	"	3 " Drab Mill'd Do.,	118 " " 2,00	236	00	1,542	25
				Am't forward			22,392	34

SALES-BOOK, FORM 6.

Philadelphia, March 27th, 1853.

S.L.F.	Consignor.									
									22,392	34
4		John Smith,		Market St.	6 m.					
✓	C. D.	B 472	1 Bale Check Cottons,		650 Yds. @ 11		71	50		
✓	"	B 474	1 " Drillings,		525 " " 10²		55	13	126	63
			29th							
5		Smith & Williams,		Broad St.	4 m.					
✓	S. & Co.	□ 27	5 Ps. Blue Blk. Cloths,		125 Yds. @ 6,00		750	00		
✓	"	□ 29	3 " Oxford Mill'd Cassimeres,		125 " " 2,32		290	00		
✓	"	"	2 " " Mix'd Do.,		80 " " 1,90		152	00	1,192	00
			31st							
4		B. Warner & Co.,		Arch St.	Note @ 4 m.					
✓	C. D.	B 477	1 Case Prints,		985 Yds. @ 10²		103	43		
✓	"	B 480	1 " Do.,		970 " " 12		116	40	219	83
5			Total month's sales, posted to Sales %.						23,930	80

In making entries in the Sales-Book, the initials of the consignors and the marks and numbers of the packages are given, as an index in transferring to the Account-Sales-Book.

Entries in this book are posted to the Sales Leger, and therefore they must in all cases be made to the debit of the individual to whom goods are sold; and if payment be made by note or cash, it must be passed to his credit on the Cash-Book. All the debits are posted daily, or as often as convenient, and at the close of the month the total sales are posted to the credit of the Sales Account.

From time to time, as convenient, the sales, as shown by this book, are transferred to the Account-Sales-Book, the items being checked as fast as transferred, to prevent omissions.

ACCOUNT-SALES-BOOK, FORM 6.

Sales for account of Charles Duncan.

Date.		To whom sold.	Time	Mark	No.	Description of goods.	Yds.	Price	Am't.	Total.
1853.										
Mar.	3	John Smith	8 m.	B	476	1 Case Prints	1,000	10	100 00	
"	"	Do.	"	"	466 468	2 Bales Drillings	900	12	108 00	208 00
"	4	E. Jones	6 m.	"	467	1 " Check Cottons	600	12		72 00
"	6	A. Edwards & Co.	"	D	532 533	2 " Do. Do.	900	10	90 00	
"	"	Do.	"	"	526 529	2 " Drillings	950	10	95 00	185 00
"	10	B. Warner & Co. (Note)	4 m.	B	469 470	2 Cases Extra Fine Prints	2,000	14	280 00	
"	"	Do.	"	D	525 528	2 " Ginghams	1,800	20	360 00	640 00
"	24	J. Thompson (Note)	6 m.	"	521 522	2 Bales Drillings	950	10	95 00	
"	"	Do.	"	"	534	1 Case Ginghams	925	16	148 00	
"	"	Do.	"	B	475	1 " Fine Prints	1,025	12	123 00	366 00
"	27	John Smith	"	"	472	1 Bale Check Cottons	650	11	71 50	
"	"	Do.	"	"	474	1 " Drillings	525	10^2	55 13	126 63
"	31	B. Warner & Co. (Note)	4 m.	"	477	1 Case Prints	985	10^2	103 43	
"	"	Do.	"	"	480	1 " Do.	970	12	116 40	219 83
		Journal folio 1.				*Charges.*				1,817 46
						Insurance		12,72		
						Freight		40,32		
						Drayage		2,37	55 41	
						Int. on $31,92 from Mar. 1st		,16		
						" $23,49 " " 5th		,10	26	
						Postage			1 31	
						Com. and Guarantee at 5 %			90 87	147 85
						Net proceeds, due Sept. 6–9 .				1,669 61

E. E. *Philadelphia, March* 31*st*, 1853. J. DUNLAP & Co.

Sales for account of Peter Kelly.

Date.		To whom sold.	Time	Mark	No.	Description of goods.	Yds.	Price	Am't.	Total.
1853.										
Mar.	3	John Smith	8 m.	C	111 112	2 Bales Tickings	900	17	153 00	
"	"	Do.	"	"	113 114	2 " Extra Do.	850	20	170 00	323 00
"	4	E. Jones	6 m.	"	115 116	2 " Do.	900	15	135 00	
"	"	Do.	"	"	117 120	2 " Do.	800	16	128 00	263 00
"	24	J. Thompson (Note)	"	"	125	1 " Do.	475	16	76 00	
"	"	Do.	"	"	119	1 " Do.	500	15	75 00	
"	"	Do.	"	"	124	1 " Do.	450	20	90 00	241 00
		Journal folio 1.				*Charges.*				827 00
						Freight		8,64		
						Drayage		1,00	9 64	
						Int. on $9,64 from Mar. 1st			05	
						Postage			94	
						Our Com. at 2^2 %			20 68	31 31
						Net proceeds, due Oct. 10–13				795 69

E. E. *Philadelphia, March* 31*st*, 1853. J. DUNLAP & Co.

Sales for account of E. Dickson and Ourselves. (*Co. R.*)

Date.		To whom sold.	Time	Mark	No.	Description of goods.	Yds.	Price	Am't.		Total.	
1853. Mar	4	E. Jones	6 m.	E	210	1 Case Satinets	600	70	420	00		
"	"	Do.	"	"	208	1 " Do.	720	65	468	00		
"	"	Do.	"	"	211	1 " Cassimeres	500	1,00	500	00		
"	"	Do.	"	"	212	1 " Ribb'd Do.	500	1,25	625	00	2,013	00
"	6	A. Edwards & Co.	"	"	209	1 " Satinets	550	70			385	00
"	10	B.Warner&Co.(Note)	4 m.	"	201 202	2 " Do.	1,200	65			780	00
"	12	Shepherd & Co.	"	"	204 205	2 " Cassimeres	800	1,50	1200	00		
"	"	Do.	"	"	203	1 " Do.	400	1,25	500	00	1,700	00
"	15	Bonnard & Bates	6 m.	"	206	1 " Satinets	425	72	306	00		
"	"	Do.	"	"	207	1 " Do.	450	50	225	00	531	00
		Journal folio 1.				*Charges.*					5,409	00
						Ins. $21,64, Fr't. $21,60, Dray. $1,00			44	24		
						Int. on $44,24 from Mar. 3d .				21		
						Postage				94		
						Com. and Guarantee at 5 % .			270	45	315	84
						Net proceeds, due Aug. 19–22					5,093	16
						E.D's ½$2,546,58,Our ½$2,546,58						

E. E. *Philadelphia, March* 31*st*, 1853. J. Dunlap & Co.

Sales for account of Merchandise.

Date.		To whom sold.	Time	Mark	No.	Description of goods.	Yds.	Price	Am't.		Total.	
1853. Mar	6	A. Edwards & Co.	6 m.	◊A	81	2 Ps. Fine Blk. Cass.	80	2,50	200	00		
"	"	Do.	"	"	"	2 " Ex. F. Blk. Do.	80	2,75	220	00		
"	"	Do.	"	"	84	4 " Su.W.D.Blk.Cloths	92	9,25	851	00		
"	"	Do.	"	"	"	5 " FineBlueBlk.Do.	120	7,50	900	00	2,171	00
"	8	John Smith	3 m.	"	86	7 " As'd. Brown Do.	175	4,75	831	25		
"	"	Do.	"	"	81	4 " Extra Blk. Cass.	160	2,75	440	00		
"	"	Do.	"	"	82	4 " Oxford Mill'd Do.	152	2,32	352	64		
"	"	Do.	"	"	83	2 " Mill'd Drab Do.	84	2,30	193	20	1,817	09
"	11	E. Jones (Check)		"	87	5 " Blue Cloths	125	5,25	656	25		
"	"	Do. "		"	"	2 " Extra Blue Do.	50	6,00	300	00		
"	"	Do. "		"	"	2 " Light Mix'd Do.	50	4,75	237	50		
"	"	Do. "		"	"	3 " Dark Do. Do.	72	4,75	342	00	1,535	75
"	12	Shepherd & Co.	4 m.	"	85	4 " Black Do.	100	6,00	600	00		
"	"	Do.	"	"	88	8 " Victoria Do.	192	4,00	768	00	1,368	00
"	17	J. Lapsley & Co.		"	89	3 " Su.Inv.Green Do.	75	7,50	562	50		
						Dis. 5 % for cash			28	12	534	38
"	19	Smith & Williams	6 m.	"	89	6 Ps.FineDrabCloths	150	3,75			562	50
		Journal folio 1.				*Charges.*					7,988	72
						Duties, $3,621,69, Ins. $135,81			3757	50		
						Freight, $65,34, Drayage, $0,75			66	09		
						Com. and Guarantee at 5 %			399	44	4,223	03
						Net proceeds					3,765	69

March 31*st*, 1853.

Sales for account of Sharpless & Co.

Date. 1853.		To whom sold.	Time	Mark	No.	Description of goods.	Yds	Price	Am't.		Total.	
Mar.	14	J. Thompson (Cash)		☐	26	6 Ps. As'd Green Cloths	150	4,75	712	50		
"	"	Do.		"	"	6 " " Brown Do.	126	5,50	693	00		
"	"	Do.		"	"	5 " " Blue Do.	125	5,25	656	25	2,061	75
"	17	J. Lapsley & Co.		"	28	2 " Su.F.OliveBr. Do.	48	7,50	360	00		
"	"	Do.		"	"	2 " " Blue Do.	48	7,50	360	00		
"	"	Do.		"	"	6 " Victoria Do.	150	4,75	712	50		
									1,432	50		
						Discount 5 % for cash			71	63	1,360	87
"	20	A. Edwards & Co.	6 m.	"	27	5 Ps. Blk. Cloths	125	6,75	843	75		
"	"	Do.	"	"	"	4 " Extra F. Blk. Do.	96	9,25	888	00	1,731	75
"	24	Bonnard & Bates	"	"	28	2 " S.F.Inv.Green Do.	48	7,50	360	00		
"	"	Do.	"	"	"	3 " Victoria Do.	75	4,75	356	25		
"	"	Do.	"	"	29	6 " Extra F. Blk. Cass.	236	2,50	590	00		
"	"	Do.	"	"	"	3 " Drab Mill'd Do.	118	2,00	236	00	1,542	25
"	29	Smith & Williams	4 m.	"	27	5 " Blue Blk. Cloths	125	6,00	750	00		
"	"	Do.	"	"	29	3 " Oxford Mill'd Cass.	125	2,32	290	00		
"	"	Do.	"	"	"	2 " " Mix'd Do.	80	1,90	152	00	1,192	00
		Journal folio 1.				*Charges.*					7,888	62
						Duties 1866,04						
						Freight 29,04						
						Drayage 38			1,895	46		
						Int. on $1,895,46 from 14th inst.			5	37		
						Postage			1	50		
						Com. and Guarantee at 5 % .			394	43	2,296	76
						Net proceeds, due July 27–30					5,591	86

E. E. *Philadelphia, March 31st*, 1853. J. Dunlap & Co.

By making this book one from which to journalize, instead of using it only for preserving copies of Account-Sales rendered, we are saved the labor of keeping in the Leger the consignment or sales accounts of the individuals for whom goods are sold, and also obtain a proof of correctness, which is described under the Journal.

Under the headings of "*Sales for ℅ of, &c.*," the sales for each consignor are copied from the Sales-Book at any convenient time, and once in three months, or as often as Account-Sales are to be rendered to the consignor, the charges on goods sold as shown by the Receiving-Book and Postage-Book, with interest on these charges, and commission for selling, &c., are placed underneath the sales, and deducted therefrom, leaving the net proceeds.

The total sales are journalized to the debit of Sales Account, the net proceeds to the credit of the different consignors, and the charges to the credit of Charges and Commission, noting the Journal folio on which the entry is made.

A space may be left after each heading, of from a part of a page to any number of pages, according to the probable amount of sales to be entered under it, and an Alphabet may be used for convenience in referring to the different Account-Sales.

When goods of various kinds are received from a consignor, and he wishes an Account-Sales rendered of each separately, "Sales for ℅ of" said consignor may be opened more than once, and numbered 1, 2, 3, &c., by way of distinction.

JOURNAL, FORM 6.

Philadelphia, March 3d, 1853.

L. F.				
3/3	Mdse. Co. R. To E. Dickson, 4 mos.			
	For our ½ Invoice of Satinets and Cassimeres rec'd this day, to be sold on his and our joint %			
	Am't of Invoice, $4,327,20,—— our ½ is		2,163	60
	5th			
1/2	Merchandise To Lovering & Bache,			
	For Broad Cloths and Cassimeres rec'd this day, pr. Invoice, amounting to £1872 11s. 5d.		8,322	54
	Sent them a Bill of Exchange, as pr. C.-B., for £900; the Balance due at 6 months			
	31st			
5	Sales Account To Sundries For Ac't-Sales rendered.			
2	Mar 31. To Chas. Duncan, due Sept. 6–9	1,817,40— 147,85	1,669	61
2	" " To Peter Kelly, " Oct. 10–13	827,00— 31,31	795	69
3	" " To E. Dickson, " Aug. 19–22	2,704,50— 157,92	2,546	58
3	" " To Mdse. Co. R. " " " "	2,704,50— 157,92	2,546	58
1	" " To Merchandise,	7,988,72—4,223,03	3,765	69
2	" " To Sharpless & Co. " July 27–30	7,888,62—2,296,76	5,591	86
		23,930,80—7,014,79	16,916	01
1	To Charges and Commission		7,014	79
			23,930	80

Any miscellaneous entries that occur, for which there is no other specific place of entry, are entered in this book directly; and periodically, say once in 3 months, the sales for account of consignors, in the Account-Sales-Book, are closed, and journalized into it. If it is wished to render an Account-Sales to any consignor before this periodical journalizing, the sales for his account must be closed, dated, and signed, and a duplicate forwarded him, but no Journal entry made until the periodical time.

The dates preceding the consignors' names, show the time when the Account-Sales were closed and entered. In the examples given, the closures are all at one time, but had any consignor's sales been closed several times before journalizing, these dates would distinctly show it.

When the Account-Sales-Book is all journalized and posted, there is in the *Sales Account* upon the Leger, a proof of the correctness of the Sales, and Account-Sales Books. Thus, in this month's operations, the total amount of sales to different persons, as shown by the Sales-Book, is $23,930,80, which sum is posted to the *credit* of the *Sales Account.* The sales having been transferred to the Account-Sales-Book, (each sale to the account of the person for whom it was made,) and from thence journalized; the total sales collected in the Journal, and from thence posted to the *debit* of the *Sales Account,* is also $23,930,80, the same amount as shown by the Sales-Book.

REMARKS ON THE LEGERS, FORM 6.

In the Key, I have given examples of two Legers for this Form, one of which is termed *Sales-Leger*, to distinguish it from the other. In the Sales-Leger are opened all accounts with persons to whom you sell goods, and the debits to them in the Sales-Book for goods sold, together with all entries, either debit or credit, which occur to these same persons in any other of the books of original entry, are posted to this Leger. The "Sales Account" is also kept in this Leger. All other entries are posted to the *main Leger*.

In houses doing a very extensive business, the Leger is soon filled, and the labor of transferring all the accounts to a new one is very considerable. But by having a Sales-Leger, this task will not be of as frequent occurrence, since each of the Legers may be made as large as can conveniently be used, and the two will contain twice as many accounts as one. Another advantage in keeping a Sales-Leger is, that an assistant may post up the Sales-Book, and thus lighten the labor of the head book-keeper. This plan of having more than one Leger is adopted in jobbing and other houses as well as in commission houses, and some jobbing houses have three, a *City-Sales-Leger*, a *Country-Sales-Leger*, and the *main Leger*.

These two or more books constitute in fact but *one Leger*, and each book is but a portion of that one Leger, bound in a separate cover. In making out Trial Balances, Balance Sheets, &c., they are to be treated as one.

Postings from the Journal should be distinguished in the Leger by being marked "J;" those from the Sales-Book should be entered "To Sales,"or in the Sales Account "By Sales;" all other postings will then be known to come from the Cash-Book.

TRIAL BALANCE, LEGER, FORM 6. *March* 31*st*, 1853.

L. F.		Dr.		Cr.	
	Sales Leger.				
4	E. Jones - - - - - - - - - - -	2,348	00		
4	A. Edwards & Co. - - - - - - - - -	4,472	75		
5	Bonnard & Bates - - - - - - - - -	2,073	25		
5	Smith & Williams - - - - - - - - -	1,754	50		
	Personal a/cs having balances due firm - -	10,648	50		
	Main Leger.				
2	Lovering & Bache - - - - - - - - -			4,322	54
2	Sharpless & Co. - - - - - - - - -			2,591	86
2	Charles Duncan - - - - - - - - -			1,669	61
2	Peter Kelly - - - - - - - - - -			795	69
3	E. Dickson - - - - - - - - - -			4,710	18
	Personal a/cs having balances firm owe - -			14,089	88
1	James Dunlap - - - - - - - - -			3,000	00
1	Samuel Robinson - - - - - - - - -			3,000	00
1	T. W. Welsh - - - - - - - - - -			3,000	00
1	Cash - - - - - - - - - - - -	5,518	52		
1	Charges and Commission - - - - - - -			1,175	87
1	Merchandise - - - - - - - - - -	4,926	85		
2	Bills Receivable - - - - - - - - -	3,301	55		
2	Interest - - - - - - - - - - -	90	81		
3	Merchandise, Co. R - - - - - - - -			382	98
3	Store Expenses - - - - - - - - - -	162	50		
	Personal a/cs due firm - - - - - - - -	10,648	50		
	Personal a/cs firm owe - - - - - - - -			14,089	88
		24,648	73	24,648	73

RECEIVING-BOOK, FORM 6.

How Received.	When Received.	Consignors.	No. of P'k'gs	Mark.	Numbers on the Packages.	Duties.	Insurance	Freight.	Drayage	Total.	Remarks.
Ship Eliza from Boston	1853. Mar. 1st	Chas. Duncan, Lowell, Mass.	20	B	461 to 480		7 27	23 40	1 25	31 92	
Brig Swan from Boston	" 5th	Do.	15	D	521 to 535		5 45	16 92	1 12	23 49	
							12 72	40 32	2 37	55 41	
Brig Ellen from Providence	Mar. 1st	Peter Kelly, Providence, R. I.	16	C	111 to 126			8 64	1 00	9 64	Shipper insured.
Bark E. Sherwood from Providence	Mar. 3d	E. Dickson, Prov. and ourselves (Co.R.)	12	E	201 to 212		21 64	21 60	1 00	44 24	
Ship Saranak from Liverpool	Mar. 5th	Merchandise	9	◇A	81 to 89	3,621 69	135 81	65 34	75	3,823 59	
Ship Thos. P. Cope from Liverpool	Mar. 14th	Sharpless & Co. Liverpool	4	□	26 to 29	1,866 04		29 04	38	1,895 46	Shipper insured.

The time and manner of receiving goods, the consignors' names, the marks, numbers, &c., together with all payments on the goods for duties, insurance, freight and drayage, are entered in this book; and when an Account-Sales is to be rendered, the charges for these items are here found.

A space may be left in this book for each consignor, greater or less, according to the probable amount of business to be transacted with him, where all his consignments can be entered in connection. Then, for ease in referring to the different consignors, an Alphabet may be used.

EXPENSE CASH-BOOK, FORM 6.

Date.				Store Exp's.		Charges.	
Mar.	1	Paid Insurance and Freight on Cons't. of C. Duncan				30	67
"	"	" Do. " " " P. Kelly				8	64
"	3	" Do. Do. " " " E. Dickson				43	24
"	5	" Do. Do. " " " C. Duncan				22	37
"	5	" Do. Do. " Merchandise				201	15
"	6	" for Stationery Grigg & Elliott		12	50		
"	12	" " 2 Tons Coal J. West		9	00		
"	14	" Freight on Sharpless & Co's Cons't.				29	04
"	25	" for Gas light		18	75		
"	31	" J. Bingham one month's wages	65,00				
"	"	" Saml. Ball " "	40,00				
"	"	" Philip Frazer " "	15,00	120	00		
"	"	" P. W. McGregor for drayage this month				5	50
"	"	" Postage for sundry persons, pr. Postage Book, this mo.				4	69
"	"	" Do. " our own a/c " " " " "		2	25		
		Ent'd on main Cash-Book, folio 1		162	50	345	30

In this book are entered the petty expenses for store, and the petty charges paid for consignors, each in a column appropriated for that purpose; and the totals of these columns are taken to the main Cash-Book, whenever a trial of the cash account is to be made.

INVENTORY-BOOK, FORM 6.

	Merchandise on hand March 31st, 1853.						
Ⓐ #81.	6 Ps. Fine Blk.	Cassimeres	240 Yds.	@	$1,24	297	60
" #82.	3 " Oxford Mill'd	Do.	114 "	"	1,24	141	36
	7 " " Mix'd	Do.	266 "	"	1,00	266	00
" #83.	1 " Drab Mill'd	Do.	42 "	"	1,22	51	24
	3 " Fine Blue	Do.	126 "	"	1,22	153	72
	3 " " " Mill'd	Do.	126 "	"	1,22	153	72
	5 " Assorted Col'd	Do.	212 "	"	1,11	235	32
" #84.	2 " Super W. D. Blk.	Cloths	46 "	"	5,00	230	00
	2 " Fine Blue Blk.	Do.	48 "	"	4,00	192	00
" #85.	4 " Black	Do.	100 "	"	3,00	300	00
	7 " Assorted Green	Do.	175 "	"	3,00	525	00
" #86.	7 " " Brown	Do.	175 "	"	3,00	525	00
" #87.	2 " Light Mix'd	Do.	50 "	"	2,50	125	00
	2 " Dark "	Do.	48 "	"	2,50	120	00
" #88.	2 " Victoria	Do.	48 "	"	2,00	96	00
	5 " "	Do.	120 "	"	2,78	333	60
" #89.	5 " Superfine Drab	Do.	120 "	"	3,00	360	00
						4,105	56
	Add 50 % for Freight, Charges, Duties and Exchange					2,052	78
						$6,158	34

INVOICE-BOOK, FORM 6.

Invoice of Cloths and Cassimeres, shipped per Saranak, Turley, bound to Philadelphia, on ac't and risk of James Dunlap & Co., Merchants there, and to them consigned, pursuant to their order.

Mark	Description		Quantity	Price	£	s.	d.
◊A #81.	6 Ps. Extra Fine Blk. Cassimeres		240 Yds. @	6*s*. 9*d*.	81	0	0
	8 " Fine Blk.	Do.	320 " "	5 7	89	6	8
" #82.	7 " Oxford Mill'd	Do.	266 " "	5 7	74	5	2
	7 " " Mix'd	Do.	266 " "	4 6	59	17	0
" #83.	3 " Mill'd Drab	Do.	126 " "	5 6	34	13	0
	3 " Fine Blue	Do.	126 " "	5 6	34	13	0
	3 " " " Mill'd	Do.	126 " "	5 6	34	13	0
	5 " Assorted Col'd	Do.	212 " "	5 0	53	0	0
" #84.	6 " Super W. D. Blk. Cloths		138 " "	22 6	155	5	0
	7 " Fine Blue Blk.	Do.	168 " "	18 0	151	4	0
" #85.	8 " Black	Do.	200 " "	13 6	135	0	0
	7 " Assorted Green	Do.	175 " "	13 6	118	2	6
" #86.	7 " " Brown	Do.	175 " "	13 6	118	2	6
	7 " " "	Do.	175 " "	11 3	98	8	9
" #87.	5 " Blue	Do.	125 " "	12 6	78	2	6
	2 " Extra Blue	Do.	50 " "	14 8	36	13	4
	4 " Light Mix'd	Do.	100 " "	11 3	56	5	0
	5 " Dark "	Do.	120 " "	11 3	67	10	0
" #88.	10 " Victoria	Do.	240 " "	9 0	108	0	0
	5 " "	Do.	120 " "	12 6	75	0	0
" #89.	3 " Superfine Inv. Green	Do.	75 " "	18 0	67	10	0
	6 " Drab	Do.	150 " "	8 4	62	10	0
	5 " Superfine Drab	Do.	120 " "	13 6	81	0	0
					1,870	1	5
	9 Packing Boxes and Drayage				2	10	0
					£1,872	11	5

Liverpool, Feb. 12th, 1853.

(Signed) LOVERING & BACHE.

NOTE.—The Inventory on the preceding page is that portion of the above Invoice that remains unsold. To save room the other Invoices are omitted.

FORM OF A CONTINUED TRIAL BALANCE.

On the opposite page is given a form for a Continued Trial Balance of the Leger, in which the *differences* only of the accounts are entered.

It will be found of great service in enabling the heads of an establishment to see at a glance the standing of the account of any individual, or of any species of property, and to compare it with the former position of that account. This sheet may be made out monthly, or once in two or three months, at discretion, and it would be well to have a book ruled for the specific purpose.

FORM OF A MONTHLY TRIAL BALANCE FOR SIX MONTHS.

L.F		January. Dr.	January. Cr.	February. Dr.	February. Cr.	March. Dr.	March. Cr.	April. Dr.	April. Cr.	May. Dr.	May. Cr.	June. Dr.	June. Cr.
1	Stock		9,288 00		9,288 00		9,288 00		9,288 00		9,288 00		9,288 00
4	Cash	5,518 04		2,324 66		825 30		1,826 57		2,763 76		2,656 97	
5	Charges and Com.		787 16		966 87		1,273 26		1,546 94		2,165 77		2,798 48
2	Merchandise	4,157 41		6,212 25		2,140 26		3,640 78		7,856 86		4,965 54	
15	Lovering & Bache		4,322 54		4,322 54								
3	Bills Receivable	3,301 55		3,125 00		6,220 75		4,366 46		6,774 54		6,774 54	
16	Sharpless & Co.		2,591 66		2,591 66		2,591 66		2,591 66		2,591 66		2,591 66
6	Prem. Int. and Dis.	467 18		189 76		460 25		475 28		286 66		125 60	
17	Chas. Duncan		1,667 25		3,187 18		3,767 45		1,767 45		1,767 45		839 15
19	Peter Kelly		795 26		2,692 62		2,692 62		692 62				
7	Mdse. Co. R.		382 06										
8	Store Expenses	162 50		322 65		556 63		693 98		893 75		1,026 84	
20	A. Edwards & Co.	4,472 75		4,472 75		2,472 75		2,472 75		2,472 75		472 75	
21	Smith & Williams	1,754 50		2,362 61		2,362 61		2,362 61		3,862 61		3,862 61	
		19,833 93	19,833 93										
10	Profit and Loss				382 06		412 33		412 33		412 33		412 33
22	E. Jones			2,348 00		2,982 99		4,345 60					
23	Bonnard & Bates			2,073 25		1,073 25		1,073 25		1,073 25		1,073 25	
				23,430 93	23,430 93								
25	T. W. Provost & Co.					930 53		1,838 40		2,452 25		5,862 50	
						20,025 32	20,025 32						
11	Bills Payable								2,000 00		3,500 00		3,850 00
26	J. & G. Henderson								4,796 68		4,796 68		4,796 68
								23,095 68	23,095 68				
27	Manning & Lord										5,582 28		5,582 28
29	Oviatt & Clark									1,667 74		3,985 90	
										30,104 17	30,104 17		
30	Taylor & Wilson												647 92
												30,806 50	30,806 50

2 I

FORM OF A RECEIVING AND FORWARDING BOOK.

Nashville, Tenn., 1853.

How Received.	Date Rec'd.	For whose ac't.	No. of Pk'gs.	Weight.	Rate.	Freight.	Storage.	Drayage.	Total.	Leger Folio.
Talleyrand fr. N. Orleans	Apr. 15.	Jas. Swanson, Williamson Co.	10	5000 Char	50 ges.	25 00 / 25 00	5 00	1 25	56 25	300
Cumberland fr. Smithland	Apr. 22.	Saml. Walker, Columbia, Tenn.	11	3000 Char	25 ges.	7 50 / 10 00	3 00	75	21 25	600

When the receiving and forwarding operations of a house are confined to regular customers, with whom the house has running accounts, it will be found convenient to post directly from this book to the Leger—the amounts extended in the total column being posted to the debit of the individuals for whose ac't received, and the footings of the Freight, Storage and Drayage columns being posted monthly to the credit of their respective accounts. The footing of the Freight column, taken to the credit of that account, should equal the amount previously debited the same account for freight and charges paid on goods when received.

When a *cash* business is done, this book will be used only as a register of particulars in relation to goods received, and no posts will be made from it. The postings will come through the medium of the Cash-Book.

FORM OF A RECEIVING BOOK.

Philadelphia, May 2nd, 1853.

Shippers.	Marks.	Consignees.	Articles.	Weight	Rate.	Charges.	Am't.
Hoffman & Co.	H &c.	P. Camden Pittsburg	8 Boxes Dry Goods # $\frac{50}{300}+\frac{60}{600}+\frac{61}{400}+\frac{62}{500}+\frac{66}{450}+\frac{67}{350}+\frac{68}{250}+\frac{70}{325}=$	3175	1,25	1 38	41 07
A. Swain & Co.	T. S.	Park & Selden	2 Crates Crockery # $\frac{71}{520}+\frac{72}{625}=$	1145	87^{2}	75	10 77
		Cincinnati	2 Boxes Hardware # $\frac{73}{450}+\frac{74}{475}=$	925	87^{2}	50	8 59

FORM OF A FORWARDING BOOK.

Philadelphia, May 3d, 1853.

	Mark.	Consignees.	Articles.	Weight
			8 Boxes	
	H &c.	P. Camden	300+600+400+500+450+350+250+325=	3175
	T. S.	Park & Selden	2 Crates 520+625	1145
			2 Boxes 450+475	925
		John Morris, Conductor, Cars No. 200, 520, 315, 626.		

The last two Forms are for houses which have regular transportation lines owned in connection with them.

In the Receiving-Book are mentioned all the particulars concerning goods received; and when goods are forwarded the weights and marks are taken down in the Forwarding-Book, also the numbers of the cars in which sent, and the name of the conductor who takes charge of them. Then, by comparison with the Receiving-Book, it can be seen whether the weights, &c., agree, and whether the goods of any consignee are all sent.

Note.—The examples given suppose the transportation line to be cars, but if it were boats, the *Forms* would answer equally well.

COMMERCIAL CALCULATIONS;

OR,

MERCANTILE ARITHMETIC.

COMMERCIAL CALCULATIONS.

INTEREST.

Interest is a premium or per-centage paid by the borrower to the lender for the use of money lent.

There are several methods of calculating interest, of which we give the following.

I. To obtain the interest, when the principal, time, and rate per cent. are given.

Rule I.

Multiply the principal by the rate per cent. per annum, and cut off two figures in the product, as decimals: the result will be the interest for one year. Multiply this interest by the number of years in the given time, and take aliquot parts for the months and days.

Rule II.

Express the time given as the fractional part of a year. Multiply this fraction by the rate per cent. per annum, and the principal by the product obtained, and in the last product point off two decimal places.

Rule III.

1*st. When the interest is at* 6 *per cent. per annum.*

Multiply the principal by one-half the number of months in the given time, and point off two places as decimals in the product. If the given time be days, multiply the principal by one-sixth the number of days, and in the product point off three decimals.

2*d. To find the interest at any rate per cent.*

Obtain the interest at 6 *per cent., as above, and take aliquot parts of the same for the required interest:—thus, if the rate per cent. be* 5, *deduct one-sixth from the interest found at* 6 *per cent.—if* 4, *deduct one-third—if* 7, *add one-sixth—if* 9, *add one-half; and so on.*

Note.—In working by rules II. and III., if the time consists of *both* months and days, get the interest for each separately, and add the amounts together to obtain the whole interest.

Examples.

1. What is the Int. on $2,954 for 3 months, 10 days, at 6 pr. ct.?

By rule I.	By rule II.	By rule III.
2954	3 mos. are $\frac{3}{12}$ or $\frac{1}{4}$ of a y'r, and	$\frac{1}{2}$ of 3 mos. is $1\frac{1}{2}$, and
6	10 d's are $\frac{10}{360}$ or $\frac{1}{36}$ of a y'r, then	$\frac{1}{6}$ of 10 d's is $1\frac{2}{3}$, then
3 mos. are $\frac{1}{4}$ of y'r 4)177,24	$\frac{1}{4}\times6=1\frac{1}{2}\times2954=44,31$ Int. 3 mos.	$2954\times1\frac{1}{2}=44,31$ Int. 3 mos.
10 d's are $\frac{1}{9}$ of 3 mos. 9)44,31	$\frac{1}{36}\times6=\frac{1}{6}\times2954=$ 4,92$\frac{1}{3}$ Do. 10 d's	$2954\times1\frac{2}{3}=$ 4,92,3$\frac{1}{3}$ Do. 10 d's.
4,92$\frac{1}{3}$	Ans. $49,23$\frac{1}{3}$	Ans. $49,23,3$\frac{1}{3}$
Ans. $49,23$\frac{1}{3}$		

2. What is the Int. on \$3,670 from Mar. 1st, 1852, to July 11th, 1853, at 7 pr. ct.?

By rule I.	By rule II.	By rule III.
3670	1853, 7, 11	$3670\times8=293{,}60$ Int. at 6 pr. ct 16 mos.
7	1852, 3, 1	$3670\times1\frac{2}{3}=$ 6,11,6$\frac{2}{3}$ Int. at 6 pr ct., 10 d's.
3)256,90 Int. 1 y'r	1 y'r 4 m. 10 d's time.	6)299,71,6$\frac{2}{3}$ whole Int. at 6 pr. ct.
12) 85,63$\frac{1}{3}$ " 4 mos.	$1\frac{1}{3}\times7=9\frac{1}{3}\times3670=342{,}53\frac{1}{3}$ Int. 16 m.	Add $\frac{1}{6}$ 49,95,2$\frac{14}{18}$
7,13$\frac{7}{12}$ " 10 d's	$\frac{1}{36}\times7=\frac{7}{36}\times3670=$ 7,13$\frac{11}{18}$ " 10 d's	Ans. \$349,66,9$\frac{8}{18}$
\$349,66$\frac{11}{12}$ Ans.	Ans. \$349,66$\frac{17}{18}$	

3. What will be the Int. for 7 months, at 9 pr. ct., on \$6,745,52?

$6745{,}52\times9=607{,}09{,}68$	$\frac{7}{12}\times9=\frac{63}{12}$ or $5\frac{1}{4}$, and	$6745{,}52\times3\frac{1}{2}=236{,}09{,}32$ Int. at 6 pr. ct.
2)607,09,68 Int. 1 y'r	$5\frac{1}{4}\times6745{,}52=$ \$354,13$\frac{98}{100}$ Ans.	Add $\frac{1}{2}$ 118,04,66
6)303,54,84 " 6 mos.		Ans. 354,13$\frac{98}{100}$
50,59,14 " 1 "		
\$354,13$\frac{98}{100}$ Ans.		

4. What Int. will accrue on \$2,184,25 for 210 days, at 12 pr. ct.?

$2184{,}25\times12=262{,}11{,}00$	* By rule II. at 365 d's to a y'r.	$2184{,}25\times35=76{,}44{,}875$ Int. at 6 pr. ct.
2)262,11 Int. 1 y'r	$\frac{210}{365}$ or $\frac{42}{73}\times12=\frac{504}{73}\times2184{,}25=$	2×
6)131,05,5 " 180 d's	\$150,80$\frac{22}{73}$ Ans.	\$152,89$\frac{750}{1000}$ Ans.
21,84,25 " 30 d's	By rule II. at 360 d's to a y'r.	
\$152,89$\frac{75}{100}$ Ans.	$\frac{210}{360}$ or $\frac{7}{12}\times12=7\times2184{,}25=$	
	\$152,89$\frac{75}{100}$ Ans.	

Note.—Add the principal and interest together to obtain the amount.

5. What Amount will be due Sept. 1st, 1853, on a Note of \$16,844, at 8 pr. ct Int., given Mar. 1st, 1852?

$16844\times8=1347{,}52$	1853, 9, 1	$16844\times9=1515{,}96$ Int. at 6 pr. ct.
2)1347,52 Int. 1 y'r	1852, 3, 1	505,32 Add $\frac{1}{3}$
673,76 " 6 mos.	1 y'r 6 m. 0 d's time.	2021,28 Int. at 8 pr. ct.
2021,28 whole Int.	$1\frac{1}{2}\times8=12\times16844=2021{,}28$ Int.	16844,00 Add princ'l
16844,00 principal	Add principal 16844,00	\$18865,28 Ans.
\$18865,28 Ans.	\$18865,28 Ans.	

* All *short* methods of computing interest for *days* assume 360 days as the year; making the calculation at so much per cent. for 360 days; and on account of the ease of this mode, it is adopted almost exclusively, although 365 days is the legal year. The above example is sufficient to show the difference in the two modes. As custom makes law, they will probably not long stand opposed to each other.

II. The principal, interest, and time being given, to find the rate per cent.

Rule. *Obtain the interest on the principal at 1 per cent. for the time given, and divide the interest given by the interest obtained: the quotient will be the rate per cent. required.*

Ex. D is worth \$30,000. At what per cent. must he loan his capital that his income may be just \$1,500 per annum?

Int. on \$30,000 one year @ 1 pr. ct. is \$300.
Then 1500÷300=5 pr. ct. Ans.

III. The principal, interest, and rate per cent. given, to find the time.

Rule. *Obtain the interest on the principal for one year, month, or day, and divide the given interest by the interest obtained: the quotient will be the time sought, either in years, months, or days.*

Ex. 1. In what time will \$2,400 gain \$360 Int., at 6 pr. ct.?

Int. on \$2400 one year at 6 pr. ct. is \$144.
Then 360÷144=$2\frac{1}{2}$ years. Ans.

Ex. 2. How long must \$1,000 be on Int. at 6 pr. ct. to gain \$6,90?

Int. on \$1000 one day at 6 pr. ct. is \$0,$16\frac{2}{3}$.
Then 6,90÷0,$16\frac{2}{3}$, or 20,70÷0,50=$41\frac{2}{5}$ days. Ans.

IV. The time, interest, and rate per cent. given, to find the principal.

Rule. *Obtain the interest of one dollar for the given rate and time, and divide the given interest by the interest obtained; and the quotient will be the principal.*

Ex. What principal is required to gain \$147 Int. in three years and a half, at 7 pr. ct.?

Int. on \$1 for $3\frac{1}{2}$ y'rs at 7 pr. ct. is \$0,24,5.
Then 147,00÷0,24,5=\$600. Ans.

DISCOUNT.

Discount is such an abatement on a note, bond, bill, or book account, that the interest on the remainder for the same length of time for which the discount is made, and at the same rate per cent., will equal the discount.

It is ascertained by the following

Rule. *Obtain the interest on* \$100 *at the given rate and time; multiply the given sum by this interest, and divide the product by the amount of* \$100 *at the same rate and time: the quotient will be the discount.*

The present worth *is obtained by deducting the discount from the given sum, or amount.*

Ex. 1. What is the discount on \$6,000, at 6 pr. ct., for 90 days.

Int. of \$100 @ 6 pr. ct. for 90 days is \$1,50.
Am't " " " " " " " " \$101,50.
Then 6000×1,50=9000,00÷101,50=\$88,$66\frac{202}{203}$. Ans.

Ex. 2. What is the present worth of \$1,675,50, due 2 years hence, discount at 9 pr. ct.?

Int. on \$100, for 2 y'rs, @ 9 pr. ct. is \$18.
1675,50×18=30159,00÷118=255,$58\frac{28}{59}$ discount.

Am't 1675,50
Less discount 255,$58\frac{28}{59}$

\$1419,$91\frac{31}{59}$. Ans.

COMMERCIAL CALCULATIONS.

BANK DISCOUNT.

Bank discount, or *interest paid beforehand*, is calculated in the same manner as interest.

Banks now generally include in their reckoning both the day when the note is discounted and the day on which the time specified in it expires, which, with *three days of grace*, makes the time for which discount is taken *four* days more than the time specified in the note.

Ex. What is the bank discount, at 6 pr. ct., on a note for $1,200, payable sixty days hence?

$60+4=64$ days, time for which discount must be reckoned.

$\frac{1}{6}$ of $64=10\frac{2}{3}\times 1200=12,80,0$. $12,80. Ans.

DISCOUNT ON BILLS AND INVOICES.

Merchants are in the habit of deducting a certain per-centage from invoices and bills of goods sold for ready pay. This is reckoned in the same manner as interest.

Ex. 1. A. purchases a bill of goods of B., amounting to $756, at a year's credit, but B offers to deduct 10 pr. ct. for ready pay. What amount is to be deducted?

$756\times 10=$ $75,60. Ans.

Ex. 2. A. sells B. a bill of goods for $1,200, and allows him 5 pr. ct. for ready pay What amount must A. receive?

$1200\times 5=60,00$ discount.

1200—60=$1140. Ans.

Ex. 3. B. purchases of A. goods amounting to $1,800, and is to be allowed a deduction of 5 pr. ct. for Cash. But finding himself short of funds, pays $1,140, for which he is to receive a discount off the bill, in the same proportion as if he had paid the whole For what Am't should he receive credit?

It is evident that he should be credited for such a sum, that, after making the 5 pr. ct discount therefrom, the remainder will be $1,140. Therefore 95 : 100 : : 1140 : the answer or, $1140\times 100=114000\div 95=$ $1200. Ans.

Note.—This will be seen to be the correct answer, by comparison with Ex. 2: for in that Ex. $1,200, the Am't of the bill, was considered as cancelled by the payment of $1,140. A very common way of working examples of this kind is as follows: $1140\times 5=57,00+1140=$ $1,197, Am't to be credited. But this is evidently incorrect; for if $1,140 pays the whole debt in Ex. 2, then in this Ex. $1,140 should pay an equivalent sum.

By discounting off the face of bills, losses are frequently sustained without suspecting it. This arises from the fact that the discount is not only made on the first cost of the goods, but also on the gains. For instance, if a profit of 30 pr. ct. be made on any article of merchandise, and then 10 pr. ct. be deducted, the gain, at first sight, would appear to be 20 pr. ct., but is in reality only 17 pr. ct.: in like manner, if 60 pr. ct. be added, and then a discount made of 45 pr. ct., the apparent profit would be 15 pr. ct., while *the real loss is 12 pr. ct.!!* For proof, see the following:

Cost of goods	$100	Cost	$100
Add 30 pr. ct. profit	30	Profit 60 pr. ct.	60
Selling price	130	Selling price	160
Deduct 10 pr. ct. disc't	13	Discount 45 pr. ct.	72
Cash price	$117	Cash price	$88
Gain 17 pr. ct.		Loss 12 pr. ct.	

This deception will be increased rapidly as the per-centage is made larger.

INSURANCE AND POLICIES.

Insurance is a contract by which one party engages, for a stipulated premium, to make up a loss which another may sustain. The premium paid is also called insurance, and is calculated in the same manner as interest.

Policy is the instrument by which the contract is effected.

Ex. 1. What is the insurance on $14,650, at 1½ pr. ct.?

14650 × 1½ = $219,75. Ans.

Ex. 2. If a policy be taken out for $7,500, at 5 pr. ct., what net amount is covered, after paying insurance?

7500 × 5 = 375,00:—then 7500–375 = $7125. Ans.

Ex. 3. If the premium is 4 pr. ct., for what amount must a policy be taken out to cover $6,144, together with the premium paid for insurance?

Note.—This question requires a solution entirely similar to Ex. 3 in *Discount on Bills.*

6144 × 100 = 614400 ÷ 96 = $6,400. Ans.

COMMISSION OR BROKERAGE.

Commission or *Brokerage* is an allowance of a certain per-centage to factors. brokers, and other agents, for their services in buying and selling stocks, merchandise, &c. It is obtained in the same manner as insurance.

Ex. A. sells for B. merchandise to the Am't of $16,000, for which B. allows him 3 pr. ct. Commission. How much must he receive?

16000 × 3 = $480,00. Ans.

LOSS AND GAIN.

I. To ascertain what is gained or lost per cent. in buying and selling goods.

Rule. *Find by subtraction the gain or loss on the articles sold (either on the whole amount, or pr. box, bale, y'd, &c.), annex two cyphers, and divide by the purchase price: the quotient will be the gain or loss per cent.*

Ex. 1. If I buy 50 Yds. of Broad Cloth at $5,25 pr. Yd., and sell it at $7 pr. Yd., what do I gain pr. ct.?

7,00—5,25 = 1,75 gain on a Yd.; to which annex two cyphers.
Then 175,00 ÷ 5,25 = 33⅓ pr. ct. Ans.

Ex. 2. Bought 1,200 Bbls. Flour at $4 pr. Bbl., and getting it damaged sold the whole for $4,000; what did I lose pr. ct.?

1200 × 4 = 4800—4000 = $800 total loss.
Then 80000 ÷ 4800 = 16⅔ loss pr. ct. Ans.

II. The gain or loss per cent. being given, to ascertain the whole gain or loss. Also to ascertain at what price merchandise must be sold to gain or lose a stipulated per cent.

Rule. 1*st. Multiply the cost by the rate per cent., and in the product point off two decimal places. The result will be the whole gain or loss.*

2d. *If a gain, add it to the cost, and if a loss, deduct it therefrom, and you will obtain the selling price.*

Ex. 1. If I sell $5,000 worth of Mdse. at $33\frac{1}{3}$ pr. ct. advance, what do I gain?

$5000 \times 33\frac{1}{3} = \$1666{,}66\frac{2}{3}$ Ans.

Ex. 2. If I buy Pork at $8 pr. Bbl., what must be my selling price to make 20 pr. ct. on the first cost?

$8 \times 20 = 1{,}60$ gain pr. Bbl., and $8 + 1{,}60 = \$9{,}60$ pr. Bbl. Ans.

III. To ascertain at what price merchandise must be bought in order to sell it at a stipulated price and make a certain rate per cent.

Rule. *Annex two cyphers to the selling price, and divide by one hundred increased by the rate per cent., and the quotient will be the purchase price.*

Ex. 1. I sell goods to the am't of $800, which includes 10 pr. ct. on the prime cost, what was the prime cost?

800, annex two cyphers, $80000 \div 110 = \$727{,}27\frac{3}{11}$ Ans.

Ex. 2. In order to sell sugar at $7,50 pr. 100 lbs., and thereby make 15 pr. ct., what must be my purchase price?

$75000 \div 115 = \$6{,}52\frac{20}{115}$ pr. 100 lbs. Ans.

EQUATION OF PAYMENTS.

The object of *Equation of payments* is to find the medium or average time for the payment of several sums of different dates, or different terms of credit, or both.

Rule I. *When the sums are of the same date, but having different terms of credit,*

Multiply each sum respectively by the time it has to run, and divide the sum of the several products obtained by the whole debt: the quotient will be the averaged time of credit.

Ex. A. purchases of B. goods amounting to $1,025, payable as follows—$200 in 3 months; $360 in 4 months; $300 in 5 months; and $165 in 6 months: but concludes to give one note for the whole. At what time shall it be made payable?

Am't.		Time.		Product.
200	×	3	=	600
360	×	4	=	1440
300	×	5	=	1500
165	×	6	=	990
$1025				4530

```
1025) 4530 (4 12 600/1025
      4100              4 mos. 13 d's.  Ans.
      ----
       430
        30
      -----
     12900
      1025
      -----
      2650
      2050
      -----
       600
```

Rule II. *Multiply each respective sum by the time intervening between the date when the* first *amount falls due, and the date on which each sum falls due. Divide the sum of the several products by the whole debt, and the quotient will be the average time of payment, to be counted* forward *from the date of the first amount falling due.*

Ex. A owes B. $2,000, for purchases at different dates, and on various credits, as below stated. Required the equated time for the payment of the whole debt.

Statement from Book Ac't.

Date of purchase.	Amount.	Time of Cr.	When due.
Jan. 16 - - -	$300 - - -	3 mos. - - -	April 16.
" 24 - - -	500 - - -	2 " - - -	March 24.
Feb. 1 - - -	250 - - -	4 " - - -	June 1.
" 15 - - -	350 - - -	3 " - - -	May 15.
March 8 - - -	600 - - -	4 " - - -	July 8.

Statement arranged as an equation.

Due.	Amount.		Time (in days.)		Product.
March 24 - - -	500	×	00	=	0000
April 16 - - -	300	×	23	=	6900
May 15 - - -	350	×	52	=	18200
June 1 - - -	250	×	69	=	17250
July 8 - - -	600	×	106	=	63600
	$2000				)105950 ($52\frac{1950}{2000}$ days.

Then 53 days from March 24, is May 16. Ans.

RULE III. *Multiply each sum respectively by the time intervening between the date on which it falls due and the date on which the* LAST *amount falls due. Divide the sum of the several products by the whole debt, and the quotient will be the equated time, to be counted* BACKWARD *from the date of the last amount falling due.*

Ex. Suppose I purchase goods at sundry times as follows:

Jan. 5 a bill of $376,40 on a credit of 6 months.
Jan. 15 " " " 125,75 " " " " 3 "
Feb. 1 " " " 295,25 " " " " 60 days.
Mar. 2 " " " 325,00 no credit: and on making the last purchase wish to give my note for the whole. When must it be made payable?

Statement as an equation.

Due.	Amount.		Days.		Product.
July 5 - - -	376*	×	00	=	0000
April 15 - - -	126	×	81	=	10206
April 2 - - -	295	×	94	=	27730
March 2 - - -	325	×	125	=	40625
	$1122				)78561 ($70\frac{21}{1122}$ days.

Then 70 days backward from July 5 is April 26. Ans.

RULE IV. BY INTEREST. *Calculate the interest on each sum respectively for the same time that you would multiply it by in working by the preceding rules. Sum up the several items of interest obtained, and find how long it will take for the whole debt to accumulate that amount of interest: the result will be the equated time, to be counted forward or backward, according to the day from which you reckon.*

NOTE.—To show that this produces the same answer as the preceding rules, we will take the three examples already given, working the first at 5 pr. ct. interest, the second at 7 pr. ct., and the third at 6 pr. ct.

* In working this equation we have omitted the cents when less than fifty, and when more than fifty called them a dollar. This will usually be found sufficiently exact.

1. Example given under Rule I.

Amount.	Months.	Int. @ 5 per ct.
$200	3	2,50
360	4	6,00
300	5	6,25
165	6	4,12,5
$1025		$18,87,5

Int. on $1025 one mo. is $4,27,1
Then 18,87,5÷4,27,1=$4\frac{1791}{4271}$ mos. or 4 mos. 13 days. Ans. as by Rule I.

2. Example given under Rule II.

Due.	Amount.	Days.	Int. @ 7 per ct.
March 24	500	00	0000
April 16	300	23	1,34,2
May 15	350	52	3,53,9
June 1	250	69	3,35,4
July 8	600	106	12,36,7

For $2000 to gain $20,60,2 Int. it requires 53 days (nearly.)
Then 53 days from March 24 is May 16. Ans. as by Rule II.

3. Example given under Rule III.

Due.	Amount.	Days.	Int. @ 6 per ct.
July 5	376	00	0000
April 15	126	81	1,70,1
April 2	295	94	4,62,2
March 2	325	125	6,77,1

For $1122 to gain $13,09,4 Int. 70 d's are required (fraction omitted.)
70 days backward from July 5 is April 26. Ans. as by Rule III.

Remarks.—In all the preceding rules we have reckoned the time from the date either of the first or last amount falling due; but any other time previous to the first date, or succeeding the last, may be chosen if preferred. Thus, in the Ex. given under Rule II., we might with equal propriety have reckoned the time from March 1st, in which case there would have been 24 days' time for the first item, and the others increased proportionally: then, in the result, the number of days obtained would have been counted forward from March 1st.

When there are a great number of small items to be equated, all those which fall due in one month are frequently summed up together and called due on the first of next month.

The days of grace (which are now almost universally allowed) may be added to the time of each item to be equated, or the equation may be first worked, and then the addition of grace made. The latter mode is much the easiest, and produces the same result.

COMPOUND EQUATION.

By *Compound equation* we ascertain at what time the *balance* of an account that contains both debits and credits becomes due.

Rule I. *First find by simple equation the averaged time when the* DEBITS *and* CREDITS *of the account fall due, without regard to their relation to each other. Then multiply the smaller side of the account, (whether it be the debit or credit,) by the number of days between the days of equated time obtained, and divide the product by the balance of the account: the quotient will be the time required for calculation. If the* EARLIER *date of equated time be affixed to the* LARGER *side, (whether debit or credit,) count the time* BACK *from the* EARLIER *date; but if the* LATER *date be affixed to the larger side, count the time* FORWARD *from the* LATER *date, and you will obtain the day on which the balance becomes due.*

Ex. 1. I have an ac't with Samuel Wells—Am'ts and times of payment as below stated—and wish to know the equated time when the balance shall be paid.

Date.	Time to run.	Due.	Amount.	Date.	Time to run.	Due.	Amount.
Jan. 4,	2 mos.	Mar. 4,	$250	Jan. 1,	6 mos.	July 1,	$500
Feb. 1,	30 d's.	" 3,	140	" 20,	60 d's.	Mar. 21,	200
" 15,	2 mos.	Apr. 15,	450	Feb. 8,	30 d's.	" 10,	350
Mar. 2,	1 "	" 2,	100	Mar. 4,	3 mos.	June 4,	240
				" 25,	2 "	May 25,	120
		Total debits	$940			Total credits	$1,410

Mode of operation.

Due.	Amount.	Days.	Product.	Due.	Amount.	Days.	Product.
Mar. 4,	250 ×	1 =	250	July 1,	500 ×	113 =	56500
" 3,	140 ×	0 =	000	Mar. 21,	200 ×	11 =	2200
Apr. 15,	450 ×	43 =	19350	" 10,	350 ×	00 =	0000
" 2,	100 ×	30 =	3000	June 4,	240 ×	86 =	20640
				May 25,	120 ×	76 =	9120
	$940		22600		$1,410		88460

940) 22600 ($24\frac{4}{94}$, 24 days from Mar. 3 is Mar. 27.
$940 due Mar. 27.

1410) 88460 ($62\frac{104}{141}$, 63 days from Mar. 10.
$1410 due May 12.

From Mar. 27, to May 12, is 46 days.

Credits	1410
Debits	940
Balance	$470

Smaller side. Days. Bal.
940 × 46=43240÷470=92 days, which, counted *forward* from May 12, bring us to Aug. 12. Ans.

Ex. 2. What is the equated time of payment for the Bal. of the following ac't.

Date.	Time.	When due.	Amount.	Date.	Time.	When due.	Amount.
Jan. 1,	6 mos.	July 1,	150	Mar. 8,	2 mos.	May 8,	150
Feb. 20,	4 "	June 20,	260	Apr. 3,	3 mos.	July 3,	340
Apr. 5,	3 "	July 5,	325	May 6,	30 d's.	June 5,	420
May 4,		May 4,	550	Aug. 2,	30 "	Sept. 1,	170
		Total debits	$1,285			Total credits	$1,080

Mode of operation.

Due.	Amount.	Days.	Int. @ 6 pr. ct.	Due.	Amount.	Days.	Int. @ 6 pr. ct
July 1,	150	58	1,45,0	May 8,	150	00	0,00,0
June 20,	260	47	2,03,7	July 3,	340	56	3,17,3
July 5,	325	62	3,35,8	June 5,	420	28	1,96,0
May 4,	550	00	0,00,0	Sept. 1,	170	116	3,28,7

For $1,285 to gain $6,84,5 interest, it requires $31\frac{247}{257}$ days.
32 days from May 4 is June 5.
$1285 due June 5.

For $1,080 to gain $8,42,0 interest, it requires $46\frac{14}{18}$ days.
47 days from May 8 is June 24.
$1080 due June 24.

From June 5, to June 24, is 19 days.

Debit	1285
Credit	1080
Bal	$205

Smaller side. Days. Bal.
1080 × 19=20520÷205=$100\frac{20}{205}$; 100 days *backward* from June 5 give Feb. 25. Ans.

RULE II. *Multiply each sum respectively by the time intervening between the date of the first amount falling due and the date on which said sum falls due. Find the sum of the several products thus obtained on the debit side, and also on the credit side—subtract one from the other, and divide their difference by the balance of the account, and you will have the time required for calculation.*

Then, if the balance of the account, and the difference between the sums of the products, both fall on the SAME *side of the account, (i. e. both on the debit or both on the credit side,) reckon this time* FORWARD *from the date on which the first amount becomes due; but if they fall on* OPPOSITE *sides, (i. e. one on the debit, and the other on the credit,) reckon it* BACKWARD *from the same date: the result will be the equated time for the payment of the balance.*

This rule may also be worked by INTEREST.

NOTE.—We give below the same examples as are given to the preceding rule.

Example 1.

Due.	Amount.	Days.	Product.	Due.	Amount.	Days.	Product.
Mar. 4,	250 ×	1 =	250	July 1,	500 ×	120 =	60000
" 3,	140 ×	0 =	000	Mar. 21,	200 ×	18 =	3600
Apr. 15,	450 ×	43 =	19350	" 10,	350 ×	7 =	2450
" 2,	100 ×	30 =	3000	June 4,	240 ×	93 =	22320
				May 25,	120 ×	83 =	9960
	$940		22600		$1,410		98330
					940		22600
					$470		75730

470)75730(161 6/47

61 days counted *forward* from Mar. 3 give, for the equated time, Aug. 11. Ans.*

Example 2.

Due.	Amount.	Days.	Int. @ 6 pr. ct.	Due.	Amount.	Days.	Int. @ 6 pr. ct.
July 1,	150	58	1,45,0	May 8,	150	4	,10,0
June 20,	260	47	2,03,7	July 3,	340	60	3,40,0
July 5,	325	62	3,35,8	June 5,	420	32	2,24,0
May 4,	550	00	0,00,0	Sept. 1,	170	120	3,40,0
	$1,285		$6,84,5		$1,080		$9,14,0
	1,080						6,84,5
	$205						$2,29,5

For $205 to gain $2,29,5 Int. it requires 67 7/41 days.

67 days *backward* from May 4, is Feb. 26. Ans.*

EQUATION APPLIED TO THE STORAGE OF PROPERTY.

Formula 1.

Received and delivered on ac't of S. B. & Co., sundry parcels of flour, as follows:

		Bbls.	Days.	Prod.
Jan. 22,	Received	125 ×	9 =	1125
" 31,	Received	1000		
		1125 ×	1 =	1125
Feb. 1,	Delivered	545		
		580 ×	14 =	8120
" 15,	Delivered	312		
		268 ×	3 =	804
" 18,	Received	420		
		688 ×	7 =	4816
" 25,	Delivered	258		
		430 ×	3 =	1290
" 28,	Delivered	220	3,0)	1728,0
Balance in Store		210		576

Formula 2.

Am'ts received and delivered the same as in formula 1.

Received.	Bbls.	Days.	Prod.	Delivered.	Bbls.	Days.	Prod.
Jan. 22,	125 ×	37 =	4625	Feb. 1,	545 ×	27 =	14715
" 31,	1000 ×	28 =	28000	" 15,	312 ×	13 =	4056
Feb 18,	420 ×	10 =	4200	" 25,	258 ×	3 =	774
				" 28,	220 ×	0 =	000
	1545		36825		1335		19545
			19545				
		3,0)	1728,0				
			576				

According to the above statements there were received 1545 Bbls. from Jan. 22, to Feb. 28, and during the same time 1335 Bbls. were delivered, leaving still in store 210 Bbls.

(*Continued.*)

* The slight differences in the answers obtained by this and the preceding rule are occasioned by the fractions that occur in working by Rule I.

In formula 1, we multiply the number of Bbls. by the days they are in store, and add the several products together, which produces 17280, the number of Bbls. on which storage should be charged for one day; then this divided by 30 gives 576, the number on which to charge storage for one month.

In formula 2, we multiply the number of Bbls. received and the number delivered, (each separately,) by the days from the time of reception or delivery, to the time the average closes, (Feb. 28,) and subtract the sums of the products, which produces 17280, the same as before.

EXCHANGE ON GREAT BRITAIN.

Table showing the nominal par value of sterling money.

£	s.	d.		$	cts.	m.	s.	d.		$	cts.	m.
1	0	0	=	4,	44,	$44\frac{4}{9}$	1	0	=	0,	22,	22
	15	0	=	3,	33,	33		9	=		16,	67
	10	0	=	2,	22,	22		6	=		11,	11
	5	0	=	1,	11,	11		3	=		5,	56
	2	6	=		55,	56		2	=		3,	70
	1	3	=		27,	78		1	=		1,	85

I. To reduce sterling to its nominal par value in federal money.

Rule I. *Bring the shillings and pence to the decimal of a pound, and annex them to the pounds; then multiply by* 40 (*the sixpences in a pound*) *and divide by* 9 (*the sixpences in a dollar*)*: the quotient will be the answer in dollars and decimals of a dollar.*

Rule II. *Find the number of sixpences in the shillings and pence, and, after multiplying the pounds by* 40, *add them to the product, and divide by* 9; *then get the value of the odd pence separately, and add it to this quotient.*

Ex. 1. What is the nominal par value in federal money of £1872 11s. 5d.?

1st method.

```
12| 5,00000
2,0|11,4166,6
   1872,57083
           40
 9)74902,83320
  $8322,53 702/1000 Ans.
```

2d method.

```
 1872
   40
 74880
    22 sixpences=11s.
9)74902
  8322,44,44
       9,26=5d.
 $8322,53 70/100 Ans.
```

Note.—To obtain the *real* value, the premium of exchange at the time of reckoning must be added.

Ex. 2. What is the value in federal money of a bill of exchange for £879, 13s. 10d., when the rate of exchange is 9 pr. ct. premium on sterling money?

```
12|10,000
2,0|13,833
   879,6916
         40
9)35187,6640
  3909,74,04 par value.
           9 pr. ct. prem.
  351,876636
 3909,7404
$4261,61 70/100 Ans.
```

```
 879
  40
35160
   27 sixpences=13s. 6d
9)35187
  3909,66,66
      7,41=4d.
  3909,74,07 par value.
   351,87,66 add prem.at 9 pr.ct.
$4261,61 73/100 Ans.
```

II. To reduce Federal to its nominal par value in Sterling money.

Rule. *Multiply by* 9 (*the sixpences in a dollar*) *and divide the product by* 40, (*the sixpences in a pound,*) *and the quotient will be the answer in pounds, and decimals of a pound, which reduce to shillings and pence.*

Ex. 1. What is the nominal par value in sterling money of $8,322,54?

```
          8322,54              £1872,571
                9                     20
      -----------             ----------
4,0)74902,8,6                s. 11,420
     £1872,571                       12
                              ----------
                             d.  5,040  £1872, 11s. 5d.  Ans.
```

Note.—The *real* value is as much less than the nominal *par* value as the premium of exchange at the time.

Ex. 2. The net proceeds of a sale amount to $4,261,62, which a factor wishes to remit to his consignor in England. For what amount will the bill of exchange be drawn, paying 9 pr. ct. premium on the same?

```
             4261,62        109 : 100 :: 958,8645
                   9                          100
          ----------                  -----------
       4,0)38354,5,8            109)95886,4500
par value   £958,8645               £879,6922=£879, 13s. 10d.  Ans.
```

INDIRECT EXCHANGE.

Owing to the difference in the rates of exchange between different countries, it is frequently more advantageous for a person wishing to remit funds to any foreign country, to purchase a bill on some other place, and direct his agent there to invest the proceeds in bills on the place to which he wishes to make the remittance. This is called *indirect exchange*, or *arbitration of exchange*, and will be readily comprehended by the following examples:

Ex. 1. Suppose the exchange of Philadelphia on London to be 10 pr. ct premium, of Do. on Hamburg $35\frac{1}{2}$ cents pr. marc banco, and of Hamburg on London $13\frac{1}{2}$ marcs banco pr. pound sterling, and a merchant wishes to remit £5,000 to London. How much would he gain by an indirect remittance through Hamburg, if his agent at that place charge $\frac{1}{2}$ pr. ct. commission for procuring the bill on London.

```
Direct to London.                   | To London through Hamburg.
  5000                              |  £     m.b.pr.£
    40                              |  5000 × 13½=67500 marcs banco
--------                            |            337,5 Com. @ ½ pr. ct.
9)200000                            |          ---------
  $22222,22,2 par.                  |            67837,5
     2222,22,2 prem. @ 10 pr. ct.   | Then
  -----------                       |     m. b.    cts. pr. m. b.
  $24444,44,4                       |  67837,5 × 35½=$24082,31,2
```

```
Cost of direct exchange    $24444,44,4
  "   "  indirect   "       24082,31,2
                    Ans.   $362,13,2
```

Ex. 2. An agent in Havana (Cuba) wishes to remit to his principal, in Paris, the amount of funds in his possession, $4,000. How much more will the principal receive (after the expenses of exchange have been deducted) by an indirect remittance through New York, than by a bill direct on Paris; provided 1 dollar Havana currency be equal to 5 francs, and the exchange of Havana on Paris be 1 pr. ct. prem., of Do. on New York 4 pr. ct. prem., and of New York on Paris 5 francs 30 centimes pr. dollar, and the agents in Havana and New York each be allowed ½ pr. ct. com. for doing the business?

To Paris through New York.

$4000 Havana cur.
20 agent's com. at Hav.
3980
153,08 prem. at 4 pr. ct.
$3826,92 am't of bill on N. Y.
19,13 agent's com. at N. Y.
3807,79
5,30 francs pr. dollar.
11423370
1903895
Francs 20181,2870 am't of bill on Paris.

To Paris direct.

$4000 Havana cur.
20 agent's com. at Hav.
3980
5 francs pr. dollar.
19900
197,03 prem. at 1 pr. ct.
Francs 19702,97 am't of bill on Paris.

Francs 20181,29 am't rec'd. via N. York.
" 19702,97 " " direct.
" 478,32 Ans.

FOREIGN COINS AND MONEYS OF ACCOUNT.*

Moneys of Account are those denominations of money in which accounts are kept, and sales and purchases usually effected. In general, money of account is represented by coin of the country, bearing the same name and equal in value with it; but in some few cases it is fictitious, that is, not represented by any coin of the country of corresponding name or value; and in other cases, of more frequent occurrence, it is (owing to excessive issues of paper currency) depreciated in value much below that of the coin of the same name.

The subjoined table exhibits the moneys of account of the principal commercial nations of the world. In every case where the money of account is represented by coin of equal value, the intrinsic value of the principal coin is given, estimated according to the United States Mint valuation of the metal (gold or silver) of which the coin is made; and an approximate value is given when the money of account is fictitious, or represented by a depreciated paper currency.

The valuation of foreign moneys by comparison of the quantity of pure gold or silver in their coins, with the quantity of these metals in the coins of our country, gives the *real* par of exchange between the United States and these countries. Different results will, however, frequently be arrived at by comparing respectively the gold and silver coinages of two countries, inasmuch as the relative values of gold and silver at their mints are various. Thus, the Louis d'or, or French 20 franc piece, of gold, containing 89.55 grains of pure gold, and the United States Eagle, or gold piece of ten dollars, containing 232.2 grains of pure gold, the Louis d'or is worth, in the currency of the United States, $3.85.64, and 1 franc of gold is worth 19.282 cents.—20 francs of silver, containing 1386 grains of pure silver, and 10 silver dollars of the United States, containing 3712.5 grains of pure silver, 1 franc of silver is worth, in the currency of the United States, 18⅔ cents. There is, therefore, a difference between the relative values of gold and silver in the two countries, of about 3.3 per cent.

Where both of the precious metals are used for the current coins of two countries, the

* For this article on Foreign Coins and Moneys of Account, which I believe to be more full and correct than any previously published in this country, I am indebted to W. Vogdes, Esq., Professor of Mathematics in the Central High School of Philadelphia, and author of the United States Arithmetic, for which work it was prepared.

real par of exchange may be said to range between the two values of their moneys estimated by comparing respectively their gold and silver coinages. The most advantageous mode of liquidating indebtedness will, of course, always be chosen; and in case of the indebtedness of the one country, a remittance will be made in gold, or should the other country be the debtor, the remittance will be in silver.

In England, the country with which the United States have the most extensive commercial transactions, the relative Mint valuation of silver to gold is not based upon the market values of the precious metals; but silver is over-valued in order to keep this coinage from being sent abroad: at the same time it is only designed to serve the purpose of small change, being a legal tender for the payment of debts to the amount of only £2 st'g. In estimating the *real* par of exchange with England, we have, therefore, to compare only the gold coinages of the two countries, which comparison gives $4.86 for the value of the Sovereign or Pound Sterling. The *nominal* par of exchange (4\frac{4}{9}$) between these two countries is retained, in quoting rates of exchange, simply because it is difficult to effect a change in the customs of nations or communities, even though such a change may be of undoubted utility.

UNITED KINGDOM OF GREAT BRITAIN AND IRELAND.

Accounts are kept in *pounds*, *shillings*, *pence*, and *farthings*. Prices of articles are also not unfrequently quoted in guineas.

4 farthings (qr) = 1 penny, (d) 12 pence = 1 shilling, (s)
20 shillings = 1 pound sterling, (£ stg.) 21 shillings = 1 guinea, (g)

The sovereign, or pound stg. in gold, is worth $4.86 United States currency. This is the *true* par of exchange; the *nominal* par is 4\frac{4}{9}$, which was established many years ago.

FRANCE.

Accounts are kept in *francs* and *centimes*. 100 centimes (c) = 1 franc (f)
The franc in silver is worth 18$\frac{2}{3}$ cts. United States currency.

BELGIUM.

Accounts are kept in *florins* or *guilders*, and *centimes* or hundredths.
The florin, in silver, is worth a trifle over 40 cts. United States currency.
The coinage of Belgium, since 1832, has been similar, in name and value, to that of France.

HOLLAND.

Moneys of account same as in Belgium.

Bremen.

Accounts are kept in *current rix-dollars*, *grotes*, and *schwares*.
5 schwares = 1 grote, 72 grotes = 1 rix dollar current = 71$\frac{1}{2}$ cts. United States currency
The old rix-dollar (silver) = 81.45 cts., that since 1840 = 71.4 cts. United States currency.

Hamburg.

Accounts are kept in *marcs*, *sols* or *schillings*, and *pfenings*, currency or lubs, (meaning of "Lubeck.")

12 pfenings = 1 schilling, 16 schillings = 1 marc.

The marc *lubs* or *currency*, which is a silver coin, = 28$\frac{1}{2}$ cts. United States currency. The marc *banco*, which is an imaginary money, based upon certificates of deposit of bullion and jewelry in the bank of Hamburg, fluctuates 2 or 3 per cent. above or below its par value, which is 23 per cent. more than the marc currency, or about 35 cts. United States currency.

Accounts are also sometimes kept, particularly in exchanges, in *pounds*, *schillings*, and *pence*, Flemish.

12 grotes or pence = 1 schilling 20 schillings = 1 pound
1 pound Flemish, banco = 7$\frac{1}{2}$ marcs banco.

FOREIGN COINS AND MONEYS OF ACCOUNT.

DENMARK.

Accounts are kept in *rix-dollars*, *marcs*, and *skillings*.

16 skillings=1 marc, 6 marcs=1 rix-dollar.

The new rix-dollar, or *rigsbank* dollar (silver) is worth about 52½ cts. United States currency. The money used in commercial transactions is bank money, which is commonly at a heavy discount.

NORWAY.

Accounts are kept in *rix-dollars* species and *skillings*.

120 skillings=1 rix-dollar species.

Value of the species dollar (silver) in United States currency $1.05. Norway has no gold coinage.

SWEDEN.

The currency of Sweden consists almost entirely of paper money, of which there are two descriptions, the one issued by the government bank, called *riksgald*, the other issued by the national bank, called *banco*, the latter being worth 50 per cent. more than the former.

Accounts are kept in *rix-dollars*, *skillings*, and *rundstycks*, either riksgald, or banco.

12 rundstycks=1 skilling, 48 skillings=1 rix-dollar.

The value of the specie dollar (silver) or coin of the realm, in the currency of the United States, is $1.06+ : that of the paper money fluctuates, but may be said to be, of the rix-dollar banco 37½ cts.; of the rix-dollar riksgald 25 cts.

RUSSIA.

Prior to the year 1840, accounts were kept in paper roubles, 3½ of which were equal to 1 silver rouble: from that period the silver *rouble*, and the *copec* of one hundredth part its value, have been adopted by law as the moneys of account.

Value of the silver rouble in the currency of the United States, 75+cts.

PRUSSIA.

Accounts are kept in *thalers* or *dollars*, *silver grochen*, and *pfenings*.

12 pfenings=1 silver grosch, 30 silver grochen=1 dollar.

The value of the dollar (silver) in the currency of the United States, is 69+cts.

AUSTRIA.

Accounts are kept in *florins* and *kreutzers*. 60 kr.=1 florin.

The florin (silver) is worth, in the currency of the United States, 48¾ cts.

Venice.

Accounts are kept in *lire* divided into 100 *centesimi*. These are imaginary moneys, of the value of the French franc and centime respectively.

SARDINIA.

Accounts are kept in *lire* and *centesimi* or hundredths; corresponding in value with the French franc and centime respectively.

The gold and silver coinages also correspond in value with those of France; differing only in name.

TUSCANY.

Accounts are generally kept in *pezze* (or dollars) of 8 rials, *soldi* di pezza and *denari* di pezza.

12 denari di pezza=1 soldo di pezza, 20 soldi di pezza=1 pezza of 8 rials.

But for transactions of small amount, accounts are kept in *lire*, *soldi*, and *denari*.

12 denari=1 soldo, 20 soldi=1 lira,

5¾ lire=1 pezza of 8 rials (silver)=90+cts., currency of the United States.

FOREIGN COINS AND MONEYS OF ACCOUNT.

PAPAL STATES.

Accounts are kept in *scudi* (or crowns) and *bajocchi*.

100 bajocchi, or 10 paoli=1 scudo (silver)=$1.00.6 currency of the United States.

Payments of greater amount than 5 scudi are made in paper money, which, not being redeemable in specie on demand, is uniformly at a discount.

NAPLES.

Accounts are kept in *ducati* and *grani*. 100 grani, or 10 carlini=1 ducat.

Value of the ducat (silver) in United States currency, a trifle under 79 cts.

SICILY.

Accounts are kept in *oncie*, *tari*, and *grani*.

20 grani=1 taro, 30 tari=1 oncia.

1 oncia=3 ducati of Naples, 1 taro=1 carlino of Naples.

The oncia (gold)=$2.48½ United States currency.

SPAIN.

Accounts are kept, at Cadiz, Malaga, and in most of the provinces of Spain, in *rials* of old plate, *quintos* and *maravedis*.

2 maravedis=1 quinto, 16 quintos=1 rial of old plate.

10⅝ rials of old plate=1 silver dollar, or $1 United States currency.

At Barcelona accounts are kept in *libras*, *sueldos*, *dineros* and *mallas*.

2 mallas=1 dinero, 12 dineros=1 sueldo, 20 sueldos=1 libra.

The libra is likewise divided into rials *de plata Catalan*, of 3 sueldos each, and into rials *ardites*, of 2 sueldos each.

1 libra=$\frac{8}{15}$ silver dollar, or 53⅓ cts. United States currency.

PORTUGAL.

Accounts are kept in *milrees* and *rees*. 1000 rees=1 milree.

In notation the milrees are separated from the rees by a crossed cypher, (⊕) and the milrees from the millions of rees, by a colon (:)—thus, 5:400⊕300 rees=5,400 milrees and 300 rees.

1 milree or crown (silver)=$1.12 United States currency.

GREECE.

Accounts are kept in *drachmè* and *lepta*. 100 lepta=1 drachmè.

Value of the drachmè (silver) in United States currency 16.6 cts.

TURKEY.

Accounts are kept in *piastres*, *paras*, and *aspers*.

3 aspers=1 para, 40 paras=1 piastre.

Some foreign merchants resident in Turkey reckon 80, others 100 aspers to the piastre, in their accounts.

The value of the piastre (silver) was depreciated from 60 cts. currency of the United States, in 1764, to 3 cts. in 1832. Its present value is about 3.8 cts. Its commercial value is about $\frac{1}{23}$ of a dollar.

EGYPT.

Accounts are kept as in Turkey. The piastre (silver)=4.8 cts. United States currency.

CAPE OF GOOD HOPE.

Accounts are kept in *pounds*, *shillings*, *pence*, and *farthings*, sterling; or in *rix-dollars*, *schillings*, and *stivers*.

6 stivers=1 schilling, 8 schillings=1 rix-dollar=1s. 6d. stg.

FOREIGN COINS AND MONEYS OF ACCOUNT.

MAURITIUS.

Accounts are kept in *dollars* and *cents* (or hundredths) currency. The current dollar or dollar of account (fictitious money) is worth 4 shillings stg., when exchange is at par. The dollar of the United States is valued at $1.08⅓ cts., currency.

EAST INDIA COMPANY'S TERRITORIES.

Accounts are kept in Company's *rupees*, *annas*, and *pice*.

12 pice=1 anna, 16 annas=1 Company's rupee.

Value of the Company's rupee, (silver) in United States currency, 44½ cts.

Notation. 1,00,000 (100 thousand)=1 lac, 1,00,00,000 (10 millions)=1 crore.

JAVA.

Accounts are kept in *florins* and *centimes*, as in Holland.

Manilla.

Accounts are kept in *dollars* and *rials* 8 to the dollar.

The dollar (Spanish)=the dollar of the United States.

Sydney, N. S. W.

Accounts are kept in sterling money.

Canton.

Accounts are kept in *taels*, *mace*, *candarines*, and *cash*.

1 tael=10 mace=100 candarines=1000 cash.

The cash is the only money coined by the Chinese government, and is made of a mixture of copper and lead. It is generally worth more than its nominal value, and when much in demand for change, a tael will sometimes purchase only 750.

Chinese is converted into United States money of account at the rate of 72 candarines per dollar; but the specie dollar of the United States generally commands a premium of 3 to 5 per cent. on this valuation.

BRITISH PROVINCES OF NORTH AMERICA.

Accounts are kept in *pounds*, *shillings*, *pence*, and *farthings*, Halifax currency. The pound=$4 United States currency.

4 farthings=1 penny, 12 pence=1 shilling, 20 shillings=1 pound.

BRITISH WEST INDIA COLONIES.

In these islands accounts are kept in *pounds*, *shillings*, *pence*, and *farthings*, of the same relative value as in England; but the value of the pound *currency* as compared with the pound *sterling*, varies very much in the different islands, and is in all cases less. The following values are affixed to the currencies of the respective islands:—£100 stg.=£135 of Barbadoes=£140 of Jamaica=£175 of the Windward islands, except Barbadoes=£200 of the Leeward islands. But exchange on England, in these several islands, is generally at from 10 to 20 per cent. premium on the values above given. Thus it would require about £160 currency of Jamaica, to purchase a bill of exchange on London for £100 stg.

CUBA AND PORTO RICO.

Accounts are kept in Spanish *dollars* and *rials* of plate 8 to the dollar. The dollar corresponds in value with the dollar of the United States.

ST. DOMINGO.

Accounts are kept in *dollars* and *centimes* or hundredths.

The dollar (silver)=about 33½ cts. United States currency. In January 1845, $2.75 currency=$1 United States currency.

FOREIGN COINS AND MONEYS OF ACCOUNT.

MEXICO.

Accounts are kept in *dollars* and *rials*.

8 rials=1 dollar (silver)=that of the United States.

VENEZUELA, NEW GRENADA, AND ECUADOR.

Accounts in these republics, formerly united under the name of Colombia, are kept in *dollars* and *rials* 8 to the dollar.

The coinage of these States is very irregular in value; some dollars (silver) being worth rather more than the dollar of the United States; some not more than $\frac{2}{3}$ its value; but most being of less value than our coin.

BRAZIL.

Accounts are kept in *milrees* and *rees* currency. 1000 rees=1 milree.

In notation the milrees are separated from the rees by ||.

The piece of 1||200 rees (silver)=99.4 cts. United States currency.

The currency of Brazil is chiefly paper and copper, redeemable in silver only at a very great discount: the rate varying very much in different provinces, and at different times in the same province. At Rio Janeiro, in December 1844, Spanish dollars were worth 2||040 rees.

Monte Video.

Accounts are kept in *dollars* currency, *rials* and *centesimos*.

100 centesimos=1 rial, 8 rials=1 dollar currency.

The dollar of account or currency=83$\frac{1}{3}$ cts. United States currency.

There is no paper currency.

Buenos Ayres.

Accounts are kept in *dollars* currency and *rials* 8 to the dollar.

The value of the dollar currency fluctuates very much. In December 1843, it was worth 6$\frac{1}{4}$ cts., United States currency, and it rarely exceeds 8 cts. in value.

CHILI.

Accounts are kept in *dollars* and *rials* 8 to the dollar.

The dollar (silver) is worth about $1.01 United States currency, but is generally estimated to be of equal value with it.

PERU.

Accounts are kept in *dollars* and *rials* 8 to the dollar.

The dollar (silver) is about equal in value with that of Chili, and the same remarks apply to it. There is a duty of 5 per cent. on dollars exported.

FOREIGN COINS MADE CURRENT IN THE UNITED STATES, AND THEIR VALUES AFFIXED BY THE SEVERAL ACTS OF CONGRESS.

GOLD COINS

Law of June 28, 1834.

	FINENESS	RATE PER DWT.	APPROXIMATE VALUES OF COINS AT RATES GIVEN.	
PORTUGAL, BRAZIL	22 carats . .	94.8 cts. . .	Moidore of 1705	$6.59
			No coin of this fineness.	
SPAIN, MEXICO, COLOMBIA	20 carats and $3\frac{7}{16}$ grains	89.9 cts. .	Doubloon of 1810—24	$15.50
			" of Republic	$15.55
			" of Bogota	$15.61

Law of March 3, 1843.

GREAT BRITAIN	$\frac{915.5}{1000}$ . .	94.6 cts. .	Sovereign, of Victoria	$4.86
FRANCE	$\frac{899}{1000}$ . .	92.9 cts. . .	Napoleon, or 20 francs	$3.85

SILVER COINS.

Law of June 25, 1834.

	FINENESS.	WEIGHT.	VALUE OF EACH.	REMARKS.
Dollar of CHILI, CENT. AMERICA.	$\frac{215}{240}$.	415 grs. .	100 cts.	Intrinsic value of a dollar of Chili, about 101 cts.; of Central America, about 100 cts.

BRAZIL. Dollars restamped in Brazil, same as above.

Law of March 3, 1843.

Pillar dollar of SPAIN and dollar of MEXICO, PERU, BOLIVIA	$\frac{897}{1000}$.	415 grs. .	100 cts.	These dollars are generally worth rather more than the value affixed.
5 Franc piece of FRANCE	$\frac{900}{1000}$.	384 grs. .	93 cts.	The value affixed is very nearly the intrinsic worth.

VALUE OF FOREIGN MONEYS OF ACCOUNT, IN COMPUTATION AT THE CUSTOM-HOUSES IN THE UNITED STATES, AS FIXED BY ACT OF CONGRESS.

By Law of March 3, 1843.

Thaler of Prussia	=	$68\frac{1}{2}$ c.
Milree of Portugal	=	$1.12
Rix-dollar of Bremen	=	$78\frac{3}{4}$ c.
Thaler of Bremen, 72 grotes	=	71 c.
Milree of Madeira	=	$1.00
" of Azores	=	$83\frac{1}{3}$ c.
Marc banco of Hamburg	=	35 c.
Rouble of Russia	=	75 c.
Rupee of British India	=	$44\frac{1}{2}$ c.

By Previous Laws.

Franc of France	=	$18\frac{708}{1000}$ c.
Austrian Guilder	=	48 c
Denmark Rix-dollar	=	$1.00
Pound Stg. Great Britain	=	$4.84
" of Halifax	=	$4.00
" of Jamaica	=	$3.00
Pezza of Leghorn	=	$90\frac{76}{100}$ c.
Ducat of Naples	=	80 c.
Rix-dollar of Prussia	=	$68\frac{29}{100}$ c.
Rial of Plate of Spain	=	10 c.
Ounce of Sicily	=	$2.46

TIME TABLE. No. 1.

January. 1st month.		February. 2d month.		March. 3d month.		April. 4th month.		May. 5th month.		June. 6th month.		July. 7th month.		August. 8th month.		September. 9th month.		October. 10th month.		November. 11th month.		December. 12th month.	
1	1	1	32	1	60	1	91	1	121	1	152	1	182	1	213	1	244	1	274	1	305	1	335
2	2	2	33	2	61	2	92	2	122	2	153	2	183	2	214	2	245	2	275	2	306	2	336
3	3	3	34	3	62	3	93	3	123	3	154	3	184	3	215	3	246	3	276	3	307	3	337
4	4	4	35	4	63	4	94	4	124	4	155	4	185	4	216	4	247	4	277	4	308	4	338
5	5	5	36	5	64	5	95	5	125	5	156	5	186	5	217	5	248	5	278	5	309	5	339
6	6	6	37	6	65	6	96	6	126	6	157	6	187	6	218	6	249	6	279	6	310	6	340
7	7	7	38	7	66	7	97	7	127	7	158	7	188	7	219	7	250	7	280	7	311	7	341
8	8	8	39	8	67	8	98	8	128	8	159	8	189	8	220	8	251	8	281	8	312	8	342
9	9	9	40	9	68	9	99	9	129	9	160	9	190	9	221	9	252	9	282	9	313	9	343
10	10	10	41	10	69	10	100	10	130	10	161	10	191	10	222	10	253	10	283	10	314	10	344
11	11	11	42	11	70	11	101	11	131	11	162	11	192	11	223	11	254	11	284	11	315	11	345
12	12	12	43	12	71	12	102	12	132	12	163	12	193	12	224	12	255	12	285	12	316	12	346
13	13	13	44	13	72	13	103	13	133	13	164	13	194	13	225	13	256	13	286	13	317	13	347
14	14	14	45	14	73	14	104	14	134	14	165	14	195	14	226	14	257	14	287	14	318	14	348
15	15	15	46	15	74	15	105	15	135	15	166	15	196	15	227	15	258	15	288	15	319	15	349
16	16	16	47	16	75	16	106	16	136	16	167	16	197	16	228	16	259	16	289	16	320	16	350
17	17	17	48	17	76	17	107	17	137	17	168	17	198	17	229	17	260	17	290	17	321	17	351
18	18	18	49	18	77	18	108	18	138	18	169	18	199	18	230	18	261	18	291	18	322	18	352
19	19	19	50	19	78	19	109	19	139	19	170	19	200	19	231	19	262	19	292	19	323	19	353
20	20	20	51	20	79	20	110	20	140	20	171	20	201	20	232	20	263	20	293	20	324	20	354
21	21	21	52	21	80	21	111	21	141	21	172	21	202	21	233	21	264	21	294	21	325	21	355
22	22	22	53	22	81	22	112	22	142	22	173	22	203	22	234	22	265	22	295	22	326	22	356
23	23	23	54	23	82	23	113	23	143	23	174	23	204	23	235	23	266	23	296	23	327	23	357
24	24	24	55	24	83	24	114	24	144	24	175	24	205	24	236	24	267	24	297	24	328	24	358
25	25	25	56	25	84	25	115	25	145	25	176	25	206	25	237	25	268	25	298	25	329	25	359
26	26	26	57	26	85	26	116	26	146	26	177	26	207	26	238	26	269	26	299	26	330	26	360
27	27	27	58	27	86	27	117	27	147	27	178	27	208	27	239	27	270	27	300	27	331	27	361
28	28	28	59	28	87	28	118	28	148	28	179	28	209	28	240	28	271	28	301	28	332	28	362
29	29			29	88	29	119	29	149	29	180	29	210	29	241	29	272	29	302	29	333	29	363
30	30			30	89	30	120	30	150	30	181	30	211	30	242	30	273	30	303	30	334	30	364
31	31			31	90			31	151			31	212	31	243			31	304			31	365

To find the time from a given date to any other date in the same year.—Subtract the sum standing opposite the *earlier* from the sum opposite the *later* date.

TIME TABLE. No. 2.

From \ To	Jan.	Feb.	March.	April.	May.	June.	July.	August.	Sept.	Oct.	Nov.	Dec.
January .	365	31	59	90	120	151	181	212	243	273	304	334
February .	334	365	28	59	89	120	150	181	212	242	273	303
March . .	306	337	365	31	61	92	122	153	184	214	245	275
April . . .	275	306	334	365	30	61	91	122	153	183	214	244
May . . .	245	276	304	335	365	31	61	92	123	153	184	214
June . . .	214	245	273	304	334	365	30	61	92	122	153	183
July . . .	184	215	243	274	304	335	365	31	62	92	123	153
August . .	153	184	212	243	273	304	334	365	31	61	92	122
September	122	153	181	212	242	273	303	334	365	30	61	91
October .	92	123	151	182	212	243	273	304	335	365	31	61
November	61	92	120	151	181	212	242	273	304	334	365	30
December	31	62	90	121	151	182	212	243	274	304	335	365

This table will be found very convenient for ascertaining the number of days between any two dates not more than a year distant; also for ascertaining with accuracy and despatch the time when notes, drafts, &c., fall due.

Each of the numbers in the table shows the length of time (in days) from any day of the month standing opposite to it on the left, to the corresponding day of that month which is over it.

Examples.

What is the number of days from March 15th to Nov. 15th?

Opposite March, and under Nov., we find 245, the number required.

What is the length of time from May 4th to August 16th?

Opposite May and under August is the number 92, showing the days from May 4th to August 4th. To August 16th it is 12 days more, which, added to 92, give 104, the answer.

How many days from December 25th to June 12th?

Opposite December and under June is 182, the number of days from December 25th to June 25th; but to June 12th is 13 days less, which, deducted from 182, gives 169, the answer.

If a note be drawn July 14th, at 90 days, when will it fall due, grace included?

In the line of figures opposite July, seek that number which is nearest in amount to the number of days for which the note is drawn. This is found to be 92, which stands under October, showing that 92 days, from July 14th, brings the time to October 14th, to which add one day, (the excess of 93 over 92,) and you have October 15th, answer.

Made in United States
Orlando, FL
21 October 2026

89529437R00160